The Complete

C++ Primer

Second Edition

The Complete
C++ Primer

Second Edition

Keith Weiskamp

Bryan Flamig

AP Professional

A Division of Harcourt Brace & Company
Boston   San Diego   New York
London   Sydney   Tokyo   Toronto

Copyright © 1992, 1990 by Academic Press
All rights reserved.
No part of this publication may be reproduced or
transmitted in any form or by any means, electronic
or mechanical, including photocopy, recording, or
any information storage and retrieval system, without
permission in writing from the publisher.

AP PROFESSIONAL
955 Massachusetts Avenue, Cambridge, MA 02139

An imprint of ACADEMIC PRESS
A division of HARCOURT BRACE & COMPANY

United Kingdom Edition published by
ACADEMIC PRESS LIMITED
24–28 Oval Road, London NW1 7DX

Library of Congress Cataloging-in-Publication Data

Weiskamp, Keith.
    The complete C++ primer/Keith Weiskamp, Bryan Flamig. —2nd ed.
        p.   cm.
    Includes index.
    ISBN 0-12-742688-4
    1. C++ (Computer program language) I. Flamig, Bryan. II. Title.
III. Title: Complete C plus plus primer.
QA76.73.C153W45   1992   92-7175
005.13'3—dc20   CIP

Printed in the United States of America
93 94 95 96 97 MV 9 8 7 6 5 4 3 2

Contents

Preface

It's no secret—C++ is rapidly becoming the language of choice for programmers interested in object-oriented programming (OOP). If you're like most programmers who have been programming with C, and you're now interested in learning how to move into the world of OOP and C++, then this book is for you. C++, developed at the AT&T Bell Laboratories by Bjarne Stroustrup, provides important extensions to the standard C language, such as classes, data abstractions, operator overloading, and inheritance. Although C++ was developed in the early 1980s, the more you work with it, the more you'll agree that this language was designed to meet the programming demands of the 1990s.

This book focuses on the C++ language and not just on OOP techniques. The programs were designed to help you learn quickly the key features of C++ programming. After a quick tour of a basic C++ program, each chapter uses a building-block approach to introduce technical programming issues. Our goal is to help you master the basics of C++ programming as quickly as possible. To this end, we've included numerous technical figures that will help clarify the programming concepts covered. As a special aid, carefully constructed translation boxes are included to show you how C++ statements and concepts translate into C code. We've also included a special appendix that covers some of the key differences between C and C++. In addition, exercises are provided in each chapter and Appendix B provides answers to selected exercises.

Who Should Read This Book

This book assumes that you're familiar with the basics of C programming. Our main goal is to show you how to program with the powerful extension that C++ provides. Whether you're programming on a personal computer, workstation, or mainframe you'll be able to try out the examples and experiment with them. If you do not have much C programming experience, we suggest that you also refer to an introductory text on C programming as you read this book and run the programs.

How This Book Is Different

Many tutorial programming books on C++ present the language in a theoretical style with incomplete code fragments. This book uses a different approach: It emphasizes the practical side of C++ programming using a hands-on, easy-to-read format. If you take a moment to look through the book, you'll see that we've included numerous notes that have been offset from the text to help you learn the critical and more subtle points of C++ programming.

We encourage you to try out as many of the program examples as you can and to feel free to modify them as you go along. Experimentation is the essence of learning; the best way to master a programming language is to roll up your sleeves and start writing programs. Wherever possible, we've written the program examples as complete programs so that you can enter and run them using your own computer. The output of the main program examples is provided to help you understand how the programs work. (If you don't want to spend your time typing in the programs, you may want to order the code disk from this book. See the end of the book for details.)

What About Standards?

This book covers Version 2.1 of C++. We have also included coverage of a new feature called templates which is supported by some of the newer C++ implementations. If you are using a compiler that currently supports templates, such as Borland C++, you'll be able to experiment with this powerful new feature.

For programmers using an earlier version of C++, you'll want to upgrade to a Version 2.1 compiler to use this book. We've included some special notes in the text to point out the new features that Version 2.1 provides.

What You'll Need

To get the most out of the material presented in this book, you should have access to a C++ compiler (Version 2.1). You can run most of the program examples presented on a variety of computers from personal computers to mainframes. The simulation program presented in Chapter 12 requires an IBM PC or a compatible computer to run. However, if you're using a different system, the program can easily be adapted to run on your own computer.

What's in This Book?

The *Complete C++ Primer* progresses from the basics of C++ programming to more advanced topics such as writing object-oriented and simulation programs in C++. Here is a short description of each chapter:

Chapter 1: *Introducing C++* presents a quick tour of C++ programming. In this chapter you'll learn how to write your first C++ program and how to use the basic features, such as classes, C++ functions, and operator overloading.

Chapter 2: *Introducing Object-Oriented Programming* begins our exploration of object-oriented programming. It explains the basic concepts of programming in the OOP style.

Chapter 3: *Introducing Classes* covers the fundamentals of defining and using classes. Here you'll learn how to use classes to combine data and functions and to create objects.

Chapter 4: *Classes in Action* puts the basic concepts presented in Chapter 3 to work. We introduce more powerful C++ concepts, such as deriving classes, virtual functions, and friends.

Chapter 5: *Introducing C++ Functions* describes the types of functions that C++ provides. Some of the topics covered include components of C++ functions, function prototypes, argument type conversions, calling C++ functions, and using default arguments.

Chapter 6: *Putting Functions to Work* expands the techniques covered in Chapter 5 and shows you how to define and use inline functions, member functions, iterator functions, and virtual functions. This chapter also introduces the powerful OOP concept called *polymorphism*.

Chapter 7: *Function and Operator Overloading* explores the basic techniques of redefining functions and operators, called *overloading*.

Chapter 8: *Working with Constructor and Destructor Functions* presents an assortment of basic and advanced techniques for working with constructors and destructors. You'll learn how these components are used to help you work with objects.

Chapter 9: *Inheritance and Class Hierarchies* examines the techniques for designing reusable and extendable classes and objects.

Chapter 10: *The C++ Stream I/O System* covers the flexible C++ I/O system, including character-level and user-defined I/O objects.

Chapter 11: *Record-Oriented File I/O* shows you how to put many of the C++ programming concepts introduced in earlier chapters to work to help you create a record-oriented file I/O application. This chapter also provides an introduction to templates.

Chapter 12: *A Simulation Project Using C++* concludes our C++ primer by showing you how to write a practical simulation program by applying OOP techniques. The program uses a number of classes, such as gauges, screen device classes, and turtle classes to draw animated figures.

Contacting the Authors

After working through this book, you might want to correspond with the authors. We'd like to encourage you to do so by using electronic mail or U.S. Mail. The quickest way to reach us is through the CompuServe Information Service. (The IDs are 72561,1536 for Keith Weiskamp and 73057,3172 for Bryan Flamig.)

You can also reach us by sending you letters to 7721 E. Gray Rd., Suite 204, Scottsdale, AZ 85260.

Acknowledgments

The authors would like to personally thank a number of individuals who helped in the preparation of this book.

◆ Jenifer Swetland, editor of Academic Press, whose commitment to publishing quality books made this work possible.

◆ Elizabeth Tustian, production editor, who has been immensely helpful in managing the production of this book.

◆ Rob Mauhar, who created the high-quality technical illustrations with loving care.

◆ Norm Atkin of LaserTypesetting, who helped with the production and printing of the final book.

◆ Loren Heiny, who read the original manuscript and provided helpful feedback.

◆ Sam Hobbs, who reviewed the first edition and provided many valuable suggestions.

Introducing C++

You've picked up this book because you have more than just a passing curiosity about C++. You probably want to learn how to program this powerful superset of the C language. And that's why we've written this book—to help you master the C++ language.

We'll start by exploring the basic features of C++. Because C++ is an extension of C, you won't have to learn a complete new syntax in order to begin writing C++ programs. As a matter of fact, you're going to see your first C++ program as soon as we give you a brief overview of the language. We'll present a working program, and then we'll quickly explore most of the main features of C++. In the last part of the chapter, we'll cover some important topics, such as working with compilers, working with source files, and type casting.

Here are some of the major highlights of this chapter:

- Techniques for learning C++
- How to write your first C++ program
- An overview of the key features of C++
- Tips for using C++ compilers

Origins

C++ was developed at Bell Laboratories by Bjarne Stroustrup. The folks at Bell Laboratories have quite a reputation for developing programming languages. After all, they developed C. The two languages that actually influenced the creation of C++ (besides, of course, C) were BCPL and Simula67. Many of the features found in Simula67, such as classes and virtual functions, are key components in C++.

Learning C++

Now that you've prepared yourself to learn a new language, you might be surprised to discover that you already know a lot about C++ if you know C! Because C++ is a superset of C, it includes all the components that C offers, including the same control statements, operators, functions, and basic data types (**int**, **char**, and so on). It also has the same standard library functions, such as **printf**() and **getc**().

The new features of C++ provide *object-oriented* programming support. The real advantage of learning C++ is that you won't have to unlearn what you already know in order to take advantage of object-oriented programming. You can learn incrementally the new features and increase your skills as an object-oriented programmer.

The major hurdle you'll encounter in learning C++ has to do more with programming style than with syntax. For example, if you know how to write a **switch** statement in C

```
switch(ch)   {
  case '.':
  case ';':
  case ',':
   return  end_of_phrase;
   break;
  default:
   return  just_another_char;
}
```

you'll be able to use the same **switch** statement in C++.

However, the real challenge is learning the object-oriented programming technique. Although you can use traditional, structured C programming techniques to write your C++ programs, you'll soon discover that the high-level, object-oriented nature of the C++ extensions opens up a new world. As you work through this book, you'll learn progressively how to navigate this new world and harness the power of object-oriented programming. In fact, because of the importance of object-oriented programming, we've devoted an entire chapter to this topic.

Advantages of Using C++

Before you start writing programs, you might want to know about some of the important advantages that C++ has over its C predecessor. Here's a list of the major advantages:

- Better type checking features are provided
- Modular programming techniques are improved
- Abstract data types are supported
- Object-oriented programming features are available
- Operators and functions can be overloaded

Without getting too technical at this point, the most unique feature that C++ provides is the *class*, which allows you to define high-level structures. So what's the big deal? After all, C allows you to declare structures.

The approach that C++ takes is different. Using classes, you can combine data and functions under one roof, so to speak. For example, let's assume that we need to develop a computer-assisted drawing program. If we were writing the program in C, we would code all the data structures needed using arrays and structures. After determining our data structures, we would then write functions to perform the major tasks, such as drawing lines, filling objects, and displaying text. Although these functions would use these structures, they would otherwise be separate from the data.

With C++, on the other hand, we can more closely link up the functions and data. For example, Figure 1.1 shows conceptually how a class can be used to represent the function and data we might need to draw lines. As you can see, data and operators (functions) are much better integrated when this approach is used.

Note: If you already have experience using other object-oriented languages like Smalltalk or Objective-C, keep in mind that C++ is a compiled language and it does not have all the dynamic features of these other languages. However, that does not detract from its usefulness! Its main advantage over these other languages is its efficiency.

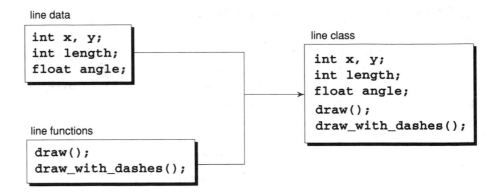

Figure 1.1. The C++ method of combining data and functions.

The Key Components of C++

We've briefly introduced classes—the main C++ component; however, there are a number of other building blocks that work together to give C++ its unique personality:

- Inheritance and derived classes
- Member functions
- Friend functions
- Inline functions
- Constructor and destructor functions
- Virtual functions
- Overloaded functions
- Overloaded operators
- Flexible stream I/O operators
- Memory management operators
- Templates

Perhaps the best way to see how each of these components operates is to examine a C++ program that uses them.

Writing Your First C++ Program

Since you're probably anxious to start using the features we have been discussing, let's put our technical discussions aside and write our first C++ program. The program asks you to enter a string, and then it provides you with three conversion options:

1. Convert string to uppercase
2. Convert string to lowercase
3. Append characters to the string

Here is the complete program:

```
// String conversion program
#include <stdio.h>
#include <string.h>

// A string class
class string {
    char data[80];
public:
    void copy(char *s) { strcpy(data,s); }
    string(char *s="") { copy(s); }
    void read(FILE *fptr);
    void write(FILE *fptr);
    void operator+=(string &s) {
      strcat(data, s.data);
    }
    friend void convert(string &s, int opt);
};

void string::read(FILE *fptr)
{
    int slen;
    fgets(data,80,fptr);
    slen = strlen(data) - 1;
    if (data[slen] == '\n') data[slen] = 0; // remove '\n'
    return;
}
```

```
void string::write(FILE *fptr)
{
    fprintf(fptr, "%s", data);
}

// Friend function of string class

void convert(string &s, int opt)
{
    string tempstr;

    switch(opt) {
      case '1': // convert to uppercase
        strupr(s.data);
      break;
      case '2': // convert to lowercase
         strlwr(s.data);
      break;
      case '3': // add to end of string
        printf("Enter a new string\n");
         tempstr.read(stdin);    // read a new string
        s += tempstr;            // call overloaded operator
      break;
        default: printf("Sorry, bad option\n");
    }
}

void main()
{
    string str;   // create a string object
    char opt;

    printf("Hello friend, enter a string please\n");
    str.read(stdin);   // invoke the string read method
    printf("Enter a conversion option\n");
    printf("1) Convert to uppercase\n");
    printf("2) Convert to lowercase\n");
    printf("3) Append to the string\n");
    opt = getchar();
    fflush(stdin);
```

```
    convert(str, opt); // call the friend function
    printf("The converted string is: ");
    str.write(stdout); // invoke the string write method
    printf("\n");
}
```

Type in the program using your favorite text editor and save it with an appropriate extension. Next, compile and link the program so that you can run it. (If you are using a C++ translator, the program must first be translated into C and then compiled.)

Here are a few sample runs of the program:

```
Hello friend, enter a string please
Mary
Enter a conversion option
1) Convert to uppercase
2) Convert to lowercase
3) Concatenate two strings
1
The converted string is: MARY

Hello friend, enter a string please
Base
Enter a conversion option
1) Convert to uppercase
2) Convert to lowercase
3) Concatenate two strings
3
Enter a new string
ball
The converted string is: Baseball
```

The structure of this program is illustrated in Figure 1.2. Note that the program contains a class called **string** and an assortment of functions. Each user-defined function used in the program is listed with a brief description in Table 1.1. The program also uses functions from the standard C library, such as **getch()**, **strcpy()**, **strcat()**, and **fgets()**. In many respects this program is not much different from a typical C program. In fact, you'll find more similarities than differences. The program is controlled by a **main()** function, which in turn calls other standard C functions, such as **printf()**, to carry out its conversion task. There are, however, many new features that we are using. We'll be exploring each one separately.

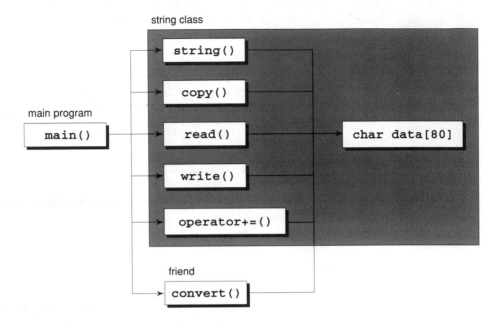

Figure 1.2. The structure of the sample C++ program.

Table 1.1. Functions used in the string conversion program

Function	Description
copy()	Member function to copy a character string
read()	Member function to read a string
write()	Member function to write a string
operator+=()	Overloaded operator function for +=
convert()	Friend function used to convert a string
string()	Constructor function to initialize a string

Note: A C++ program follows the basic format of a C program. You can use any of the C language statements, such as **for**, **do-while**, **if**, **switch**, and so on. You can also make calls to any of the standard C library functions.

Comments

The first line of our program contained a statement that you probably haven't seen before. C++ has a new syntax for comments.

```
// String conversion program
```

Note: The symbols // define a comment line in C++.

In fact, we didn't even use the old form for C comments.

```
/* String conversion program */
```

C++ allows you to use both styles but, to be consistent, we'll use the // notation throughout this book.

Classes

Classes give C++ its object-oriented personality. It is through this component that all of the object-oriented features are implemented. In our string conversion program, we defined the following class:

```
class string {
    char data[80];
public:
    void copy(char *s) { strcpy(data,s); }
    string(char *s="") { copy(s); }
    void read(FILE *fptr);
    void write(FILE *fptr);
    void operator+=(string &s) { strcat(data, s.data); }
    friend void convert(string &s, int opt);
};
```

What does this class actually accomplish? It defines a new type called **string**, which is a "template" for **string** objects. This class combines a character array, along with the functions used to manipulate the array, into one neat package. An instance of such a package is called an *object*.

Classes are used to declare objects in C++ programs just like C structures are used to declare variables in C programs. For example, the statement

```
string str;
```

declares a variable named **str**. In C++, we call this type of variable an *object* because it can be used to access both data and functions.

Each component of a class is called a class member. As Figure 1.3 shows, a class can have both data and function members.

```
class string{                          private data member
  char data[80];
public:
  void copy(char *s)  {strcpy(data,s);}
  string(char *s="")  {copy(s);}
  ...
  friend void convert(string &s,int opt);
};
                                       friend

public function members
```

Figure 1.3. Class members.

Classes incorporate another important feature: information hiding (sometimes referred to as *encapsulation*). They accomplish this by having public and private members. The keyword **public** designates selected members as being accessible to any program that uses the class definition. For example, because the function **read()** is listed in the public section, it can be freely accessed. Our **string** class also contains a private member called **data**. Because this member is not listed in the public section, it can only be accessed by other class members, such as **copy()**, **read()**, and **write()**.

Note: The **struct** keyword is still available in C++ and is actually a special case of a **class**. The only difference between a **class** and a **struct** is that the **struct** members are public by default, whereas class members are private by default. We'll be using the terms *structure* and *class* interchangeably, unless otherwise noted.

Member Functions

C++ provides a new set of functions called *member functions* to support classes. How are they different from standard C functions? They can access the other members of the class in which they are defined. Also, they can be called only by using an object. Let's take a closer look.

As an example, notice the following statement in the **string** class declaration:

```
void write(FILE *fptr);
```

Because this statement is inside the class declaration, it indicates that **write()** is a member function of the class **string**. It also serves as the function prototype for **write()**. Of course, we'll also need to define the function. We happened to define it outside the class as shown:

```
void string::write(FILE *fptr)
{
    fprintf(fptr, "%s", data);
}
```

You might notice something unusual in the first line.

```
void string::write(FILE *fptr)
```

Here, we are attaching the class name **string** with the name of the function. This makes **write()** belong to the **string** class. The symbol **::** combines the two components, and is used as a scoping operator. It allows **write()** to access directly other class members, such as **data**.

```
fprintf(fptr, "%s", data);
```

Although **data** belongs to the class structure, we didn't have to reference it using the dot operator. That is, we didn't have to write:

```
fprintf(fptr, "%s", str.data);
```

As you can see, there is no structure variable in our function to reference the **data** component. So how can this work? To answer that, we must consider how the **write()** function is called.

Member functions are called differently than standard C functions. If you remember from our string conversion program, we used the notation shown here to call **write()**:

```
str.write(stdin);
```

We can interpret this as two operations: Select the object **str** and call its function **write()**. Functions associated with objects are sometimes referred to as *methods*, and the process of calling a function is sometimes referred to as *message passing*. Now, the object that **data** is part of is the object selected in the function call, that is, the object **str**.

Friend Functions

Next in our list of C++ features are *friend functions*. These functions are more like standard C functions. Friend functions are not intimately tied to a class definition; however, they can be used to access private class members. For example, we declared **convert()** to be a friend function.

```
class string {
    char data[80];
public:
    friend void convert(string &s, int opt);
    // other member functions
};
```

To make a function a friend of a class, we must include the function's prototype inside the class and prefix it with the **friend** keyword. Unlike member functions, friend functions must be explicitly passed objects of the class. In our example, notice that we pass in the **string** object **s**. (We'll explain the **&** symbol shortly.) Because the function is passed an object, it can access any member of the class, including private members. Here's an example of how we access a member of the **string** class:

```
void convert(string &s, int opt)
{
    // ...
    case '1':              // convert string to uppercase
      strupr(s.data); // access private member
```

```
        break;
        // ...
    }
```

Note: Friend functions provide a bridge between standard C functions and member functions.

Reference Variables

Our friend function also incorporates another new feature: *reference variables*. A reference variable is simply an alias for another variable. It is like a pointer, except that, once initialized, it can never be changed, and whenever used, it is automatically de-referenced. We declare reference variables using the **&** operator, as we did in our function prototype for **convert**().

```
void convert(string &s, int opt);
```

Note how we can then use **s** as though it were just a normal structure variable, as in

```
strupr(s.data);
```

rather than using

```
strupr(s->data);
```

In short, a reference variable is like a constant pointer that is always de-referenced when used. It simply becomes another name for a variable. In our example, the reference variable serves as a name for the actual parameter being passed. More importantly, it allows a parameter to be passed by address, rather than by value, and thus eliminates the overhead of copying data.

Constructor and Destructor Functions

Another useful feature that C++ provides are constructor and destructor functions. What are they? Recall that the **string** class contained the following member function:

```
string(char *s="") { copy(s); }
```

Notice that this function has the same name as the **string** class. Could this be a mistake? No. C++ actually treats such a function as a *constructor*. The constructor **string()** is automatically called whenever an object of type **string** is declared. For example, the declaration

```
string str("This is a test");
```

will cause the object **str** to be created and initialized so that it contains the string "This is a test".

Note the unusual syntax in the following constructor argument:

```
string(char *s="");
```

This is an example of how default arguments are used. In this case, if a constructor for **string** is used without any argument specified, that argument is given the default value of "" (which is a null string). Recall how in our program we used

```
string str;
```

In this case, when **str** is created, it is initialized to a null string. Note that default arguments are available for any function, not just constructors.

Constructors have opposites called *destructors*. They are used to perform the cleanup work after an object is no longer needed. A destructor has the same name as the class, except that its name is preceded by a ~ symbol. As an example, we might change our **string** class to store our string dynamically and to use a constructor and a destructor to allocate and de-allocate the storage:

```
class string {
    char *data;   // now just a pointer
public:
    // constructor to allocate and initialize string
    string(char *s) { data = strdup(s); }
    // destructor to free up storage--note the ~ symbol!
    ~string(void) { free(data); }
    // other class members go here
};
```

Constructors and destructors provide a convenient method for initializing and cleaning up after objects. Whenever an object with a constructor is declared, you can always be certain that the object will be initialized. In addition, the object's destructor guarantees that the necessary cleanup operations are performed after the object is no longer used.

Inline Functions

C++ also has *inline functions*, which are similar to macros because they can be used to eliminate the overhead of a function call. Whenever an inline function is used, the code that makes up the function is inserted *inline*. Unlike macros, however, inline functions use the same scoping rules as other functions.

There are two ways to declare an inline function. One way is to include the complete function definition in a class declaration, as we did for the member function **copy**().

```
class string {
    char data[80];
public:
    void copy(char *s) { strcpy(data,s); } // inline
    // other members
};
```

Inline functions can also be declared explicitly using the **inline** keyword.

```
class string {
    char data[80];
public:
    inline void copy(char *s);
    // other members
};
```

In this case, the function body is given outside the class.

```
inline void string::copy(char *s)
{
    strcpy(data, s);
}
```

Figure 1.4 presents a translation box that illustrates how C++ inline functions are translated into C code. Throughout this book we'll be presenting different translation boxes to help you understand how C++ features correspond with C code.

C   C++

```
typedef struct {              class clock {
  int hr,min,sec;               int hr,min,sec;
} clock;                      public:
                                void set(int h,int m,int s)
clock bigben;                   {
                                    hr = h; min = m; sec = s;
bigben.hr = 12;                 }
bigben.min = 0;               };
bigben.sec = 0;
                              clock bigben;

                              bigben.set(12,0,0);
```

Figure 1.4. Translation box for an inline function.

Note: Inline functions do not have to be class members. Any function is a candidate. Since an inline function is copied whenever used, it should be kept short.

Overloaded Functions and Operators

One of the more unique features of our string conversion program is that it allowed us to process **string** objects as if they were built into the language (like integers and characters). For example, if you look closely at the function **convert()**, you'll notice the statement:

```
s += tempstr;
```

Now remember that **s** and **tempstr** are both **string** objects. So, how can we get away with using the **+=** operator to process them? Our favorite C compiler would go crazy with error messages if we tried to write such a statement in C.

Actually, what we've done is overloaded the **+=** operator by using the following function:

```
void string::operator+=(string &s) {
   strcat(data, s.data);
}
```

When the **+=** operator is used in an expression, such as

```
s += tempstr;
```

the expression is translated into the following function call:

```
s.operator+=(tempstr);
```

The **+=** operator has another use besides its original one; therefore, we call it an *overloaded operator*.

Operators aren't the only components that can be overloaded—we can also overload functions. For example, we might declare two forms of the member function **copy()**:

```
class string {
   char data[80];
public:
   // copy null terminated string
   void copy(char *s)        { strcpy(data, s); }
   // copy a bound character array
   void copy(char *m, int n) { strncpy(data, m, n); }
   // other members
};
```

Because the function **copy()** was declared twice, it is an *overloaded function*. It can be used in one of two ways—to copy a null-terminated string or to copy an array of bytes of a given length. In our example, notice that each version of **copy()** has a different set of arguments. Based on the number and type of the arguments provided in a call to **copy()**, the C++ compiler knows which version to use.

Inheritance and Derived Classes

One of the more interesting and useful features of C++ classes is the ability to derive new classes from existing classes. A derived class incorporates all the features (code and data) of the existing class. That is, it *inherits* the features, and it can also add new features of its own. Inheritance and derived classes provide a powerful method for reusing and sharing code.

As an example, we can derive a new **string** class from our existing **string** class. This new class contains all of the features of **string**, but we'll add a slight twist. It will be able to process strings that will not have any whitespace, such as blanks, tabs, or newlines. That is, they'll just contain words. Here's the new class definition:

```
class word : public string {
public:
    word(char *w="") { copy(w); }
    void read(FILE *fptr);
};


void read(FILE *fptr)
// Reads up to the next whitespace character
{
    fscanf(fptr, "%s", data);
}
```

The syntax **word : public string** instructs the C++ compiler that **word** uses all the members in the **string** class. To be more specific, we can say that the class **word** is derived from class **string**.

The most striking feature of this new class is that it has few members. At least that's what you might think at first. All we have is the constructor **word()** and the function **read()**. However, **word** also contains all the functions and data members of the class **string**! For instance, it has **read(), copy(), write(),** and **operator+=()**, and it has the data member **data**. Our new class inherited all these members from class **string**.

There's also one other thing going on. Recall that class **string** had a **read()** member function. But so does **word**. What this means is that **read()** is overloaded. However, we are soon going to make it a special kind of overloaded function called a *virtual function*.

Virtual functions are different from other functions. When a function related to an object is called, it is usually linked up to the object at compile-time. The function is said to be *statically bound* to the object. With virtual functions, this binding doesn't take place until run-time, and it is called *dynamic binding*. For example, suppose we have a pointer to a string object **strptr** and we call its **read()** function:

```
strptr->read(stdin); // call a virtual function
```

Unlike most pointers, it turns out that **strptr** can point to two different types of objects: either a **string** object or a **word** object. This is allowed because **word** was derived from **string**. Now when **read()** is called, which function is used, the one from **string** or the one from **word**? It depends on what **strptr** is pointing to. This is illustrated with the following examples:

```
string str;          // declare string object
word wrd;            // declare word object
string *strptr;      // declare pointer to string

strptr = &str;          // point to string object
strptr->read(stdin);    // call string's read() fctn

strptr = &wrd;          // point to word object
strptr->read(stdin);    // call word's read() fctn
```

Thus, we can make the calls to **read()** have different behaviors. We can either allow character strings, including blanks, to be read, or allow only words to be read. The ability to take on different characteristics is called *polymorphism*, which means to take on many shapes. As you become acquainted with C++, you'll find that virtual functions, polymorphism, inheritance, and derived classes make a powerful combination.

To use virtual functions, you must declare properly. For instance, to make the **read()** function virtual, we must not only declare it in class **word**, we must also change our **string** class declaration. The change involves using the keyword **virtual**.

```
class string {
    char data[80];
public:
    void copy(char *s) { strcpy(data,s); }
    string(char *s="") { copy(s); }
    virtual void read(FILE *fptr); // note new keyword!!
    void write(FILE *fptr);
    void operator+=(string &s) {
      strcat(data, s.data);
    }
    friend void convert(string &s, int opt);
};
```

Note: Inheritance, derived classes, virtual functions, and polymorphism are the features that make C++'s style of object-oriented programming so useful.

Stream I/O Operators

The I/O operations were performed in our sample program using standard C library functions, such as **getch()** and **printf()**. C++ provides another means to accomplish I/O, through a set of classes designed for stream-oriented I/O.

For example, just when you thought we were going to spare you from the "Hello World" program, we decided to sneak it in with this new form of I/O.

```
#include <iostream.h>
void main()
{
    cout << "Yet another hello world program\n";
}
```

This program introduces a new twist. The **<<** operator replaces the **printf()** statement, and **cout** replaces **stdout**. The **<<** operator serves as the C++ output operator. In this case it sends the string to the output stream designated as **cout**. As the next program illustrates, there is a companion input operator **>>**.

```
#include <iostream.h>
void main()
{
    int value;

    cout << "Input a number ";
    cin >> value;
    cout << "The number is " << value;
}
```

This time we are using **cin** to designate the input stream. In addition to **cin** and **cout**, there is a **cerr** stream, and you can declare your own streams much the same way you can open up standard I/O files in C.

Note: In C++, the basic I/O declarations for the stream system are declared in the header file **iostream.h**. You must include this file in all programs that use this new system.

Memory Management Operators

Recall that our sample string conversion program didn't use dynamic memory. We allocated storage for our string data using a static array:

```
char data[80];
```

We could, however, change this member so that it serves as a pointer and allocate and de-allocate memory for it dynamically.

```
char *data;
data = malloc(strlen("Input String"));
free(data);
```

As shown here, C++ has all the standard allocation routines of C. However, it has a new way of allocating dynamic storage that you should become familiar with—the operators **new** and **delete**.

```
data = new char[strlen("Input String")];
delete[] data;
```

What's important about these new operators is that they automatically call any constructor and destructor that an object might have; **malloc()** and **free()** don't. This means you can couple the allocation of storage for an object with the initialization and cleanup of the object.

Another important feature of **new** is that it looks at the type of the object being allocated to determine the amount of storage to use. For example,

```
char *c;
c = new char;
```

allocates one byte of storage, whereas

```
double *d
d = new double;
```

allocates eight bytes of storage on most systems. Contrast this with having to write

```
double *d;
d = malloc(8); // easy to give the wrong number
```

Type Casting

Another new feature of C++ is the way that type casting can be handled. Recall that in C you can type cast a variable using syntax like

```
i = (int)some_float_num;
```

You can also use the same syntax in C++. However, there is an alternate form available:

```
i = int(some_float_num);
```

That is, you can treat the type cast like a function call. There is a good reason for this, as you'll find out later in this book—you can link up your own type conversions with special functions.

C++ in Practice

Now that we've written our first C++ program and briefly explored the major features of C++, we'll need to look at a few programming issues before we turn you loose.

A Matter of Style

There's an old saying that certainly applies to C++ programming—"A little bit of style goes a long way!" Because C++ adds many new powerful features, there is a tendency for newcomers to get carried away and use every feature possible, even though it might not be warranted for their particular application. You should always strive to keep your data structures and functions as simple as possible. Use the complex features only when they're really needed. A good style is a simple style.

One feature we do encourage you to use all the time is function prototyping. The function prototypes that are now supported by the ANSI C standard were actually inherited from C++. Many of the new features of C++ require that you use function prototypes. We strongly recommend that you get into the habit of using them.

Working with Compilers

Before you start programming in C++, you should take a close look at what type of implementation you have. Because C++ is a compiled language, you program using the same edit–compile–link–run cycle that you've always used with your C programs. Figures 1.5 shows the basic steps required to write, compile, and run a C++ program.

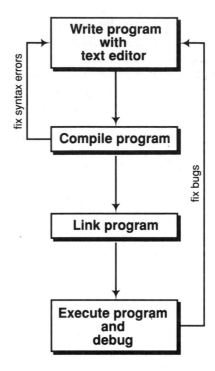

Figure 1.5. The C++ program development method.

Working with Source Files

Because C++ has not been standardized across computing platforms, a few different conventions have emerged for naming source files. Most UNIX implementations of C++ use the extension **.c** to name both C and C++ source files. There are, however, other programming environments that use extensions like **.cxx** or **.cpp** for C++ files. You'll also find the same kind of differences in the way header files are named. Some environments stick to the standard **.h** naming conventions, while others use **.hxx** or **.hpp**.

Note: Throughout this book we'll be using the extensions **.cpp** and **.hpp** for our code and header files. Before you try running any of the programs in this book, be sure to consult the documentation with your implementation of C++ to find out what extensions you should use.

When using header files in C++, you must take into account two of the new features of C++: classes and inline functions. Class declarations are just like structure declarations in C. If you're using header files, you should include your class declarations there. However, you shouldn't include any class member functions in the header file, just as you wouldn't include functions in C header files. There is, however, one exception. Many class declarations contain inline functions. Fortunately, inline functions can be placed in header files (remember, they're similar to macros). In fact, if you want your inline functions to be global, they must be placed in a header file.

Note: If an inline function is to be global or if it is in a class declaration to be used by several source modules, it must be placed in a header file. Be sure to include both the function's prototype and body.

Summary

We've now seen many of the new features that C++ has to offer, including classes, member functions, friend functions, inline functions, overloaded operators and functions, and other components. What's important to keep in mind as you learn more about C++ is that you can build upon your C programming experience.

The more you use C++ you'll discover that the real challenge to learning this language doesn't involve memorizing the set of new features. The challenge is learning how to think in the object-oriented programing style that C++ supports. To help you get started on the right path, we'll present a hands-on introduction to object-oriented programming in the next chapter.

2

Introducing Object-Oriented Programming

Software developers and researchers have used many different languages to come up with a better way of modeling real-world problems. Although most programmers can't agree on which method is best for solving a given problem, most would agree that any method that supports a high level of abstraction is worth considering. Because the world is complex and the work of modeling real-world problems is tricky business, it helps to have techniques for reducing the complexity of representing both data and the operations that are used to process the data. And that's where object-oriented programming (OOP) comes in.

We have several goals in this chapter. First, we want to explain the basic concepts involved in object-oriented programming for those of you who are new to this programming methodology and style. We'll use many of the features of OOP throughout this book as we present C++ programming techniques, and that's why it's important to understand the basics of OOP. Our second goal is to show you how the fundamental OOP components and processes such as objects, classes, inheritance, and message passing can be represented with C++. Keep in mind that this chapter is designed to be a quick introduction. We'll take up many of the topics introduced here in later chapters.

After you complete this chapter, you will know:

• How OOP provides a system for packaging program data and code
• The five key components associated with OOP languages

- How OOP techniques can enhance the programs you develop
- How many of the fundamental OOP components such as objects, classes, and messages are implemented in C++
- How to bridge the gap between traditional programming and OOP

What Is Object-Oriented Programming?

Object-oriented programming has been getting a lot of attention lately. In fact, many programming language experts feel that in the 1990s OOP is going to have an impact similar to structured programming in the 1970s. Because OOP means so many different things to different programmers, it is difficult to come up with a single definition for OOP. However, it is fair to say that OOP is a programming style that uses objects as the essential building blocks.

Although the idea of using objects to create computer programs might not seem like such a revolutionary idea, the high-level nature of objects provides numerous benefits. As you work through this chapter, you'll start to see many of these benefits, such as the ability to create reusable code. Actually, objects are a lot like the *abstract* or *user-defined data types* widely used by programmers in the 1970s and early 1980s with structured languages (Pascal and Modula-2). However, the concept of an object extends beyond that of the classical definition of user-defined types, as we'll discover. Like user-defined data types, an object is a collection of data items, along with the associated functions used to operate on that data. But the real power of objects is in the way objects can be used to define other objects. This process is called *inheritance*; it is the mechanism that helps you build programs that are easily modified and adapted to different applications.

We can't answer our original question—What is object-oriented programming?—by just introducing objects. After all, OOP involves many other programming concepts. Fortunately, we can divide these concepts into five areas: *objects*, *classes*, *inheritance*, *messages*, and *methods*. As you work through this chapter, you'll learn how these components work together and how they can be represented with C++.

Note: C++ programs written in the object-oriented style provide objects that communicate with each other by passing messages.

Working with Objects

With conventional programming methods, we're taught to split up a program into two components: procedures and data. Each procedure acts as a *black box*. That is, it's a component that performs a specific task such as converting a set of numbers or displaying a window. If the black boxes are partitioned correctly, we can write the code for each one without worrying about what the other black boxes are doing internally. The main advantage for using this approach is that it helps us to develop programs that are modular and portable.

However, it could be argued that this method of programming is outdated and needs to be extended. It allows us to package program code into procedures, but what about the data? The data structures used in programs are often global or are passed around explicitly with parameters. More importantly, they are often treated separately from the procedures that work on them.

When object-oriented programming techniques are used, a program is divided into components that contain both data and procedures. Each component is considered an *object* and functions like a miniature program. Let's look at an example to see how OOP is different from conventional programming. Assume that the following four operations are required to move a visual object, such as a window, across the screen:

1. Move the visual object to the right.
2. Move the visual object to the left.
3. Move the visual object up.
4. Move the visual object down.

Using conventional programming methods, we can write a separate procedure for each operation as shown in Figure 2.1. These procedures serve as the black boxes. This approach provides a built-in mechanism for dividing operations. Unfortunately, the data that defines the object is separate from each of the procedures.

Let's now look at how we can process the visual object using object-oriented methods. Applying this method, we combine data and procedures into one package. Our first step is to create an object called *window*. This window object, shown in Figure 2.2, contains the procedures that define how the window moves. When the window receives a command, such as *move right*, the appropriate procedure executes.

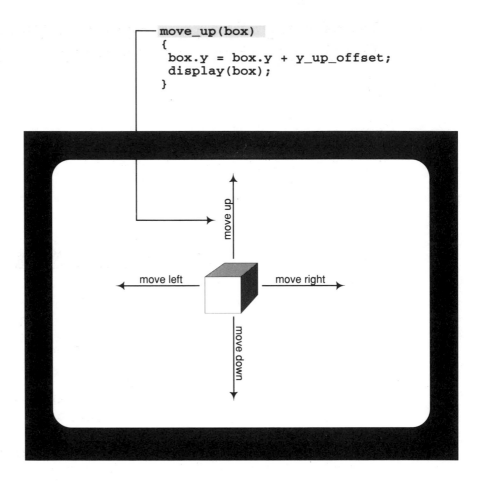

```
move_up(box)
{
  box.y = box.y + y_up_offset;
  display(box);
}
```

Figure 2.1. Moving the visual object with procedural techniques.

By combining procedures and data into objects, we can increase the level of abstraction of our programming tools. Hidden inside each object are the *methods* and data structures needed to manipulate and process the object. The outside world talks to the object by sending it what are commonly called *messages*. The important distinction here is that a message tells an object what task it should perform, not how the task should be performed. Essentially, objects function like independent little programs. The main program unit serves as a manager that controls these little programs.

As you gain more experience working with objects, you'll learn that objects have the following features:

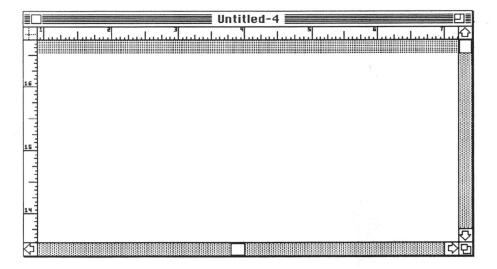

Figure 2.2. The window object.

- They are grouped into types called *classes*.
- They have internal data that defines their current state.
- They support *information hiding*.
- They can *inherit* properties from other objects.
- They can communicate with other objects by passing *messages*.
- They have *methods,* which define their *behavior*.

We'll examine each of these features as we continue this chapter.

Classes

To take advantage of the power and flexibility that objects provide, we need to come up with a way of categorizing objects. Usually, an object is categorized by its *type*. For example, our window object can be categorized as a graphics interface type object. Other objects that might fit into this category include pop-up windows, menus, help messages, and dialog boxes, as shown in Figure 2.3. We can group these objects under the graphics, or user interface, category because they have many attributes in common. That is, they can move across the screen, they can be displayed in different colors and sizes, and they provide a means for communicating with the user of a program.

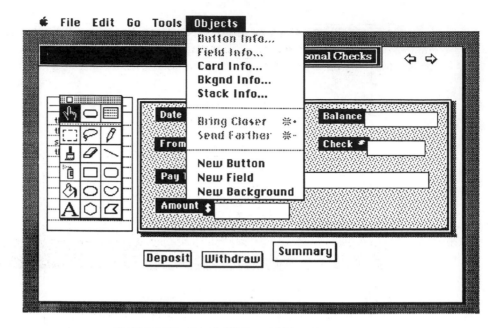

Figure 2.3. User-interface type objects.

In traditional OOP, each object type is called a *class*. A class is a user-defined type that determines the data structures and operations associated with that type. Fortunately, C++ provides a special statement that enables us to define a class easily. To see how this statement is used, let's represent our window as a class in C++. Here is the code required:

```
class window {
   int xpos, ypos;
   int window_type;
   int border_type;
   int window_color;
public:
   move_hz(int dir, int amt);
   move_vt(int dir, int amt);
};
```

Notice that this class defines the attributes for a window, such as a horizontal and vertical position, the window type, and color. Figure 2.4 shows the relationship between this class and an actual window object. The C++ class is essentially an extension of the C structure. In our example, we are using the keyword **public** to define the two functions **move_hz()** and **move_vt()** so that they can be accessed by any program that uses the **window** class.

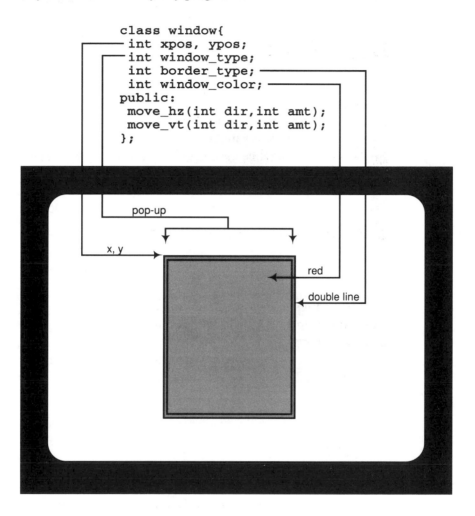

Figure 2.4. Relationship between a window class and a window.

Classes are useful devices that describe how certain types of objects are constructed. Each time we build an object from a class, we are creating what is called an *instance* of that class. Thus, objects are nothing more than instances of classes. In general, the terms *object* and *instance of a class* can be used interchangeably.

Note: Don't be misled into thinking that classes and objects are the same. A class is simply a device used to describe one or more objects having the same type.

Internal Data

One important property of objects is that they store *state* information in the form of internal data. The state of an object is simply the set of values of all the variables contained within the object at any given time. For the purpose of this book, we'll call these variables *state variables*. In our window example, the state variables might be the current coordinates of the window and its current color attributes.

In many cases, state variables are only used indirectly. To illustrate, let's return to our window example. Assume that a typical command to the window is

```
shrink by 5 rows and 6 columns
```

This means that the window should be reduced in size by five rows and six columns, as shown in Figure 2.5. Fortunately, we don't have to keep track of the current position because the window object does this for us. The current position is stored in a state variable that the window maintains internally. Of course, we might want to access this state variable from time to time by sending a message such as

```
tell us your current position
```

Information Hiding

In order to maintain the black box-like characteristics of OOP, we must consider how an object is to be accessed when we design the object. Usually, it is good practice to restrict access to the object's state variables and other internal information that is used to define the object. When an object is used we don't need to know about all of the specific implementation details. This practice of limiting the access to certain internal information is called *information hiding*.

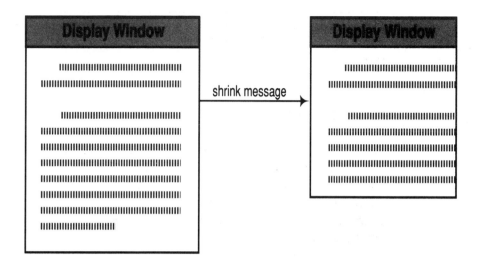

Figure 2.5. Resizing a window object.

In our window example, the user doesn't need to know how the window is implemented, only how it is used. The internal details of the implementation can and should be hidden. By taking this approach, we are free to change the window's design (perhaps to improve its efficiency or to get it working on different hardware) without having to change the code that uses it.

Note: C++ supports information hiding features with the **public**, **private**, and **protected** keywords. You'll see these in action throughout this book.

Inheritance

Another important property of both objects and classes is *inheritance*. Inheritance is the property that allows classes to be built from other classes. The real advantage of using this technique is that you can build upon what you already have. The key to understanding how inheritance applies to objects is found when we consider objects that are hierarchical in nature. Let's return to our window example to clarify this point.

Assume that you are working with different types of windows. Some of the windows are used to display warning messages, some are used to edit text, and others are used to list files. While there can be implementation differences among these windows, they all share common traits, such as the ability to accept messages like

"Change your border attributes to a single line drawn in a red foreground and black background."

We can define a main window and assign it the standard traits such as move, shrink, grow, and so on, and then we can create *instances* of this main window for each *specialty window* (warning window, edit turtle, and browse window). Because of inheritance, each specialty window will automatically receive the attributes of the main window.

Inheritance also allows us to create a hierarchy of classes where each subclass can inherit or share properties with its parent. In other words, you can have general classes from which more specific classes are derived. In C++ terminology, a general class is called a *base class*. The classes derived from base classes are called *derived classes*. These derived classes can inherit code and data from its base class, adding its own special code and data to it, or perhaps changing those items that need to be different.

Message Passing

In a previous section we mentioned that objects perform actions when they receive messages. You're now probably wondering what a message is. A message is essentially a command that is sent to an object to instruct the object to do something. The technique of sending messages to objects is called *message passing*. As an example, you might send a window object a message such as *Scroll up 5 lines*. Messages play a critical role in OOP. Without them, the objects that we define wouldn't be able to communicate with each other.

From a conventional viewpoint, message passing is nothing more than calling a function. In fact, that is exactly what happens when a message is sent in a C++ program. But what's important is not how message passing is implemented, but how messages are used. Programming in an object-oriented style requires a shift in viewpoint. To help you master this shift in viewpoint, we've devoted a complete section to it later in this chapter.

Let's consider our window object again. Assume that we want to change its size, so we send it the message

```
Shrink by 3 columns to the right
```

Note that you don't tell the window how to change its size; the window handles that itself. In fact, you could send the same message to different kinds of windows and expect each one to perform the same action. How the window changes is its own business.

Methods and Behavior

We've now covered all the critical OOP components except one—*methods*. What is a method? It is the code that describes how an object should respond to a given message. In classic OOP terminology, the manner in which an object responds to a message is called its *behavior*. Different objects can have different methods associated with a message and thus have different behaviors.

In C++, methods are implemented with what are called *member functions*. For instance, in our window class:

```
class window {
   int xpos, ypos;
   int window_type;
   int border_type;
   int window_color;
public:
   move_hz(int dir, int amt);
   move_vt(int dir, int amt);
};
```

the functions **move_hz()** and **move_vt()** are the names of messages that you can send to a window object. The content of the messages is stored in the parameters to the functions. The code that implements these functions are the methods associated with those messages. Figure 2.6 shows how this class corresponds with the functions **move_hz()** and **move_vt()**. Using inheritance, we can derive different classes of windows by changing the definitions of some of these member functions, thus allowing different behaviors to occur.

In summary, objects, classes, internal data, information hiding, inheritance, message passing, and methods are all components of OOP. Figure 2.7 presents a translation box to show the relationships between OOP and traditional programming terminology.

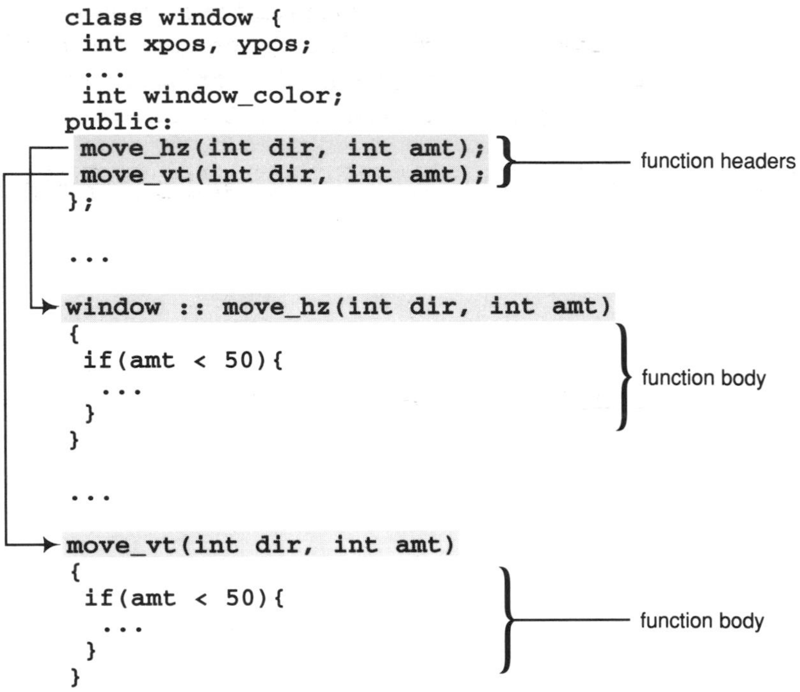

```
class window {
  int xpos, ypos;
  ...
  int window_color;
public:
  move_hz(int dir, int amt);  ⎫
  move_vt(int dir, int amt);  ⎬ ──── function headers
};                            ⎭

...

window :: move_hz(int dir, int amt)
{
  if(amt < 50){       ⎫
    ...               ⎬ function body
  }                   ⎭
}

...

move_vt(int dir, int amt)
{
  if(amt < 50){       ⎫
    ...               ⎬ ──── function body
  }                   ⎭
}
```

Figure 2.6. Relationship between window class and member functions.

A Shift in Viewpoint

Now that we've discussed the different components of OOP, it's time to see how OOP techniques can be applied. We've been emphasizing the point that OOP involves more that just using objects in a program. To program in the OOP style, you must learn first how to think in a different paradigm. Our goal in this section is to help you change your viewpoint.

When we program in a conventional language such as C, we typically start by determining our data requirements, and then we build data structures and write functions to process the data structures. This approach involves using parameters to pass data to functions. To return data, function return values are typically used. In this sense, the data is subservient to the functions.

With OOP, we take the reverse approach. The data is still grouped into structures (now called objects); however, these structures contain functions as well. By placing a function in an object, the function's job is to describe the behavior of the object. This change in viewpoint might seem subtle, but it turns out to be quite powerful for many applications. To see why, let's look at an example that we'll code in both C and C++.

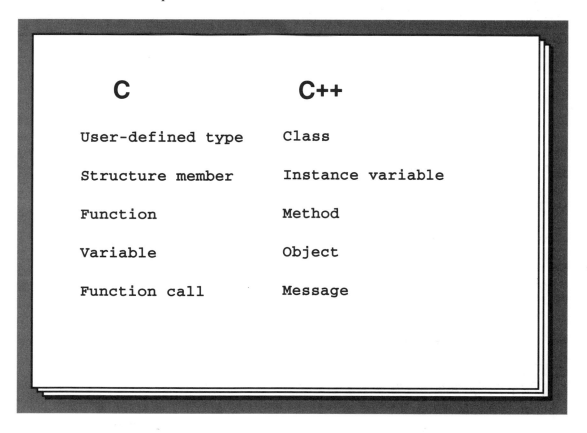

C	C++
User-defined type	Class
Structure member	Instance variable
Function	Method
Variable	Object
Function call	Message

Figure 2.7. Relationships between OOP and traditional programming terminology.

A Button Event Driver in C

Suppose that you're writing a user interface for a new program you've been developing. The interface is mouse-based and supports windows, icons, and buttons. Now, assume that one of your input screens is assigned three buttons, as shown in Figure 2.8. Each button controls a different activity. When a button is selected with the mouse, the action assigned to the button is carried out. For example, the first button might pop up a message, the second scrolls the screen window, and the third closes the window and terminates the program. A typical way to program such an interface is to write an event loop, which handles the selection of buttons. In C, this code will do the job:

```c
enum kind_of_button { popup, scroll, quit };
typedef struct {
    kind_of_button btype;
   /* other button data ... */
} button;

int handler(button *b)
{
    switch(b->btype) {
        case popup : popup_handler(); return 1;
        case scroll: scroll_handler(); return 1;
        case quit  : return 0;
        default: ;
    }
}

button *b;
int r;
/* code to set up buttons goes here ... */
do {
    b = wait_for_button_activation();
    r = handler(b);
} while(r);
```

In this code we create a user-defined type called **button**, which is implemented as a structure. The **button** structure holds the subfield **btype,** which is an enumerated type called **kind_of_button**. The event loop is a **do-loop** that first calls the **wait_for_button_activation()** function to wait for a button to be selected. This function returns a pointer to the button selected. The pointer is then passed to our button handler function. Note that **handler()** is essentially a **switch** statement with one case statement for each button type.

Although this technique works, it is not easy to extend. To add a new button type, you must modify **kind_of_button** to take on more values. You must also add more cases to the **switch** statement in the button handler. This means you must modify the handler each time a new button is added. Now suppose you're a software vendor and you've compiled your button handler and driver and put it in a object code library, which was then sent to your customers. What if your customers want to add their own kind of buttons? They can't do this unless you release the source code to the handler.

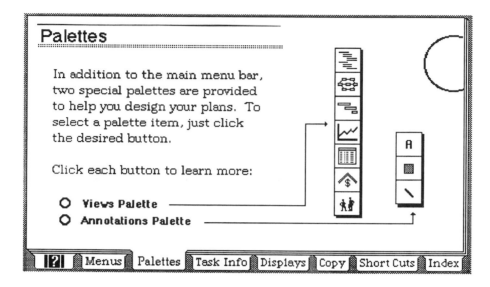

Figure 2.8. Example of screen buttons.

With objects, you can get around this problem. It is possible to write and compile a button handler, tuck it away in an object library, and then later add other types of buttons without ever having to recompile the original button handler code. This is the principle of *code reusability*; it is one of the many benefits of OOP. Let's next explore how we can write the button handler in C++.

Note: The most difficult obstacle in learning C++ is learning to change your programming approach from a traditional viewpoint to an object-oriented one.

The Event Driver in C++

In C++, our button example can be coded as follows. (Recall that in C++, comments can be denoted by // markers as well as the usual C brackets.)

```
// Define a general kind of button and its handler
class button {
public:
    virtual int handler();
  // other data and functions ...
};

int button::handler() {
    // do default action here (basically nothing) ...
    return 1;
};

// Derive different types of buttons and their handlers
class popup_button: public button {
public:
    int handler(); // defined below
    // other data and functions ...
};

int popup_button::handler() {
    // popup code goes here ...
    return 1;
};

class scroll_button: public button {
public:
    int handler(); // defined below
    // other data and functions
};

int scroll_button::handler() {
    // code for scrolling goes here ...
    return 1;
};

class quit_button: public button {
public:
    int handler(); // defined below
    // other data and functions
};
```

```
int quit_button::handler() {
   // cleanup code on exit goes here ...
   return 0;
}

// C++ Event Driver

button *b;
int r;

// Set up buttons here ...

do {
   b = wait_for_button_activation();
   r = b->handler();
} while(r);
```

Don't worry if you can't understand every line of code at this point. Just note the way that we have defined each button type. Instead of having one structure with a tag field like we did in the C code, we've defined several kinds of structures. These structures are called *classes* in C++. As we discussed earlier in this chapter, classes are used to define different types of objects. In our button example, we even went one step further and *derived* special button classes from a general button class. That is, we defined a general kind of button and then made special cases of it. This concept is illustrated in Figure 2.9. Each special kind of button has its own handler, but it inherits all other properties from the general button class.

At first glance, you might think that the C++ code is more complicated than the C version, but look at it more carefully, particularly the event loop driver:

```
// C++ Event Driver

button *b;
int r;

// Set up buttons here ...

do {
   b = wait_for_button_activation();
```

```
    r = b->handler();
} while(r);
```

Notice that the button handler is called with the statement:

```
r = b->handler();
```

If you're not familiar with C++, this statement might look a little strange. What we're doing here is calling the handler function of the button to be activated. This handler is a member of the structure holding the button and can be accessed just like any other member of a structure. In other words, C++ structures hold data, as well as functions. This is what we meant when we said earlier that objects can *contain* functions.

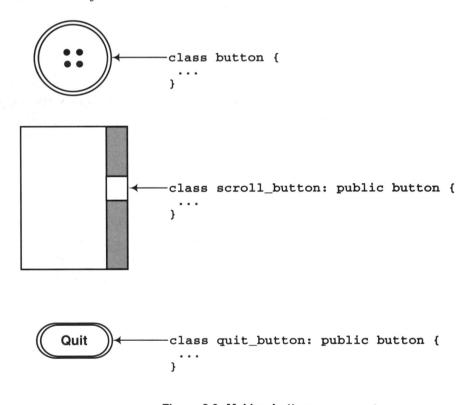

```
class button {
    ...
}
```

```
class scroll_button: public button {
    ...
}
```

```
class quit_button: public button {
    ...
}
```

Figure 2.9. Making buttons.

Each button has its own handler, and what we're doing is telling the button to call that handler. In a sense, we're sending a message to the button to activate itself. Instead of having one function to handle all types of buttons and passing the button to activate as a parameter, we let each button have its own function and simply "send a message to it" by calling that function. This is the fundamental shift in viewpoint, which is summarized in Figure 2.10.

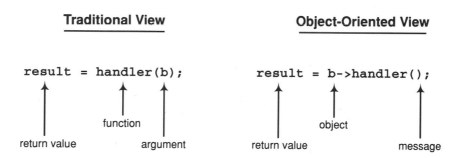

Figure 2.10. Fundamental shift in viewpoint.

You should study this figure carefully, for in it lies the key to understanding what is behind the object-oriented method. With this key, you can unlock a much more powerful and maintainable programming style.

Extending the Button Handler

We haven't said yet what is so powerful about this shift in viewpoint. Think back to our problem of the software vendor who wanted to allow his customers to add more types of buttons without needing the source code to the driver and button handler. Well, with the C++ code given earlier, this is possible. To add a new kind of button, the customer only needs to derive the button's definition from the general definition and then code up a special handler for that button. For instance, we might define a button that beeps when activated:

```
class beep_button : public button {
public:
    int handler();
  // other class members go here
};


int beep_button::handler() {
```

```
    beep();
  return 1;
}
```

Once this is done, the precompiled driver will work with this type of button just as though it knew about it all along. How is this possible? With the statement

```
r = b->handler();
```

the button driver does not have any idea what the button handler does; it merely has a pointer to it so that it can call it. This is not the case with our C version, which has the call

```
r = handler(b);
```

Here, there is one handler, which was coded to have a switch statement to handle each kind of button. If this handler were precompiled and tucked into an object library, it would be difficult to add a case to that **switch** statement.

Summary

In this chapter you've learned about the basic principles and components of object-oriented programming. Here are most of the key points that we covered:

- Object-oriented programming incorporates these five important components:

  Objects
  Classes
  Methods
  Messages
  Inheritance

- Classes are used as a higher-level mechanism for grouping objects.
- An object derived from a specific class is called an *instance* of that class.

- The technique of placing data and functions inside objects so that they cannot be directly accessed is called *information hiding*.
- *Inheritance* is the property that allows objects to inherit traits from other objects.
- Objects communicate with each other by passing messages.
- *Methods*, the code that describes how objects react to messages, are implemented with *member functions* in C++.

Exercises

1. Describe in detail the difference between an object and a class.

2. List five advantages that OOP has over conventional programming.

3. Assuming that a window's size is determined by using both the length of the longest string to calculate the width and the number of lines displayed to calculate the height, describe how the window object might use state variables to store its size.

4. Explain the way information-hiding techniques are useful for developing portable programs.

5. Describe the difference between a C++ *base class* and a *derived class*.

3

Introducing Classes

No matter what type of program you are developing, from a simple data conversion program to a desktop presentation application, you'll need a way to represent your data. In high-level languages like C and Pascal, built-in language statements (structures and records) are provided to help organize and represent program data. These data storage devices are especially useful because they allow us to create user-defined types by combining data components that are of different data types into a single structure. As we make the transition to object-oriented languages, in particular C++, more functional user-defined types can be created by using a component called *classes*. Classes are especially useful because they allow us to add functions to our structures.

In this chapter we introduce C++'s flexible classes for representing data and functions. We'll start by showing you how basic classes are defined. We'll also look at the similarities and differences between C++ classes and C structures. Our goal is to explain all of the basics of classes so that you can start using them in your C++ programs. For instance, you'll learn how to define a class, how to access class members, and how to define functions that serve as class members. In the next chapter, we'll present the more advanced topics related to classes, such as techniques for creating dynamic objects and deriving functions, data hiding techniques, and the basics of using virtual functions and friend functions.

After you complete this chapter you'll know:

- The basic principles of abstract data types
- How the scoping operator :: is used to access class members

- The basic scoping rules for accessing the members of classes
- How function bodies can be defined inside and outside of classes
- How to access the data and function members of classes
- How to define and use static class members
- How classes relate to C structures and unions

Creating Data Types in C++

Because C++ is an extension of C, you can use any of the built-in data storage devices that C provides, including variables, arrays, structures, and unions. Figure 3.1 shows the different ways these constructs are stored in memory. Notice that as we progress from the simple memory variable to the union, the flexibility of the storage device increases. For instance, with a memory variable we can only store a single value having a specified data type, whereas, with structures and unions, we can combine an assortment of data elements of different data types, including pointers. These data structures are useful for creating more complex types such as linked lists and binary trees.

Now you're probably wondering about the advantages C++ provides for creating user-defined data types. The best way to answer this question is to look at an example. Suppose that you are writing a program that monitors the performance of the machines used in a factory. Your program must read data from the different machines and display it on the screen so that an engineer can monitor them. A good way to display the information is to use a set of gauges and dials, as shown in Figure 3.2. One way to represent these dials in a language like C is to define a data structure for each dial. For example, the following structure could be used to represent a temperature dial:

```
struct temp_dial {
    int low;            /* low temperature range */
    int high;           /* high temperature range */
    int dial_inc;       /* the dial increment */
    int xloc, yloc;     /* the position of the dial */
    int diameter;       /* size of the dial */
};
```

So far so good, but how do we get the dial to do something? That is, how do we get the needle on the dial to move? After all, structures can only store data, and a real dial is more than just a set of data components. Its whole purpose is to display data, and we need functions to do that. If we continue to write a C program to process our dial, we'll need to build functions that take our dial structure as arguments. As an example, the following function displays either the current temperature or a warning message if the current temperature is outside the dial's low and high temperature ranges:

```
void display_temp(struct temp_dial *d, int temp)
{
    if (temp <= d->low)
        printf("Brrr...it's $%&*#$ cold out!\n");
    else if (temp >= d->high)
        printf("We must be in Phoenix, Arizona!\n");
    else
        printf("The current temperature is %d\n", temp);
}
```

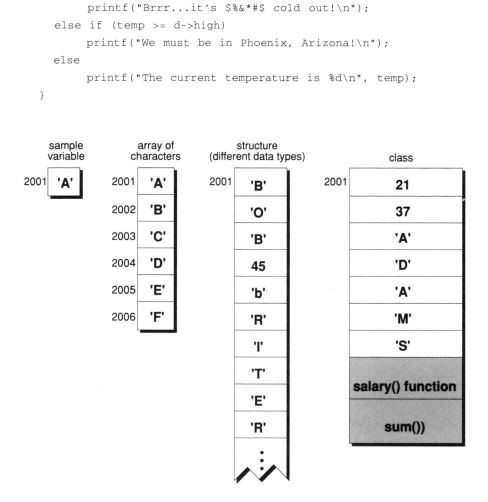

Figure 3.1. Representations of storage devices.

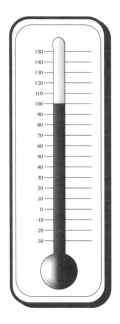
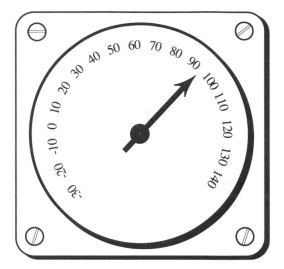

Figure 3.2. Gauge and dial.

Now we have two separate pieces: a dial structure and a function to process the dial. These components taken together make up what is known as an *abstract data type*. The main attraction of the abstract data type is that it provides a mechanism for combining both data and operations.

But hold on a second. We really haven't done anything to combine the **temp_dial** structure and the **display_temp**() function. Actually, we can't if we continue to use C. With C++, on the other hand, we can use classes to combine data structures and functions.

Note: Abstract data types are used by programmers to package data elements with the operations to be performed on the data. The term *user-defined types* is often used to refer to abstract data types.

Getting Started with Classes

As we just discussed, classes are used to combine data and operations. That is, they are used to create user-defined data types. To support the object-oriented programming style, C++ provides classes so that objects can be constructed.

As you begin to work with classes, keep in mind that classes and C structures have much in common. In Figure 3.3, we've included a checklist to show you that all of the features supported by structures, such as defining arrays of structures or passing structures to functions, are available with classes.

☑ Classes can be used as array types.

☑ Class objects can be passed to functions.

☑ Class objects can be returned by functions.

☑ Pointers can be used to access class objects.

☑ Classes can be nested.

☑ Memory can be allocated dynamically for class objects.

Figure 3.3. Features of classes.

But keep in mind that classes are much more powerful than C structures. They provide a number of extensions that allow us to build abstract data types and support object-oriented programming. Some of these extensions include:

- A facility for information hiding with **public**, **private**, **protected**, and **friend** declarations
- The ability to have functions as members
- A facility for conveniently initializing and cleaning up objects using special functions called *constructor* and *destructor* *functions*
- A facility to support *inheritance* with *derived classes* and *virtual functions*

We'll be explaining how these extensions are used throughout this book.

Note: In C++ you use classes the way you would use structures: to describe the data representations of a given type. Remember that a class can do anything a C structure can.

Creating a Simple Class

Let's return to our previous dial example and develop a class for it. Here's a
C++ program that uses a class to process the dial:

```cpp
#include <stdio.h>
class temp_dial {      // the dial is now a class
    int low;           // low temperature range
    int high;          // high temperature range
    int dial_inc;      // the dial increment
    int xloc, yloc;    // the position of the dial
    int diameter;      // size of the dial
public:
    void display_temp(int temp);
    void set_temp_range(int l, int h) { low = l; high = h;}
};

void temp_dial::display_temp(int temp)
{
    if (temp <= low)
        printf("Brrr...it's $@&*#$ cold out!\n");
   else if (temp >= high)
        printf("We must be in Phoenix, Arizona!\n");
   else
        printf("The current temperature is %d\n", temp);
}

void main() {
    temp_dial dial;
    int l, h, ctemp;
    printf("Enter the low and high temperature ranges\n");
    scanf("%d%d", &l,&h);
    printf("Enter the current temperature\n");
    scanf("%d", &ctemp);
    dial.set_temp_range(l,h);
    dial.display_temp(ctemp);
}
```

A sample run of the program would look like:

```
Enter the low and high temperature ranges
22 105
Enter the current temperature
106
We must be in Phoenix, Arizona!
```

As you scan the sample program, you might notice some unfamiliar syntax. But don't worry if you can't follow each line of code just yet. We'll be explaining the basics of defining and using classes next. Essentially, this program shows how a class is defined and used. The unique feature of the class is that we are able to place functions inside the class definition. In this case, **display_temp**() and **set_temp_range**() are defined as class members.

Class Components

Now that we've written a class, let's step back a moment and look at the components provided for defining classes. We'll start by studying a general class definition, and then we'll look at how classes are used in C++ programs. A class is defined in much the same way as a C structure, except it has extra keywords to support information hiding. Here is the basic syntax:

```
class <classname> {
private:
    // private members go here
protected:
    // protected members go here
public:
    // public members go here
};
```

Like a structure, a class contains one or more members. However, a class can also contain three levels of information hiding and, for this, the class members are divided into three corresponding groups: private, protected, and public. A private member plays a role similar to that of a local variable in a function. That is, it can only be accessed by other members of the class, much like a local variable is only available inside the function in which it is defined.

Note: The **private**, **public**, and **protected** keywords are optional. By default, all members are private unless otherwise specified. These keywords can be placed in any order and may be included more than once.

Protected members have a level of data hiding that's between private and public members. They are normally used when deriving a new class from a predefined class. To the outside world (that is, outside of the class), they are private. However, they are accessible inside the class they were defined in and in any class derived from the original class. Private members do not work this way. That is, a private member of a base class cannot be accessed by derived classes of the base class.

To better understand the difference between private and protected members, examine Figure 3.4. Here we are showing two classes where the second class is derived from the first class. Notice that the private member in the first class cannot be accessed by the second class, whereas the protected member in the first class can be accessed by the second class. We'll defer further discussion of protected members until we reach the chapters that cover inheritance and class hierarchies, where the explanation will be more relevant.

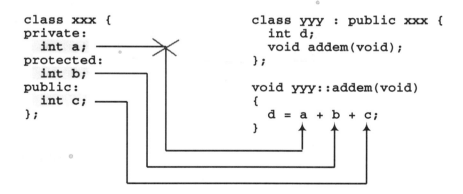

```
class xxx {                      class yyy : public xxx {
private:                             int d;
   int a;                            void addem(void);
protected:                       };
   int b;
public:                          void yyy::addem(void)
   int c;                        {
};                                   d = a + b + c;
                                 }
```

Figure 3.4. Deriving classes.

Public members, on the other hand, are declared after the **public** keyword and are accessible to any user of the class.

The members of a class can be simple data types such as **int**, **char**, and so on; object types of another class; or functions. For example, here's a class definition we can use to represent rectangles. To create this class we'll use both private and public members, as shown:

```
class rectangle {
  int wd, ht;
public:
  void set_size(int w, int h) { wd = w; ht = h; }
  int area(void) { return wd * ht; }
};
```

Note that we are also using both data and functions in this class definition. The name of this class is **rectangle**. The data members, **wd** and **ht**, are declared just like they are in a C structure. Because the data members are listed before the **public** keyword, they are private by default and can only be accessed by the other members of this class, including **set_size()** and **area()**.

Figure 3.5 summarizes the different components of a class definition including private and public members. Notice also that the class contains private and public functions.

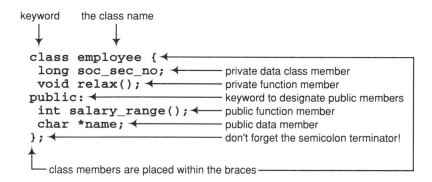

Figure 3.5. Components of a class definition.

Note: Remember to include a semicolon after the last curly brace in a class definition. If you forget it, you'll encounter a compiler error.

Functions are included in a class definition by enclosing their definitions within the body of the class, as we've done for **set_size()** and **area()**. Here we've put both the function headers and function bodies inside the class. A function declared in this manner is called an *inline function*—a special type of function that's treated much like a macro. It's also possible (and more typical) to define the function body outside of the class, like this:

```
class rectangle {
   int wd, ht;
public:
   void set_size(int w, int h);
   int area(void);
};

void rectangle::set_size(int w, int h)
{
   wd = w; ht = h;    // note scoping of wd and ht
}

int rectangle::area(void)
{
   return wd * ht;    // note scoping of wd and ht
}
```

The function headers are still defined within the class declaration and serve as function prototypes for type-checking purposes. The function bodies are declared outside by placing the class name in front of the function name and including the **::** scoping operator. This operator is used to denote member functions and serves to indicate to which class a function belongs. Figure 3.6 shows the format for a function definition.

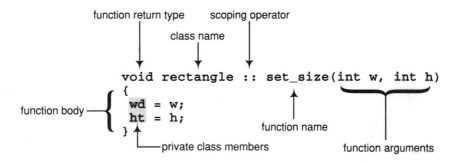

Figure 3.6. Format for a member function definition.

Note: The scoping operator :: joins a class name with a function that is a member of the class.

Note the scoping used in the example functions. Even though the function bodies are defined outside the class declaration, the class data members can be accessed by the functions by merely specifying their name (without any need for additional qualification), as shown above in functions **set_size**() and **area**(). For example, in the function **set_size**(), the statements

```
wd = w; ht = h;
```

set the variables (class members) **wd** and **ht** to the values stored in the parameters **w** and **h**. Later in this chapter and in the next chapter, we'll have more to say about the scoping rules of classes.

Another feature of classes introduced by our **rectangle** class is the concept of information hiding. The member functions **set_size**() and **area**() are public. That is, they are accessible on the outside, because they are declared after the **public** keyword. The members **wd** and **ht**, by virtue of not having an access specifier (**public** or **private**), are private and cannot be used outside the class. Only the functions **set_size**() and **area**() can access them because they are also members of the class. If the class was redefined as

```
class rectangle {
public:
    int wd, ht;
    void set_size(int w, int h);
    int area(void);
};
```

then the members **wd** and **ht** could be accessed by any statement or function included in a program that uses the class definition.

Note: When you define a class, you should make all the members private that do not need to be accessed outside of the class. This practice helps you write modular programs by hiding the implementation details of the class.

Making Objects from Classes

Now that you've seen how a class is defined, you might be wondering how a class definition is used in a C++ program. Because classes, like structures, represent user-defined data types, they can be used just like any other built-in type such as **int** or **char** to declare variables. For example, we can declare a **rectangle** variable as follows:

```
rectangle window_brd;
```

Although **window_brd** is a variable, in object-oriented terms it is usually referred to as an object because it contains both data and functions.

Note: Objects are like miniature programs that can be pieced together like building blocks.

Note the distinction between a class and an object. Class **rectangle** defines a type of object, and **window_brd** is an instance of that type. Throughout this book, the terms *object* and *variable* will be used interchangeably; they both mean *instances of a class*.

Objects can be treated like any C variable. The main difference is that we can call any of the functions belonging to an object; that is, we can send a message to it. For example, we can send a message to our **window_brd** object to set its size and then command it to give us back its area:

```
// Declare the object
rectangle window_brd;

// Define the object's size
window_brd.set_size(10,5);

// Calculate the object's area
printf("Area is: %d\n", window_brd.area());
```

Accessing a Class Member

The data members of a class are accessed in much the same way that structure members are accessed. If you have the following structure in C:

```
struct list_node {
    char key[10];
```

```
      int size;
};
```

and you declare a memory variable for this structure such as

```
struct list_node lst1;
```

you can access either member of the structure using the syntax

```
structure_name.member_name
```

For example, both of the following statements are legal:

```
strcpy(lst1.key, "harry");
new_val = lst1.size;
```

Fortunately, to access public class members that are data variables, you use the same technique. For example, using the following class definition and object declaration:

```
class list_node {
public:
   char key[10];
   int size;
};
list_node lobj1;
```

either class member can be referenced using the standard notation as shown:

```
strcpy(lobj1.key, "harry");
new_val = lobj1.size;
```

Private data members, on the other hand, cannot be accessed by a main program using this notation. Also, a function cannot access a private member unless the function is a member of the class. Later, when we present a discussion on the scoping rules for class members, you'll learn more about how both private and public data members are accessed.

We've now seen how data members are accessed, but what about function members? Recall that the rectangle class we defined earlier contained the two functions **set_size()** and **area()** as members:

```
class rectangle {
    int wd, ht;
public:
    void set_size(int w, int h);
    int area(void);
};
```

Because these functions are defined as public members, we can access them by calling them from a main program or another function. To do this we use the notation

```
<object_name>.<function_name>(<arguments>)
```

As an example, the following program declares two rectangle objects and calls the class member functions **set_size()** and **area()**:

```
#include <stdio.h>
void main() {

    rectangle rect1, rect2;
    rect1.set_size(10,20);
    rect2.set_size(100,200);
    printf("The area of the first rectangle is %d\n",
            rect1.area());
    printf("The area of the second rectangle is %d\n",
        rect2.area());
}
```

Although it appears that each rectangle object **rect1** and **rect2** has its own copy of the **set_size()** and **area()** functions, this is really not the case. As Figure 3.7 illustrates, there is only one copy of each function stored in memory; however, the notation

```
rect1.set_size(10,20);
```

informs the C++ compiler which object you are using to call the function specified by your code.

This approach to calling functions is different from the method used to call functions in C. In C++, it is as though we are sending an object a message when we call a member function. That is, the **set_size()** function sends a message to the object **rect1**.

```
class rect{
 int wd, ht;
public:
 void set_size(int w, int h);
 int area(void);
};
```

memory for functions

memory for object

| wd | ht |

```
void rect :: set_size(int w, int h)
{
 wd = w; ht = h;
}
```

```
int rect:: area(void)
{
 return wd * ht;
}
```

Figure 3.7. How function members are stored.

Note: In C++ the **.** operator is used to access a class member just like it is used in C to access a structure member. The **->** operator also works in a similar fashion.

Creating and Using a Complete Class

Now that we've seen how classes are defined and accessed, we're ready to roll up our sleeves and begin writing more complete classes. As an example we'll create a class for representing clocks and then show how the clock can be used. This clock keeps track of hours, minutes, and seconds, which you can set and display. You can also instruct the clock to start ticking, which, when performed in succession, runs the clock. Here's the complete program:

```
#include <stdio.h>
// The clock definition
class clock {
```

```
   int hr, min, sec;    // private members
public:
  void set(int h, int m, int s);
  void tick(void);
  void display(void);
};

// Member function to set the clock
void clock::set(int h, int m, int s)
{
  hr = h; min = m; sec = s;
}

// Member function to cause clock ticks
void clock::tick(void)
{
  if (sec++ == 60) {
     sec = 0;
     if (min++ == 60) {
        min = 0;
        hr++;
     }
  }
}

// Member function to display the current time
void clock::display(void)
{
  printf("%02d:%02d:%02d\n", hr, min, sec);
}

// The main clock program
void main() {
  clock big_ben;
  int i;

  big_ben.set(12, 0, 0);
  for (i=0; i<3600; i++) {
    big_ben.tick();
```

```
        big_ben.display();
    }
}
```

Let's discuss this code in detail. The first thing we've done is set up the **clock** class. Here, we've defined clocks to have the private members **hr**, **min**, and **sec**. These members serve as state variables for clock objects. In essence, they are its memory. By making them private, we force the user of a clock to access them indirectly through the public functions **set()**, **tick()**, and **display()**.

This arrangement keeps the data private and the functions public, and is typical of well-designed objects. We want to treat the objects as black boxes. The way to do this is to hide the details of how they are implemented and to allow only the behavior (i.e., the input/output response produced by the functions) to be known.

Each function is defined using the special **::** syntax to indicate that it belongs to **clock**. By doing so, the functions automatically have access to the state variables **hr**, **min**, and **sec**.

After defining the class **clock**, the main program creates a clock object called **big_ben**. Notice that this object is declared with the same syntax required to declare a C variable:

```
clock big_ben;
```

We've also declared the integer variable **i**, which is used in our loop to run the clock.

Before running the clock, we send a message to **big_ben** telling it to set the time to twelve o'clock. After this, we run **big_ben** for 3600 seconds (one hour) by sending it a command to tick one second at a time. We also command **big_ben** to display its current time after each tick so that we can see what's happening.

Note the terminology we are using to describe how this program works. Instead of making statements like "call the tick function" and "call the display function," we use statements like "tell the clock to tick" and "tell the clock to display its current time." This subtle difference reinforces the object-oriented approach. Our clock objects aren't simply a collection of data and functions; they are independent, self-contained entities.

Using Multiple Objects

Just as we can define and use multiple structure variables in a program, we can also define and use multiple objects from a single class definition. To illustrate how this is done, let's put together a program that uses objects to represent a simple hierarchical menu system. The program includes a definition for a general menu class called **menu**, and this class is used to declare two objects called **topmenu** and **submenu**. Here is the complete program:

```
#include <stdio.h>
#include <string.h>
#include <stdarg.h>
// base class for a menu definition
class menu {
   char name[15];
   char msg[50];
   int num_items;
   char items[5][15];
public:
   int item_selected;
   void init(char *n, char *msg, int nitems, char *item1, ...);
   void disp(void);
   void process(void);
};

void menu::init(char *n, char *m, int nitems, char *item1, ...)
{
   va_list arg_ptr;
   char *cur_arg;
   int i=0;

   item_selected = 0;              // indicates no item selected
   strcpy(name, n);                // set the menu's title
   strcpy(msg, m);                 // set the menu's message
   num_items = nitems;
   va_start(arg_ptr, item1);   // process variable arguments
   strcpy(items[i++], item1);
   while (--nitems > 0) {
       cur_arg = va_arg(arg_ptr, char *);
       strcpy(items[i++], cur_arg);    // store menu items
```

```
      }
   va_end(arg_ptr);
}

void menu::disp(void)
{
   int i;

   printf("%s\n\n", name);
   printf("%s\n", msg);
   for (i = 0; i < num_items; i++)
      printf("(%d) %s\n", i+1, items[i]);
}

void menu::process(void)
{
   printf("\n\nPlease select a menu item __");
   scanf("%d", &item_selected);
   printf("\n");
}

// The main menu program
void main()
{
   menu topmenu, submenu;

   topmenu.init("File Options", "Select a file command",
                4, "Open file", "Close file", "Save file",
                "Delete file");

   submenu.init("File Types", "Select a file type",
                3, "Source file", "Document file", "Other");
   topmenu.disp();
   topmenu.process();

   // process the selected menu item
   switch (topmenu.item_selected) {
     case 1 : submenu.disp();
              submenu.process();
              // add code to process submenu item
```

```
                  break;
    case 2 : printf("\nReady to close the file");
             break;
    case 3 : printf("\nReady to save the file");
             break;
    case 4 : printf("\nReady to delete a file");
             break;
    default : printf("\nInvalid item selected");
  }


}
```

And here is a sample run:

```
File Options

(1) Open file
(2) Close file
(3) Save file
(4) Delete file


Please select a menu item __1

File Types

Select a file type
(1) Source file
(2) Document file
(3) Other


Please select a menu item __3
```

First notice how the two menu objects are declared:

```
menu topmenu, submenu;
```

Each of these objects contains the set of members included in the class **menu**. The first object, **topmenu**, represents the highest level menu. The other object, **submenu**, represents the menu that is activated when one of the menu items from **topmenu** is selected. Figure 3.8 shows how each object is represented and stored in memory. Notice that each object allocates memory space to store the data members. We've made the member **item_selected** public so that it can be accessed from the body of the main program.

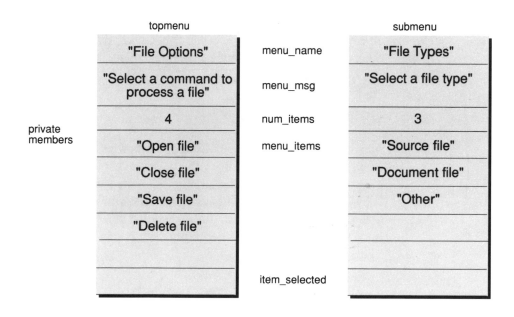

Figure 3.8. How menu objects are stored in memory.

The class definition contains three public functions, **init()**, **disp()**, and **process()**. These functions should be easy to follow; however, in order to process different sized menus, **init()** accepts a variable number of parameters, as indicated by its definition:

```
void menu::init(char *n, char *m, int nitems, char *item1, ...)
```

Inside the body of the function we are using the standard C functions **va_arg()**, **va_start()**, and **va_end()** to access the variable arguments. (If you are not familiar with using variable arguments, we discuss this subject in more detail in Chapter 5.)

The main program contains a simple **switch** statement to process the menu items. For this example, we've limited the number of menu items in the main menu to four, in order to keep the example simple. If you needed to expand the program by adding more entries, you could easily do so by declaring other menu items.

Note: When multiple objects are created from a single class definition, each object receives its own copy of the public and private data members. To reduce overhead, the function members are not actually stored in each object.

Static Members

As we've stated, each object declared in a program normally receives a copy of all the data members of its class. However, it's possible to declare class members in such a way that all objects created from the class share the same copy of the data members. These members, which are called *static members*, are declared by placing the **static** keyword before the member declarations. For example, here's a class definition that contains a static member:

```
class window {
    static list popup_stack; // static member declaration
    int x, y, wd, ht;
    char *save_image;
public:
    void put_char(int c);
    void print(char *s);
    void popup(int x, int y, int wd, int ht);
    void unpop(void);
};
list window::popup_stack;  // must allocate outside the class
window edit_win, error_win;
```

We've declared **popup_stack** to be a static **list** member. Therefore, the two objects, **edit_win** and **error_win**, created from this class will share this member, as shown in Figure 3.9. Notice, however, that the other members are not shared because they are not declared to be static.

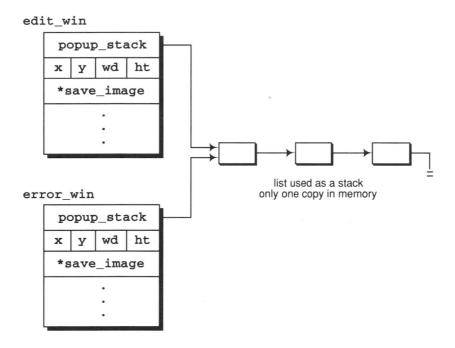

Figure 3.9. Representing static members.

Static members are useful when objects of the same class need to access the same data, as shown here with our window objects. Each window is stored on a pop-up stack, and it's useful for each window to be able to access that stack directly, perhaps to communicate with the base window or other windows on the stack. It's necessary for each window to use the same stack. This can be accomplished by making the stack a static member.

In the previous example notice the statement

```
list window::popup_stack;   // must allocate outside the class
```

which appears after the class declaration. What does this statement do? As it turns out, static data members must be allocated somewhere, and that is what this statement does. Notice the syntax where we provide the type of the member (**list**), then the name of the class (**window**), followed by **::**, and then the name of the member (**popup_stack**). You'll notice that this syntax is similar to that used for member functions.

Why must we add this extra statement to allocate the static member **popup_stack**? Why doesn't the declaration for the member inside the class suffice? The reason is this: Class declarations typically go into header files. If the inclusion of a static member declaration inside the class were to also allocate that member, then in effect we would be allocating data in a header file—something that should never be done. Typically, the allocation of the static member is placed in the same source file as the method of the class.

After studying this example you might be wondering why you couldn't have used a global variable to represent the window stack. Indeed, you could have. However, if the variable belongs to the class, why not include it as a member? By making it a member you get the benefit of both the single copy of the global variable and the modularity of a class member.

Let's put together a program that actually uses a static class member. In this program, we'll define point objects to represent screen coordinates. Each object has an (x,y) coordinate that is represented as an offset from a common origin point that the object stores. Because the origin is shared, it's a good candidate to be a static member. Here is the complete program:

```
#include <stdio.h>

class point {
public:
    static int xo, yo; // origin shared between all points
    int x, y;
    int abs_x(void) { return x + xo; } // absolute coords.
    int abs_y(void) { return y + yo; }
};

int point::xo = 0; // Allocate and initialize the
int point::yo = 0; // static members

void main()
{
  point a, b;

    // set common origin
```

```
point::xo = 5; // note you can use class name here!!
point::yo = 6; // but only for static members

// set up relative coordinates
a.x = 17;   a.y = 42;
b.x = 55;   b.y = 75;

// print absolute coordinates
printf("a's absolute coordinates: (%d, %d)\n",
       a.abs_x(), a.abs_y());
printf("b's absolute coordinates: (%d, %d)\n",
       b.abs_x(), b.abs_y());

// change origin, using a, note how it affects b
a.xo = 0;   a.yo = 0;
printf("b's absolute coordinates: (%d, %d)\n",
       b.abs_x(), b.abs_y());
}
```

Here's what you'll see when you run the program:

```
a's absolute coordinates: (22, 48)
b's absolute coordinates: (60, 81)
b's absolute coordinates: (55, 75)
```

Figure 3.10 shows how the two objects share a common origin. Notice that it's possible to set static members using three different methods. The first method involves initializing the members at the time they are allocated, as in:

```
int point::xo = 0;
int point::yo = 0;
```

The second method involves setting the values of the members in assignment statements, using the name of the class to qualify the member names, as in:

```
point::xo = 5;
point::yo = 6;
```

Note that in both of these methods, an object was not referred to. Because **xo** and **yo** are common to both point objects, we don't need to include object references.

The statements

```
a.xo = 0;   a.yo = 0;
```

show the third way that a static member can be set. In this case, by setting the static members in one of the objects, they are automatically set in the other object. Thus, **b**'s origin is also changed to (0,0).

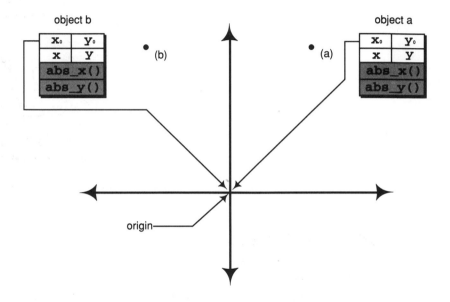

Figure 3.10. Representation of the point objects.

Note: C++ allows you to define static member functions in addition to static data members. You'll learn how to do this in Chapter 5.

What about Pointers?

Up until now we haven't used any pointers with the objects that we have constructed. But just as with regular C variables, you can also use pointers to reference objects. For example, the declaration

```
clock *big_ben_ptr;
```

creates a pointer to a clock object as shown in Figure 3.11. This pointer can then be used like any other C pointer that references a variable. That is, you can allocate memory for the pointer object, pass the pointer to a function, or dereference the pointer using the **->** operator. We won't be using many pointer objects in our example programs in this chapter; however, in the next chapter, we'll explore pointers in more detail when we discuss dynamic objects.

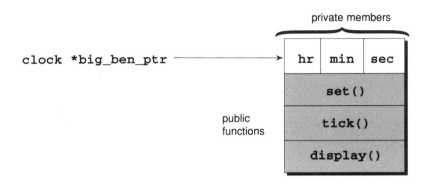

Figure 3.11. Declaring a pointer to an object.

Working with C++ Structures

As we've seen in this chapter, classes are extensions of basic C structures. But it turns out that even structures in C++ are more powerful than their C counterparts. In fact a C++ structure can have all the features of a C++ class. It can include functions as members, and it can also inherit properties from a base class. A C++ structure can also have private, public, and protected members.

Note: A structure in C++ is defined simply to be a class where all the members default to being public.

For example, the structure

```
struct rectangle {
   int wd, ht;
};
```

is equivalent to the class

```
class rectangle {
public:
   int wd, ht;
};
```

Because a C++ structure is a class, it can be used to define user-defined types. In contrast to C, you do not usually need to use the **struct** keyword when declaring a variable using a C++ structure. For instance, in C the following statement is required to declare a structure variable:

```
struct rectangle my_rect;   /* C's way */
```

A typical way in C to get around using the **struct** keyword in variable declarations is to use a **typedef** declaration. For example, we might say

```
typedef struct {   /* C's way of declaring a type */
   int wd, ht;
} rectangle;

rectangle my_rect;
```

In C++, the **typedef** declaration is not necessary. We can declare the variable **my_rect**, as shown:

```
rectangle my_rect;              // C++'s way
```

However, you can use the **struct** keyword in C++ if you wish. (This is to keep upward compatibility with C.) That is, it's legal to say

```
struct rectangle my_rect; // Also legal in C++
```

To summarize the similarities and differences between C structures and C++ structures and classes, we've included the translation box in Figure 3.12.

C structure	C++ structure	C++ class
```typedef struct { int wd,ht; } rect;```	```struct rect { int wd,ht; };```	```class rect { public: int wd,ht; };```

Figure 3.12. Translation between C structures and C++ classes.

Throughout this book, we'll use mostly classes to demonstrate C++ and object-oriented programming techniques. However, don't get the idea that structures can't be used instead of classes. Classes are shown to reinforce the concept of programming with objects.

How Unions Relate to Classes

You might also be wondering about how unions relate to C++ classes. Basically, a C++ union is a structure where all data members have the same address. Like a C++ structure, functions can be included as members as well.

Unlike structures, there are some restrictions to using unions. One is that unions can't have private or protected members. Another is that you cannot create a class hierarchy with unions, that is, you cannot derive a class from a union. Yet another is that objects of a class with special constructor and destructor functions (to be discussed later) cannot be members of a union. We'll explain how these rules apply when we cover more of the advanced features of constructors and destructors in Chapter 8.

Scoping of Class Members

C++ sports a similar scoping convention to that of Cs; however, classes that contain function members introduce a new scoping twist. To illustrate these new scoping rules, let's return to the clock class we introduced earlier. To refresh your memory, here is the definition of this class:

```
class clock {
   int hr, min, sec;
public:
   void set(int h, int m, int s);
   void tick(void);
   void display(void);
};

void clock::set(int h, int m, int s)
{
   hr = h; min = m; sec = s;
}
```

Note that we've also included the code for the function **set()**, which sets the clock's time. The most unusual feature of **set()** has to do with the way the member variables **hr**, **min**, and **sec** are referenced. Note that they are accessed without us having to designate where they came from or to whom they belong. What's going on here? To answer this question, we must understand how scoping works in C++.

Because **set()** is a member of the same class that the variables **hr**, **min**, and **sec** are, it can access them without having to name the class in which they are defined. One way to remember how this scoping works is to pretend that the function was defined inside the curly braces surrounding the class members. Then the variables are global to the member functions, but not available anywhere else outside the class. The curly braces are a scoping mechanism, much the way they are in conventional C programming. Figure 3.13 illustrates this scoping concept.

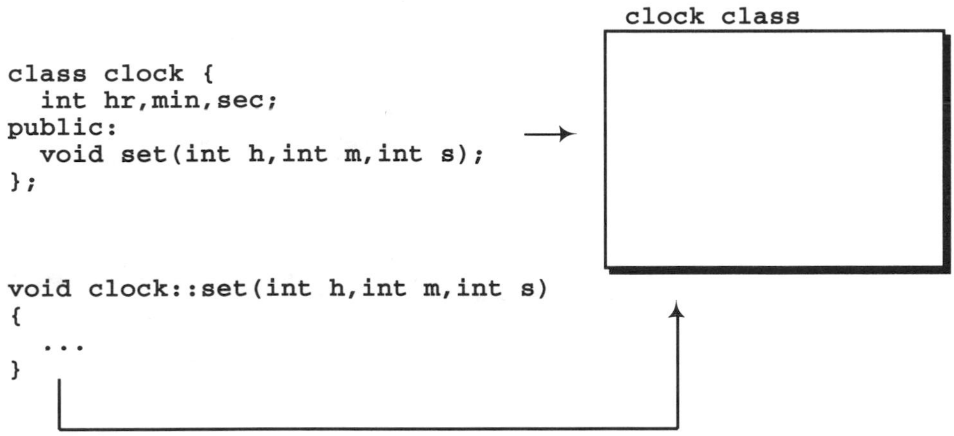

clock class

```
class clock {
   int hr,min,sec;
public:
   void set(int h,int m,int s);
};


void clock::set(int h,int m,int s)
{
   ...
}
```

Figure 3.13. Scoping of class member functions.

Scoping with Multiple Objects

By now you should be familiar with the basic scoping rules involved in accessing the members of a single object. Unfortunately, the scoping becomes slightly more complex when multiple objects are declared from a class definition. As an example, suppose that we have declared pointers to two clock objects:

```
clock *big_ben, *rolex;
```

When the **hr** variable inside **set()** is accessed, which clock does it come from, **big_ben** or **rolex**? To answer this question, we must review how **set()** is actually called. Here are some examples:

```
big_ben->set(12, 0, 0);
rolex->set(10, 2, 4);
```

Note that the name of the object is specified before the function's name. The operator -> is used to combine the pointer to the object with the member function.

Keep in mind the differences between calling functions in C and C++. In C we could call **set()** directly and pass a pointer to the object **big_ben**. In C++, we turn this around and call **set()** using the object pointer **big_ben**. Actually, to put this in object-oriented terminology, what we're really doing is sending the object a message. For example, the two statements elicit similar results:

```
/* the C approach */
set(big_ben, 12, 0, 0);


// the C++ object-oriented approach
big_ben->set(12, 0, 0);
```

So, to answer the question as to which **hr** variable is used, it's the one associated with the object that was sent the message!

The Hidden Argument in Member Functions

At this point you might be wondering how member functions are implemented in C++. Could it be that an extra argument is added to access the other class members, as we suggested a C program might do? The answer is yes.

Member functions do indeed have a hidden argument. This argument is a pointer to the object from which the function is called. This pointer has a special name, **this**. Normally, a C++ programmer does not need to worry about this pointer. Although it's redundant, you can use **this** when accessing class members inside a function. For example, the following function uses the **this** pointer to access the data members of the **clock** class:

```
// Redundant use of this in a C++ member function:
void clock::set(int h, int m, int s)
{
    this->hr = h; this->min = m; this->sec = s;
}
```

It turns out that the example above is very close to how the member function is actually implemented. Here is an example of what the function would look like in C:

```
// set() in C
void set(clock *this, int h, int m, int s)
{
    this->hr = h; this->min = m; this->sec = s;
}
```

The pointer **this** points to the clock object passed as the first argument. The members **hr**, **min**, and **sec** are obtained by explicitly de-referencing this clock pointer. The clock being pointed to is the one that was sent the message.

By closely studying this example, you should be able to better understand the scoping rules of member functions in C++. Just remember the hidden argument. This is summarized in Figure 3.14, using our earlier rectangle class as an example.

C	C++

```typedef struct {```
``` int wd,ht;```
```} rect;```
 	
```int area(rect *r) {```
``` return r->wd*r->ht;```
```}```
 	
```rect r;```
 	
```printf(area(&r));```
	```class rect {```
	```public:```
	``` int wd,ht;```
	``` int area(void);```
	```};```
	
	```int rect::area(void)```
	```{```
	``` return wd*ht;```
	```}```
	
	```rect r;```
	
	```printf(r.area());```

Figure 3.14. Translation box for member functions.

By now you might be thinking that if you can code member functions in C using this method, why bother with C++ at all? While it is true that you can code in an object-oriented style in C, it's much easier to do so in C++. Although there are many reasons, just the ability to use member variables in member functions without explicit structure de-referencing is reason enough. Although it can sometimes be confusing to figure out which variables belong to which structure, in a well-designed program the code actually becomes more readable, since it's less cluttered with repeated structure de-references.

Name Qualifying

You might be wondering what happens if you have a global variable that was the same name as a class member. Wouldn't the code (or you) get confused? For instance, consider the following sample program:

```
#include <stdio.h>
int a;           // global variable
class add_test {
    int a, b;       // member variables
public:
    void setem(int x, int y) { a = x; b = y; }
    int addem(void) { return a + b; }
};

void main() {

    add_test addobj1;
    a = 100;
    addobj1.setem(a, 200);
    a = 400;
    printf("The result is %d ", addobj1.addem());
}
```

Here the variable **a** is declared as both a global variable and a data member for the class **add_test**. Note that it is also used in the functions **setem()** and **addem()**. When either of these functions executes, which variable **a** is used, the global variable or the member variable? The answer is the member variable. This means that when **setem()** is called with the arguments **a** and 200, the member variables get set to 100 and 200, respectively. Although the statement **a = 400;** changes the value stored in the global variable **a**, it does not have any effect on the **addem()** function, which is executed after this assignment statement. The result returned by **addem()**, in this case, is 300 (100 + 200).

Now suppose that you want a member function to access a global variable that has the same name as a member variable. This can be accomplished by using the C++ binary scoping operator (**::**). You've already seen how this operator is used to define member functions outside a class declaration. For instance, the expression

```
ccc::xxx
```

indicates that **ccc** is the class name and **xxx** is the name of the class member function. If you leave off the first argument to the operator (effectively making it unary), then it means "use the global version." This same trick works for class data members as well.

Therefore, we can modify our **addem()** function to use the global variable **a** by coding:

```
int addem(void) { return ::a + b; }   // uses global a
```

With this in mind, what result will now be produced by our modified program?

```
#include <stdio.h>
int a;          // global variable
class add_test {
    int a, b;       // member variables
public:
    void setem(int x, int y) { ::a = x; b = y; }
    int addem(void) { return ::a + b; }
};

void main() {

    add_test addobj1;
    a = 100;
    addobj1.setem(300, 200);
    a = 400;
```

```
    printf("The result is %d ", addobj1.addem());
}
```

If you guessed 600, then you're on the right track. You might want to experiment with this sample program by changing the :: operator and the values of the global variable **a** to make sure that you understand how this scoping system works.

Note: The :: scoping operator used as a unary operator instructs the C++ compiler to use the global version of the variable or function.

Usually, it's best not to do this with variables because you could end up with confusing code. However, there is some advantage to using the scoping operator to access global functions. For instance, you might want to build a high-level file class that, among other things, has an **open**() function. No problem here, but suppose you wanted to call the system I/O function of the same name inside your own function? For instance, consider the following class definition for **file_mgr**:

```
#include <io.h>      // has open() definition
class file_mgr {
    char *table[20]; // names for 20 files
    int indx;
    // ... other private data members go here
public:
    int open(char *file, char *mode);
    // ... other public members go here
};

int file_mgr::open(char *file, char *mode)
{
    ::open(file, mode);         // call system function
    strcpy(table[indx++],file);    // add name to table
}
```

In this example, the **file_mgr**'s version of **open**() simply calls the system level version and then does some extra processing, like adding the file name to an internal table. If we hadn't qualified the system level call with the :: operator, an infinite recursive call to **file_mgr::open**() would have resulted. While we could give the **open()** function for **file_mgr** a different name, it's more convenient to just use the name **open()**. By using the scoping operator, you don't have to keep inventing new names for the open operation every time you use it in different classes.

Chaining function calls in this manner is very typical in certain C++ applications. You'll see more examples of this technique in later chapters.

Another scoping problem that you might encounter is illustrated by the next example. This scoping problem occurs when the name of a function argument is the same as a member name in a class. For example, note that the variable **x** is both a private member and an argument for the function **setit()**:

```
class number {
    int x;
public:
    void setit(int x) { number::x = x; }
    int getit(void) { return x; }
};
```

We can eliminate the scoping problem by using the **::** operator, as shown. In **setit()**, we qualified the member name **x** in order to keep it from being confused with the parameter name.

Nested Classes and Objects

Just as C lets us place structure variables inside other structures, C++ allows us to nest classes and objects. Here's an example:

```
class window {
public:
    box border;   // a "box" object
    cursor curs;  // a "cursor" object
    scroll bar sb; // a "scroll" bar object
};
```

We're assuming that **border**, **curs**, and **sb** are class variables (objects) declared elsewhere.

It's also possible to include the class definitions of these objects right inside the **window** class. Recall that in C you can declare nested structures, as shown in this program:

```
#include <stdio.h>
struct dial_entry {
    char name[80];
    struct phone_num {
        char area_code[3], prefix[3], num[4];
    } phone;
};

void main()
{
    struct dial_entry clients[100];
    strcpy(clients[0].name, "Bill Gates");
    strcpy(clients[0].phone.area_code,"206");
    strcpy(clients[0].phone.prefix, "957");
    strcpy(clients[0].phone.num, "3142");
    printf("%s: 1-%s-%s-%s", clients[0].name,
            clients[0].phone.area_code,
            clients[0].phone.prefix,
            clients[0].phone.num);
};
```

When run, the program produces:

```
Bill Gates: 1-206-957-3142
```

As you might expect, the same program would work in C++. In fact, because classes are just extensions of C structures, classes can also be nested using a similar technique. The information-hiding feature of classes also allows us to hide classes within another class. As an example, consider the following class definition:

```
class dial_entry {
    char name[80];
public:
    class phone_num { // Is this name hidden?
    public:
        char area_code[3], prefix[3], num[4];
    };
    phone_num phone;
};
```

This class definition defines the class **phone_num** along with a **phone_num** object, **phone**. Both of these names are hidden in the class. The inner class name **phone_num** is only accessible if qualified with the name of the outer class, **dial_entry**. For example:

```
phone_num my_fax_machine;            // Illegal, phone_num hidden
dial_entry::phone_num my_fax_machine; // Legal with qualifier
```

Note that for nested class names, the access keywords **public**, **private**, and **protected** take effect, as they do for all names in classes. If we had defined **phone_num** in the private section of **dial_entry**, then we couldn't have accessed it.

One point to keep in mind is that a nested class has no special access to the members of the enclosing class, nor vice versa. The scoping does *not* work the same as it does for nested code blocks, where an inner block can access outer block variables. As it turns out, a nested class can only access the members of the outer class through objects of that outer class. Also, an outer class can only access members of a nested class through objects of the nested class. For instance:

```
class outer {
public:
  int outer_num;
  class inner {
  public:
    int inner_num;
    int twosum(void) {
      return inner_num + outer_sum; // Illegal access to
                                    // outer_num
    }
    int twosome(outer *a) {
      return inner_num + a->outer_num; // Legal access thru
                                       // object
    }
  };
  int addup(void) {
    return outer_num + inner_num; // Illegal access to
                                  // inner_num
  }
  int addem(inner_num *a) {
```

```
                  return outer_num + a->inner_num; // Legal access thru
                                                   // object
      }
};
```

Of course, in this example, had **outer_num** been declared private, then the function **twosome()** could not have accessed the member. Likewise, if **inner_num** had been declared private, the function **addem()** wouldn't have worked either.

Nested Type Definitions

Just as you can define a class inside another class, you can also define other types inside a class. For example, we can use **typedef** to define a new type, as well as declare an enumerated type inside a class. The rules for accessing these new types are the same as those for nested classes. For example, the following code fragment shows some nested type definitions and some legal and illegal accesses to those types:

```
class file_mgr {
   typedef long btree_ptr;
public:
   enum xlat_mode { text, binary };
   typedef long record_ptr;
   // ... Other members
};

xlat_mode xm;              // Illegal, xlat_mode hidden
file_mgr::xlat_mode xm;    // Legal with qualifier
record_ptr rp;            // Illegal, record_ptr hidden
file_mgr::record_ptr rp;  // Legal with qualifier
btree_ptr bp;             // Illegal, btree_ptr hidden
file_mgr::btree_ptr bp;   // Illegal, btree_ptr private
```

Note: The rule for nesting class and type definitions is new to V2.1 of C++. Earlier versions of C++ had different rules, which basically made nested class and type definitions behave as though the definitions were flattened out and defined outside the enclosing class.

Summary

In this chapter we've covered the basics of defining and using classes. We've explained how data and function members can be combined in a class definition to create a data type that includes both data and the operators that process the data. We've also discussed how C++ structures and classes relate to C structures and unions, and how multiple objects can be declared using a single class definition. Now that we've covered the basics we're ready to move on and explore some of the more advanced features of classes in the next chapter.

Exercises

1. Write a short program that uses a class to represent an expression evaluator. The class will consist of two data members to store some operands and contain functions such as **add()**, **subtract()**, **multiply()**, and so on, to evaluate the expressions. For instance:

```
evaluator e;

e.setleft(17.0);
e.setright(25.0);
printf("%f\n", e.add());
```

2. Modify the menu program presented earlier in this chapter so that each main menu item will display a submenu when selected. To perform this task, you might consider declaring an array of objects using the following definition:

```
menu submenu[4];
```

You can then access each submenu object with a syntax of the form:

```
submenu[1].disp_menu();
submenu[1].process_menu();
```

3. Define a function **menu_error()** that can be added to the class definition for the menu program. This function should display an error message if the user selects an invalid menu item number.

4. Examine some of the C code you have written in the past, particularly your data structures. See if you can convert some of your smaller programs to the object-oriented style by packaging functions and data into classes.

Classes in Action

In the previous chapter we explained the basics of how classes are defined and used in C++ programs. Now that you are familiar with classes, it's time to move ahead and explore some of the more advanced features that classes provide.

Our goal in this chapter is to show you how to create and use more complex classes. We'll begin by discussing information-hiding techniques. As we explore this topic, we'll introduce a new type of function called a *friend function*. In the second part of this chapter we'll explore how classes are dynamically created and initialized. We'll also examine how classes are created using existing classes. This technique is important because it enables us to reuse classes that we have developed for other applications. For example, if we have a class that we are using to display pop-up windows, we can use it to create another class that we might use to display error messages on the screen.

The major topics covered in this chapter include:

- Techniques for information hiding
- How to create read-only variables
- How to use friend functions
- How to use constructors and destructors
- Techniques for using dynamic variables
- Techniques for deriving classes
- How to write a virtual function

Information Hiding

The first topic we need to cover in this chapter before we move on to dynamic objects is information hiding. As we noted in the previous chapter, information hiding is an important feature of C++ classes that helps you to create modular programs.

Information hiding is accomplished by using the **public**, **protected**, and **private** keywords. To see how this works, let's return to the basic form of a class definition:

```
class class_name {
private:
  // private members go here
protected:
  // protected members go here
public:
  // public members go here
};
```

The members of the class are partitioned into *private*, *protected*, and *public* members. Private members are accessible only to other members of the class, that is, they are private to the class. For example, suppose we used the following class to define employee payroll data:

```
class employee_data {
  double wage;
public:
  int soc_sec_no;
  void set_wage(double w);
  double pay(int hrs);
};

void employee_data::set_wage(double w)
{
  wage = w;
}

double employee_data::pay(int hrs)
{
```

```
        return hrs * wage;
}
```

Here, **wage** is private to the **employee_data** class, while **soc_sec_no** and **pay()** are public, much like the way they would be in a typical company setting. The only places that **wage** can be used are in the functions **set_wage()** and **pay()**, because they are the only functions related to the class.

Note: Any number of public, private, and protected sections can appear in a class, and they can be in any order.

What does it mean that a member is private? What happens if you try to use it outside the class? The answer is that the compiler will generate an error. Because C++ is a compiled language, the compiler must perform the type checking and access calculations statically, before the program runs. For example, the following program fragment generates an error:

```
employee_data john_doe;

john_doe.wage = 25;  // Compiler error! Illegal access
```

This is different from other object-oriented languages, such as Smalltalk, which allow objects to be defined at run-time. In such a language, it is generally not possible to tell when an illegal access is taking place until the program is actually running. While this feature adds more power and flexibility, it also means that error handling must be done at run-time. This often takes the form of annoying messages to the user, such as "Illegal access to object X."

Because these types of errors are of concern only to the developer, why not make it so the errors are caught *before* the user gets hold of the program? This is what C++ does when it catches such errors at compile-time and is one of the reasons (the main one being efficiency) that C++ was designed *not* to support the creation of classes dynamically.

You should also keep in mind that a member can never be truly private. Nothing stops you from pointing at it by using type casting and changing its value by de-referencing that pointer. Also, because the class declaration that contains the private member must either appear in a header file or be present in the module that uses it, the fact that the member exists is available to anyone who wishes to find out. In the spirit of C, the designers of C++ assumed that programmers are honest. C++ enforces the private accessibility only to the point of making it an inconvenience to anyone trying to circumvent it.

A Simulated Computer Network

Now that you know a little more about information hiding, let's write a program that uses this feature. Our program performs a simulation of a supercomputer network. The network is represented as a class called **cray_network**. This network supports a system of 10 users and provides password security. It also contains functions to allow you to log-on and log-off the system.

Although we're simulating a network with our own simple functions, there's no reason the **cray_network** class couldn't be a front end to a real network. In this capacity, it could serve as an interface to the network for other computer applications on the local system, such as an inventory system or a top secret research project. We could then write functions such as **check_passwd()** and **logon()** to provide hooks into the real network. Security problems aside, it is still wise to make such information private so that the interface to the network doesn't have to change if the implementation details change.

Here is the complete network simulation program:

```
// A simulated supercomputer network.
#include <stdio.h>
#include <string.h>
struct acct_info {  // password entry structure
    char passwd[16];
    char name[80];
};

class cray_network {
    acct_info accts[10]; // private password info
    int passwd_lookup(char *name, char *passwd);
    int check_passwd(char *name);
    int find_acct(char *name);
    int new_acct(char *name);
    void start_session(int acct);
    void logon(void);
public:
```

```
    void install(void);
    void operate(void);
};


void cray_network::install(void)
{
    int i;
    for (i = 0; i<10; i++) {
        strcpy(accts[i].name,"");
        strcpy(accts[i].passwd,"");
    }
}


void cray_network::operate(void)
{
    do {
        logon();   // break out with ctrl-c
    } while(1);
}


int cray_network::find_acct(char *name)
// Returns 1-10, or returns 0 if can't find acct.
{
    int i;

    for(i = 0; i<10; i++) { // look for name match
        if (!strcmp(name, accts[i].name)) return i+1;
    }
    return 0;
}


int cray_network::new_acct(char *name)
// Returns 1-10, or 0 if error.
{
    int acct;

    if ((acct = find_acct("")) == 0) {    // look for empty
                                          // account
        printf("Sorry, the network is full\n");
    }
```

```
    else {
       strcpy(accts[acct-1].name, name);
       printf("Enter new password: ");
       gets(accts[acct-1].passwd);
    }
    return acct;
}

int cray_network::passwd_lookup(char *name, char *passwd)
// Returns acct number if found, else returns 0.
{
    int i;
    for (i = 0; i<10; i++) {
        if (!strcmp(name, accts[i].name)) {
            if (!strcmp(passwd, accts[i].passwd))
                return i+1;
             else return 0;
        }
    }
    return 0;
}

void cray_network::start_session(int acct)
{
    char command[80];

    printf("%s, you're now logged on ...\n\n",
            accts[acct-1].name);
    do {
       printf("%% "); // famous Unix prompt
       gets(command);
       printf("okay\n");
       // do commands here
    } while (strcmp(command, "logoff"));
    printf("\nLogging off user %s ...\n\n",
            accts[acct-1].name);
}

void cray_network::logon(void)
{
    char passwd[80], name[80];
```

```
        int acct;
        printf("Welcome to the Number Five Network ...\n\n");
        printf("Please logon: ");
        gets(name);
        acct = find_acct(name);
        if (acct == 0) {
            printf("\n'%s', you must be a new user ...\n", name);
            acct = new_acct(name);
            if (acct != 0) start_session(acct);
        }
        else {
            printf("Please enter your password: ");
            gets(passwd);
            if ((acct = passwd_lookup(name, passwd)) == 0) {
                printf("Sorry, wrong password\n\n");
            }
            else start_session(acct);
        }
    }

void main()
{
    cray_network teknon;

    teknon.install();
    teknon.operate();
}
```

Here's a sample output from the program:

```
Welcome to the Number Five Network ...

Please logon: flamig

'flamig', you must be a new user ...
Enter new password: bry
flamig, you're now logged on ...

% rm -r /usr
okay
```

```
% format c:
okay
% logoff
okay
Logging off user flamig ...


Welcome to the Number Five Network ...


Please logon: flamig
Please enter your password: sly
Sorry, wrong password


Welcome to the Number Five Network ...


Please logon:
```

C Files versus C++ Classes

A good way to see how information hiding works is to compare it with a topic you're already familiar with—C files. A C++ class is analogous to a C source file that contains variables and functions. The variables and functions declared as static (local) are the C file's private members. Figure 4.1 illustrates this relationship. To see this analogy clearly, let's explore an example. Here is a C++ program that uses a class to represent a savings account:

```c
#include <stdio.h>
class nest_egg{
    int savings;
public:
    void open(void)        { savings = 0; }
    void deposit(int amt)  { savings += amt; }
    int withdraw(int amt);
    int balance(void)      { return savings; }
};
int nest_egg::withdraw(int amt)
{
    if (savings < amt) {
        amt = savings;
```

```
        printf("Sorry, you're broke!\n");
    }
    savings -= amt;
    return amt;
}

void main()
{
    nest_egg bank;
    int amt;

    bank.open();
    printf("How much to deposit?: ");
    scanf("%d", &amt);
    bank.deposit(amt);
    printf("How much to withdraw?: ");
    scanf("%d", &amt);
    amt = bank.withdraw(amt);
    printf("You have %d left\n", bank.balance());
}
```

file1.c

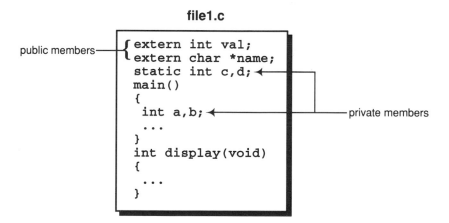

Figure 4.1. Relationship between a file and a class.

Typically, the functions of a class are used to provide an interface into the internal workings of the class. They allow objects created from classes to be treated as black boxes. The functions representing the behavior of the objects are the only visible component to the outside world. We keep the internal details of the class hidden.

For example, the internals of the savings bank, which in this case is an integer variable (**savings**) that holds the total savings, are not directly accessed. Instead, the functions **open**(), **deposit**(), and **withdraw**() are used to modify the **savings** variable indirectly. These functions act as messages to the bank, instructing it what to do.

In contrast to the C++ way of packaging functions in objects, stop and think for a minute how you would do the same in C. Take our nest egg example. In C you would probably place all the functions and code in a single file, making those parts to be kept internal as statically scoped. Here's how you might code it:

```c
/* C's form of modularity control */
/* First, a header file containing external names */
external void open(void);
external void deposit(int amt);
external int withdraw(int amt);

/* Then the C source file */
static int savings;      /* make it internal to file */

void open(void) { savings = 0; }
void deposit(int amt) { savings += amt; }

int withdraw(int amt)
{
    if (savings < amt) {
        amt = savings;
        printf("Insufficient funds\n");
    }
    savings -= amt;
    return amt;
}
```

Here, our only form of modularity control is the fact that variables and functions declared **static** are only accessible to the file in which they reside. In this respect they are like the private members of a class. The functions are declared external, so that they can be used outside the file. Thus, the entire file serves as the class definition and represents one black-box object. The functions declared as external represent the methods of this object.

Remember that classes are used as templates to create objects, and we can create multiple objects from the same template. For instance:

```
nest_egg dream_vacation_acct;
nest_egg that_home_in_the_pines_acct;
```

But in our C version, the equivalent of a class is a whole file. How can we create multiple objects from that? The answer is that you can't, at least not easily. Thus, C++ supports object-oriented programming, where C doesn't. The class mechanism is a major reason for this.

Of course, a dedicated C programmer might say, "Well, you've declared your functions wrong. You should be passing the savings amount as an argument instead of using a global variable." That's true. For our C version, we could write the **deposit()** function as

```
void deposit(int *savings, int amt)
{
    *savings += amt;
}
```

and not make **savings** global in the file.

While this approach works, it makes it hard to extend our banking example. For example, you'll soon learn about inheritance and how you can use it to modify existing code incrementally. In our C example, the objects are not conveniently packaged into the kind of building blocks that support this.

Read-Only Variables

Another advantage of information hiding is that it gives us the ability to have read-only variables. What do we mean by this? Take another look at our savings bank class:

```
class nest_egg{
    int savings;
public:
    void open(void)        { savings = 0; }
    void deposit(int amt)  { savings += amt; }
```

```
      int withdraw(int amt);
      int balance(void)          { return savings; }
};
```

Notice how we handle the account balance. Because the **savings** variable is private, we can only access it by using the **balance**() function. This function returns the value of **savings**. In a sense, **savings** is a read only variable. We can look at its value, but we can't change it, at least not directly. We have to change it indirectly with the functions **deposit**() and **withdraw**().

You might be thinking now, why not just make **savings** public and be done with it? The reason is that by making it private, it gives our class control over how it is handled. For example, this class might be used by a big banking firm and it might have rules about when deposits take effect, how much you can withdraw at once, and so on. In addition, functions like **withdraw**() act as an official teller, making sure the customers don't take more than their share when withdrawing cash.

Introducing Friends

In previous examples we stated that only class members can access legally the private parts of a class. But that's not quite true. Sometimes a function that is not a member of a class needs to access a private member of the class. To help you get around this obstacle, C++ provides a unique facility called *friends*. This feature is used to declare a type of function called a *friend function*.

A friend function is essentially a standard C function that is not a member of a class. Friend functions can access the private members of a class, even though they are not members themselves.

Declaring Friend Functions

Friend functions are declared by placing their function prototype in the class they are to be friends with, preceded by the **friend** keyword. For example, in the following class definition, the function **irs**(), which represents the Internal Revenue Service, is a friend of the class **employee_data** (one could argue the friend status). As such, it can access the private member **wage**, allowing it to take out its share of taxes.

```
class employee_data {
    double wage;
    friend void irs(employee_data *e);     // declare "friend"
public:
    int soc_sec_no;
    void set_wage(double w);
    double pay(int hrs);
};

double tax_rate = 0.35;      // 35% tax rate
void irs(employee_data *e)
{
    e->wage -= e->wage*tax_rate;   // some friend!!
}
```

Although we've shown the friend declaration in the private part of the class, it can be placed anywhere in the class. The declaration is an actual function prototype whose scope is the outermost scope of the module it resides in (not just the class), just like any other normal function declared in the module.

Because it is not a class member, the body of **irs()** is not specified with the **class::func()** syntax. In essence, it operates just like any other standard function, except that it has access to the private member **wage**. But it can't access **wage** directly as class members can. We must pass a pointer to an **employee_data** object in order to access the private members of the object. Figure 4.2 shows the components labeled for the definition of the friend function.

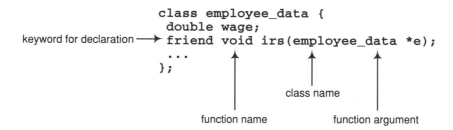

Figure 4.2. Components of a friend function.

The friend status is one-way. A class determines who its friends are and not the other way around. A non-member function cannot access the members of a class unless the function has been listed as a friend inside the body of the class definition. Therefore, once you've defined a class and compiled it into object code, it is no longer possible to attach other friends to it without changing the class declaration and recompiling it.

As a further example of friends, the following code shows the difference between member functions, friend functions, and regular functions:

```
class my_class {
   int private_data;
public:
   int public_data;
   void insider(int p);
   friend int buddy(my_class *a);
};

void my_class::insider(int p) {
   private_data = p;                  // legal, insider() is
}                                      // a class member

int buddy(my_class *a) {   //
   return a->private_data; // legal, buddy() is a friend
}

int outsider(my_class *a) { // error: outsider() not
   return a->private_data;    // a friend
}
```

The functions **insider()** and **buddy()** can access the private member **private_data**, but **outsider()**, which is not a class member or friend, cannot. All the functions can access **public_data**, however.

When to Use Friends

In our tax example, you might argue that **irs()** should not be a friend of the class **employee_data**! But seriously, there are cases where a function needs to access private members but should not otherwise be a member of the class.

As an example, suppose you're building a 3-D CAD system and you need a class to represent drawing coordinates. Shown next is such a class. For simplicity, the points are measured from some implied common origin.

```
#include <math.h>
class point {
  double x, y, z;
public:
  void place(double xm, double ym, double zm);
  double dist_from_origin(void);
};

// Initialize the point in 3-D.
void point::place(double xm, double ym, double zm)
{
  x = xm; y = ym; z = zm;
}

// Compute the distance from the origin.
double point::dist_from_origin(void)
{
  return sqrt(x*x+y*y+z*z);
}
```

We've included two member functions: one for placing the point and one for computing the distance of the point from the origin. Using good design practices, we've made the representation for points private. In this case, we've represented them with Cartesian coordinates, but we could have also represented them with polar coordinates.

Now suppose we need to add a function that computes the distance between two points? That function could be written

```
double dist_between_pts(point *a, point *b)
{
    return sqrt( (a->x - b->x) * (a->x - b->x) +
                 (a->y - b->y) * (a->y - b->y) +
                 (a->z - b->z) * (a->z - b->z) );
}
```

The problem is, where do we put this function? Since the private members **x**, **y**, and **z** are used, you might think we should make the function a class member.

```
class point {
    double x, y, z;
public:
    void place(double xm, double ym, double zm);
    double dist_from_origin(void);
    double dist_between_pts(point *a, point *b);
};
```

There's only one catch. Because it's a member function, we can only access it using a **point** object. In object-oriented terms, this means using message passing, as in

```
point p, q;
p.dist_between_pts(&p, &q); // send message to point p
```

But to which object do we send the message? We could have just as well sent it to **q**.

```
q.dist_between_pts(&p, &q); // send message to point q
```

Either way, it seems awkward and artificial. We don't want to send a message to an object; we just want to use two **point** objects. It makes more sense just to write

```
dist_between_pts(&p, &q);   // what we really want
```

The solution then is to make **dist_between_pts()** a friend of the class.

```
class point {
    double x, y, z;
public:
    void locate(double xm, double ym, double zm);
    double dist_from_origin(void);
    friend dist_between_pts(point *a, point *b);
};
```

Now **dist_between_pts()** can access legally the **x, y,** and **z** coordinates of the points **a** and **b** without having to be called through a **point** object.

This problem surfaces with other types of C++ functions as well. The most common type of problem occurs when the special class of functions called *operator functions* is used. These functions are associated with overloaded operators, such as + and <, and they are discussed in Chapter 7. Declaring operator functions as friends is most helpful in these situations.

In general, friend functions should be used whenever a function needs to operate on two or more objects of the same type and must access the private members of the objects. If message passing (that is, accessing the function using an object) doesn't provide the best approach, then the function could be defined and used as a friend.

Friend Classes

Not only can a function be a friend of a class, but an entire class can also be a friend of another class. What this means is that all the functions in the friend class can access the private parts of the other class. Let's explore an example. The following two classes are used to implement a linked list data structure:

```
class node {
    friend list;   // declares list class as friend of node
    node *next;
public:
    int data;
};

class list {
    node *head;
public:
    void add(int i);
    node *find(int i);
    // other methods
};

// Typical list functions
void list::add(int i)
{
    node *n = new node;
    node *p = head, *q = head;
    n->data = i;
    n->next = 0; // accessing private node member next
    while (p != 0) { q = p; p = p->next; }
```

```
        q->next = n;
};

node *list::find(int i)
{
    node *p = head;
    while (p != 0 && p->data != i)
        p = p->next; // accessing hidden member
    }
    return p;
}
```

The two classes we have defined are **node**, which represents the nodes in the list, and **list**, which represents the list as a whole. Because we have hidden the **next** pointer in the **node** class, we had to make the **list** class a friend of the **node** class. The relationship between the two classes is illustrated in Figure 4.3. With this arrangement, the functions **add()** and **find()** can access the **next** pointer even though these functions are members of the **list** class. Note the **new** operator used in **add()**. It allocates memory for a new node object.

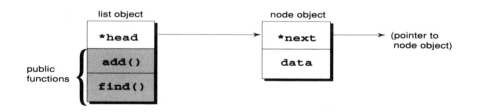

Figure 4.3. Relationship between node and list classes.

Note: Friend classes are useful whenever you have a class of objects that is managed in some way by another class.

Techniques for Creating and Initializing Objects

In the previous chapter we saw that objects could be declared and initialized like C structures. The objects shown served as static objects. That is, they were declared at the beginning of a program and they remained until the program finished. As another example, consider the following program:

```c
#include <stdio.h>
// Class definition to store employee information.
class employee {
    char name[30];
    int age;
    float salary;
public:
    void get_emp_data(void);
    void compute_wage(void);
};

void employee::get_emp_data(void)
{
    printf("Enter the employee's name\n");
    gets(name);
    printf("Enter the employee's age\n");
    scanf("%d", &age);
    printf("Enter the employee's salary\n");
    scanf("%f", &salary);
}

void employee::compute_wage(void)
{
    int num_hours;
    float week_pay;

    printf("How many hours did %s work this week? ", name);
    scanf("%d", &num_hours);
    week_pay = (salary / 2080) * num_hours;
    printf("Annual salary is %.2f\n", salary);
    printf("%s's pay this week is %.2f", name, week_pay);
}

void main()
{
    employee emp1;
```

```
        emp1.get_emp_data();
        emp1.compute_wage();
    }
```

Here the class **employee** is used to define the object **emp1**. When the C++ compiler encounters the statement

```
    employee emp1;
```

it allocates memory to store the data members **name**, **age**, and **salary** contained in the object as shown in Figure 4.4. In simple programs such as the one in our example, this memory allocation scheme works well. If, on the other hand, we are writing programs that use many different objects, we may need to allocate memory dynamically for our objects. This would enable us to create objects as we need them and delete the objects when they are no longer being used. Fortunately, C++ also provides features for creating and initializing objects so that we can take advantage of the dynamic nature of objects.

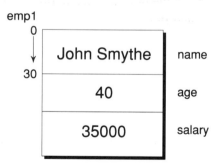

Figure 4.4. The employee object.

In this section we'll explore the more advanced techniques for creating and deleting objects. Essentially, there are two basic issues that we'll be covering: how to create and delete dynamic objects, and how to automatically initialize objects and perform clean-up tasks after objects have been deleted. Although we've listed these topics as two separate processes, they are often combined. For instance, when an object is created dynamically, we can initialize the object at the same time.

Dynamic Objects

One important difference between C++ and C is found in the way objects (variables) can be allocated dynamically. As you know, C provides the **malloc()** family of functions for allocating memory space for dynamic variables. These functions are difficult to use and prone to error because they can't determine the size of the variable to be allocated on their own. To allocate memory for a C variable dynamically, you must specify explicitly the size of the variable you are allocating.

```
cptr = malloc(sizeof(struct employee));
```

C++ improves the memory allocation system by providing the operators **new** and **delete**, which correspond roughly to the **malloc()** and **free()** functions of C. Although **new** and **delete** should be used whenever possible, for compatibility, the **malloc()** and **free()** functions are still available in C++.

Note: You can use both the **malloc()** family of memory management functions and the **new** and **delete** operators in your C++ programs. However, only **new** and **delete** will cause constructors and destructors to be called (see Chapter 8), so avoid using the **malloc()** family.

The new Operator

To allocate memory for a variable or object during the execution of a program, we can use the **new** operator. Here's a quick example that illustrates how this operator is used:

```
#include <stdio.h>
#include <string.h>

struct employee {
    char name[30];
    int age;
    float salary;
};

void main()
```

```
{
        employee *ptr;   // declare pointer

        ptr = new employee; // allocate storage for structure
        strcpy(ptr->name, "Norba Wiercheker");
        ptr->age = 28;
        ptr->salary = 42000.99;
        printf("The salary for %s is %f\n", ptr->name,
                ptr->salary);
        printf("This employee's age is %d", ptr->age);
}
```

The **new** operator in C++ differs from its C **malloc()** counterpart because it automatically determines the amount of memory to allocate by considering the type of object. In our example program, the compiler determines the amount of space needed to store the structure and allocates the required number of bytes. A pointer of the appropriate type is returned from the operation. You can then use this pointer to access the members of the structure just as you would if it were initialized with **malloc()**.

You can also allocate an array of objects by using square brackets. The following code allocates memory for a pointer variable that references 10 integers:

```
int *p;
p = new int[10];     // allocate array of integers
```

In C++, **new** is an operator, but you can also use standard function notation when using it. For example, the following statement performs the same memory allocation operation that our previous example performed:

```
p = new(int[10]);
```

It's also possible to allocate an array of pointers to objects. For this, the syntax is a bit strange. The following example allocates 10 pointers to integers and returns a pointer to a pointer:

```
int **p;                // define pointer to a pointer
p = new int *[10];   // allocate array of pointers
```

This statement allocates memory, as shown in Figure 4.5.

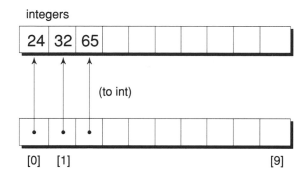

integers

Figure 4.5. Memory allocation for array of pointers.

Note: C++ will not automatically de-allocate memory for objects that have previously been allocated but are no longer used. After you allocate memory for an object, it is up to you to free up this memory.

The delete Operator

Now that we've seen how to use the **new** operator to allocate memory, we're ready to explore the **delete** operator, which frees up this memory. This operator is similar to the C **free()** function. The following code shows an example:

```
int *p = new int;    // declare and allocate storage
*p = 25;             // assign 25 to the location pointed by p
delete p;            // remove the object
```

You should never attempt to delete an object that has not been created with **new**, just as you should never use **free()** to delete an object that has not been created with **malloc()** or **calloc()**.

You must use an alternate form of the **delete** syntax when deleting an array of objects, as shown:

```
int *p = new int[10];  // declare and allocate array
delete[] p;            // free the array
```

In this case, notice that the array subscript is placed between the **delete** operator and the object name. This signals to **delete** that an array of objects is being deleted. Note also that no array size is passed to **delete**, since it knows the size automatically. (This has changed for C++ version 2.1.)

C++ allows you to customize the actual tasks performed by **new** and **delete**. The main advantage of this feature is that it enables you to build powerful applications that can take advantage of special cases for efficient memory storage.

To review how the **new** and **delete** operators are used, let's modify our previous program, which stored and processed employment data for an employee. In this new program we'll use the dynamic memory allocation features of C++ to support more than one employee. Here is the complete program:

```c
#include <stdio.h>

// class definition to store employee information
class employee  {
    char name[30];
    int age;
    float salary;
public:
    void get_emp_data(void);
    void compute_wage(void);
};

void employee::get_emp_data(void)
{
    printf("Enter the employee's name\n");
    gets(name);
    printf("Enter the employee's age\n");
    scanf("%d", &age);
    printf("Enter the employee's salary\n");
    scanf("%f", &salary);
    fflush(stdin);
    printf("\n");
}

void employee::compute_wage(void)
{
```

```
        int num_hours;
        float week_pay;

        printf("How many hours did %s work this week? ", name);
        scanf("%d", &num_hours);
        week_pay = (salary / 2080) * num_hours;
        printf("Annual salary is %.2f\n", salary);
        printf("%s's pay this week is %.2f", name, week_pay);
    }

void main()
{
    employee *emp_ptr;
    int num_emp, i;

    printf("Enter the number of employees to process\n");
    scanf("%d", &num_emp);
    fflush(stdin);
    emp_ptr = new employee[num_emp]; // allocate an array for
    for (i = 0; i < num_emp; i++) {   // the set of employees
        emp_ptr[i].get_emp_data();
    }
    do {
        printf("\nEnter employee's number to compute pay "
                "(0 to quit)\n");
        scanf("%d", &i);
        if (i == 0) break;
        emp_ptr[i-1].compute_wage();
    } while(1);
    delete[] emp_ptr; // remove the array of objects
}
```

And here's a sample run:

```
Enter the number of employees to process
2
Enter the employee's name
Jack Wright
Enter the employee's age
32
```

```
Enter the employee's salary
30000

Enter the employee's name
Bill Thomas
Enter the employee's age
25
Enter the employee's salary
45000

Enter employee's number to compute pay (0 to quit)
2

How many hours did Bill Thomas work this week? 45
Annual salary is 45000.00
Bill Thomas's pay this week is 973.55
```

Notice that we are using an array of **employee** objects so that we can input and process data for more than one employee. Because the number of employees is determined when the program executes, we must use the **new** operator to allocate storage space for the array of employees.

To access each employee, we now use a statement of the form

```
emp_ptr[i].get_emp_data();
```

where the variable **i** references the employee number.

Initializing and Cleaning up after Objects

One major advantage that a C++ variable has over a C variable is the ability to have a special user-defined initialization routine attached to it. This is done by including a special member function called a *constructor function* in the class to which the variable belongs. This function is called whenever the variable comes into scope, that is, when the program execution reaches the statement where it was declared. A constructor can do a variety of things, like initialize internal variables, allocate dynamic memory, and so on.

A class can also have a corresponding *destructor function*. This function is called when the program execution leaves the scope of a class variable (e.g., on a function return). It can also do a variety of housekeeping tasks and typically is used to free dynamically allocated memory associated with the variable. We'll explore both constructor and destructor functions next.

Constructor Functions

A constructor function is declared by using the following special naming convention:

> Any member function that has the same name as the class
> itself is treated as a constructor function.

For example, we could extend our **clock** class introduced in the previous chapter to have a constructor, as follows:

```
class clock {
   int hr, min, sec;
public:
   void set(int h, int m, int s);
   void tick(void);
   void display(void);
   clock(int h, int m, int s);   // constructor declared
};


// The constructor function defined
clock::clock(int h, int m, int s)
{
   set(h, m, s);
}
```

In this case the function **clock()** will execute whenever an object is defined of the type **clock**. For example, when the following declaration is encountered

```
clock timex(10,2,4), rolex(6,0,0);
```

the **clock()** function is called, and the values included as parameters are used to set the clock. Figure 4.6 shows the relationship between the declaration of the **clock** objects and the constructor function **clock()**.

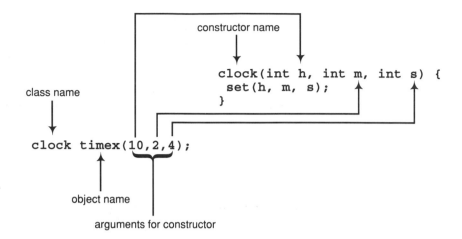

Figure 4.6. The clock object and its constructor.

Constructor functions can basically do what any other function can do, like call other functions, as **clock**() does by calling **set**(). Constructors can have parameters, as we've shown, but unlike other functions, no return type can be specified, and the function cannot contain a return statement.

Parameters to the constructor are set by including them with the object declaration. When the objects **timex** and **rolex** come into scope, the constructor function for clocks is called for each object, using the respective parameters given. So not only can we declare objects, we can also initialize them at the same time, using a routine we have specified. Thus, C++ offers you great flexibility in initializing objects.

In the clock example, the constructor initializes internal variables but it does not allocate additional memory. For some objects, you might want to have additional memory allocated off the heap. For example, you might want a character array whose length is determined dynamically. This can be accomplished in the constructor function, as shown:

```
class string {
   char *data;
public:
   string(int sz); // constructor function
   // other members
};

string::string(int sz)
```

```
{
    data = new char[sz]; // allocate storage
}
```

The constructor function uses the **new** operator to allocate **sz** bytes of heap storage for the array. Now you can declare **string** objects having different lengths, such as

```
string small_string(2), big_string(500);
```

This feature is particularly useful when the objects occur in functions that have a parameter determining the appropriate length of the array, as in

```
void my_func(int n)
{
    string str(n);
    ...
}
```

The trouble with the function above is that storage is allocated on the heap for **str** when the function is executed, but when the function returns, that storage is not freed. What's needed is a way to de-allocate that storage space automatically. This is where *destructor functions* come into play.

Note: Make sure that you don't name a function using the same name as the class name, unless you want the function to serve as a constructor function.

Destructor Functions

A destructor can be specified for a class by naming the function with the class name preceded by a ~ symbol, as shown for the **string** class:

```
class string {
    char *data;
public:
    string(int sz);   // constructor
    ~string(void);    // destructor
};
```

```
string::string(int sz)
{
    data = new char[sz];
}
string::~string(void)
{
    delete[] data;
}
```

Here, we have included both a constructor and a destructor. The constructor allocates memory for a character array, and the destructor frees up the memory used to store the array.

Constructors and destructors defined outside the class body have the form shown in Figure 4.7. This syntax may seem strange at first; however, with a little practice, you'll be able to spot constructors and destructors easily.

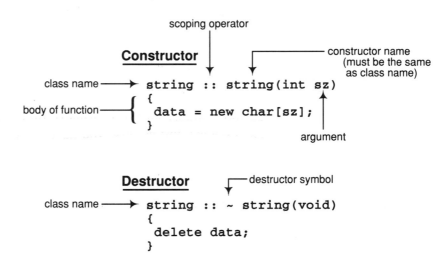

Figure 4.7. Form for a constructor and a destructor.

The destructor function is called when the routine that declares the object containing the destructor terminates. For example, consider the following function (here we've assumed that **data** is a public member of **string**):

```
void check_psswd()
{
    string s1(20);
```

```
      printf("Please enter your password\n");
      scanf("%s", s1.data);
      if (pass_lookup(s1.data) == 0)  {
        printf("Your password is correct\n");
        enter_system();
      }
      else  {
        printf("Sorry, wrong password\n");
        logout();
      }
  }
```

When **check_psswd()** is called, the constructor function **string()** executes, and storage is allocated for the string **data**. The advantage of this is that you don't have to worry about allocating memory directly for the data. When the function terminates, the allocated memory is freed because the destructor function **~string()** takes over and executes the statement

```
  delete data;
```

Destructor functions have no arguments and return type. Although you can have them perform almost any task, usually they are used to free dynamically allocated storage. Just because you have a constructor does not mean you need a destructor. This is especially true when no dynamic data is involved.

Constructors and destructors, if set up properly, can alleviate a lot of headaches, especially when dynamic data is used. This is particularly true when objects local to a function are used. For example, Figure 4.8 shows the difference between a function written in C and C++ that performs a string processing operation.

Notice that the C++ routine requires fewer statements. In the C routine, we must explicitly allocate and de-allocate storage for the string. The C++ function, on the other hand, relies on a constructor and destructor function to allocate and de-allocate memory. In large C programs this memory management is hard to maintain properly. If you forget to allocate memory for a variable, you know what you get—a nasty bug that might keep you up all night! In the C++ version, this memory management is handled automatically, if you set it up correctly with constructors and destructors.

```
        C                        C++

void my_func(int n)        void my_func(int n)
{                          {

  struct string str;
                             string str(n);
  str.data = malloc(n);      // memory allocated
  /* use the data */
                             // use the data
  free(str.data);
                             // destructor called
}
                           }
```

Figure 4.8. Translation of constructors and destructors.

Keep in mind, however, that our example is deceptively simple. There are many caveats to consider when using constructors and destructors, especially when dealing with dynamic memory. We've only scratched the surface here. Be sure to read Chapter 8 carefully before trying to use dynamic memory with constructors!

Deriving Classes

Probably the most powerful feature of classes is that they can be used to *derive* other classes. This is called *inheritance*. Applying this technique, you can use the definition of a class to define a new class. A derived class *inherits*, or takes on, all the attributes of the class from which it is derived. The derived class can also change any of the attributes that it inherits, or add new attributes.

In C++ terminology, the class used to derive a new class is called the *base class*, the derived class is called a *subclass*. This terminology is illustrated in Figure 4.9, which shows how a more complex window class can be derived from a simple window class. Notice that the derived window contains all the attributes from the first window. In addition, some new attributes have been added, such as a title and a scroll bar. We've also modified one of the attributes—the window border has been changed from a single-line border to a double-line border.

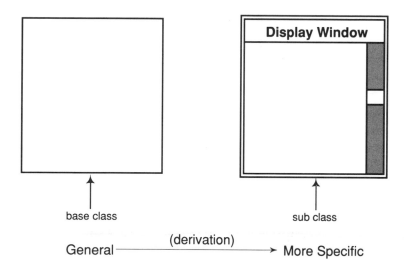

Figure 4.9. Deriving a window class.

Although this concept of deriving classes seems straightforward, the code required to create and use derived classes can get a little tricky. But don't get scared away just yet. In this section we'll cover the basics to whet your appetite and then, in Chapter 9, when you have more knowledge about classes and C++ functions, we'll take up this topic again.

Derived classes are declared using the : operator. The basic syntax required is

```
class <subclass name> : [<public>]<base class name> {
// class members go here
};
```

The : operator is used to join the base class name with the new subclass name that is being created. Notice that the **public** keyword is optional. If it is included, all the members declared as public in the base class will be declared as public in the derived class, otherwise they will be private. The rest of the derived class definition follows the same rules as those used to define a base class. That is, the **public** keyword can be used to define the public members, and both data and function members can be included in the class definition. Here's an example that illustrates how a derived class is created:

```
// The base class
class pen {
public:
    int x, y, status;
};

// The subclass
class colored_pen : public pen {
public:
    int color;    // additional member
};
```

The relationship between the base class and the subclass is illustrated in Figure 4.10. Here, we've made a base class representing drawing pens. These pens have an (x,y) location, along with an up/down status. The base class, however, does not provide a component that allows the color of a pen to be changed. Therefore, we've derived a new pen class that does.

The class **colored_pen** is derived from the class **pen** using the : operator. The **public** keyword used before the base class name makes all the public members of the base class also public in the derived class. This means that any of the members defined in the base class can be accessed by the derived class. By default, the members from a base class are private. (The access rules for base class members are covered in detail in Chapter 9.)

The new derived class adds another public data member, which stores the color of the pen. The colored pen still has the variables **x**, **y**, and **status**; therefore, we can execute any of the following statements:

```
colored_pen papermate;

papermate.x = 15;
```

```
papermate.y = 1;
papermate.status = UP;
```

as well as statements like

```
papermate.color = RED;
```

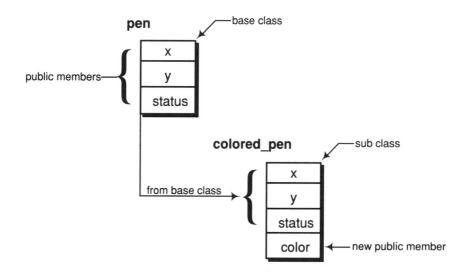

Figure 4.10. Relationship between a base class and a subclass.

Notice that the first three statements access the members that the subclass inherited from the base class. Again, because these members are public, we can access them using the standard notation used to access class members. The last statement shows that the member defined in the **colored_pen** class can be accessed in the same way.

In addition to adding new data members, you can also add function members. These can access all the public members of the base class, as well as any additional members of the derived class.

Note: When a subclass is derived from a base class, you cannot take out members. All the members of the base class are included in the subclass as well.

A Quick Look at Virtual Functions

In the previous section we stated that functions can be added to derived classes. In addition, a function inherited from a base class can also be modified. This is accomplished by making the function a *virtual function*. Virtual functions are important in C++ and are especially useful for supporting the object-oriented programming style, as we shall see.

A virtual function is created by using the **virtual** keyword. Let's look at an example:

```
class error_msg {
public:
    virtual void display(void) { printf("An error has
                                          occurred!\n"); }
};
```

This class definition can be used to create a general message object. Note that we've included a function called **display()** for our general **error_msg** class. In this example we arbitrarily made the function an inline function, but it doesn't have to be one. If you are creating virtual functions that are more complex, you can define them outside the body of the class, as well.

Now, suppose we wished to derive a class for a syntax-related error message. The following class definition illustrates how this can be accomplished:

```
class syntax_msg : public error_msg {
public:
    void display(void) { printf("Semicolon missing in
                                  statement\n"); }
};
```

By declaring **display()** in the derived class **syntax_msg**, we've told the compiler to override its original definition. Thus, whenever **display()** is used for **syntax_msg**, the program prints "Semicolon missing in statement" instead of "An error has occurred!" The following sample program illustrates how the virtual function operates:

```
void main() {
    // declare objects
```

```
        error_msg *msg_lst[2];
        error_msg msg;
        syntax_msg smsg;
        msg_lst[0] = &msg;      // print to the general error obj
        msg_lst[1] = &smsg;     // print to the syntax error obj
        msg_lst[0]->display();
        msg_lst[1]->display();
}
```

This code produces the following output when executed:

```
An error has occurred!
Semicolon missing in statement
```

Let's see how. The first thing we did was create an array of pointers to **error_msg**. (You can point to objects just like any other variable.) Then we set them to point to **msg** and **smsg**—the two message objects we created. Note that it is possible for a base class pointer to point to any object created from a derived class, without the need for explicit type casting. Needless to say, you can't do this in C!

When the first **display()** message is sent, at run-time the program determines that the base class version of **display()** should be used, so the general error message is printed. The program also detects that the second **display()** message refers to the **syntax_msg** version. Determining which function to execute is accomplished by inspecting a pointer inside the object, which points to the appropriate function. This process is illustrated in Figure 4.11. This special pointer is used by C++ to implement virtual functions.

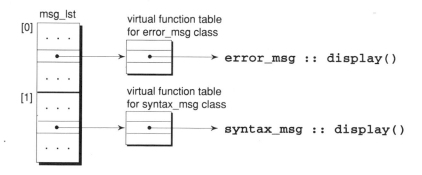

Figure 4.11. Reference pointer for virtual functions.

~ (Tilde)

It's possible for a subclass also to act as a base class for a sub-subclass. Thus, you can set up a whole hierarchy of classes. These and other issues about deriving classes are discussed in detail in Chapter 9.

Note: For a virtual function to work properly, it must be declared virtual in the base class using the **virtual** keyword. This keyword is optional in the derived class but the function remains virtual with or without the keyword.

Deriving Buffers

Now that we've covered some of the basics of deriving classes, let's see how we can use this feature. Our final example program converts a buffer of characters to uppercase. What's unique about the program is that we've designed a general buffer class so that we can derive memory and file buffer classes. Pointers to each buffer are passed to an uppercase conversion routine, which calls the virtual functions **get**() and **put**(). By defining these functions as virtual, we've made our conversion routine more general purpose. It can accept any combination of file and memory buffers for input and output! Our example shows two such combinations. Here's the listing:

```
#include <stdio.h>
#include <string.h>
#include <ctype.h>
#include <stdlib.h>
// General buffer class
class buf {
public:
    virtual int eob(void)    { return 1; }
    virtual int get(void)    { return 0; }
    virtual void put(int c) { ; }
};

// Derived memory buffer class
class charbuf : public buf {
    // added data
    char *data;
    int cursor, len;
public:
```

```
    // added methods
    charbuf(char *s);
    ~charbuf(void)        { delete data; }
    char *inspect(void) { return data; }
    // overridden methods
    int eob(void)     { return cursor >= len; }
    int get(void)     { return !eob() ? data[cursor++] : 0; }
    void put(int c) { if (!eob()) data[cursor++] = c; }
};

charbuf::charbuf(char *s)
{
    data = new char[len = strlen(s) + 1];
    strcpy(data, s);
    cursor = 0;
}

// Derived file buffer class
class filebuf : public buf {
    // added data
    FILE *f;
public:
    // added methods
    int open(char *name, char *mode);
    int close(void) { return fclose(f); }
    // overridden methods
    int eob(void)     { return feof(f); }
    int get(void)     { return fgetc(f); }
    void put(int c) { fputc(c, f); }
};

int filebuf::open(char *name, char *mode)
// Returns 0 on error
{
    if ((f = fopen(name, mode)) != NULL)
        return 1; else return 0;
}

// General purpose uppercase converter
void convert_to_upper(buf *in, buf *out)
```

```
{
   while(!in->eob()) {
     out->put( toupper(in->get()) );
  }
}

void main()
{
   // memory to file conversion
   charbuf a("enemy warship, range 300 kilometers\n");
   filebuf b;

   if (b.open("radar.dat", "w")) {
      convert_to_upper(&a, &b);
      b.close();
   }
   // memory to memory conversion
   charbuf c("sunny and cold, highs near 110");
   charbuf d("                              ");
   convert_to_upper(&c, &d);
   printf("Forecast for today: %s\n", d.inspect());
}
```

Note how we've typed the arguments to the conversion routine as pointers to **buf**, rather than as pointers to **charbuf** or **filebuf**. We did this so we can keep the routine general. Note also that we did not need to type cast our **charbuf** and **filebuf** pointers because they were from derived classes of **buf**. By the way, you might notice that our **buf** class doesn't seem to do much of anything. This is actually an important technique, that of defining *abstract classes*, which are meant to be at the top of a class hierarchy. You'll see this term again in Chapter 9 when we discuss inheritance and class hierarchies.

Summary

We've now completed our whirlwind tour of C++ classes. In the previous two chapters, we covered most of the fundamental and many of the advanced features of classes. We've seen how classes are a powerful extension of C structures and that they are used as the main building block to support object-oriented programming.

In this chapter we introduced the more advanced features of classes, including information hiding, accessing members with friend functions, techniques for working with dynamic objects, initializing objects with constructor and destructor functions, and techniques for deriving classes. Because of the importance of these advanced features, we'll be exploring them in detail in later chapters.

Exercises

1. Using classes, write a program to implement a linked list. Include functions to add, delete, and search for nodes in the list. Taking information hiding into consideration, which members in the list class should be made private?

2. How could you use a constructor and a destructor to help initialize and clean up the linked list implemented in the previous exercise? Add the constructor and destructor to the list class.

3. Which function, **add1**() or **add2**(), will produce an error? What is the error? (Hint: Remember that friends only provide a one-way access to class members.)

```
class numb1 {
   int a;
   friend class numb2;
public:
   int b;
   void add1(numb2 w) { a = w.z + w.y; }
};

class numb2 {
   int z;
public:
   int y;
   void add2(numb1 x) { z = x.a + x.b; }
};
```

4. Given the following definition for a **circle** class, derive a new class to represent a cylinder class. Include a member function, **volume()**, to calculate the volume of the cylinder.

```
class circle {
public:
    int radius, xo, yo;
};
```

5. Modify the linked list program that you developed in Exercise 1 to support a dynamic stack. Add functions **push()** and **pop()** to add and remove elements from the stack. When you alter the linked list class, make sure that you redefine the internal list processing functions so that they are private. The only member functions that the user should have access to are **push()** and **pop()**.

6. What is wrong with the statement that uses the **delete** operator in the following code?

```
class phone_num {
    int prefix, area, num;
public:
    phone_num(int p, int a, int n) {
      prefix = p; area = a; num = n;
    }
};

phone_num *yellow_pages = new phone_num[1000];
delete yellow_pages;
```

5

Introducing C++ Functions

Can you imagine writing a useful C program without using functions? If you wrote a substantial program without functions, your program would be a nightmare to maintain. As you transition from a procedural language like C to an object-oriented language like C++, you'll rely heavily on functions. In previous chapters we've seen how we can use classes to define high-level data structures for representing program data. We now need a mechanism for processing that data, and that's where functions come in.

In this chapter we'll explore the basics of defining and using C++ functions. We'll begin by briefly introducing the types of functions that C++ provides. Next, we'll show you how to work with the basic function components such as function prototypes, arguments, reference variables, and return values.

After you complete this chapter you'll know:

- The types of functions that C++ provides
- The basic techniques for defining and calling a function
- How to use function prototypes
- How to pass arguments to functions
- How to use default arguments
- How to use a variable number of arguments in a function call

A Look at C++ Functions

You should already know how to define and use functions, since you're familiar with C programming. As a quick review, Figure 5.1 shows a typical C function with its components labeled, including the return type, function name, argument list, and function body.

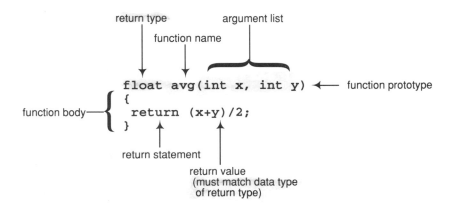

Figure 5.1. A C function with its components labeled.

The basic structure of C++ functions is similar to the structure of C functions; however, C++ has many more types of functions. The complete set of C++ functions is shown in Figure 5.2. Notice that the functions are divided into two groups—*class member functions* and *nonmember functions*. The class member functions include the seven kinds of functions that can be included in a class definition. (Remember that functions, as well as data, can serve as class members.) The nonmember functions include C++ functions that are not defined inside a class.

Here is a quick overview of each class member function type:

- *Standard functions*. These functions are used to access class members. They don't have any other special properties.
- *Virtual functions*. These are functions that can be overridden in derived classes.
- *Constructor and destructor functions*. These functions are used to initialize and clean up the objects that are created and destroyed in a program.

- *Operator functions*. These functions are used to change the functionality of a standard operator. For instance, the + operator can be overriden to support complex numbers.
- *Static functions*. These functions are used to operate on static data members (as described in Chapter 3). They are also used to write member functions that can be accessed without the use of an object.
- *Constant functions*. These functions are used when manipulating objects declared as being constant.

The class member functions, which we'll call *member functions*, are used to perform operations on a class's data members. These functions are also called *class methods*. Throughout this chapter, we'll be exploring a number of different techniques for writing efficient member functions.

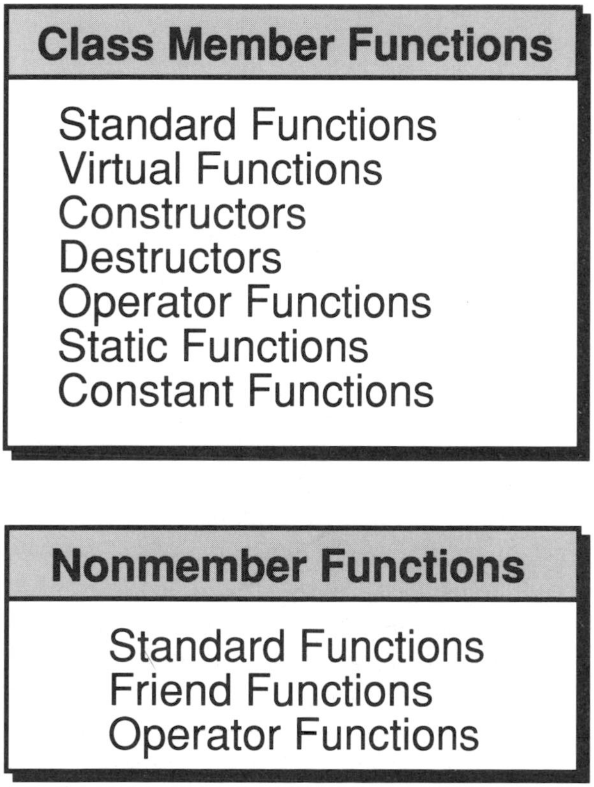

Class Member Functions

Standard Functions
Virtual Functions
Constructors
Destructors
Operator Functions
Static Functions
Constant Functions

Nonmember Functions

Standard Functions
Friend Functions
Operator Functions

Figure 5.2. The types of C++ functions.

Nonmember functions are simpler than member functions. These functions can be of two types: functions that are not related to a class and friend functions, which can access hidden class members.

Both C++ member and nonmember functions are more powerful than standard C functions because they can have special attributes assigned to them. Table 5.1 shows the different attributes that can be assigned to each function type.

Table 5.1. C++ function attributes

Attribute	Member Function	Nonmember Function
Virtual	Yes	No
Inline	Yes	Yes
Friend	Yes	Yes
Overloaded	Yes	Yes
Operator	Yes	Yes

Note: Member functions are defined in conjunction with classes and nonmember functions are defined independently of classes.

Components of a C++ Member Function

As we stated, C++ functions are similar in form to C functions. The main difference is that a class specifier is included with member functions. Figure 5.3 illustrates the general form of a C++ member function. Here we've labeled the main components, including the return type, class name, function name, argument list, and scoping operator. This syntax should be familiar to you. Notice the use of the **::** operator. This C++ operator serves as a scoping operator. In this case it is used to connect the function's name to the class to which the function belongs. The function definition shown in Figure 5.3 indicates that the function **draw_rect()** is a member of the class **rectangle**.

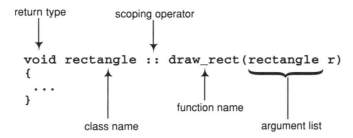

Figure 5.3. General form of a C++ member function.

A function body contains one or more statements written using standard C syntax. The function can also access the private members of the class if the function is a class member. Figure 5.4 shows the relationship between a member function and a class. Note that this function uses local variables, global variables, and class members.

```
class window {
public:
  int xo,yo;
  void move(int n);
  void draw(winmgr *m);
};

void window::move(int n)
{
  int i;          ◄─────────────── local variable

  for (i=0;i<n;i++) {
    xo++;         ◄─────────────── data member
    draw(mgr);
  }
}
```
function member   global variable

Figure 5.4. Relationship between a member function and a class.

Note: If a function is not a member function, don't include a class name in the function's definition. The function is defined using the standard C notation

```
<return type> <function name>(<argument list>)
```

Function Prototypes

C++ uses the ANSI C standard for function headers. (Actually, the standard for representing function headers was borrowed from C++.) An example of the old C programming style is

```
int avg(x, y)
int x,y;
{
    return((x+y)/2);
}
```

You can still use this old style with some C++ implementations, but the new syntax is better.

```
int avg(int x, int y)
{
    return((x+y)/2);
}
```

Here the function arguments are listed in the function header, along with their data types. Why is this so important? This style enforces type checking on the arguments by using a function prototype. A *function prototype* is a declaration that tells the compiler the number of actual arguments required and the data type of each argument. For example, the complete prototype for the **avg()** function is

```
int avg(int x, int y);  // function prototype
```

This statement declares that **avg()** returns an integer and takes two integer arguments. The names of the arguments are ignored by the compiler; however, they are useful for documenting the names of arguments used in a function. Because they are ignored, we can obtain the same results by writing the prototype as

```
int avg(int, int);
```

We'll use the first style throughout this book because of its built-in documentation features.

If a function is used differently than the way it is defined by the prototype, the compiler will issue a warning or error message. For example, if we call **avg()** with

```
result = avg(5);
```

the compiler will inform us that an incorrect number of arguments is specified.

Note: In C++, a function must be declared before it can be called. The old style of function headers is considered obsolete in Version 2.1 and may not be supported by your implementation.

In general, function prototypes increase the reliability of programs; they should be used whenever possible. Usually they are declared before a function is actually defined, typically in a header file. A prototype that is placed before a function definition is called a *forward declaration*. Alternatively, the function header provided with the function body can serve as the prototype. In this case, any code using the function must come after the function in the source file so that the type checking will work properly. Also, any function headers included in a class declaration will serve as prototypes for their corresponding functions.

Note: A function prototype looks like a function definition without the function body.

Type-safe Linkage

Type-safe linkage is a technique for catching typing errors in function calls at link-time. It can catch errors that occur when you specify function prototypes incorrectly. As an example, consider the following two C files:

```
/* file mymath.c */
double mysqrt(double d)
{
    /* do sqrt */
}


/* file myprog.c */
```

```
extern double mysqrt(int d); /* Argument has wrong type */
double f;
int d = 55;
f = mysqrt(d);
```

The prototype used for **mysqrt()** (in myprog.c) does not match the one used in mymath.c. A C compiler would not detect this error. The compiler can't tell that the **extern** declaration for **mysqrt()** has the wrong argument type (**int** instead of **double**). Also, the linker would link up the function call in the file myprog.c with the function definition in the file mymath.c. (The linker only sees the name **mysqrt**.) Therefore, the call to **mysqrt()** returns an erroneous answer because the **int** variable **d** was not properly cast to a **double**.

In C++, these types of errors are detected by the compiler because it encodes each function name with argument-typing information. This type of encoding is called *name mangling*. As an example, our two previous square root functions might be assigned the following mangled names, with **d** representing **double**, and **i** representing **int**. (The actual encoding used is implementation-dependent.)

```
mysqrt@d    // for double mysqrt(double d)
mysqrt@i    // for double mysqrt(int d)
```

When the compiler sees the definition for **mysqrt()** in the first source file, it uses the mangled name **mysqrt@d** to refer to the function. Then, when the compiler sees the erroneous call to **mysqrt()** in the second source file, it uses the second mangled name **mysqrt@i**. As far as the compiler is concerned, everything is okay. However, when the linker attempts to find the object code for **mysqrt@i**, the linker generates an "undefined function" error, since the only function it can find has a different name: **mysqrt@d**.

Name-mangling is a valuable technique because it makes the linker's job easier. The linker doesn't have to be "smart" in determining argument types. The linker simply compares the names of the functions. However, this type of linkage isn't entirely safe. If you'll notice in the mangled names, the return type is not encoded. This means that the mistake in the following scenario, where the return types are not specified correctly, would not be caught:

```
// file yourmath.cpp/
double mysqrt(double d)
{
    // do sqrt
```

```
}

// file yourprog.cpp
extern int mysqrt(double d); // wrong return type
int r;
int d = 55;
r = mysqrt(d);
```

In this case, both references to **mysqrt()** are given the same name, **mysqrt@d**, so the linker would not detect the error.

This situation can be improved. Simply ensure that both the function definition and function call see the same function prototype. How is this done? Place the prototype in a header file and include the header file in both source files, as follows:

```
// file yourmath.h
double mysqrt(double d);

// file yourmath.cpp
#include "yourmath.h"
double mysqrt(double d)
{
    // do sqrt
}

// file yourprog.cpp
#include "yourmath.h"
int r;
int d = 55;
r = mysqrt(d);
```

When the compiler sees the call to **mysqrt()** and sees that an integer is being used to hold the return value, it will make the appropriate conversion from **double** to **int**.

Name mangling is also used with member functions. For example, the following two functions

```
void window::move(int dx, int dy);
void turtle::move(int dx, int dy);
```

might be assigned the following mangled names:

```
window@move@ii
turtle@move@ii
```

The linker can tell the two functions apart because the class name is encoded in the function name.

Calling C Functions in C++

The type-safe linkage scheme (name mangling) presents a problem if you try to call functions from another language. For example, if you try to call a C function from C++, the linker will never find the function, because the C function name isn't mangled. To easily work around this problem, you can specify the language type of a function, effectively turning off the name mangling.

As an example, the following statement declares the function **sin**() to be a C function and tells the compiler not to mangle the function name:

```
extern "C" double sin(double a);
```

You can declare a group of functions (such as those declared in a header file) by using double quotes to enclose them in a linkage specification. For example:

```
extern "C" { // here's a linkage specification
#include <stdlib.h>        // all functions included are "C"

void myfunc(int a);        // so are these
{
    int myadd(int x, int y);
}
;
```

Note: To link assembly language routines into a C++ program, try using the **extern "C"** specification.

Argument Type Conversions

We've now seen that function prototypes are valuable because they help the compiler check the data types of arguments that are passed. Function prototypes also have another important use: They instruct the compiler to perform type conversions when a function is called. Let's look at an example to see how this works. Assume that we have the following prototype defined:

```
double range_check(double d); // function prototype
```

Here's the main program that calls this function:

```
main()
{
    int k;
    double d;

    printf("Input a number to check\n");
    scanf("%d", &k);
    d = range_check(k); // k converted to a double before
                        // the function call
    printf("The returned value is %d", d);
}
```

The argument **k** is converted to a **double** before it is passed to **range_check**().
Without prototyping, this conversion would not take place. We would have to perform the conversion using a type cast; otherwise, we might end up with the wrong results.

Function prototypes are a necessity for *overloaded* functions. These are functions that have the same name but different arguments—a feature not supported in C but available in C++. The compiler determines which function to actually call by examining the argument types and matching them with the calling types. Without function prototypes, this would not be possible.

Calling C++ Functions

Let's now shift gears and look more closely at how C++ functions are called. Actually, the manner in which a function is called depends on whether or not the function serves as a member function. If a function is not a class member, you call it just like you would any C function. Here's an example:

```
popup_menu(1,10,"File Menu", opt_lst);
```

To call a class member function, you combine the call with an object. Here's an example:

```
turtle tommy;      // define an object
tommy.move(5);     // call move() in object tommy
```

We've defined an object named **tommy** using the class **turtle**, and then we've called the function **move()**. In object-oriented programming, this type of function call is considered the act of *passing a message*. In this case, the message **move(5)** is passed to the object **tommy**. When the object receives the message, it responds by executing the function **move()**.

Next, we'll examine the common techniques available for calling any type of C++ function, including member and nonmember functions. These techniques include:

- Passing arguments by value versus passing arguments by reference
- Passing arrays as arguments
- Using return values
- Using default arguments
- Passing a variable number of arguments

Passing Arguments by Value versus Passing by Reference

By default, function arguments in C++ are passed by value (except for arrays). This means that the arguments are copied before they are actually passed to a function. This technique is illustrated in Figure 5.5. Because a function uses only copies of the arguments passed, the arguments retain their initial value after the function returns. This is true even if the function modifies the arguments. You can verify this by running the following program:

```
#include <stdio.h>
void mess_with_args(int x, int y);   // function prototype
```

```
void mess_with_args(int x, int y)
{
    x = x + y;
    y = y * y;
    printf("\nThe variable x is now %d", x);
    printf("\nThe variable y is now %d", y);
}

main()
{
    int x, y;

    printf("\nPlease enter two numbers");
    scanf("%d", &x);
    scanf("%d", &y);
    mess_with_args(x,y);
    printf("\nThe numbers are %d and %d", x,y);
}
```

Notice that the function **mess_with_args**() changes the contents of both **x** and **y**. However, these variables will keep the values that you typed in before the function **mess_with_args**() is called.

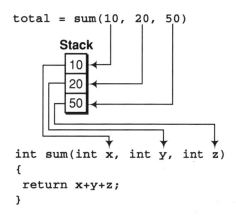

Figure 5.5. Arguments passed by value.

This argument-passing technique works well with simple variables, such as numbers and characters. For larger objects, such as arrays and structures, it is usually more efficient to pass the address of the object. When an address is passed, you can instruct the function to look up the address to determine the contents of the variable. The variable is not copied, and that means less overhead is involved. For instance, if you pass a structure that has a lot of members, only one reference to the structure is required—the address to the beginning of where the structure is stored in memory. In traditional programming practices, this approach to passing arguments is called *pass by reference*. Besides being more efficient, the pass-by-reference method also allows us to change the value of the arguments. To illustrate, let's modify our previous sample program so that it passes its arguments by reference.

```c
#include <stdio.h>
void mess_with_args(int *x, int *y);
void mess_with_args(int *x, int *y)
{
    *x = *x + *y;
    *y = *y * *y;
    printf("\nThe variable x is now %d", *x);
    printf("\nThe variable y is now %d", *y);
}

void main()
{
    int x, y;

    printf("\nPlease enter two numbers ");
    scanf("%d", &x);
    scanf("%d", &y);
    mess_with_args(&x, &y);
    printf("\nThe numbers are %d and %d", x,y);
}
```

Notice that this program uses pointers to carry out the pass-by-reference method. When **mess_with_args()** is called, the addresses of the variables **x** and **y** are passed instead of their contents. Because we define the function header with the statement

```c
void mess_with_args(int *x, int *y)
```

we must take the address of **x** and **y** in the call

```
mess_with_args(&x, &y);
```

Remember that the address-of operator (**&**) in C produces the address of a variable. This technique for passing arguments is the standard method used in C programs. However, C++ provides a type of variable called a *reference variable* that also allows us to pass arguments by reference.

Reference Variables

A reference variable (or reference, for short) contains the address of another object. In this respect, a reference variable works like a pointer. However, it is different because it cannot be changed after it has been initialized. Also, reference variables are automatically de-referenced when they are used, as we shall soon see.

Figure 5.6 shows the syntax required to define a reference variable. Notice that the address-of operator (**&**) is used. The notation <*data type*>**&** y translates to "the variable **y** is a reference variable of the specified data type." The following program shows how a reference variable is defined and used:

```
#include <stdio.h>
void main()
{
    int i = 17; // here's an integer set to 17
    int &p = i; // make reference p, which points to i

    p = 55; // set p to 55, which also causes i to be 55
    printf("i = %d, p = %d\n", i, p);
}
```

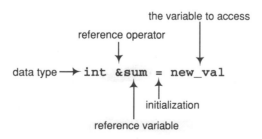

Figure 5.6. Defining a reference variable.

After **p** is initialized, it points to the same location that **i** does. When it is used in the **printf()** call, it is automatically de-referenced to produce the value of 55. Because of this automatic de-referencing, it's as though **p** were simply another name for **i**. Indeed it is, and, in fact, **p** is called an *alias* for **i**. Note that once it's set to point to **i**, the value of **p** cannot be changed to point to any other variable. That is, it cannot be initialized twice, although the *value* it points to can change as often as you like.

Note: A reference variable is like a constant pointer that is automatically de-referenced when used.

Using Reference Arguments

Now that we've seen how reference variables are defined, you might be wondering what they have to do with passing arguments to functions. Well, you can also declare arguments to be reference variables. Arguments declared in this manner are said to be *passed by reference*, and are called *reference arguments*. For example, here is a function with a reference argument, along with a typical call to it:

```
#include <stdio.h>
void set_value(int &i) { i = 17; }

void main()
{
    int z = 25;

    set_value(z);
    printf("%d\n", z);
}
```

This program prints out the value 17. To see how, let's examine it step by step. First, we declare the function **set_value()** to have the formal argument **i**. This argument is declared to be a reference variable by using the **&** operator. In effect, we've told the program that **i** points to the argument passed to the function when called. That is, the argument is passed by reference.

The body of the function assigns the value 17 to the memory location referenced by the argument **i**. In **main()**, we've declared an integer variable **z**, which is set to 25 before **set_value()** is called. When this function returns, **z** will have the value 17, as set in the function. Unlike when using pointers, we did not have to take the address of **z** explicitly when calling **set_value()**, nor did we have to de-reference the argument **i** inside the function using the C pointer notation ***i**.

To summarize the application of reference arguments, Figure 5.7 shows how the example we just presented might be translated into C.

C	C++

```
void set_value(int *v)
{
   *v = 25;
}

int t;

set_value(&t);
```

```
void set_value(int &v)
{
   v = 25;
}

int t;

set_value(t);
```

Figure 5.7. Translation box for reference arguments.

Figure 5.7 illustrates how reference variables are more convenient than pointers when arguments are passed by reference. The pointer method is awkward because the pointer arguments must be explicitly de-referenced each time they are used. Using reference variables helps you get around this problem. For those of you familiar with Pascal, we should mention the similarities between C++ reference arguments and Pascal **VAR** parameters. As an example, the C++ function definition

```
void count_numbers(int a, int b, int &result)
```

is equivalent to the following Pascal procedure definition:

```
Procedure Count_Numbers(A, B : Integer;
                        VAR Result: Integer);
```

When to Use Reference Arguments

In the previous example we learned how to define a reference variable so that it can be modified inside a function's body. Although you might think that this is the best way to use reference arguments, it turns out that in many situations it is preferable *not* to use reference variables like this. Why? Well, consider the following function call:

```
set_value(z);    // the C++ way
```

Without actually knowing what **set_value**() does, there is no way for us to tell if **z** might be changed by the function. (Admittedly, in this example the function name is a dead giveaway.) In a long program, this situation could cause a lot of headaches, especially if you are trying to maintain a program that was written by someone else. If our sample program was written in the C style, we would have passed the address of the argument, as shown:

```
set_value(&z);    // the C way
```

Here, the **&** operator tells us that **z** might be modified because its address is being passed. You might say that the **&** operator raises a big red flag. If you are used to relying on this red flag when debugging your C code, you're going to be in for a lot of surprises if you use reference arguments in C++.

Okay, so when *should* reference variables be used for passing arguments? If you're passing a large structure to a function, then it is a likely candidate. For example, here's a function that passes a big structure by value:

```
int func(big_struct x)
{
```

```
        return x.some_member + 1;
    }
```

This same function can be passed by reference, as shown:

```
    int func(big_struct &x)
    {
        return x.some_member + 1;
    }
```

Except for the appearance of the **&** in the latter version, the functions look identical. However, the second version is more efficient because the structure's data is not passed to the function—only the address of the structure is passed.

Not only do the functions look the same, each function is also called using the same form. Here's an example:

```
    k = func(x);  // could be used with either version above
```

You don't need to know if **x** is passed by reference or by value because **x** is not changed by the function. In cases like this, it's a good idea to document the fact that the argument should not be changed. You can do this and include additional security by using the **const** keyword in the argument list, as shown:

```
    int func(const big_struct &x)
    {
        x.some_member = 25;         // compiler error
        return x.some_member + 1;   // okay
    }
```

Combining the **const** keyword with reference arguments gives you the best of both worlds: You can pass arguments efficiently and you don't have to worry about an argument being changed accidently.

Array Arguments

Arrays are the only arguments that are passed by reference, unless the **&** operator is used with the argument. When an array argument is used, the address of the first element of the array is passed so that the array can be accessed. Let's examine a short program to see how arrays are passed.

```
#include <stdio.h>
int numbers[8] = {100, 12, 205, 11, 19, 74, 500, -1 };
int sum(int *nums)
// sum up array of numbers until you reach a
// negative value
{
    int s = 0;

    while (*nums >= 0) s += *nums++;
    return s;
}


void main()
{
    printf("The sum is: %d\n", sum(numbers));
}
```

This program sums up an array of numbers. Because the address of the array argument **numbers** is passed, a pointer is used to access the members of the array. Figure 5.8 illustrates how the pointer ***nums** is used to access the array **numbers** in our sample program.

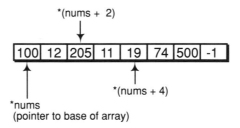

Figure 5.8. Using a pointer to access an array.

This built-in argument-passing mechanism is fine for cases where we want to pass an array argument by reference, but what do we do if we want to pass the array by value? Although you might think that this can't be done, there is a simple trick that we can apply. We'll place the array inside a structure, as shown:

```
#include <stdio.h>
struct num_trick {
```

```
        int numbers[8];
};

num_trick na = {100, 12, 205, 11, 19, 74, 500, -1};

int sum(num_trick nums)
// sum up array of numbers until you reach a
// negative value
{
    int i = 0, s = 0;

    while (nums.numbers[i] >= 0) s += nums.numbers[i++];
    return s;
}

void main()
{
    printf("The sum is: %d\n", sum(na));
}
```

Here, the argument **nums**, which holds the array, is copied before it is passed. The trouble is that it costs us an extra structure de-reference to access the array. Also, the array length must be predefined because the size of the structure must be known at compile-time.

If you're passing an array by value because you want to ensure that the members of the array cannot be changed, a better method is available. You can pass the array using a pointer argument that is defined with the **const** keyword. Here's an example:

```
int myfunc(const int *v)
{
    v[1] = 25;    // generates compiler error
    return v[1]; // okay
}
```

Notice that the statement **v[1] = 25;** is illegal because the argument **v** was declared to be a pointer to an array of constant integers, which can't be modified.

Getting down to Size

One disadvantage to the way array arguments are passed in both C and C++ is that the size of the array is not passed. If you're working with character arrays that are zero-terminated, as shown in Figure 5.9, this is not a problem, because the array's length can be determined using the standard library function **strlen()**. But what about other types of arrays, such as arrays of integers or structures?

Figure 5.9. Representation of a zero-terminated character array.

Fortunately, there are two possible solutions. We can pass the length of the array with another argument, or we can package up the array inside a structure that maintains the length of the array. As an example, the next function sums up the elements in an integer array. The length of the array is passed using the argument **size**.

```
int sum(int *v, int size)
{
    int i, sum = 0;
    for (i = 0; i<size; i++) sum += v[i];
    return sum;
}
```

Using the structure approach instead, we could write

```
struct int_array {
    int size;
    int *data;
};

int sum(int_array *v)
{
    int i, sum = 0;
    for (i = 0; i<v->size; i++) sum += v->data[i];
    return sum;
}
```

The first method is slightly more efficient (it doesn't perform structure de-referencing), but it's not as object-oriented, because the size of the array is separated from the array itself. Also, if you're working with multidimensional arrays, you'll need to pass sizes for each array dimension. This could quickly get out of hand. For this reason, the second method is preferred.

Multidimensional Arrays

As we just noted, multidimensional arrays are more difficult to work with than one-dimensional arrays because of the additional size information required to process the array. However, if the size of the array is fixed, it's relatively easy to pass and reference the elements of a multidimensional array argument. For instance, we could easily write a function to sum up 3 x 5 matrices, as shown:

```
int  m[3][5];
int  sum_up_3_by_5(int  m[3][5])
{
    int  sum = 0;
    for (int i = 0;  i<3;  i++) {
        for (int j = 0;  j<5;  j++)  sum += m[i][j];
    }
    return sum;
}
```

In the function definition, the syntax **m[i][j]** is just syntactic sugaring for the actual address calculations that are performed to access an array element, as shown in Figure 5.10. Notice that in the equivalent address arithmetic, only the size of the last dimension, 5, is needed to calculate the location of any given element **m[i][j]**. The size of the first dimension, 3, is not used. Because of this, we could have just as well written the function heading as

```
int  sum_up_3_by_5(int  m[][5]);
```

The method of passing a multidimensional array is similar to that of passing an array of one dimension. For example, if we had an array called **num** that was defined as a two-dimensional 3 x 5 array, we could pass it, as shown:

```
result = sum_up_3_by_5(num);
```

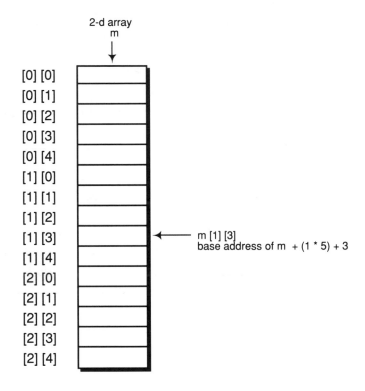

Figure 5.10. Address calculations used to access an array element.

The trouble comes when the size of either dimension is not known at compile-time. In this case, the syntax we just introduced won't work. We must somehow pass in the size. For example, in the following code sample we've allocated a matrix dynamically before we pass it to a function to sum up its elements. We can do this by passing the size as arguments, as shown:

```
int nr = 5, nc = 7;
int *m = new int[nr*nc];

int matrix_sum(int *m, int nr, int nc)
{
    int sum, i = 0, j = 0;
    for (i = 0; i<nr; i++) {
        for (j = 0; j<nc; j++) {
            sum += m[i*nc+j];
        }
```

```
    }
    return sum;
}
```

However, now we've thrown our modular design out the window. The extra arguments aren't what you would call elegant programming style. Also, every time we need to access an element **m[i, j]** in the function, we must use the address calculation **i*nc+j**. This is clumsy and prone to errors.

Working toward Objects

A better solution is to use a structure to enclose the matrix, as we showed earlier when we were working with one-dimensional arrays. And while we're at it, we could treat the matrix more like a class, hiding the address calculations and providing automatic allocation and de-allocation for the array as well. Check out the next program to see how this is accomplished.

```
#include <stdio.h>
struct matrix {
    int nr, nc;             // matrix dimensions
    int *data;              // pointer to data
    matrix(int w, int h);   // constructor
    ~matrix();              // destructor

    // use the following to store element
    void elem(int i, int j, int v)
    {
        data[i*nc+j] = v;
    }

    // use the following to retrieve element
    int val(int i, int j)
    {
        return data[i*nc+j];
    }
};

matrix::matrix(int w, int h)
```

```
{
    nr = w; nc = h;        // automatically size
    data = new int[nr*nc];  // and allocate storage
}

matrix::~matrix()
{
    delete[] data;   // automatically free up storage
}

int matrix_sum(matrix &m)   // note use of '&'
{
    int sum, i = 0, j = 0;
    for (i = 0; i< m.nr; i++) {
        for (j = 0; j< m.nc; j++) {
            sum += m.val(i,j);
        }
    }
    return sum;
}

void main()
{
    matrix m(17,15); // declares and allocates storage
    ...                    // initialize matrix via elem()
    printf("%d\n", matrix_sum(m));
    // destructor implicitly called here to free up storage
}
```

The first thing you probably noticed is the unusual structure definition.

```
struct matrix {
    int nr, nc;                // matrix dimensions
    int *data;                 // pointer to data
    matrix(int w, int h);   // constructor
    ~matrix();                 // destructor
    ...
};
```

What's going on here? Recall that C++ structures are really classes and that we can include functions in them. Here, we've included two functions, **matrix(int w, int h)** and **~matrix()**, to serve as the constructor and destructor functions, respectively. When a variable is declared of the structure **matrix**, as shown:

```
matrix m(17,15);
```

The constructor function is called automatically and memory is allocated for the two-dimensional array. The destructor function is called right before the main program terminates, and it frees up the memory allocated for the array. Notice that we haven't made any direct calls to the destructor inside the body of the main program.

There are also several important things to note about our matrix program. First, we've accessed the matrix dimensions directly from the structure in the **for** loops used in the function **matrix_sum()**. Also, the line that sums up the matrix elements in the function is now

```
sum += m.val(i,j);   // structure hiding method
```

instead of

```
sum += m.data[i*m.nc+j];   // direct
```

The address calculations are hidden from view. Even though there is an extra structure de-reference and function call, the function **val()** was declared inline, causing the following code to be inserted:

```
sum += m.data[i*m.nc+j];   // inline code expanded
```

Thus, the overhead is really just some structure de-referencing; the gain is that the code is more modular and easier to read. By packaging the matrix in a structure complete with constructors and destructors, we can conveniently declare differently sized matrices and take care of the storage handling automatically.

Since we passed the matrix with a reference argument, we eliminated the need to use the **&** operator in the call to **matrix_sum()**. We could just as well have passed a pointer to the matrix. If we had done so, the function and its corresponding call would have looked like the following code:

```
// pointer way to pass matrix
int matrix_sum(matrix *m)
```

```
{
    int sum, i = 0, j = 0;
    for (i = 0; i< m->nr; i++) {
        for (j = 0; j< m->nc; j++) {
            sum += m->val(i,j);
        }
    }
    return sum;
}


...
s = matrix_sum(&m);
```

Here the structure members are referenced with the arrow operator (->) instead of with the dot operator (.). The arrow operator is used because we're now pointing to a structure. In contrast, the reference argument technique allows us to access the structure directly.

Which method should you use, reference arguments or pointer arguments? Well, it doesn't really matter. Use the one that is more natural to you.

There is a more elegant way to code up the matrix access functions **elem()** and **val()**. To see how, we need to discuss how values are returned by C++ functions.

Note: Constructor and destructor functions can be included in structure definitions just as they can be included in class definitions. That's because structures are classes in C++.

Function Return Values

C++ plays by the same basic rules that C follows when it comes to function return values. You can pass back simple types (such as integers and doubles), structures, pointers to structures, and pointers to functions. The differences with C++ include the following:

- A function can return objects and pointers to objects
- A function can return references to objects

C++ allows functions to pass back objects and pointers to objects. This feature is a natural consequence of the fact that C++ extends the notion of structures to the more powerful class mechanisms.

Using Reference Return Types

The most intriguing feature that C++ offers when it comes to returning values from functions is the ability to pass back references in the return value. For instance, we can write

```
int &no_op(int &k)   // note & in return type
{
    return k
};
```

Here, **no_op()** returns the address of **k**, which also happens to be passed to the function as a reference. So what does this particular function do? Not much. For instance, the following two statements are equivalent:

```
i = no_op(k);     <===>  i = k;
```

But don't be disappointed. There *are* some extremely useful applications for reference return types. One is the ability to have a function call appear on the *left side* of an assignment without a pointer de-reference—something not possible in C. The translation box shown in Figure 5.11 shows an example of this technique. As another example, we can call a function that returns the address of an array element, and then we can set the address of the element to a new value. Here's the example:

```
int &elem(int *v,int i)
{
    return v[i];
}

int v[10];

elem(v,2) = 42;   // sets element #2 to 42
```

```
          C                          C++

  int x,y;                    int x,y;

  int *pick(int n,int *a,     int &pick(int n,int &a,
                int *b)                       int &b)
  {                           {
    if (n==1)                   if (n==1)
      return a;                   return a;
    else return b;              else return b;
  }                           }

  *(pick(2,&x,&y)) = 42;      pick(2,x,y) = 42;
```

Figure 5.11. Translating C++ reference arguments into C.

The neat thing about this technique is that the assignment operation can be performed with a single expression. To further illustrate the power of using reference return types, let's modify the matrix structure that we presented earlier.

```
struct matrix {
    int nr, nc;          // matrix dimensions
    int *data;           // pointer to data
    matrix(int w, int h);   // constructor
    ~matrix();           // destructor

    // Use the following to both store and retrieve
    // element. Don't need separate val() function
    int &elem(int i, int j)
```

```
    {
        return data[i*nc+j];
    }
};
```

Here we were able to use just one access function for both storing and retrieving matrix arguments. Thus, we can code expressions like

```
m.elem(3,4) = 5; // would have used m.elem(3,4,5) before
k = m.elem(6,7); // would have used k = m.val(6,7) before
```

Using our newly modified **elem()** function in the second expression is more efficient than using the old **val()** function. With **val()**, we would have set **k** equal to a *copy* of the element **m[6,7]**, whereas the new **elem()** function uses the element directly. Thus, less actual data is copied, which is important, especially if you are using arrays with large elements.

There is one more important consideration. As with pointers, you should never return the address of local variables using references. For instance, never do things like

```
double &mint(void)
{
    double gum;
    return gum;        // Never do!
}

int &eger(void)
{
    return 1;          // Equally bad!
}
```

In both cases, an address to data that's stored on the function-calling stack is returned. This stack space can get reused at any time, so you've just pointed to data that may not be there the next time you try to access it.

You have seen just a glimpse of what is possible using reference return types. The most common use of them is in conjunction with operator functions. You'll see examples of this later in the material on operator functions in Chapter 7.

Default Arguments

Unlike C, but like other languages such as BASIC, C++ allows you to set default values for unspecified parameters. This is performed by initializing the parameters in the formal argument list, as in

```
void func(int i, int j = 12)
{
    ...
}
```

If a call is made to **func()** without specifying **j**, as in **func(14)**, then **j** takes on the *default value* of 12. If **j** is specified, as in **func(14,15)**, then **j** takes on the value given in the call, in this case 15.

Here's a more complete example, where default values are used in a function that sets the date:

```
#include <stdio.h>
struct date { int mo, day, yr; };

void set_date(date *dt, int m=12, int d=25, int y=92)
{
    dt->mo = m; dt->day = d; dt->yr = y;
}

void prt_date(date *d)
{
    printf("%02d/%02d/%02d\n", d->mo, d->day, d->yr);
}

void main()
{
    date birthday, Christmas;
    set_date(&birthday, 8, 19, 57);
    set_date(&Christmas);
    prt_date(&birthday);
    prt_date(&Christmas);
}
```

In **set_date()**, **m** gets the default value of 12, **d** gets 25, and **y** gets 92. Whenever **set_date()** is called with some of the arguments missing, they are set to these default values. In the first call to **set_date()**, the defaults are overridden, since all the arguments are supplied by the call. In the second call, since no date arguments are given, all of the defaults are used. When run, this program prints out the following:

```
08/19/57
12/25/92
```

Here, we've specified either all the parameters or none of them. It's also possible to specify just part of them, as in

```
date payday;
set_date(&payday, 1, 15);
prt_date(&payday);
```

which prints out 01/15/92. Note that you can only leave the rightmost trailing parameters unspecified. For instance, it's not possible to use the default value for **mo** while overriding the defaults for **day** and **yr**. This also implies that only trailing arguments can be given defaults, as shown here:

```
int aaa(int x, int y=0, int z=0); // fine
int bbb(int x=0, int y, int z);   // illegal
```

When using a function prototype along with a function definition, there's one more rule you should know about involving default arguments: The values for the default arguments should be specified only in the prototype, and not in the actual function. For instance:

```
// Correct way
int elem(int *a, int indx, int ofs = 0); // specify default
                                          // value here

int elem(int *a, int indx, int ofs)       // not here
{
    return a[indx + ofs];
}

// Incorrect way
```

```
int elem(int *a, int indx, int ofs = 0);

int elem(int *a, int indx, int ofs = 0)   // can't specify
                                           // twice
{
    return a[indx + ofs];
}

// Another incorrect way
int elem(int *a, int indx, int ofs);

int elem(int *a, int indx, int ofs = 0) // specified in wrong
                                        // place
{
    return a[indx + ofs];
}
```

You should specify the default values in the prototypes, and not in the function definitions. Remember that the prototypes will most likely appear in header files and may be the only syntax the compiler can check against when processing a call to a function. If that function needs default arguments, the compiler needs the prototype to determine the values to use. Without the prototype, the compiler would not know that defaults were even being used and might generate a compiler error due to the supposedly missing arguments.

Using a Variable Number of Arguments

Before we drop the curtains and turn down the lights on our introduction of C++ functions, we need to take a quick look at how we can define and call functions that use a variable number of arguments. Actually, this topic is similar to the one we just explored (default arguments), except that now we are interested in creating functions that can have any number of arguments. As with C, you can specify a variable number of arguments to a function by using the ellipses notation, as in:

```
int argsum(...);
```

This is the extreme form. By specifying just ellipses for the arguments in the function definition, you can call the function with any number of arguments of any type. Since the compiler does not know how many arguments are needed, nor their types, it cannot perform type checking. It is up to the function to interpret the arguments. Typically, at least the first argument is specified (so that it's type checked), which can be used by the function to interpret the other arguments, as is done in **printf()**:

```
int printf(char *fmt, ...);
```

The character string **fmt** contains format codes that are used by **printf()** to tell what other arguments have been passed to the function. For example, in

```
printf("Name %s  Id %d\n", "Loren", 5127);
```

the **%s** and **%d** codes tell **printf()** to expect two more arguments; the first argument is a character string and the second is an integer. Although **printf()** expects to be passed these arguments, the compiler does no checking to ensure that these arguments are actually supplied. If they are not supplied, you'll get unexpected results, as you've probably encountered when using **printf()** improperly.

Note: In C++, a function declaration of the form **f()** means the same as **f(void),** whereas in C it means **f(...)**—a function with unspecified arguments. When mixing C and C++ code, always use **f(void)** to indicate a function with no arguments and **f(...)** to indicate a function with unspecified arguments. This will avoid any confusion.

You should keep in mind that more than one argument can be specified, with an unspecified remainder of arguments, as in:

```
void print_menu(char *title, int no_entries, ...);
```

To access the unspecified arguments in your functions, it helps to understand how the argument stack works. Figure 5.12 shows the relationship between a sample function call that uses a variable number of arguments and the argument stack. Notice that a memory location (stack address) is reserved for each argument. Fortunately, C++ provides a standard set of macros to help you access the unspecified parameters placed on the argument stack. These macros, listed in Table 5.2, are also provided with C. To use them you must include the header file **stdarg.h** in your programs. The advantage of using these built-in macros is that your code will be able to run on different computer systems even though each computer may use an entirely different internal system for passing arguments on the stack.

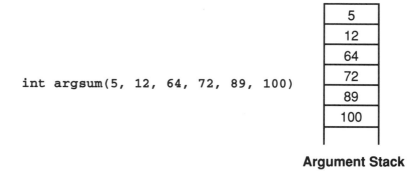

Argument Stack

int argsum(5, 12, 64, 72, 89, 100)

Figure 5.12. Passing variable arguments.

Table 5.2. Macros for accessing unspecified parameters

Macro/Type	Description
va_list	Declares an argument list type
va_start(va_list v,arg)	Used to point to first argument
va_arg(va_list v,type)	Used to access current argument
va_end(va_list v)	Used to clean up the arguments

Let's put together a sample program so that we can see how the built-in macros are used. We'll write a function that prints a menu from a list of character strings representing menu entries. Assuming the menu entries are known when we write the program, we can pass each entry as an argument. Of course, we'll want to define the function so that it can accept a variable number of arguments to allow us to call it with different menu entry lists. Here is the complete program:

```
#include <stdio.h>
#include <stdarg.h>
void print_menu(char *title, int n, ...)
{
```

```
        va_list arg_ptr; // holds arg info
        int i;
        char *entry;

        va_start(arg_ptr, n); // point to first entry
        printf("%s\n\n", title);
        for (i = 0; i<n; i++) {
            entry = va_arg(arg_ptr, char *); // access entries
            printf("%d. %s\n", i+1, entry);
        }
        va_end(arg_ptr); // clean up arguments
    }

void main()
{
    print_menu("Lunch Specials", 3,
            "Chicken", "Beef", "Veggies");
}
```

In this example, we've specified the first two arguments of **print_menu()** for type checking purposes. These arguments hold the menu title and number of entries, respectively. The latter is used in the **for loop**, which walks through and prints out each of the remaining unspecified arguments. The arguments are interpreted with **va_arg()** as character strings.

When run, the program produces

```
Lunch Specials

1. Chicken
2. Beef
3. Veggies
```

In case you're wondering how the **va_list, va_start(), va_arg()**, and **va_end()** macros work, here's how one MS-DOS compiler implements them:

```
typedef char *va_list;

#define va_start(ap, arg)
        ((ap) = (va_list)&(arg) + sizeof(arg))
```

```
#define va_arg(ap, arg_type)  (*((arg_type *)ap)++)
#define va_end(ap)
```

We see that **va_list** is simply defined to be a character pointer type. The macro **va_start()** sets the supplied **va_list** pointer **ap** to point to the location just after the specified argument **arg**. To access the current argument, **va_arg()** de-references **ap** and then increments it the appropriate number of bytes to point to the next argument. It uses **arg_type** to determine the argument's size and return type.

Keep in mind that there is no guarantee that all C++ systems will implement these macros in the same way. For example, the macro **va_end()** we used was defined as a no-op. Thus, it wouldn't be strictly necessary to use it, even though we did in our menu example. However, some systems might define **va_end()** differently in order to allow the stack to be cleaned up properly. Thus, it's strongly recommended that you end your argument accesses with **va_end()**.

Summary

You now have been introduced to the basics of using C++ functions. In the first part of this chapter we presented an overview of the types of functions that C++ supports. We've seen how to define both standard and class member functions. We also have learned how to use function prototypes, call functions, define reference arguments and default arguments, return values, and use variable length arguments. Also, you've learned how C++ uses type-safe linkage to make function calling safer.

In the next chapter we'll explore the more advanced features of C++ functions. You'll learn how to write more complex programs that take advantage of techniques such as virtual functions and polymorphism.

Exercises

1. Change the **vector_len()** function so that it passes its argument with pointers instead of by reference. Remember to make the necessary changes to the function call as well.

```
#include <stdio.h>
struct vector {
   int x, y;
   vector(int a, int b) { x = a; y = b; }
};

int vector_len(vector &v)
{
   return sqrt(v.x * v.x + v.y * v.y);
}

void main()
{
   vector dist(100, 42);
   printf("vector length: %d\n", vector_len(dist));
}
```

2. What value does this program display when it executes? (Hint: Review how reference variables work.)

```
void main()
{
   int i = 42;
   int &p = i;
   int &q = p;

   q = 17;
   i = 55;
   printf("The result is: %d\n", i - q);
}
```

3. The following code segment produces an error. Can you find it?

```
int i = 13;
int &p = i;

&p = 34;
```

4. Why won't the following function compile?

```
int ultimate_answer(int i = 42, int j, double d = 13)
{
  return i - d;
}
```

6

Putting Functions to Work

In the previous chapter we covered the basics of C++ functions. In this chapter we'll continue our discussion and cover other important types of functions including:

- Inline functions
- Member functions
- Static and constant member functions
- Iterator functions
- Virtual functions

Because of the complexity of the other function types introduced in the previous chapter, such as constructors, destructors, and operator functions, we'll cover them in more detail in the following two chapters.

In this chapter we'll start by working with inline and member functions. Both of these functions are used to define class methods—the operations that are applied to the class data members. You'll learn how inline and member functions are defined inside and outside the body of a class. Next, we'll examine two special types of member functions: static and constant member functions. We'll also explain how iterator functions can be used to access sequences of objects. We'll then move on to discuss virtual functions.

Here are some of the key topics we'll be exploring:

- How inline functions relate to C macros
- When to use inline functions
- How member functions are stored

- How to use iterator functions to process linked lists
- How to declare and use virtual functions
- How to apply *polymorphism*

Inline Functions

Whenever you need to use a constant or a simple expression in a program multiple times, you can define a macro to represent the constant or expression. Although macros are helpful, they have serious limitations. C++ provides *inline functions* to extend the power of macros. Inline functions work especially well as class members. They can help you write efficient code, and they support the modular, object-oriented programming style.

Note: An inline function does not have to be a member function. Any short function is a good candidate for an inline function.

Inline functions can be declared two ways: Use the **inline** keyword in the function declaration or include the entire function definition inside a class declaration. The second method makes the inline function a member function. Let's start with an example that illustrates how the first method is used. The following simple program contains an inline function called **plus_one**:

```
#include <stdio.h>
inline int plus_one(int n) { return n+1; }
void main()
{
    int i = 15, j;

    j = plus_one(i);
    printf("The value of j is %d", j);
}
```

When compiled, the statement **j = plus_one(i);** is expanded to

```
j = i+1;  // this code is inserted inline
```

A function call does not actually take place. Instead, the code in the function is inserted at the location of the call, and the appropriate variables are renamed. As you can see, inline functions operate like macros. However, there is an important difference. Unlike macros, an inline function has the same scoping and argument-passing semantics as standard functions.

To see the difference between inline functions and macros, consider the following program:

```
#include <stdio.h>
#define MAC(i) ++i;
inline int func(int i) { return ++i; }
int j[1] = { 17 };
void main()
{
    int k;

    k = func(*j);    // k gets 18, *j still 17
    printf("k = %d, *j = %d\n", k, *j);
    k = MAC(*j); // k gets 18, *j gets 18 !!
    printf("k = %d, *j = %d\n", k, *j);
}
```

On the surface, it seems that both **MAC()** and **func()** do the same thing—return the value of **(*j) + 1**. However, **MAC()** causes a side effect: It changes the value of ***j**, which was probably not intended! When expanded, **MAC()** becomes:

```
k = ++*j;
```

In comparison, **func()** makes a copy of ***j** before it increments the variable, leaving the original ***j** intact. How is it implemented inline? One way is to use a temporary variable to hold a copy of the passed argument. Here is an example of how the call **k = func(*j);** might be written in C:

```
int tmp;
tmp = *j;
k   = ++tmp;
```

There are two other important differences between macros and inline functions. One is that type checking is performed with inline functions, just as it is for any function having a prototype. Another is that you can have a pointer to an inline function. This means that you can pass an inline function as an argument to other functions.

How can we use a pointer to reference inline code? After all, isn't the code inserted as text? It depends. If the compiler determines that you're setting a pointer to the address of an inline function, the code for that function is stored as an actual function. The pointer will then point to this code. When the pointer is de-referenced, an actual function call takes place. This process is illustrated in Figure 6.1. To see how this process works, let's use a pointer to access the function **func()** we introduced in our previous example.

```c
#include <stdio.h>
inline int func(int i) { return ++i; }
void main()
{
    int (*my_pointer)(int i); // declare function pointer
    int z, j = 41;

    my_pointer = func;       // point to func()
    z = (*my_pointer)(j);    // make indirect call to func()
    z = func(j);             // inline code used here
    printf("z = %d\n", z);
}
```

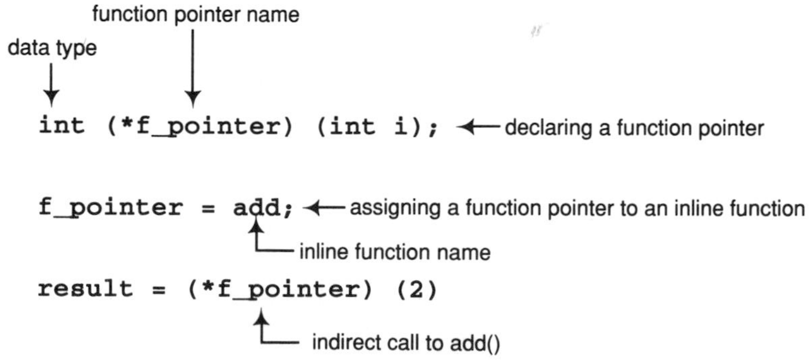

Figure 6.1. Using a pointer to access an inline function.

When **my_pointer** is de-referenced, a call to the stored form of **func()** is made, as shown in Figure 6.2. However, when **func()** is called directly, as in the statement **z = func(*j);**, the compiler can generate inline code. Thus, you get the best of both worlds.

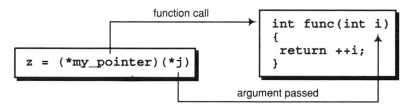

Figure 6.2. Accessing the function func().

Inline Member Functions

We've now seen how inline functions can be declared as standard functions, but don't forget that they also can be defined as member functions. To make an inline function a class member, we can define both its prototype and body in the class declaration.

For example, in class **clock** shown next, **set()** serves as an inline member function because it's defined inside the class:

```
class clock {
public:
    int hr, min, sec;
    void set(int h, int m, int s)
    {
      hr = h; min = m; sec = s;
    }
};
```

Alternatively, you can use the **inline** keyword and define the function outside the class:

```
class clock {
public:
    int hr, min, sec;
    inline void set(int h, int m, int s);
};
```

```
inline void clock::set(int h, int m, int s)
{
    hr = h; min = m;
    sec = s;
}
```

Normally, you won't have to declare inline member functions this way. They are usually small (at least they should be), and it's easier to package them with the class declaration.

Note: A function that has more than a few statements should probably not be declared inline. Otherwise, the overhead of copying the text each time the function is called will be too great.

When to Use Inline Functions

Inline functions provide a useful extension to the C language. In situations where a macro might be used in C, you can probably use an inline function in C++ and receive the benefits of proper scoping in the process. In fact, you should try to avoid using macros if you can define an inline function instead to do the job.

Probably the most important use of inline functions is with classes. A well-designed class that takes advantage of the black-box design approach usually has public functions whose only purposes are to access selected private class members. Often these functions are short. In fact, they sometimes just have a single statement to return the value of a private member.

To support a modular design in C, a set of functions could be used to hide the processing of the variables and data structures on which you were operating. This might include reading the values of variables that should otherwise be hidden or performing simple arithmetic operations. Since C does not support inline functions, you would introduce the overhead of a function call every time you performed these simple computations. In critical sections of code, this cost can be high, forcing you to dispense with the modular design altogether.

In C++, you don't have to give up the benefits of a modular design. The short access functions can be made inline, giving you not only a flexible interface to the class, but an efficient one as well.

Let's look at an example. Suppose we needed to create a class to implement a stack of integers. We might start with the following class definition:

```
class stack {
    int data[20];        // max size of stack is 20
    int *top;            // top of stack
public:
    stack(void)     { top = data; }
    void push(int x) { *top++ = x; }
    int  pop(void)   { return *--top; }
};
```

We can then define a stack object and perform stack operations, as shown:

```
stack s; // declares and initializes stack
int k;   // variable to keep track of stack position

s.push(25);        // put a number on the stack
k = s.pop();       // remove a number from the stack
```

To simplify matters, we've left out all error handling code. Two functions are provided in the class to push and pop integers from the stack. A constructor function is also provided to initialize the top of the stack. Note that we've implemented these functions inline. The stack is accessed with high-level functions; however, no function calls actually take place. Instead, short code statements for the **push()** and **pop()**expressions are inserted into the code.

```
*(s.top++) = 25;
k = *(--s.top);
```

This code would be much more efficient than making a function call if **push()** and **pop()** were frequently called in a time-critical loop.

Unlike other functions, an inline function is the only function type that may appear in a header file. In C, recall that you should never place a function definition in a header file. This causes the function to be compiled every time the header file is accessed, and, therefore, duplicate code will be generated. The same is true in C++, with the exception of inline functions.

Inline functions are not a problem because their text is copied in each call. Also, inline function definitions must be included in header files because inline functions typically appear in class declarations, which in turn are often placed in header files.

> **Note:** Unlike other functions, the bodies of inline functions must be visible to any source module that uses them. This usually means including them as header files in a well-designed program.

One final but important note. A function declared as inline will not always be implemented as one. The compiler may process it as a standard function. The **inline** keyword only informs the compiler that you would like the function to be inline. In this respect, the **inline** keyword operates like the **register** keyword, which is used to tell the compiler that variables are being used in time-critical code and that they should be stored in registers, if possible.

Member Functions

Next, we'll concentrate on functions that serve as class members. Member functions are an important component of C++ programs, especially for programs written in the object-oriented style. After all, they provide the means for implementing class *methods.* When considering the object-oriented viewpoint, we can say that a member function defines the *behavior* of an object. The member function is also used as the device to pass *messages* to an object.

C++ supports different types of member functions. They can be classified into these six groups:

- Access functions
- Constant functions
- Static functions
- Iterator functions
- Virtual functions
- Constructor and destructor functions

When we explored the basics of classes in Chapter 3, we introduced each of these types of functions, except for iterator, constant, and static functions. In this section we'll cover the features that are common to all the member functions, and then we'll discuss constant and static member functions. We'll also explore virtual functions and iterators. Constructors and destructors are covered in Chapter 8.

Declaring Member Functions

A function can be defined as a class member by enclosing its function header within the body of the class declaration. Here's an example:

```
class piggy_bank{
    int savings;
public:
    void piggy_bank(void);
    void deposit(int amt);
    int withdraw(int amt);
};
```

In this case, **piggy_bank()**, **deposit()**, and **withdraw()** are member functions. The actual code for member functions is usually provided outside the class declaration. The basic syntax for this is shown here:

```
<return type> <class> :: <function> (<parms>)
{
    // the function body goes here
}
```

Figure 6.3 shows a sample member function with its components labeled. Applying this format, let's write the code for each of the functions in our **piggy_bank** class.

```
void piggy_bank::piggy_bank(void)
{
    savings = 0;  // constructor to initialize bank
}

void piggy_bank::deposit(int amt)
{
    savings += amt;
```

```
}

int piggy_bank::withdraw(int amt)
{
    if (savings < amt) {
        amt = savings;
        printf("Insufficient funds\n");
    }
    savings -= amt;
    return amt;
}
```

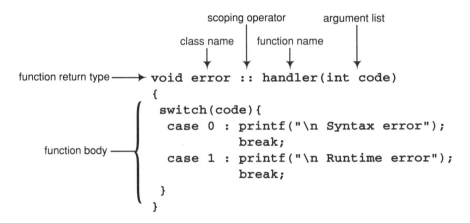

Figure 6.3. A sample member function.

Notice that we have combined the class name, **piggy_bank**, with each function name. Why? The class name informs the compiler that the function is a class member. As discussed in Chapter 4, the **::** operator is used as a scoping mechanism. In this case, it places each function within the scope of the class to which the function belongs. The scoping allows each member function to enjoy special access privileges to class members; they can use any other class member without having to specify the class name. For example, the member function **withdraw**() can directly access the private class member **savings**.

Note: Class member functions and friend functions are the only functions that can access the private members of a class.

Member functions can also easily be declared *inline*. This is done either by using either the **inline** keyword or by including the entire function inside the actual class declaration. As an example, here's a new version of the **piggy_bank** class we presented earlier that defines **piggy_bank()** and **deposit()** as inlinc functions:

```
class piggy_bank {
    int savings;
public:
    void piggy_bank(void) { savings = 0; }  // inline
                                            // function

    void deposit(int amt)
    {
      savings += amt;                 // also inline
    }
    int withdraw(int amt);            // not inline
                                      // no function body
};
```

Where Are Member Functions Stored?

We've now presented most of the key features of member functions; however, we haven't explained how member functions are stored in memory. Because a member function is called through an object, the slight overhead of a structure de-reference is required when a member function is actually called. But what about storage? Do member functions take up room in an object?

The answer is that, except for virtual functions, they do not take up any room *inside* the object. Figure 6.4 shows how a C++ class containing a member function is translated into a C structure. Notice that only one copy of the function **sum()** is stored, regardless of the number of objects created from the class definition. This means that you can define arrays of objects without having to worry about incurring additional storage overhead for any functions the objects use, regardless of how many and how complicated those functions are.

Keep in mind that virtual functions take up memory, but the memory taken up is minimal, as we'll discuss later in this chapter.

```
           C                          C++

typedef struct {              class num {
  int a;                      public:
} num;                          int a;
                                int sum(int i);
int num_sum(num *n,int i)     };
{                             int num::sum(int i)
  return n->a+i;              {
}                               return a+i;
                              }
void main()
{                             void main()
  num n;                      {
  int s;                        num n;
  n.a = 17;                     int s;
  s = num_sum(&n,3);            n.a = 17;
}                               s = n.sum(3);
                              }
```

Figure 6.4. Translation of a C++ class.

Constant Member Functions

Let's now move on and explore a special type of function called *constant member functions*. These functions are used to support constant objects. To understand how to use constant member functions, we'll need to review constants.

In C++, you can declare a variable to have a constant value, as shown:

```
const int nelems = 10;
int j = nelems; // Legal--just accessing the constant
nelems = 25;    // Illegal
```

The third statement is invalid; we are trying to assign a new value to **nelems**, which was declared as a constant and assigned a value of 10.

An object can also be declared as being constant. In this case, the definition of a constant must be generalized. Basically, *a constant object is an object whose data members cannot be changed once they are initialized.* (To initialize the data members, a constructor is used.) This definition introduces some interesting consequences for an object's member functions. Let's take a look at a simple **point** class to see what's involved in making a constant **point** object. Try typing in and running the following program:

```
#include <stdio.h>
class point {
    int x, y;
public:
    point(int a, int b) { x = a; y = b; }
    int x_pos(void) { return x; }
    int y_pos(void) { return y; }
    void move(int dx, int dy) {
      x += dx; y += dy;
    }
};

void main()
{
    const point p(40, 12); // a constant point object
    printf("Coordinates: (%d, %d)\n", p.x_pos(), p.y_pos());
    p.move(1, 1);
}
```

We've declared **p** to be a constant **point** object. However, the compiler will complain that we are calling the **point** functions **x_pos()**, **y_pos()**, and **move()**. Why? The compiler can't tell if the functions might be modifying the members **x** and **y** of object **p**, which would be illegal since **p** is a constant. Since **x_pos()** and **y_pos()** don't actually change any members, we should be able to use them. Unfortunately, the compiler won't let us.

How can we get around this problem? We can declare **x_pos()** and **y_pos()** to be *constant member functions.* A member function is declared constant by attaching the keyword **const** after the function arguments, but before the function body, as shown:

```
class point {
    . . .
```

```
     int x_pos(void) const { return x };
     int y_pos(void) const { return y };
     ...
};
```

By placing the **const** keyword before a function body, we are stating "this function is guaranteed not to modify any data members of the class." The compiler will then allow us to call the function, even if the function is for an object declared as a constant. The only member functions that can be called from a constant object are constant member functions. Thus, **p.x_pos()** and **p.y_pos()** can be called, but **p.move()** cannot.

Note that we can't declare **move()** to be a constant member function. For a constant member function, the hidden **this** argument is treated as a pointer to a constant object, and thus any attempted updates to the object's data are flagged as errors. The following proposed change to **move()** will not compile:

```
class point {
    ...
    void move(int dx, int dx) const
    {
      x += dx; y += dy; // error, illegal updating
    }
    ...
};
```

You must be careful when calling other functions inside a constant member function. These other functions cannot be allowed to modify any of the data members. This is ensured by the following compiler trick: *When inside a constant member function, each data member is typed as though it were a constant.* Thus, the only legal ways to pass the members to another function are either by value or by using pointers to constants or references to constants. To see this in action, take the following code fragment. Here, we have introduced a new member function **random_walk()**, which calls the function **random()** to assign the coordinates random values.

```
void random(int &v)
{
    // set v to some random value
}
```

```
class point {
  ...
  void random_walk(void) const {
    random(x);
    random(y);   }
  ...
};
```

We've incorrectly declared **random_walk()** to be a constant function. The code won't compile because the calls to **random()** require integer references, when, in fact, **x** and **y** are typed as constants. We can change **random()** to be acceptable to the compiler by changing its argument type, as shown:

```
void random(const int &v)
{
    // can't really change v here
}
```

This prevents **random()** from changing the value of the coordinate.

The same rule about calling other functions inside constant functions applies to calling other member functions. A constant member function can only call other constant member functions. It can't call standard member functions, since they might update the object's data.

You could find a way to get around the restrictions for constant member functions by using clever programming techniques. For instance, you could use type casts and pointers to trick the compiler into letting you change the constants. There is no guarantee that a constant member function won't change the data members. C++ doesn't stop you from violating the rules, it only prevents accidental misuse.

Note: You can use constructors and destructors with constant objects, and unlike with other member functions, you don't have to declare them as constants.

Static Member Functions

Earlier in this book, we introduced static data members. Recall that they are members in which only one copy exists for every object declared from a particular class. C++ also provides *static member functions* to correspond with static data members.

When a static member function is associated with a class, you don't need to use an object to access the function. One example is creating a static member function to operate on the static data of a class. Since static data members don't belong to any particular object, they are perfect candidates to be manipulated by a static member function.

Let's borrow an example from Chapter 3 which used static data members to process points (coordinates). We'll now add a static member function to set the origin.

```
class point {
public:
    static int xo, yo; // origin global to all points
    int x, y;          // coordinates relative to origin
    // a static member function to set the origin
    static void set_origin(int a, int b);
    // some normal member functions
    int abs_x(void) { return x + xo; }
    int abs_y(void) { return y + yo; }
};

int point::xo; // don't forget to allocate static data
int point::yo;

void point::set_origin(int a, int b)
// define static member function to set origin
{
    xo = a; yo = b;
}
```

We've defined the static member function **set_origin**() by using the **static** keyword in the class declaration. Note that we don't use the keyword when we define the function outside the class. Recall that the **static** keyword is also used to make the scope of a variable or function local to the module in which it was declared. Here, we want to make the function "global" to all objects of the **point** class. It's unfortunate that the meaning of **static** is overloaded like this.

Notice that we must allocate the static member data outside of the class. Unfortunately, our static member function can't do this for us.

Just as there are two ways to access static data members (with or without an object), there are two ways to call a static member function. For example:

```
point p;

point::set_origin(1,1); // call via class name qualifier
p.set_origin(1,1);      // call via object
```

Since static member functions can be called without using an object, this means that they have no hidden **this** pointer. After all, what object would **this** point to. Therefore, a static member function cannot access directly the normal data members of an object. It can, however, access any static data members, since they don't require an object. Our **set_origin()** function did just that when setting the static members **xo** and **yo**.

In order for a static data member function to access normal data members, it must be given an object (or objects) to work with. One way to do this is to pass an object as a parameter. Here is a modification of **set_origin()** that sets the origin to the location of the point object passed in

```
void point::set_origin(point p)
// set origin to location of point p
{
    xo = p.x;  yo = p.y;
}
```

Our static member function accesses both static member data, **xo** and **yo**, as well as the members **x** and **y**. All of these data members are accessed with the point object **p**.

There is little advantage in passing an object to a static member function if both the object and member function belong to the same class. It would be better to use a standard member function and dispense with the explicit passing of the object argument. For example, we could modify **set_origin()** to be non-static and take no arguments:

```
class point {
    ...
    void set_origin(void); // No longer static
    ...
};
```

```
void point::set_origin(void)
{
    xo = x; yo = y;
}
```

Here, our **set_origin**() function is interpreted as "set the origin to the location of this object."

Iterator Functions and Objects

Our next stop on our tour of C++ functions is *iterator functions*. An iterator function is used to step through (iterate) a sequence of objects such as an array, a linked list, and so on. Recall that with object-oriented programming, our goal is to hide the actual implementation details of the objects that we use. For example, if we are processing a list of objects, we want to perform commands such as initializing the list, adding objects to the list, or searching for objects without having to know how the list is implemented. The advantage of this approach is that we can change the implementation details of the list without having to change the code that accesses the list.

Iterator functions are not really a part of the C++ language—at least not in the way that virtual functions, inline functions, and operator functions are. They are a coding technique used by C++ programmers for iterating through a sequence of objects. A typical use of iterator functions is with linked lists. To illustrate how an iterator function works, let's write a program that allows us to add elements to a linked list. We'll also use an iterator function to access the elements that we have added. Here is the complete program:

```
#include <stdio.h>
// singly linked integer list node
class int_node {
    int_node *next;        // let's hide this pointer
    friend class int_list; // so that only int_list can use
public:
    int data;              // let data be public, though
};

// singly linked list
class int_list {
    int_node *head;        // keep track of start of list
```

```
      int_node *cursor;   // keep track of iteration position
public:
    int_list(void) { head = 0; }  // constructor
    ~int_list(void);              // and destructor
    void add(int i);              // to add integers to list
    void reset_iter(void) {
      cursor = head;              // reset the iteration
  }
    int_node *iter(void);         // the iterator function
};

int_list::~int_list(void)
// destructor for list, deletes all nodes in the list
{
    int_node *p = head, *q;

    while(p != 0) {
      q = p;
      p = p->next;
      delete q;
    }
    head = 0;
}

void int_list::add(int i)
// add an integer to end of list
{
    int_node *p = head, *q = head, *r;

    while(p != 0) { q = p; p = p->next; }
    r = new int_node;
    r->data = i; r->next = 0;
    if (head) q->next = r; else head = r;
}

int_node *int_list::iter(void)
// iterator function
{
    int_node *p = cursor;
```

```
            if (cursor) cursor = cursor->next;
            return p;
    }

    void main()
    {
        int_list my_list;
        int_node *p;

        my_list.add(5); my_list.add(6); my_list.add(7);
        my_list.reset_iter();   // must do this first!!
        while((p = my_list.iter()) != 0) printf("%d ", p->data);
    }
```

Notice that this program uses two classes: a node class (**int_node**) to hold integers and next pointers, and a list class (**int_list**) to represent a sequence of list nodes. Each list node holds an integer data item.

The program starts by inserting three numbers in the list: 5, 6, and 7. For this task, the member function **add**() is used. After the elements have been added, we print the elements using a simple **while** loop, which calls the iterator function **iter**() to access each list element. The first thing you've probably discovered is that we didn't need to use statements such as

```
    p = list->next;
```

in the main program to step through the list.

The iterator function, **iter**(), is assigned to the **int_list** class definition. We've also included a second function called **reset_iter**() to reset the iterator so that we can start at the top of the list when we need to access the list elements. The **cursor** pointer is required to keep track of our current position in the list as we perform the iteration. Figure 6.5 shows how the list is implemented. Each time the **iter**() function is called, the **cursor** pointer advances to the next element in the list.

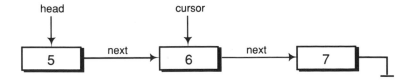

Figure 6.5. Implementation of the linked list.

Although our list implementation is simple and provides us with a high-level way to access list elements, it has several drawbacks. First, we can only support one iterator at a time for a given list object. That is, we can't use two iterators to scan a list starting at different positions. Why? We only have one state variable for the itcrator: **cursor**. If we wanted to add additional iterators, we would have to define more state variables.

A second drawback is that we must remember to call **reset_iter()** before using **iter()**, so that the **cursor** pointer is initialized properly. (In our example, we initialize it to point to the head of the list.) Even in simple programs this is easy to forget.

We can correct these problems by modifying our approach. The new approach involves recognizing that our iterator should be an object. It has a state variable, doesn't it? In fact, it is common to implement iterators not as functions but as complete objects. The idea is to define an iterator for a given linked list or array class (or however you've implemented the list) in such a way that it can be attached to the list or array. This ensures that each iterator has its own cursor; thus, more than one iterator can be used at the same time. Also, since we've made the iterators objects, they can be initialized automatically by skillful use of constructors.

Let's modify our list example so that it uses iterator objects. Here is the new program:

```
// example of iterator objects
#include <stdio.h>
// Singly linked integer list node
class int_node {
    int_node *next;
    friend class int_list; // int_list needs to access this
    friend class int_list_iterator; // so does iterator
public:
    int data;
};

// singly linked integer list
class int_list {
    int_node *head; // keep track of start of list
    friend class int_list_iterator; // needs to access head
public:
    int_list(void) { head = 0; }
    ~int_list(void);
```

```
      void add(int i);
};
int_list::~int_list(void)
// destructor for singly linked integer list
{
    int_node *p = head, *q;

    while (p != 0) {
      q = p;
      p = p->next;
      delete q;
    }
    head = 0;
}


void int_list::add(int i)
// add integers to the list
{
    int_node *p = head, *q = head, *r;

    while(p != 0) { q = p; p = p->next; }
    r = new int_node;
    r->data = i; r->next = 0;
    if(head) q->next = r; else head = r;
}
// iterator class
class int_list_iterator {
    int_list *l;  // keep track of what list you belong to
    int_node *cursor;  // and the current node
public:
    void reset(void) { cursor = l->head; }
    int_list_iterator(int_list *li) {
      l = li; reset(); // point to list, initialize cursor
    }
    int_node *next(void);
};


int_node *int_list_iterator::next(void)
// iterator function
{
```

```
      int_node *p = cursor;
      if (cursor) cursor = cursor->next;
      return p;
}


void main()
{
   int_list my_list;
   int_node *p;

   my_list.add(5);
   my_list.add(6);
   my_list.add(7);

   // declare and initialize iterator to point to our list
   int_list_iterator x(&my_list);
   while ((p = x.next()) != 0) {
     printf("%d ", p->data);
   }

}
```

In this example, we've defined the class **int_list_iterator**, which is used to create iterator objects for our linked list. This class contains a constructor for initializing an iterator object to point to a specified list and to reset the cursor. Note that we don't have to initialize the list pointer (**cursor**). The initialization occurs automatically when we declare the iterator object!

Now that we've made our iterators objects, we can declare more than one for a given list. For instance, we can implement a cross product for a list of integers using two iterators, as shown:

```
#include <stdio.h>
// include class definitions for lists and iterators ...
int cross_product(int_list *l)
// compute cross product of list
{
   int_list_iterator x(l), y(l); // make two iterators
   int_node *p, *q;
   int cp = 0;
   while ((p = x.next()) != 0) {
```

```
      y.reset(); // must restart the inner one each time
      while ((q = y.next()) != 0) {
        cp += p->data * q->data;
      }
    }
    return cp;
}

void main()
{
    int_list my_list;
    int_node *p;

    my_list.add(5);
    my_list.add(6);
    my_list.add(7);
      printf("%d\n", cross_product(&my_list));
}
```

When executed, this program produces the following result:

```
324
```

Iterator objects provide another important advantage: They can be combined with operator functions. These are functions that can be attached to the standard C++ operators so that the operators can be used in new ways. A good example is the ++ operator, which is usually thought of as an increment, or "next" operation. We can use this operator to serve as our iterator function **iter()** discussed earlier. The following example shows how:

```
// modified iterator class using the ++ operator
class int_list_iterator {
    int_list *l;  // keep track of what list you belong to
    int_node *cursor;  // and the current node
public:
    void reset(void) { cursor = l->head; }
    int_list_iterator(int_list *li) {
      l = li; reset(); // point to list, initialize cursor
    }
    int_node *operator++(int);
```

```
};
int_node *int_list_iterator::operator++(int)
// iterator function
{
    int_node *p = cursor;
    if (cursor) cursor = cursor->next;
    return p;
}
```

Don't worry if you don't understand the syntax for operator functions yet; you'll learn more about operator functions in the next chapter. For now, just think of the operator function as you would any other function, except that it has a unique name that happens to be an operator—in this case, the operator **++**.

Here is an example of our cross-product function, using our new iterator operator:

```
// compute cross product of a list using the ++ operator
int cross_product(int_list *l)
{
    int_list_iterator x(l), y(l); // make two iterators
    int_node *p, *q;
    int cp = 0;

    while ((p = x++) != 0) { // note ++ operator !!
      y.reset(); // must restart the inner one each time
      while ((q = y++) != 0) { // note ++ operator !!
        cp += p->data * q->data;
      }
    }
    return cp;
}
```

While it's usually advantageous to use objects for iterators, there are some disadvantages. One is that you must declare a different iterator class for each class on which you wish to iterate. This is mostly a problem when using class hierarchies where classes are derived from other classes. Often (but not always) you must develop special iterator classes for each of these derived classes.

Virtual Functions and Polymorphism

One of the most important features of object-oriented programming is the ability to have objects respond to similar commands differently. This feature is called *polymorphism*, and objects that have it are called *polymorphic objects*. In C++, polymorphism is achieved by one of two methods: with *function overloading* or *virtual functions*. In this chapter we'll be working with virtual functions. Overloaded functions are covered in depth in the next chapter. However, we'll introduce overloaded functions so that you can see how they are used to support polymorphism.

To see how polymorphism is implemented, let's write a simple program that contains objects that respond to the same commands in different ways. Suppose we have two different types of robot objects: obedient and disobedient robots. Both robots are programmed to add two numbers.

```
#include <stdio.h>
class obedient_robot {
public:
    void add(int a, int b) {
      printf("Yes master, the answer is: %d\n", a+b);
    }
};

class disobedient_robot {
public:
    void add(int a, int b) {
      printf("I don't feel like adding, maybe tomorrow\n");
    }
};

void main()
{
    obedient_robot number_five;
    disobedient_robot hal;

    number_five.add(40, 2); // command number five to add
    hal.add(2,2);           // command hal to add
}
```

Our two robots respond differently to the same command:

```
Yes master, the answer is: 42
I don't feel like adding, maybe tomorrow
```

In this case, the polymorphism is created using *function overloading*. If you create two or more functions with the same name but with different parameters, the functions are said to be *overloaded.* For example, in the following code fragment, **concatenate()** is overloaded because it comes in two versions with different arguments:

```
string concatenate(string a, string b);
list concatenate(list a, list b);
```

Our two robot **add()** functions are also overloaded, although it doesn't look like they are, because they appear to have the same arguments—**int a** and **int b**. However, recall that they are member functions with a hidden first argument, so their function headers really look like

```
int add(obedient_robot *this, int a, int b);
int add(disobedient_robot *this, int a, int b);
```

Because they have different argument types (in the first arguments), they are overloaded.

In our robot program, the compiler determines which **add()** function to call at compile-time because it knows which robot is involved. That is, the function is bound to the robot object at compile-time. This is known as *early* or *static binding*. Another type of function binding, called *dynamic* or *late binding,* is the direct opposite of static binding. In this case, the compiler can't tell at compile-time which object is being used when a function is called. Here's an example:

```
obedient_robot *robot_ptr = new obedient_robot;
robot_ptr->add(35, 7);
```

The compiler doesn't know which object is being referenced when pointers to objects are involved. The function and its object aren't bound together until the program runs. For example, the function **add()** is bound to the robot pointed to by **robot_ptr** at run-time.

This form of late binding is powerful. C++ provides an even more powerful form of late binding that is achieved by using inheritance and virtual functions. But before we can show you how this technique works, we need to explain the basics of virtual functions. We'll then revisit overloaded functions to show you how they relate to their virtual function cousins. In particular, we'll introduce some of the common mistakes that can occur if you unintentionally use overloaded functions in place of virtual functions. These mistakes are related to this more powerful form of late binding.

Declaring Virtual Functions

Virtual functions go hand-in-hand with inheritance, which is the system of deriving a new class from a base class. The derived class inherits the base classes' data and function members. By making a base member function virtual, we can have the derived class override the function and provide its own version.

The word *virtual* does not best describe the true nature of virtual functions. A better word might be adaptable. A virtual function can be overridden in a derived class and thus adapted to fit new situations. This adaptability is what makes inheritance such a powerful tool. To use inheritance, you'll need to learn how to declare virtual functions.

A class member function can be made virtual by declaring it with the **virtual** keyword in the base class. A derived class can then override and define its own version. Figure 6.6 shows how a virtual function is declared. Let's write a program that uses a simple virtual function.

```
#include <stdio.h>
class obedient_robot {
public:
    virtual void add(int a, int b) {
      printf("Yes master, the answer is: %d\n", a+b); }
};

class disobedient_robot : public obedient_robot {
public:
    void add(int a, int b) {
      printf("I don't feel like adding, maybe tomorrow\n");
    }
};
```

```
void main()
{
    obedient_robot number_five;
    disobedient_robot hal;

    number_five.add(35, 7); // command number five to add
    hal.add(2,2);           // command hal to add
}
```

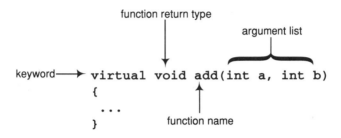

Figure 6.6. Declaration of a virtual function.

Note: The **virtual** keyword need only be used in the base class. That is, the virtual function in the derived class that overrides the base class version does not require the **virtual** keyword.

This program produces results that are the same as the results of the previous program.

```
Yes master, the answer is: 42
I don't feel like adding, maybe tomorrow
```

At first glance, you might not notice any difference between this program and the one we gave earlier. However, look closely and you'll see that, instead of creating two separate robot classes, we derived one from the other, as shown in Figure 6.7. We made the function **add()** virtual.

By making **add()** virtual, any derived class of **obedient_robot** can override this function, as we've done with the derived class **disobedient_robot**. Because it didn't change the output of the program (the same messages were displayed as before), you might wonder why we bothered with the **virtual** keyword. Why didn't we just overload the function? The reason has to do with the more powerful form of late binding, as we'll show you next.

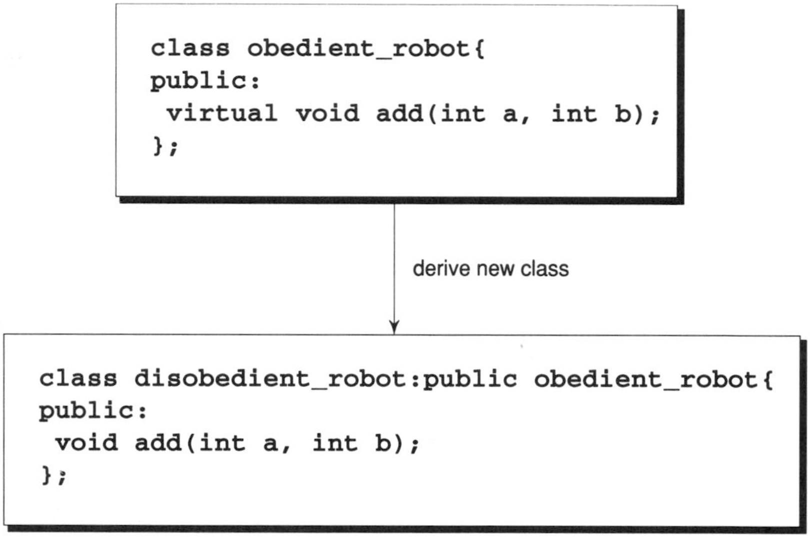

```
class obedient_robot{
public:
 virtual void add(int a, int b);
};
```

derive new class

```
class disobedient_robot:public obedient_robot{
public:
 void add(int a, int b);
};
```

Figure 6.7. Deriving a robot class.

Late Binding with Virtual Functions

Let's start by modifying our robot example to work with robot pointers. We'll be using a trick that's available with derived classes: We can point to a derived class object with a base class pointer without using explicit type casting. This next program shows how:

```
#include <stdio.h>
class obedient_robot {
public:
    virtual void add(int a, int b) {
        printf("Yes master, the answer is: %d\n", a+b);
    }
};

class disobedient_robot : public obedient_robot {
public:
```

```
      void add(int a, int b) {
        printf("I don't feel like adding, maybe tomorrow\n");
      }
};
void main()
{
    // note how we're using pointers of same type
    // but pointing to different type robots
    obedient_robot *number_five = new obedient_robot;
    obedient_robot *hal = new disobedient_robot;
    number_five->add(40, 2); // command number five to add
    hal->add(2,2);           // command hal to add
}
```

Late binding occurs because we're now using pointers. However, it's a little different from before. To link up each robot with its own **add()** function, the compiler must know the type of robot that is being pointed to because each type has its own version of **add()**. But how can the compiler know this when we're using similar pointers for the robots? (Note that both robots were pointed to with pointers of type **obedient_robot ***.) The compiler can determine this because we made **add()** virtual. This causes the compiler to store an extra pointer inside the object that points to a function lookup table for that object. Thus, not only must the compiler de-reference a pointer to get to the actual robot, it must de-reference another pointer stored with the robot to actually call the function. This is shown in Figure 6.8.

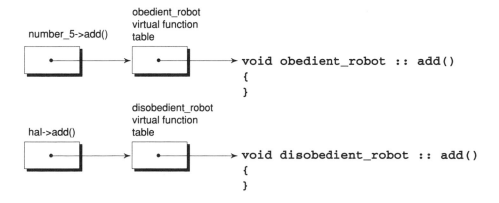

Figure 6.8. Late binding with virtual functions.

Note: Each object having a virtual function keeps track of its own version of that function by pointing to a function lookup table.

You're probably wondering why we went to all this trouble. Why didn't we simply use pointers of different robot types, as in:

```
obedient_robot *number_five = new obedient_robot;
disobedient_robot *hal = new disobedient_robot;

number_five->add(40,2);
hal->add(40,2);
```

Wouldn't this solve all the problems? Wouldn't the robots respond with the right messages? In this case, yes. But it can get trickier. Suppose you have an array of robots and want the array to store both **obedient_robots** and **disobedient_robots**, as shown in Figure 6.9. We'll run into a problem, because arrays can only store objects of the same type. That is, we could have an array of **obedient_robots** or an array of **disobedient_robots**, but not an array of both objects. The solution is to use an array of **obedient_robot** pointers instead, and have these pointers point to either type of robot, as in:

```
robot *clan[2];

clan[0] = new obedient_robot;
clan[1] = new disobedient_robot;
```

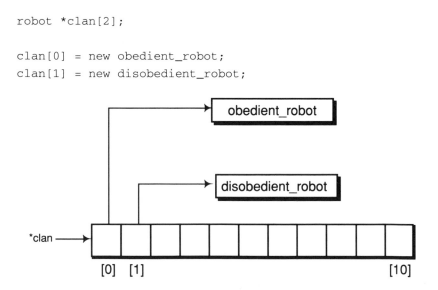

Figure 6.9. An array of robots.

This declares an array of two **robot** pointers. Each array element is then assigned a pointer to a different **robot** type. If we use robots with virtual **add()** functions, we can be assured that a robot will give the appropriate response when commanded to add. In contrast, if the **add()** functions are just overloaded, we can get erroneous results. To see this, type in and run the following program:

```
#include <stdio.h>
class obedient_robot {
public:
    // note no virtual keyword !!
    int add(int a, int b) {
      printf("Yes master, the answer is: %d\n", a+b);
    }
};
class disobedient_robot : public obedient_robot {
public:
    int add(int a, int b) { // overloaded, not virtual
      printf("I don't feel like adding, maybe tomorrow\n");
    }
};

void main()
{
    obedient_robot *clan[2];

    clan[0] = new obedient_robot;
    clan[1] = new disobedient_robot;
    clan[0]->add(40,2); // which add function is called?
    clan[1]->add(40,2); // which add function is called?
}
```

The output to the program might surprise you:

```
Yes master, the answer is: 42
Yes master, the answer is: 42
```

What happened to our disobedient robot? Did it decide to behave? The compiler, seeing a pointer to an **obedient_robot**, used the **add()** function from this class. The compiler did this because **add()** was not virtual; the compiler did not have a pointer to access the proper **add**() function. Because we're using an **obedient_robot** pointer, the compiler just assumed that **obedient_robot::add**() is the function to use.

Note: If you call a nonvirtual function with a pointer to an object, the type of object the pointer points to determines which function to call, not the object itself!

A more powerful type of late binding is used when virtual functions are involved. This late binding is achieved with an extra indirection when calling member functions. This indirection is essential in any situation where you are pointing to objects having virtual functions.

Common Mistakes Using Virtual Functions

As we've seen, both overloaded and virtual functions provide forms of polymorphism. However, these forms are slightly different. This difference becomes crucial when pointers to derived class objects are involved. Because of the differences, it's easy to make mistakes when using virtual functions.

You must remember the following rules to declare a virtual function properly:

1. The **virtual** keyword must be used in the base class.
2. Both base class and the derived class functions must have the same parameters and types; that is, their function prototypes must be equivalent.

If you define a function with the same name in both the base class and the derived class, but you haven't followed these rules, you've only overloaded the function. You have not made it virtual, even if you used the **virtual** keyword. The following program (involving a different species of robots from the ones you've seen before) provides an example of this common mistake:

```
#include <stdio.h>
class robot {
public:
    virtual void greeting(void) {
        printf("At your command, master!\n");
```

```
    }
};

class robot_from_2001 : public robot {
public:
    void greeting(int unused_arg) { // note parameter!
      printf("Daisy, Daisy, . . .\n");
    }
};

void main()
{
    robot *robbie = new robot;
    robot *hal    = new robot_from_2001;
    robbie->greeting();
    hal->greeting();
}
```

Instead of **hal** responding "Daisy, Daisy, ...", it outputs the same text that **robbie** outputs:

```
At your command, master!
At your command, master!
```

What went wrong? The problem is that **greeting()** is declared with a **void** argument in the **robot** version and an **int** argument in the **robot_from_2001** version. Although we declared the function virtual, we didn't override it properly—it is just overloaded. Figure 6.10 shows what happened. The compiler noticed that the derived class did not change the virtual function and, thus, set **hal's** function pointer to the same function that **robbie** had.

Note: If objects of derived classes do not work properly, you probably forgot to use the **virtual** keyword when you were supposed to or you mixed up the function argument types in the derived class.

Note from Figure 6.10 that **hal** has two **greeting()** functions. One is called with a pointer and points to the base class version of **greeting()**. The second is called whenever an object of class **robot_from_2001** is used directly. For example, suppose we used the robots just shown (with the virtual function declared improperly):

```
robot *hal = new robot_from_2001; // from improper class
hal->greeting();     // base class version used!
robot_from_2001 hal_no_2;  // no pointers here!!
hal_no_2.greeting();        // derived class version used
```

The output produced by these statements is

```
At your command, master!
Daisy, Daisy, ...
```

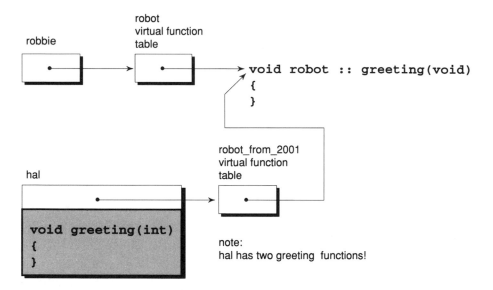

Figure 6.10. Calling the wrong function.

In the first case, the base class function **robot::greeting()** was used because we didn't declare the virtual function correctly in the derived class—we simply overloaded it. In the second case, the derived class function **robot_from_2001::greeting()** is used.

What this example implies is that you don't have to override a virtual function, because the base class version is always available. As an example, here we've created a new derived class called **robot_clone** that does not contain a definition for the **greeting()** function:

```
class robot_clone : public robot {
public:
    // doesn't do anything different from robot
};
```

If we then create an object and use it as shown:

```
robot_clone X117J5;
X117J5.greeting();
```

the message displayed would be

```
At your command, master!
```

Even if you declare a virtual function properly, the original base class version is still accessible to the derived class. You can get to the original by using the :: scoping operator. The following program shows how:

```
#include <stdio.h>
class robot {
public:
    virtual void greeting(void) {
      printf("At your command, master!\n");
    }
};

class robot_from_2001 : public robot {
public:
    void greeting(void) { // note declared properly!
      printf("Daisy, Daisy, ...\n");
    }
};

void main()
{
    robot_from_2001 hal;

    hal.greeting();        // use robot_from_2001 version
    hal.robot::greeting(); // use base robot version
}
```

The messages displayed now are

```
Daisy, Daisy, ...
At your command, master!
```

Although using the original function definition in this manner may seem strange, there are many situations where it is actually useful. We'll explore this topic in more depth later in this chapter.

Doing Menus, Object-Oriented Style

Now that you know how to use virtual functions properly, you'll want to see how you can put them to use in a practical setting. We'll do this by developing an object-oriented menu system.

When we first introduced classes in Chapter 3, we wrote a program that illustrated how menus could be represented with classes. The example was written in the procedural programming style used by most C programmers. Recall that the program used a **switch** statement to process each menu item. To refresh your memory, here's a rough outline of the **switch** statement:

```
switch(selected_item) {
    case 1:
      // process menu item #1
    break;
    case 2:
     // process menu item #2
    break;
   case 3:
      // ...
}
```

Remember that in Chapter 2 we presented a simple event handler that processed dialog buttons. We introduced a similar **switch** statement, and then we showed how we could eliminate the **switch** statement by using objects. The object-oriented method was better because our objects could be extended. (We were able to add new types of buttons without having to alter the **switch** statement.)

Using virtual functions and polymorphism, we can do the same for a menu system. Let's implement one that is modeled after the simple button example. To get started, we'll need to consider the components that make up the menus. As shown in Figure 6.11, a menu typically has a label or name, a set of menu items, and an action that is associated with each menu item. Notice that a menu item really has two parts: data (a label) and an operation (an action that is implemented as a function). That sounds suspiciously like an object, doesn't it? Indeed, we can take advantage of the power of object-oriented programming and define both the menu and each menu item as objects.

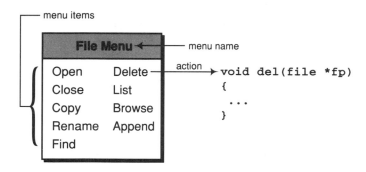

Figure 6.11. A menu with its components labeled.

To get even fancier, we can define the menu and its associated items as the same kind of object! After all, why can't a menu item be a menu? Certainly, you've seen menu systems that display different submenus when an item is selected from a main menu. Can we make a general purpose menu object to cover all of these cases? We can if we use inheritance and virtual functions.

First, we'll need a name for the menu item object. We'll call it a button, because the item performs an action when selected. An action might consist of opening a file, changing a color, or popping up a submenu. To set up the menu buttons properly, we'll first define a general purpose type of button from which the more specialized menu buttons can be derived. Here is the code for the general **button** class:

```
class button { // general button class
public:
    char label[20];
    virtual void display_label(void) { printf("%s", label);
}
```

```
   virtual void activate(void) {
      printf("No operation defined for this button");
   }
};
```

We've defined a general class that contains a label and two functions—
display_label() and **activate**(). The first function is used to display a label,
and the other function activates the button. Note that the **button** class as
defined wouldn't generate very interesting buttons; in fact, it does little.
While this may seem strange, it's actually an example of an important
technique used in object-oriented programming—that of using *abstract
classes*. (Our button class isn't precisely an abstract class. See Chapter 9 for
the exact definition of an abstract class.)

Note: An abstract class is a general class that sets the stage for a hierarchy of
classes. It isn't really meant to be used by itself. Instead, other classes are to
be derived from it, and these classes are the ones that are actually used.

In our **button** class we made **activate**() virtual. Why? So that we can
then make our buttons adaptable, deriving new types of buttons with
different actions. By doing this, we can get rid of the infamous **switch**
statement, as you'll soon see.

Now that we have a **button** class, let's move ahead and define a special
type of button—a menu. We do this by deriving a **menu** class from the
button class, as shown:

```
class menu : public button {
    button **entries;   // dynamic array of button pointers
    int num_items;      // how many in the array
public:
    int curr_item;         // the currently selected item
    menu(char *name, int nitems, ...); // constructor
    ~menu(void) { delete[num_items] entries; } destructor
    void display_entries(void); // new function
    void activate(void);        // overridden function
};
```

In this new class, we've added several new members not present in the
button class. We've added an array of button pointers, a counter

(**num_items**) to keep track of the number of button pointers in the array, a function to display the menu, and constructor and destructor functions to initialize and clean up the menus. The most noteworthy of these additions are the button pointer array and the **activate()** function.

The button pointer array is used to store the list of menu items. Notice that we're using an array of **button** pointers instead of just buttons. Remember this same trick from previous sections? We do this so we can have an array that encompasses different types of buttons. For instance, some buttons might be objects to clear the screen, open a window, or format your hard disk. Other objects might be menus. By using pointers of type **button** in our array, we can store these different types of buttons and then rely on virtual functions to ensure that the appropriate operations are used. For example, we might have something like:

```
button **entries;
button panic;
menu lunch_specials;

entries = new button *[2];
entries[0] = &panic;
entries[1] = &lunch_specials;
entries[0]->display();
entries[1]->display();
```

In this case, the different button types actually come from the same class hierarchy. Note that we didn't have to do any type casting to access different types of buttons. In particular, we didn't have to type cast **lunch_specials**, even though it is of type **menu**. We can get away with this because **menu** is derived from class **button**.

Now, imagine such an array representing a menu. Once the appropriate menu item is selected, we can call its **activate()** function like that shown here:

```
entries[selected_item]->activate();
```

This one statement takes the place of the **switch** statement we used in our original menu example. Because this statement does not include any reference to the types of menu entries we have, it can be left as is, even when we add new types of menu entries. All we have to do is define these new types by deriving them from the **button** class. And this can be done long after the previous statement has been compiled.

Now that we've toured the features of our menus, we're ready to show all the code. The menu displayed contains two types of menu entries; the first displays a message and the second displays a menu.

```
// object-oriented menu example
#include <stdio.h>
#include <string.h>
#include <stdarg.h>

// a general button class -- doesn't do anything useful
class button {
public:
    char label[20];
    virtual void display_label(void) { printf("%s", label);
    }
    virtual void activate(void) {
      printf("No operation defined for this button");
    }
};

// a special type of button -- a menu
class menu : public button {
    button **entries;  // array of button pointers
    int num_items;     // how many in the array
public:
    int curr_item;     // currently selected item
    menu(char *name, int nitems, ...);  // constructor
    ~menu(void) { delete entries; }     // destructor
    void display_entries(void);
    void activate(void);
};

menu::menu(char *name, int nitems, ...)
// constructor to initialize menu system. The variable
// arguments should be pointers to buttons
{
    va_list arg_ptr;
    int i;
```

```
    strcpy(label, name);
    // initialize button pointer array
    entries = new button *[num_items = nitems];
    va_start(arg_ptr, nitems);
    for (i = 0; i<num_items; i++) {
      entries[i] = va_arg(arg_ptr, button *);
    }
    va_end(arg_ptr);
    curr_item = 0;
}


void menu::display_entries(void)
{
    int i;

    printf("%s\n\n", label);
    for (i = 0; i < num_items; i++) {
      printf("(%d) ", i+1);
      entries[i]->display_label();
      printf("\n");
    }
}
void menu::activate(void)
{
    display_entries();
    printf("\n\nPlease select a menu item: ");
    scanf("%d", &curr_item);
    printf("\n");
    if (curr_item > 0 && curr_item <= num_items) {
        // note polymorphism here!!
        entries[curr_item-1]->activate();
    }
    else {
      printf("Invalid selection, try again");
      activate();
    }
}


// a simple type of button that doesn't do much
// except report on what it might do
```

```
class sample_button : public button {
    char report[80];
public:
    sample_button(char *name, char *rep);
    void activate(void) { printf("%s\n", report); }
};

sample_button::sample_button(char *name, char *rep)
// constructor to initialize sample button
{
    strcpy(label, name);
    strcpy(report, rep);
}

void main()
{
    // define sub menu
    sample_button source(
        "Source File", "Source File Selected");
    sample_button document(
        "Document File", "Document File Selected");
    sample_button other(
        "Other", "Other file type selected");
    menu submenu(
        "File Types", 3, &source, &document, &other);

    // define main menu
    sample_button close_button(
        "Close File", "Ready to close file");
    sample_button save_button(
        "Save File", "Ready to save file");
    sample_button del_button(
        "Delete File", "Ready to delete file");
    menu topmenu(
        "File Options", 4, &submenu, &close_button,
        &save_button, &del_button);
    topmenu.activate(); // start the menus
}
```

Here's a sample run of the program:

```
File Options

(1) File Types
(2) Close File
(3) Save File
(4) Delete File

Please select a menu item: 1

File Types

(1) Source File
(2) Document File
(3) Other

Please select a menu item: 2

Document File selected
```

Chaining Virtual Functions

Next we'll explore a useful object-oriented technique called *function chaining*, which is often used with virtual functions. This technique involves chaining function calls together, such as having a function from a derived class call a related base class function. This chaining process is shown in Figure 6.12.

A virtual function that has been overridden in a derived class can call the original base class definition. How is this done? Use the scoping operator, as we showed you earlier in this chapter. You can actually chain the function calls together. In this case, the original function is used to perform the initial processing work. Then, the overriding function can be used to finish off the job.

Note: Just as an overloaded base class function does not disappear, neither does an overloaded virtual function.

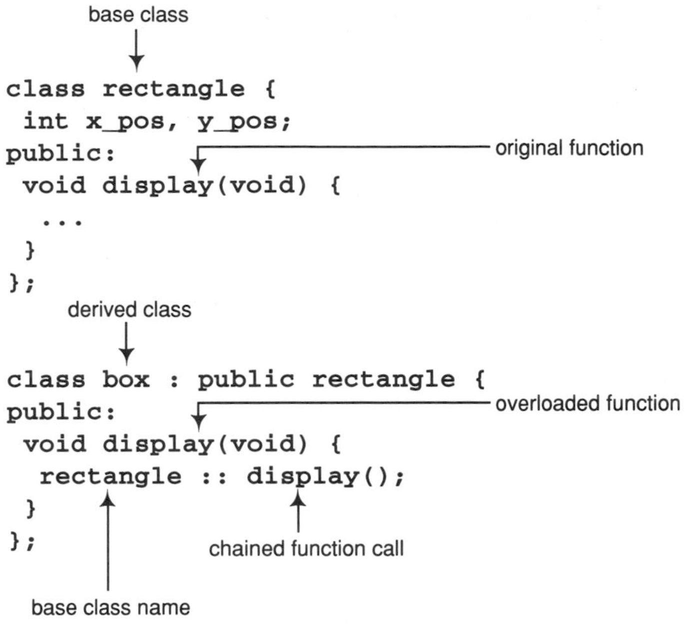

```
                         base class
                            │
                            ▼
        class rectangle {
          int x_pos, y_pos;
        public:                              ──── original function
          void display(void) {
            ...
          }
        };
                  derived class
                       │
                       ▼
        class box : public rectangle {
        public:                              ──── overloaded function
          void display(void) {
            rectangle :: display();
          }
        };
                                    chained function call

             base class name
```

Figure 6.12. Chaining virtual functions.

The best way to see how functions are chained is to write a program. In the next example, we'll simulate a dishonest cash register. Take note of the function **takein()** in the derived class and how it chains back to the original version in the base class.

```
// dishonest cash register simulation
#include <stdio.h>
// class for honest and fair cash registers
class cash_register {
    double amt;
public:
    cash_register() { amt = 0; }  // constructor
    virtual double balance(void) { return amt; }
    virtual double takein(double a) { return amt += a; }
    virtual double payout(double a);
};
double cash_register::payout(double p)
{
    if (p > amt) {
```

```
        printf("Insufficient funds!\n");
        p = amt;
    }
    amt -= p;
    return p;
}


// a derived class for dishonest cash registers
class dishonest_cash_register : public cash_register {
    double embezzled_funds;  // aren't we crooked!!
public:
    dishonest_cash_register(void) { embezzled_funds = 0; }
    double takein(double a); // override takein function
    double steal(double a);  // add function to steal with
};


double dishonest_cash_register::takein(double a)
{
    // take a percentage off the top
    embezzled_funds += 0.10*a;
    // put rest in the cash register
    cash_register::takein(0.90*a); // chaining functions!
    return a;
}


double dishonest_cash_register::steal(double p)
{
    if (p > embezzled_funds) {
        printf("Not so greedy!\n");
        p = embezzled_funds;
    }
    embezzled_funds -= p;
    return p;
}


void main()
{
    dishonest_cash_register john;
    printf("Dishonest John at work ...\n\n");
    printf("Initial balance   $%6.2f\n", john.balance());
```

```
    printf("Taking in          $%6.2f\n",
            john.takein(100.0));
    printf("Paying out         $%6.2f\n",
            john.payout(25.0));
    printf("New \"Balance is\"  $%6.2f\n",
            john.balance());
    printf("Stealing           $%6.2f\n",
            john.steal(10.0));
}
```

Here are the results produced by the program:

```
Dishonest John at work ...
Initial balance   $    0.0
Taking in         $  100.0
Paying out        $   25.0
New "Balance is"  $   65.0
Stealing          $   10.0
```

The first thing you'll notice is that you probably wouldn't want to have Dishonest John working for your company. But aside from that, let's examine how this program works.

There are two classes : **cash_register** and **dishonest_cash_register**. The first class keeps track of the amount of money in the cash register. Notice that access functions are provided, such as **balance()** and **takein()**, so that the private member **amt**, which stores the money, can be accessed. The **dishonest_case_register** class is derived from the **cash_register** class, as you can see from its basic definition:

```
class dishonest_cash_register : public cash_register {
    ...
}
```

So far, we haven't done anything tricky. The dishonest cash register class adds two extra members, **embezzled_funds** and **steal()**, which are used to store and retrieve monies embezzled whenever money is added to the register. Of course, because the **embezzled_funds** member is private, no other object (including the IRS) can examine what **John** is up to. To embezzle the money, we have modified **takein()** from its base class definition. It uses the statement

```
embezzled_funds += 0.10*a;
```

to take a percentage off the top.

Now the fun begins. Look carefully at the overridden definition for **takein()** in the **dishonest_cash_register** class. We had to call the base class's version of **takein()** in order to change **amt**. As mentioned earlier, private members of a base class are not directly accessible by a derived class. They are available only through access functions, like **takein()**, for instance. To call **takein()**, we had to qualify the name as shown so that we could access the version from the **cash_register** class.

```
cash_register::takein(0.90*a);
```

If we hadn't done so, an infinite loop would have occurred, because the version in the **dishonest_cash_register** class would be called recursively. As Figure 6.13 illustrates, the statement

```
john.takein(100.0);
```

first calls the function assigned to the **dishonest_cash_register**, and this function then calls the **takein()** function in the **cash_register** class.

```
                         dishonest_cash_register john

john.takein(100.0);      ┌──────────────────────────────────────────────┐
                         │  embezzled funds                             │
                         │           . . .                              │
                         ├──────────────────────────────────────────────┤
              calls      │  dishonest_cash_register :: takein()         │
        ─────────────────▶│  {                                          │
                         │    . . .                                     │
                         │    cash_register :: takein()                 │
                         │    . . .                                     │
                         │  }                                           │
                         └──────────────────────────────────────────────┘
```

Figure 6.13. Order of function calls.

This method of chaining functions is common in many applications. As an example, suppose that we have a series of keyboard handlers that process keys from the keyboard. Figure 6.14 shows such an arrangement. The first handler does the low-level processing of keys. It handles the status of the shift keys, changing the input character to uppercase, and so on. The later processes can then build on this information, adding their own modifications or blocking anyone else from receiving a key.

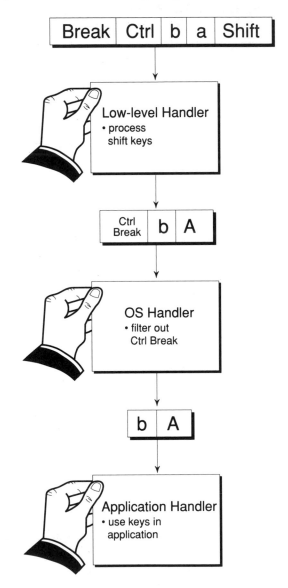

Figure 6.14. Chaining keyboard handlers.

When to Use Virtual Functions

In the cash register program we declared **balance**() and **payout**() as virtual functions; however, they were not changed in the derived class. Why did we need to make them virtual? We did this so that we could later override the functions. For instance, if Dishonest John really got greedy, we could make sure that he got all of the cash by overriding the **balance**() function:

```
double dishonest_cash_register::balance(void)
{
    embezzled_funds += amt;   amt = 0;
    return amt;
}
```

Because a virtual function must be declared virtual in the base class, you must decide initially what operations you're going to allow to be overridden. Once you've compiled the base class and placed it in an object code library, no further modifications are possible to any nonvirtual functions—without recompiling, that is.

There is a trade-off to be made, however. Virtual functions add a slight run-time overhead both in execution time and memory, as you'll soon see. You must use your programming experience and judgment to determine which functions should be virtual. Of course, it helps to know what happens when a virtual function is called. How does the program know where to find it? Is it found at run-time or at compile-time? Does the program step through the chain of derived classes, perhaps all the way back to the base class, looking for a function to call? We'll answer these questions next.

How Virtual Functions Are Implemented

To understand how to use virtual functions, it's instructive to see how they are implemented. Our discussion here is based on the system used by most current C++ compilers. Keep in mind that your compiler might use a different technique.

Virtual functions are usually implemented with a table of function pointers. Each class that has one or more virtual functions has such a table. This table holds pointers to the actual functions used for each virtual function, and it has as many elements as there are virtual functions (see

Figure 6.15). The pointers are computed at compile-time by examining which functions were overridden and which were not. The overridden functions point to the derived class functions; those not overridden point to the base class functions.

To show you how this works, we've constructed a pointer table for the **cash_register** and **dishonest_cash_register** classes used in our previous example. In this case, because the **takein()** function has been overridden in the **dishonest_cash_register** class, the table for **dishonest_cash_register** points to the derived version of this function. On the other hand, the **balance()** and **payout()** functions were not overridden; therefore, the table points to the base class definitions of these functions, as shown in Figure 6.16.

Keep in mind that only one table is required for each defined class, regardless of how many objects are instantiated from the class. Instead of storing copies of the table, each object has its own pointer to the table for its class. Each time a virtual function is called, the pointer is de-referenced to this table. Then, the appropriate function is called by yet another de-reference. Because of this double de-referencing, calling a virtual function is slightly slower than calling a regular function.

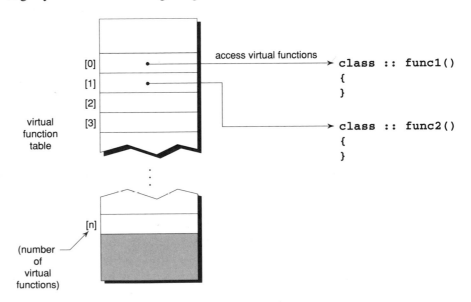

Figure 6.15. Virtual function table.

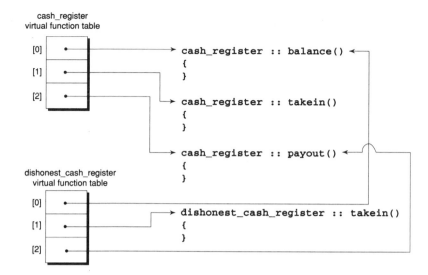

Figure 6.16. Pointer table for the cash_register class.

Because a pointer must be added to an object if it has virtual functions, virtual functions also add a slight memory overhead—the storage for a single function pointer. But this isn't too bad, since this cost doesn't increase regardless of how many virtual functions an object has. The number of virtual functions does cause the virtual function table to be larger, but there is only one table per class, not per object.

Figure 6.17 shows a translation of virtual functions from C++ into C.

Summary

We've now completed our exploration of both the basic and advanced features of C++ functions. You have seen that C++ functions are much more powerful than C functions, because they provide object-oriented programming features. Because C++ functions can be interconnected with classes, they can provide access to class members.

In the next three chapters, we'll be covering many of the function-related topics that we introduced in this chapter and the previous chapter. Our goal is to show you how to use the more advanced features, including constructors, destructors, overloaded functions, and inheritance, so that you can build more powerful C++ programs.

C	C++
| ```c
typedef struct {
  int d;
  int (**vp)();
} calc;

int (*calc_vtbl[1])() =
{
  (int(*)())calc_mult
};
void calc_store(calc *this,int i)
{
  this->d = i;
}
void calc_mult(calc *this,int i)
{
  return this->d*i;
}

void main()
{
  calc c;
  c.vp = calc_vtbl;

  calc_store(&c,25);
  (*((int(*)())(c.vp[0])))(&c,17);
}
``` | ```cpp
class calc {
public:
  int d;
  void store(int i);
  virtual int mult(int i);
};




void calc::store(int i)
{
  d = i;
}
void calc::mult(int i)
{
  return d*i;
}

void main()
{
  calc c;

  c.store(25);
  c.mult(17);
}
``` |

Figure 6.17. Translation box for virtual functions.

Exercises

1. Find a case where the following macro, which is suppose to square its argument, won't work properly:

```c
#define SQ(x)    x*x
```

Rewrite this macro as an inline function. Why would the inline function be better?

2. Change the iterator we used in the linked list program so that instead of always returning the next node in the list, it returns the node containing the data that matches an input argument. That is, the iterator should serve as a search iterator. For example, the statement

```
p = x.next(5);
```

searches the list until element 5 is found. The pointer **p** is then assigned to the node that contains element 5.

3. Find the subtle mistake in the virtual function **sound**(). How would you correct the error?

```
class clock {
public:
    virtual sound(int iii);
};

class radio : public clock {
public:
    void sound(int iii);
};
```

4. What does the following program output? How would you fix it so that the label's display function is executed? Explain the difference in terms of static and dynamic binding.

```
#include <stdio.h>
class form {
public:
    virtual void display(void) { printf("First name: "); }
};

class label : public form {
public:
    void display(void) { printf("Well, what is your name?");
}
```

```
};

void doit(form f)
// note pass by value
{
    f.display();
}

void main()
{
    label l;
    doit(l);
}
```

Function and Operator Overloading

C++ provides a rich set of features for writing high-level programs. In previous chapters we've seen how we can use components, such as classes, constructor and destructor functions, inline functions, and virtual functions, to build programs that are modular and embrace the spirit of object-oriented programming. The more you work with C++, the more you'll rely on these powerful features.

Now that we know how to construct user-defined data types using classes and functions, we'll need a way to process them in expressions. Fortunately, C++ provides the tools so that we can define our functions and operators that use the same name or symbol as a built-in function or operator. These functions and operators are called *overloaded functions* and *overloaded operators*. They're useful because they can be used to redefine existing functions and operators.

In this chapter we'll explore the basic techniques of overloading functions and operators. We'll start by introducing the basics of overloading, and then we'll show you how to use overloading in your programs. Although most of the chapter concentrates on operator overloading, we'll be covering topics related to function overloading as well.

Some of the highlights of the chapter include:

- How to declare overloaded functions
- How to resolve ambiguities in overloaded function names
- How to define and call operator functions

- How to overload difficult operators such as the assignment, subscript, and function call operators
- How to use conversion functions and type casting operators

A Quick Look at Overloading

We'll be exploring three interconnected topics: overloaded functions, overloaded operators, and type casting operators. Let's start by examining how these topics are related, and then we'll present each one in more detail as we work through this chapter.

Function overloading occurs when two or more functions are given the same name. The function name is *overloaded* because it can be interpreted in more than one way. As an example, we can have two **add()** functions, one to add integers and one to add strings.

```
int add(int a, int b);              // for integers
string add(string a, string b);     // for strings
```

As this example illustrates, overloaded functions are useful in cases where several functions perform similar operations. You might say that our **add()** function is like a switch-hitter because it can handle integers or strings. If we call **add()** with the arguments

```
result = add(21, 45);
```

the C++ compiler knows which version of the function to use—the integer one. Although the two **add()** functions work with different data types, they perform similar operations: They add two objects together. As you can see, this abstraction allows you to increase the flexibility of the functions you write.

Note: Overloaded functions have the same name. However, they must have a different number of arguments or different types of arguments, or both.

Function overloading is especially useful with special types of functions called *operator functions*. These are functions that can be attached to the built-in operators to extend their meanings. For instance, we can extend the + operator to perform string concatenation for a **string** class by writing

```
string operator+(string a, string b);
```

Then, instead of calling the concatenation function, we can use the more concise + operator, as shown:

```
string a, b, c;
a = b + c;
```

Because the + operator has a built-in definition, that of adding numbers together, our redefinition shows an example of how the + operator can be overloaded or assigned a new meaning. This process of redefining an operator is called *operator overloading.*

In addition to operators such as + and =, C++ also provides *type casting operators*. You can specify type casts with the syntax **Type(X)**, as well as with the older C style **(Type)X**. The type specifiers are called type casting operators, or casting operators for short. The syntax **Type(X)** makes casting operations look like function calls, and, in fact, like all function calls, you can overload them. The overloading is accomplished by using special forms of operator functions.

For example, suppose you defined a class that stored numbers in Binary Coded Decimal (BCD) and you wanted to provide a conversion from BCD numbers to ordinary integers. This could be accomplished as shown:

```
class bcd {
    // class members go here
    operator int() {
      // compute and return proper value
    }
};
```

You could then write statements such as

```
bcd my_bcdnum;
int i;
i = int(my_bcdnum);
```

By declaring the function **operator int()**, we have, in effect, overloaded the casting operation for integers to include conversions from BCD numbers.

Declaring Overloaded Functions

Functions can be overloaded by defining two or more functions with the same name. These functions can be standard functions, class member functions, and operator functions.

Here is an example of how the **add**() function is declared as an overloaded function:

```
int   add(int a, int b);        // for integers
char *add(char *a, char *b);    // for strings
```

You can also overload member functions. The following example shows how the **set**() function is overloaded:

```
class point {
    int x, y;
public:
    // set point location with specified parms
    void set(int xp, int yp) {
      x = xp; y = yp;
    }
    // or, copy another point's location
    void set(point &p) {
      x = p.x; y = p.y;
    }
};
```

To call one of these functions, we must first declare an object and then use the object to access the function, as shown:

```
point p, q;
p.set(42, 17);
q.set(p);
```

Overloaded member functions are often used with constructor functions. Next to overloaded operator functions, this is probably the most common application of function overloading. Because we'll be discussing constructor functions in detail in Chapter 8, we'll defer most of the examples of overloading constructor functions until then.

Now that we've seen how a simple overloaded functions is declared, let's put together a working program that uses the overloaded function **add()**. With this one overloaded function, the following program can handle both integer and string data types:

```
#include <stdio.h>
#include <string.h>

int add(int a, int b)       { return a + b; }
char *add(char *a, char *b) { return strcat(a, b); }

char msg_a[80] = "The answer to life, the universe, ";
char msg_b[]   = "and everything.";

void main()
{
    printf("%d: %s", add(35, 7), add(msg_a, msg_b));
}
```

When you run the program, you'll see the output:

```
42: The answer to life, the universe, and everything.
```

Of course, you can easily expand this program by declaring other **add()** functions that use different arguments. For example, you may want to include a function that can add two matrices together. The rest we'll leave to your imagination.

Note: Overloading functions helps relieve the burden of inventing many different names for similar operations. You can instead give similar operations the same name.

Resolving Ambiguities in Overloaded Functions

When an overloaded function is called, the compiler must determine which function to use. It does this by looking at the number and type of arguments being passed. The compiler can easily determine which function to use if the candidate functions use different number of arguments. The compiler's job isn't quite as easy if the functions use the same number of arguments or if they use default arguments.

Note: The compiler does not look at the function return types when determining which overloaded function to call. Consequently, it's illegal for overloaded functions to differ only in their return type.

Here is the basic algorithm used to determine which overloaded function should be used:

1. Select the functions that have both the correct function name and the correct number of arguments. Note that possible default arguments must be taken into account.

2. From the functions chosen in (1), narrow down the choices to the functions that have argument types that are compatible to the arguments used in the call. To be compatible, the argument types must match, or there must exist conversions to make the argument types match.

3. From the functions chosen in (2), select that function that provides the "best match." What factors are used to determine the best match? Argument types that match exactly are considered better than those that require conversions. When the overloaded functions have more than one argument, the best matching function is the one which, looking at every argument, has at least as good a match as any of the other candidates, and which has at least one argument that matches better than any of the others. If this does not occur, the overloaded function call is said to be *ambiguous* because there is no best matching function. Ambiguous calls are illegal and will be flagged as errors.

Figure 7.1 shows some examples of matching arguments to overloaded functions.

Here is an example of an ambiguity where the compiler can't determine which overloaded function to call:

```
void myfunc(double d);
void myfunc(char *p);
...
myfunc(0); // ambiguous: should we call myfunc((double)0)
           // or myfunc((char *)0)?
```

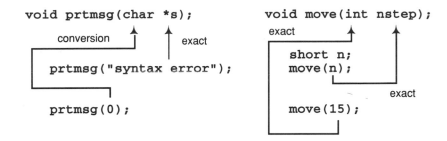

Figure 7.1. Examples of overloaded functions.

Note that ambiguous overloaded functions can be used in a program; however, you *can't* call them in an ambiguous way. For instance, given the previous overloaded functions, the following two calls would be legal:

```
myfunc(3.1416);     // Okay, no ambiguity
myfunc("A string"); // Okay, no ambiguity
```

Matching Arguments

The heart of the argument-matching algorithm involves determining what constitutes a best match for an argument. There are five ways that a match can take place. Figure 7.2 shows these methods, ordered in terms of performance from one to five. Let's take a closer look at each method.

> 1. Exact Matches and Trivial Conversions
>
> 2. Promotions
>
> 3. Standard Conversions
>
> 4. User-Defined Conversions
>
> 5. Match with Ellipses

Figure 7.2 Argument type matching precedence.

Exact Matches

An exact match occurs when the argument types are identical, or when a trivial conversion exists between the types. For example, a literal 0 is considered an exact match for **int**, and a literal character is considered an exact match for **char**. The following program shows some exact matches:

```
#include <stdio.h>
void hex_dump(char c) { printf("%02X ", c); }
void hex_dump(int i)  { printf("%04X ", i); }
void hex_dump(long l) { printf("%08lX ", l); }

void main()
{
    char c = 16;
    int i = 0x1234;
    long l = 0x56789ABCL;

    hex_dump('A'); // uses char version
    hex_dump(c);   // uses char version
    hex_dump(0);   // uses int version
    hex_dump(i);   // uses int version
    hex_dump(l);   // uses long version
}
```

When you run the program, you should get the output:

```
10 41 0000 1234 56789ABC
```

Trivial Conversions

Trivial conversions are considered almost as good as, and sometimes equal to, exact matches. Here are a function prototype and function call that show an example of a trivial conversion:

```
void f(int *x); // takes a pointer to an int
..
int v[25];
f(v);           // passing an int array
```

We are passing an **int** array to a function requiring an **int** pointer. Since an array name is a pointer, the argument can be converted easily.

There are numerous trivial conversions. The following conversions are considered to be equivalent to exact matches:

From	To
`T[]`	`T*`
`T`	`T&`
`T&`	`T`
`T`	`const T`
`T`	`volatile T`
`F(args)`	`(*F)args`

The last example represents a conversion from a function name taking a particular set of argument types to a pointer to a function taking the same set of argument types. For example:

```
void myfunc(int (*f)(char c, double d));
int somefunc(char c, double d);
...
myfunc(somefunc); // okay
```

The next best conversions to the trivial ones just discussed are

From	To
`T*`	`const T*`
`T*`	`volatile T*`
`T&`	`const T&`
`T&`	`volatile T&`

Note that it is not possible to distinguish between a function taking an argument of type **T** and one taking a reference argument of type **T&**. Thus, overloaded functions such as the following are ambiguous:

```
void f(int i);
void f(int &i); // ambiguous
```

In a similar vein, functions taking an argument of type **T** versus **const T** or **volatile T** are also ambiguous, such as:

```
void f(int i);
void f(const int i);      // ambiguous
void f(volatile int i);   // ambiguous
```

However, it's okay to declare overloaded functions differentiated by an argument of type **T&** to type **const T&** and **volatile T&**, such as in the following:

```
void f(int &i);
void f(const int &i);     // okay now
void f(volatile int &i);  // okay now
```

The same idea holds true between pointers and pointers to constants or volatiles:

```
void f(int *i);
void f(const int *i);     // okay
void f(volatile int *i);  // okay
```

Promotions

Promotions follow exact matches and trivial conversions in order of precedence. Promotions include such conversions as **char** to **int, short** to **int, int** to **long**, and **float** to **double**. Promotions also include converting enumerated types to **int** or **unsigned int** (depending on the number of enumerations used). Note that the exact promotions allowed or used are implementation-dependent.

Standard Conversions

Next in order of precedence are standard conversions. These conversions consist of arithmetic and pointer conversions. Arithmetic conversions include conversions from **int** to **float, float** to **int, int** to **double, double** to **int**, and **signed** to an **unsigned** type, or vice versa. Pointer conversions include converting a pointer of any type to a **void** pointer (but not the other way around without a cast), and converting derived class pointers to base class pointers. The same holds true for references. Note that it's possible to convert 0 to a null pointer, but that it's more preferable to match 0 with an integer.

Here is a short program showing some standard conversions in use:

```
#include <stdio.h>
void prt(float f) { printf("%f ", f); }
void prt(void *p) { printf("%p ", p); }

void main()
{
    int i = 42;
    char buf[20];

    prt(i);    // uses conversion i -> float
    prt(&i);   // uses conversion int * -> void *
    prt(buf);  // uses conversion char * -> void *
}
```

User-Defined Conversions

C++ allows you to define your own type conversions, and these conversions come next in argument matching precedence. Although user-defined conversions will be discussed in detail later in this chapter, let's look at a simple example now. In the following **gadget** class, the constructor shows an example of converting from **char *** to **gadget,** and, thus, the constructor is in fact a conversion function:

```
class gadget {
public:
    int data;
    gadget(char *);
};
```

This conversion function could then be utilized when attempting to match overloaded function arguments, as in:

```
void compute(int v);
void compute(gadget g);
compute("A gadget"); // convert char * -> gadget
```

In an attempt to match the call to **compute()** to one of the overloaded functions, the compiler converts the character string **"A gadget"** into a **gadget**, so that the second **compute()** function can be used.

One thing to note about using conversions during argument matching is that the compiler will only do one level of user-defined conversions. Therefore, the compiler will have trouble with the following program:

```
class gadget {
public:
    int data;
    gadget(void);
    gadget(char *s);
};

class widget {
public:
    int data;
    widget(void);
    widget(gadget);
};

class tinkertoy {
public:
    int data;
    tinkertoy(void);
};

void manufacture(widget w);
void manufacture(tinkertoy t);

widget w;
gadget g;
tinkertoy t;

void main()
{
    manufacture(w); // okay, exact match
    manufacture(g); // okay, calls manufacture(widget(g));
    manufacture(t); // okay, exact match
```

```
    manufacture("F14 Fighter Jet"); // can't do
}
```

The first and third calls to **manufacture()** are valid because the argument types match exactly. The second call is valid because there is a conversion from **gadget** to **widget**, which allows the first overloaded function to be called. The last call is illegal, because there is no direct match possible, and it would take two conversions, from **char *** to **gadget** to **widget**, to find a match. Figure 7.3 illustrates this conversion procedure.

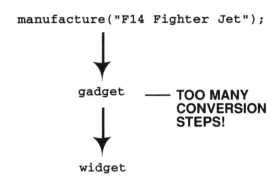

Figure 7.3. Converting a gadget to a widget.

Using Ellipses

The lowest form of argument matching is when ellipses are used to denote "any number of arguments of unspecified types." Matching to ellipses is only used as a last resort. For instance, in the following code, the function specifying ellipses as the second argument is used only when there is no other alternative:

```
void doit(int a, int b);
void doit(int a, ...);
...
doit(2, 3); // calls first overloaded function
doit(2, "three"); // calls second overloaded function
```

Keep It Simple

Although you might not think it, we have simplified the rules used for argument matching. The exact rules are quite complex and would require much discussion about C++ topics that haven't been introduced. However, we have shown you the basic rules, the algorithm matches the arguments in an intuitive fashion, preferring exact matches over those requiring complex conversion sequences.

When the overloaded functions have many arguments, the compiler can't easily determine which function should be called, if any. Thus, try to keep your overloaded functions as simple as possible.

Note: To help the compiler, use explicit type casts to uniquely identify the data type of the arguments passed to overloaded functions.

Operator Functions

Now that we've discussed overloaded functions, we're ready to move on and explore a related topic—operator functions. Overloaded functions are commonly used as operator functions. At this point, you may be wondering how to define operator functions. They are simply functions that can be used to extend the built-in set of operators that C++ provides. An operator function is attached to a predefined operator so that when the operator is used in an expression, the corresponding operator function is called. You can have more than one operator function for any given operator. That is, you can even *overload the operators*!

Let's start by examining the basic syntax used to declare an operator function.

```
<return type> operator<op>(<arg1, arg2, ...>)
{
    <function body>
}
```

Operator functions have the same syntax as any function except that the name of the function is **operator<op>**. The following example declares a function to overload the + operator, allowing you to add two **clock** objects and return the result:

```
class clock { // ...  }
clock operator+(clock a, clock b)
{
    // code to add a and b together goes here
}
```

In this case, the function name is **operator+**. This function can be called in two ways, either by using the + operator with its usual precedence or by calling the operator function explicitly. For example, the following assignment statements are equivalent.

```
clock a, b, c;
a = b + c;          // function called implicitly
a = operator+(b,c); // function called explicitly
```

Note that you can only define operator functions for operators already in the C++ language. Therefore, by declaring an operator function, you are automatically overloading an existing built-in operator.

Note: When the C++ compiler processes a source file, it checks the arguments to each operator to see if an operator function should be substituted.

An Operator-Overloading Example

It's time to write our first program that uses operator functions. We'll expand the **clock** class from the previous chapter and develop a set of operator functions for it. The **clock** class represents the time in seconds and has appropriate functions for handling the time in a standard hours–minutes–seconds (hms) format. Our example includes two operators for addition that are slight variations of each other. Here is the complete program:

```
#include <math.h>
#include <stdio.h>
class clock {
    double data; // time stored in seconds
public:
    clock(double h, double m, double s);
```

```
        void hms(double &h, double &m, double &s);
        friend clock operator+(clock a,clock b);
        void operator+=(clock t);
};


// constructor converts from hms to seconds
clock::clock(double h, double m, double s)
{
    data = h*3600.0 + m*60.0 + s;
}


// a member function to convert seconds to hms
void clock::hms(double &h, double &m, double &s)
{
    h  = (data/3600.0);
    s  = data - h*3600.0;
    m  = (s/60.0);
    s -= m*60.0;
}


// declare += operator to add one time to another
void clock::operator+=(clock t)
{
    data += t.data;  // add t's time to self
}


// declare friendly + operator for addition as well
clock operator+(clock a, clock b)
{
    clock t(0,0,0);

    t.data = a.data + b.data;
    return t;
}

void main()
{
    double h, m, s;
    clock casio(12,0,0), timex(3, 30, 0);
    casio = casio + timex; // one way to add
```

```
        casio.hms(h,m,s);
        printf("Time is %02.0f:%02.0f:%02.0f\n", h,m,s);
        casio += timex;    // another way to add
        casio.hms(h,m,s);
        printf("Time is %02.0f:%02.0f:%02.0f\n", h,m,s);
}
```

When you run the program, the following output is generated:

```
Time is 15:30:00
Time is 19:00:00
```

Initially, you may not see how the operator functions and their associated operators are related, but don't worry; you'll learn that soon enough. To get you started, our two addition statements are translated into the following expressions:

```
casio = operator+(casio, timex);  // casio = casio + timex
casio.operator+=(timex);          // casio += timex;
```

We've purposely included two ways to add times. The first method uses a friend function, and the second uses a member function. Later, we'll discuss the difference between these two approaches.

The **clock** class serves as a concise but excellent example of how C++ operator functions are defined and used. Throughout this chapter, we'll be extending this class to include other operators. For instance, we'll show you how to write expressions that allow you to mix floating-point numbers with **clock** objects and how to provide output functions for such objects.

Restrictions on Operator Functions

Before you get too excited about using operator functions, you should be aware of the following restrictions:

- New operator symbols cannot be defined
- The precedence or arity of an operator cannot be changed
- At least one argument of the operator function must be a user-defined class object, or the operator function must be a class member
- Operators cannot be combined to create new operators

The first two restrictions surface because of the way operator functions are implemented. If you could define your own operator symbols or change the syntax of the built-in ones, the parser used to process C++ code would have to be modified on the fly for each program. Also, if C++ allowed you to change the precedence or arity of a built-in operator, you would end up with a program that would be difficult to be read by others. If fellow programmers had to maintain your programs, they would have to learn the precedence rules all over again—not a pleasant task!

The reason behind the third restriction may not be as obvious. By forcing at least one argument of the operator function to be a user-defined object, or at least making sure the operator function is a class member, you won't be able to override how the operators work for built-in types.

The fourth restriction keeps you from combining overloaded operators. Recall that in C we can write expressions such as **a += b**. The += operator combines the addition and assignment operators. Now suppose that we had a class where the operators = and + were overloaded. Could we then write expressions such as **object1 += object2**? The answer is no. Every operator we overload must have an operator function defined for it, including operators such as +=. The compiler or translator won't combine the + and = operations for us. The reason: The ambiguity problems are too complex to handle. For example, you might have three overloaded operator functions for + and two for =. What should the compiler use for +=? Which of the six combinations of + and = should it use? You get the idea.

Here are some examples of legal and illegal operator functions to show you what is possible:

```
complex operator+(complex a, complex b);    // ok
void clock::operator++(clock t);            // ok
char *operator+(char *a, char *b);          // can't do!
void operator@(menu bar1, menu bar2);       // can't do!
menu operator++(menu a, menu b);            // can't do!
void string::operator+=(char *s);           // ok
```

The first two functions are valid because they contain class objects as arguments. The second function shows how an operator function that is a class member is declared. In this case, the function is a member of the class **clock**. The third function is illegal because it does not use class objects as arguments. The fourth example is illegal because **@** is not a valid C++ operator. The fifth example is illegal because you can't change the arity of the operators. The ++ operator is unary, not binary. Finally, in the last example, even though **operator+=** doesn't use a class object in the argument list, it is a member function, so it's perfectly legal.

Before you move on to the next section, take another look at the third example:

```
char *operator+(char *a, char *b);
```

When we presented overloaded functions earlier in this chapter, we wrote a function to concatenate two strings. But note that we cannot turn this function into an operator function, because it does not work with user-defined types! Fortunately, there are ways to get around this problem. For instance, you can declare a string class that encompasses a character pointer and then write operator functions that take these strings as arguments.

```
class string {
public:
    char *str;
};
char *operator+(string a, string b);
```

Table 7.1 lists all of the C++ operators that can be overloaded. In addition to those given in the table, you can also define your own casting operators, and you can overload the built-in type casts such as **int(x)**. As you look over this table, two of the operators, [] and (), might seem strange to you. They are the subscript and function call operators, respectively. You wouldn't normally think of these as operators, but they are. We'll later present examples of how they can be overloaded.

Table 7.1. C++ operators for overloading

Op	Description	Type	Associativity	Precedence
,	Comma operator	binary	Left	1
=	Assignment operator	binary	Right	2
+=	Assignment operator	binary	Right	2
-=	Assignment operator	binary	Right	2
*=	Assignment operator	binary	Right	2
/=	Assignment operator	binary	Right	2

Table 7.1. C++ operators for overloading (continued)

Op	Description	Type	Associativity	Precedence
!=	Assignment operator	binary	Right	2
^=	Assignment operator	binary	Right	2
&=	Assignment operator	binary	Right	2
%=	Assignment operator	binary	Right	2
<<=	Assignment operator	binary	Right	2
>>=	Assignment operator	binary	Right	2
||	Logical OR	binary	Left	4
&&	Logical AND	binary	Left	5
|	Bitwise OR	binary	Left	6
^	Bitwise XOR	binary	Left	7
&	Bitwise AND	binary	Left	8
==	Equality	binary	Left	9
!=	Inequality	binary	Left	9
<	Less than	binary	Left	10
<=	Less than/equal	binary	Left	10
>	Greater than	binary	Left	10
>=	Greater than/equal	binary	Left	10
<<	Left shift	binary	Left	11
>>	Right shift	binary	Left	11
+	Addition	binary	Left	12
-	Subtraction	binary	Left	12
*	Multiplication	binary	Left	13
/	Division	binary	Left	13
%	Modulo	binary	Left	13
->*	Pointer to member	binary	Left	14
++	Increment	unary	Right	15
--	Decrement	unary	Right	15
!	Logical NOT	unary	Right	15
~	Bitwise NOT	unary	Right	15
+	Unary plus	unary	Right	15
-	Unary minus	unary	Right	15
*	Pointer de-reference	unary	Right	15
&	Address of	unary	Right	15
()	Type cast	binary	Right	15
new	Allocate	binary	Right	15

Table 7.1. C++ operators for overloading (continued)

Op	Description	Type	Associativity	Precedence
delete	De-allocate	binary	Right	15
->	Member selector	binary	Left	16
[]	Array index	binary	Left	16
()	Function call	binary	Left	16

Note: The following operators cannot be overloaded:

.	Dot operator
.*	Pointer to member operator
::	Scoping operator
?:	If–then–else operator
#	Preprocessor command symbol
##	Macro concatenation symbol

Calling Operator Functions

As with standard C++ operators, operator functions are grouped into two categories: unary and binary. Further, the manner in which an operator function is called depends on whether or not it is a class member. If you are overloading a unary operator, you must also know if the operator is used as a prefix or postfix operator. We've provided Tables 7.2 and 7.3 to show you how overloaded operators are translated into corresponding operator function calls.

Table 7.2. Calling binary operator functions

Member Status	Syntax	Actual Call
Member	X Op Y	X.operatorOp(Y)
Nonmember	X Op Y	operatorOp(X,Y)

Table 7.3. Calling unary operator functions

Member Status	Syntax	Actual Call
Member	Op X	X.operatorOp();
Member	X Op	X.operatorOp(int);
Nonmember	Op X	operatorOp(X);
Nonmember	X Op	operatorOp(X, int);

Both Table 7.2 and Table 7.3 point out the differences between calling operator functions that are class members and nonclass members. The binary operator functions that are members have only one explicit argument in their function declaration. The other argument is the hidden argument **this**, which is included automatically in all member functions. Likewise, in unary prefix operators that are members, no arguments are given explicitly, since **this** takes up the single slot.

For example, you might overload the assignment operator = to work with string objects, as shown:

```
class string {
    char *data;
    //...
    void operator=(string &s);
  //...
};

void string::operator=(string &s)
{
    strcpy(data, s.data);
}
```

Remember that the statement **strcpy(data, s.data)** could also be written **strcpy(this->data, s.data)**. The pointer **this** is the first operand to the = operator. The object **s** is the second operand. With this overloaded operator, you can write expressions such as

```
string a, b;
a = b;
```

The assignment is translated into the call

```
a.operator=(b);
```

Prefix and Postfix Unary Operators

All unary operators in C++ are prefix operators (which come before the operand), with the exception of the increment and decrement operators, **++** and **--**. The increment and decrement operators, on the other hand, can also be postfix operators; they can appear before or after the operand. For example:

```
y = ++x;
y = x++;
```

These statements perform different operations. The first statement, which uses a prefix **++** operator, increments **x** before assigning its value to **y**. The second statement assigns the value of **x** to **y** and *then* increments **x**.

A problem occurs if you want to overload the **++** or **--** operators. How can you distinguish between prefix and postfix usage? The answer lies in Table 7.3. You'll notice that the operator function syntax given for postfix operators has an additional **int** argument as compared to the prefix operator function syntax. This **int** argument is a "dummy." It is used only to signal that the operator function is for postfix usage. For example, here's how we might declare prefix and postfix **++** operators for our familiar **clock** class:

```
class clock {
    ...
    void operator++(void); // prefix usage
    void operator++(int);  // postfix usage
};
```

Here are some sample calls to these two operator functions:

```
clock c;
++c; // calls c.operator()
c++; // calls c.operator(0); // note "0" dummy argument
```

Note how an extra argument, set to 0, is passed in the second call.

We'll revisit the **++** and **--** operators next and show you to implement them for **clock** objects.

Using Friend Operators

We've seen how operator functions can be defined to enhance the power of the standard set of C++ operators. However, there is one major problem that can occur when a binary operator is overloaded. If you use a binary operator function with regular variables (that is, variables of a built-in type—**int**, **char**, and so on), you must exercise caution if the operator function serves as a class member. The following example shows why:

```
class string {    // the class definition
public:
    char *str;
    operator+(string s1);
};

// declare string class objects
string str1, str2;
str1 = 1 + str2; // oops!
```

The problem is that the last statement is translated into

```
str1 = 1.operator+(str2); // what?
```

where the two operands are 1 and **str2**. Operand 1 isn't a user-defined object and, in particular, not a **string** object. So how can we fix this problem? We can define the operator as a friend function instead. Here's how this is done:

```
class string {
    char *str;
    friend string operator+(string a, string b);
};
```

This solution works only if both operands are **string** objects. It wouldn't work if the first operand were a 1. We can define another friend operator function to handle this case, as shown:

```
friend string operator+(int a, string b);
```

Now you can write expressions such as **1 + str2**. The problem is that you have to provide a separate operator function for each possible combination of argument types.

Fortunately, there is a better solution. You can provide either user-defined conversion functions or user-defined type casting operators and you'll need only a few operator functions for each operator. We'll show you how to do this later in this chapter.

Note: You might consider defining your overloaded operators as friend functions to make them as flexible as possible. You also might need to supply appropriate conversion functions so that the operator can handle operands of different data types.

Here is one last point to keep in mind as you define operator functions: Some operators are best left as class members. One example is the **++** operator. Since **++** takes a single argument—the object to be incremented—it is most appropriately a member function. Here's how we might define the prefix **++** operator for the **clock** class:

```
class clock {
    double data;
    // ..
    void operator++(void) { data++; }
};
```

If you declare the **++** operator as a friend, you must pass the **clock** object by reference. Why? You must make sure the actual **clock** object is incremented, instead of a copy of the object. Here's an example:

```
class clock {
    // ...
    friend void operator++(clock &t) { t.data++; }
};
```

Examples of Operator Overloading

Let's explore how overloaded operators can be defined for different C++ operators before we move on to a different topic. We'll work with the five operators that are probably the most confusing to overload. These operators include:

++	Increment operator
--	Decrement operator
=	Assignment operator
[ ]	Subscript operator
( )	Function call operator

Before we get started, let's discuss a few general principles about overloading C++ operators.

Tips on Overloading C++ Operators

When overloading a C++ operator, keep in mind the standard usage of the operator. You can use an overloaded operator to perform any operation you wish. However, you should consider using an operation that is in some way analogous to the normal usage of the operator. For example, let's assume that we need to overload the += operator. We wouldn't *have* to make += mean "add one object's value to another and assign the result to the first object." The overloaded operator could perform an operation such as popping up a window. The problem with this approach is that the new meaning assigned to the operator might confuse you and other programmers who are trying to read your programs.

Note: In general, you'll want to keep the meanings of the overloaded operators similar to their built-in counterparts. That way, other programmers can follow your code.

Overloading the Increment and Decrement Operators

The ++ and -- operators are tricky to overload because they can be used in both prefix and postfix form. As an example, let's implement an overloaded

++ operator for the **clock** class. (The implementation for -- would work in a similar fashion.) The code shown here provides an example:

```c
#include <math.h>
#include <stdio.h>
class clock {
    double data;
public:
    clock(double h, double m, double s);
    void hms(double &h, double &m, double &s);
    clock &operator++(void); // prefix usage
    clock operator++(int);    // postfix usage
};


clock::clock(double h, double m, double s)
// constructor
{
    data = h * 3600.0 + m * 60.0 + s;
}


void clock::hms(double &h, double &m, double &s)
// convert internal data back to hours, minutes, seconds
{
    h = floor(data / 3600.0);
    s = data - h * 3600.0;
    m = floor(s / 60.0);
    s -= m*60.0;
}


clock &clock::operator++(void)
// prefix increment operator function
{
    data++;
    return *this; // return reference to this clock
}


clock clock::operator++(int)
// postfix increment operator function
{
    clock temp = *this; // copy the clock
```

```
        data++; // increment original clock's data
        return temp; // return copy of clock
    }

void main()
{
    clock a(12, 30, 0), b(0, 0, 0), c(0, 0, 0);

    b = ++a; // call a.operator++(void)
    c = a++; // call a.operator++(int)

    double h, m, s;
    a.hms(h, m, s);
    printf("a's time is: %02.01f:%02.01f:%02.01f\n",
            h, m, s);
    b.hms(h, m, s);
    printf("b's time is: %02.01f:%02.01f:%02.01f\n",
            h, m, s);
    c.hms(h, m, s);
    printf("c's time is: %02.01f:%02.01f:%02.01f\n",
            h, m, s);
}
```

When run, this program should output:

```
a's time is: 12:30:02
b's time is: 12:30:01
c's time is: 12:30:01
```

Let's take a closer look at the operator functions. First, the prefix **++** function:

```
clock &clock::operator++(void)
// prefix increment operator function
{
    data++;
    return *this; // return reference to this clock
}
```

True to the semantics for pre-increment, our operator function first increments the value of the **clock** and then returns the updated **clock**. Note how we are returning a reference to the **clock**, rather than a copy. This allows statements such as the following to work as expected:

```
clock c(12,30,0);

++(++c);
```

The object **clock c** should have a new time of 12:30:02. Here's how the last statement would be translated into explicit function calls:

```
(c.operator++()).operator++();
```

The **clock** is incremented in the first call, and then a reference to the **clock** is returned. This reference is used to make the second call.

The post-increment function is trickier: We must preserve the original value of the **clock** before incrementing it, and then return this preserved value. To do this, we make a copy of the **clock** to return:

```
clock clock::operator++(int)
// postfix increment operator function
{
    clock temp = *this; // copy the clock
    data++; // increment original clock
    return temp; // return copy of clock
}
```

You might wonder why we didn't return a reference. The reason is that we are using an object stored on the stack. As we explained in Chapter 5, you should never return a reference to a location on the stack. Doing so may cause your program to crash. Instead, we must make a copy of that stack object. (This means that we are actually performing two copies in the function, as explained in the code.)

Because we are returning a copy for postfix **++** expressions, statements such as the following won't work as expected:

```
clock c(12, 30, 0);

(c++)++;
```

You would expect **clock c** to have a time of 12:30:02 after the statement executes. However, it has a time of 12:30:01. Why? It only gets incremented once. But who gets the second increment? The copy of the **clock** that is returned by the first increment operation. As an example, here's how the sample code is translated:

```
clock c(12, 30, 0);

clock temp = c.operator++(0);
temp.operator++(0);
```

A temporary **clock** object is created and is then incremented. This temporary **clock** has no other use and is destroyed sometime after the statement.

There is no easy way around this postfix copying problem. Fortunately, constructs such as (c++)++ do not occur very often.

Overloading the Assignment Operator

The assignment operator = is often overloaded to help process class objects, particularly when such objects use dynamic memory. If you use an assignment statement to copy one object to another of the same class, a member-wise copy operation is performed. That is, each member of the object is copied in turn. When pointers are included in the object, the data items that the pointers reference are not actually copied—only the pointers are copied. Figure 7.4 illustrates how an object that contains pointers is copied. Because the actual data is not copied, you might encounter problems when you attempt to use the copied object. Let's look at an example. The following function, called **window_setup()**, uses the = operator to copy an object:

```
void window_setup()
{
    // allocate memory for each window buffer
    char *window_buff1 = new char[4096];
    char *window_buff2 = new char[4096];

    window_buff1 = window_buff2;   // be careful!
    get_screen(window_buff1);
    get_screen(window_buff2);
```

```
        delete window_buff1;          // okay
        delete window_buff2;          // trouble!
    }
```

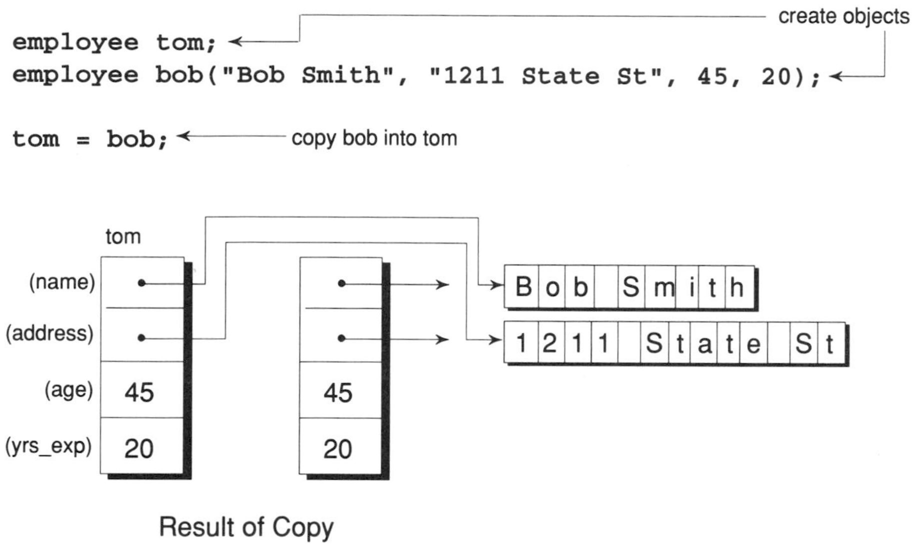
create objects
employee tom;
employee bob("Bob Smith", "1211 State St", 45, 20);
tom = bob;
copy bob into tom
tom
(name)
(address)
(age)
(yrs_exp)
45
20
45
20
B o b S m i t h
1 2 1 1 S t a t e S t
Result of Copy

Figure 7.4. Copying an object that contains pointers.

This example introduces two problems. Can you find them? First, the pointer to the memory allocated for **window_buff1** is lost when the following assignment is executed:

```
window_buff1 = window_buff2;
```

The **window_buff1** object now points to the same memory location as **window_buff2**. Second, before **window_setup()** terminates, the two **delete** statements attempt to free up the data pointed to twice by **window_buff2**. This action might cause a serious memory allocation error, and you might find yourself reaching for your computer's reset button.

To solve the pointer problem, let's package the window buffers into class objects and overload the assignment operator. By overloading this operator, we can insure that the actual data in the window buffer object is copied when an assignment is made. The following code illustrates how this is done. To keep the code simple, let's assume that the windows are always the same size.

```
#include <string.h>
class window_buffer {
    char *data;
public:
    window_buffer(void) { data = new char[4096]; }
    ~window_buffer() { delete data; }
    void operator=(window_buffer &w);
};


void window_buffer::operator=(window_buffer &w)
// assignment that copies the data
{
    memcpy(data, w.data, 4096); // assume buffers are the
                                // same size
}


void activate_window(window_buffer &w)
{
    // do something here
}


void main()
{
    window_buffer base_window, menu_window;

    activate_window(base_window);  // call function to use
                                   // window
    menu_window = base_window;     // copy the window
    activate_window(menu_window);  // use the copy
}
```

When the two window buffers are declared, the constructor function **window_buffer()** automatically allocates memory for them. Then, when the following assignment takes place:

```
menu_window = base_window;
```

the data from **base_window** is copied to **menu_window** rather than just the pointers. Finally, the destructors for each window buffer are safely called when **main()** is exited, and the memory is de-allocated for each window object.

Recall how operator functions work when they are defined as class members. Notice that the **operator=()** function has only one explicit argument, the source operand. The destination operand is the object being assigned into and is a hidden argument. Thus, the statement

```
menu_window = base_window;
```

translates into

```
menu_window.operator=(base_window);
```

With this example, we could have made the operator function a friend function instead of a member of the **window_buff** class. Let's modify our class definition to show how the friend function can be written.

```
class window_buff {
    char *data;
public:
    window_buffer(void) { data = new char[4096]; }
    ~window_buffer() { delete data; }
    friend void operator=(window_buff &a, window_buff &b);
};

void operator=(window_buff &a, window_buff &b)
{
    memcpy(a.data, b.data);
}
```

Our assignment statement would then translate into

```
operator=(menu_window, base_window);
```

Now you might be wondering if there is any advantage to using a friend function instead of an operator function. With this example, it doesn't really matter. However, there are operator functions, such as the subscript and function call operators, that *must* be defined as class members. We'll be exploring these operators shortly.

Note: An overloaded assignment operator is often used to help make class objects that use dynamic data more robust.

Overloading the Subscript Operator

Our next stop is the binary subscript operator []. From your C programming experience, you're probably aware that this operator is normally used to index arrays. Actually, the subscript operator performs a useful function: It hides pointer arithmetic for us. For example, if we have the following array:

```
char names[20];
```

and we execute a statement such as

```
ch = names[12];
```

the [] operator directs the assignment statement to add 12 to the base address of the array **names** to locate the data stored in this memory location. This process is illustrated in Figure 7.5.

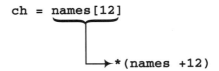

Figure 7.5. The subscript operation.

In C++, we can also overload this operator and provide many useful extensions to the subscripted array concept. Because [] is a binary operator, it requires two arguments. But where do these arguments come from? To answer this question, let's consider an expression such as

```
p = x[i];
```

Here [] is the operator, **x** is the first argument, and **i** is the second argument. You can think of the first argument as the object that is indexed; the second argument is the index.

Based on the discussion we presented earlier about how overloaded operators are translated into function calls, you might be thinking that **x[i]** is translated into **operator[](x,i)**. Well, it doesn't work like this. One important restriction imposed on an overloaded subscript operator is that the corresponding operator function can *only* be a class member. As we illustrated earlier with Table 7.2, a binary operator function that is a class member is translated as

```
X Op Y  ------>  X.operatorOp(Y)
```

Therefore, you should be able to see that the translation for the subscript operator is

```
x[i]   <===>  x.operator[](i)
```

Although [] is a binary operator, the actual function call has only one explicit argument. The other argument is the hidden **this** pointer, as it is for all member functions.

Let's put together a working program that illustrates how the [] operator is overloaded. Suppose we have a string class that represents strings of different lengths and we wish to provide bounds-checking for array subscripting operations on the strings. To keep the example simple, we'll support strings that are statically allocated and can hold a maximum of 255 characters. The overloaded subscript operator allows us to support the bounds-checking feature. Here's the complete program:

```
#include <stdio.h>
#include <stdlib.h>
class string255 {
    char data[255];  // maximum size
    int size;        // actual size
public:
    string255(int sz);          // constructor
    char &operator[](int i);    // subscript function
};

string255::string255(int sz)
```

```
{
    size = sz;    // merely indicate size
}

char &string255::operator[](int i)
{
    if (i < 0 || i >= size) {
        printf("Subscript out of bounds\n");
        exit(1);        // fatal error
    } else
        return data[i]; // the normal [] operation used here
}

void main()
{
    string255 a(10); // declare array with 10 elements
    char c;

    // sample uses
    a[5] = 17;         // set the 5th element
    c = a[7];          // retrieve the 7th element
    c = a[26];         // subscript error!
}
```

The first two statements result in valid subscripting operations, and the appropriate assignments are performed. The last statement, however, results in a subscripting error, as determined by the **operator[]()** function. In this case, the program is aborted.

To help you understand how the operator function is called, here's how the three assignments of **main()** are translated from subscript operator syntax into function calls:

```
a.operator[](5) = 17;
c = a.operator[](7);
c = a.operator[](26);
```

In each case, the hidden first operand is a pointer to the object being subscripted—the object **a**.

As you examine **operator[]()**, notice that the function passes back a reference to a character. We do this so that we can use it on both sides of an assignment statement as we did in the example.

Overloading the Function Call Operator

One of the more unusual operators is the function call operator, (). You may not have been aware that the set of parentheses in a function call could be used as an operator. In many respects, this operator is similar to the subscript operator, [], which we just explored. Like the subscript operator, the () operator can only be overloaded by an operator function that is a class member. Unlike the subscript operator and the other C++ operators, the function call operator can be unary or binary, or even can take multiple arguments. Here are some translations of function call operators with different numbers of arguments:

```
x()       <===> x.operator()()
x(i)      <===> x.operator()(i)
x(i,j)    <===> x.operator()(i,j)
x(i,j,k)  <===> x.operator()(i, j, k)
```

Notice how () is the syntax used in formal math for denoting subscript operations, as opposed to the [] operator used in C++ and other languages. One of the potential uses of overloading () is to provide subscripting for multiple dimensions. Remember that the [] operator can only subscript a single dimension because it is a binary operator, and the first operand must be an object. While the () operator must also have an object as its first operand, it can have any number of operands following. This allows it to be used for subscripting two or more dimensions.

Let's explore an example of overloading the function call operator. Here is a two-dimensional matrix class that we borrowed from an earlier chapter. We've modified it by using the () operator to add a subscripting function:

```
#include <stdio.h>
class matrix {
    int nr, nc;
    int *data;
public:
    matrix(int w, int h);
```

```
    ~matrix(void);
    int &operator()(int r, int c);
};

matrix::matrix(int w, int h)
{
    data = new int[nr = w, nc = h];
}

matrix::~matrix(void)
{
    delete[] data;
}

int &matrix::operator()(int r, int c)
// implement () to mean two-dimensional subscripting
{
    return data[r*nc + c];
}

void main()
{
    matrix m(3, 5);

    m(0, 0) = 1;
    m(1, 1) = m(0, 0) + 1;
    m(2, 2) = m(1, 1) + 1;
    printf("%d\n", m(2, 2));
}
```

Take a closer look at the **operator()** function. Note how it is declared as a class member (it must be). It cleverly returns a reference to the **matrix** element selected:

```
int &matrix::operator()(int r, int c)
// implement () to mean two-dimensional subscripting
{
    return data[r*nc + c];
}
```

By returning a reference, we can call the function on both sides of an assignment statement, as we did in statements such as

```
m(1,1) = m(0, 0) + 1;
```

This latter statement translates to

```
m.operator()(1,1) = m.operator()(0, 0) + 1;
```

We've made our subscripting operation compute the appropriate element from a one-dimensional array. We could also provide error checking:

```
int &matrix::operator()(int r, int c)
// Implement () to mean two-dimensional subscripting
{
    if ((r < 0 || r > nr-1) ||
        (c < 0 || c > nc-1)) {
        printf("Subscript error\n");
        exit(1);
    }
    else return data[r*nc + c];
}
```

Conversion Functions and Type Casting Operators

Like any overloaded function, the main problem that a C++ compiler has with overloaded operators is knowing which operator function to call. The ambiguities are resolved by using the same algorithm that we outlined earlier in this chapter. Remember that part of this algorithm involves looking for any type conversions that may apply. An example is given in Figure 7.6. In addition to the built-in conversions, you can also define your own. Specifically, two methods are available for declaring your own type conversions: *conversion functions* and *type casting operators*.

Conversion Functions

Conversion functions are special types of constructor functions that contain a single argument. The argument must be an object that has a different type than the constructor's class. For instance, recall our **clock** class. We could extend this class so that it has a second constructor, which converts a variable of type **double** to a **clock** variable.

```
class clock {
    double data;
public:
    clock(double h, double m, double s);
    clock(double s) { data = s; }     // new constructor
};
```

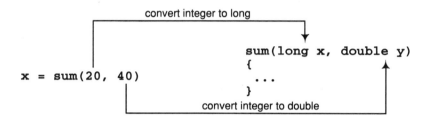

Figure 7.6. Matching function arguments.

Using our new class definition, we can include the following declarations in a program:

```
clock stop_watch = clock(0,0,0);
clock egg_timer  = clock(30.0);
```

The first declaration causes the original constructor to be called because the constructor contains three arguments. The second declaration, on the other hand, causes our new constructor to be called because only a single argument is used. In this context, the new constructor can be interpreted as a conversion function because it takes an argument that is a **double** and turns it into a **clock** object. (In fact, you might argue that the first constructor is also a conversion function. It takes hours–minutes–seconds objects and turns them into clock objects.)

This conversion process is perhaps easier to see when constructors are used in the middle of expressions. For example, with the appropriate operators defined for **clock**, we can write expressions such as:

```
clock elapsed_time(0,0,0), timer(0,55,17);
elapsed_time = timer - clock(42.0);
```

Note: Because conversion functions are actually constructor functions, we'll be exploring them in much greater detail in Chapter 8. We've included them in this chapter so that they can be compared with type casting operators—the other method used to perform conversions.

While useful and powerful, conversion functions have one limitation. Because they are class members, additional conversions cannot be added without changing the class declaration. If the class you're dealing with has already been compiled or is a standard class you don't wish to alter, this can be a problem. Typically, when you first define a class you don't know ahead of time all of the possible conversions that might be needed. And what about all of the new types that are created long after the class is defined?

Another problem with conversion functions relates to built-in types, such as **int** and **double**. Because these types are not classes (that is, they are not user-defined), we cannot define constructor functions for them to serve as conversion functions.

Type Casting Operators

Fortunately, there is a way to get around the limitations of constructor conversion functions. We can use type casting operators. A type casting operator, or casting operator for short, is an operator function that happens to have the name of a type as its own name. For instance, let's define a casting operator that converts our **clock** object to a **double**. This operation is just the reverse of the conversion function we wrote in the previous section. We've included a fragment of the class declaration for **clock** to show the extension.

```
class clock {
    double data;     // number of seconds
    // class members go here
    operator double() { return data; } // casting operator
};
```

Now, here are a few lines of code that illustrate how this casting operator can be used.

```
clock mickey(2,45,15);
double seconds;

seconds = double(mickey)
```

In this case the conversion is simple. We merely return the value of the member **data**, because it's already of type **double** and has the appropriate number of seconds.

Since **double()** is a unary operator function that is defined as a class member, the statement above is translated into

```
seconds = mickey.double();
```

As this example indicates, type casting operators must be class members. Also, no return type is declared for the function. (Actually, the return type is the name of the function!)

If we had declared the function outside the class, it would look like

```
clock::operator double()
{
    return data;
}
```

Recall how type casts are denoted in C (see Figure 7.7). It's also possible to use this alternate syntax for casting the operators you've defined in your C++ programs. For instance, we could write

```
seconds = (double)mickey;
```

```
int result;
double x;

result = (int) x;
```

type cast

Figure 7.7. A C type cast.

The new C++ way—that is, to denote the type cast as a function call—is preferred, since it alleviates problems with precedence and usually requires fewer parentheses. For instance, the expression

```
long(45.5 + 67.8)
```

is clearer and less prone to errors than

```
(long)(45.5 + 67.8)
```

or

```
(long) 45.5 + 67.8;  // not the same as above, or is it?
```

Implicit Type Conversions

So far we've shown type conversions that use explicit type casts. It's also possible for implicit type conversions to take place, even for overloaded type casts and conversion functions. For instance, in our earlier clock example we could have written

```
seconds = mickey;
```

This results in an implicit type cast since the compiler detects that **seconds** is of type **double**, and it is able to find an appropriate casting operator from **mickey's** type, **clock**, to **double**. It's as though we had written

```
seconds = double(mickey)
```

Conversion functions can also be called implicitly. For example, given the conversion function we created earlier for **clock**, an implicit call takes place in the statement shown next to convert 42.17 to a **clock** object.

```
clock t(0,0,0);

t = 42.17;    // t = clock(42.17)
```

Implicit type conversions can also be performed in the middle of any arbitrary expression. For instance:

```
seconds = 3600 + mickey;
```

They can also occur when values are returned from a function or passed as arguments.

```
double duty(clock t)
{
    t.data += t.data;
    return t;      // casting operator called
}

double dutyII(double d)
{
    return d += d;
}

clock dutyIII(void)
{
    return 33.33;     // conversion function called
}

clock mickey(0,0,0);
double make_time;

make_time = duty(mickey);    // conversion on return
make_time = dutyII(mickey); // conversion passing arg
mickey = dutyIII();          // conversion on return
```

Except in the function **dutyIII**, the **clock::double()** casting operator is called wherever the type conversions take place. For **dutyIII**, the conversion function **clock::clock(double)** is called.

As another example, the following is a class that stores two byte integers with the low- and high- order bytes reversed, as illustrated in Figure 7.8. The class also contains a casting operator to convert such a number into a normal integer. These types of operations are common when transferring data between different machines. Of course, the definition of what's normal depends on what machine you're used to working with. Here's the program:

```
#include <stdio.h>
class reversed_int {
```

```
    int data;
public:
    reversed_int(int i);
    operator int();
    int dump() { return data; }
};

int reverse(int i) // note: not a member!
// actual function to do the byte reversal
{
    return ((i & 0xff) << 8) + ((i & 0xff00) >> 8);
}

reversed_int::reversed_int(int i) { data = reverse(i); }
reversed_int::operator int() { return reverse(data); }

void main()
{
    int i = 0x1234, k, q;
    reversed_int j(i); // constructor does conversion
    printf("J contains: %04x\n", j.dump());
    k = j;     // implicit type cast
    printf("K contains: %04x\n", k);
    q = 0x00ff & j; // implicit type cast
    printf("Q contains: %04x\n", q);
}
```

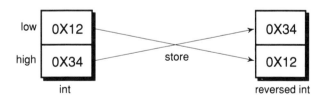

Figure 7.8. The integer representation.

In this example, we've defined a nonmember function that knows how to swap the bytes of a two-byte integer. Then, with two class members, we've defined conversions that work both ways. The constructor function is used to convert a normal integer into a reversed one. The **operator int()** function is used to convert the reversed integer back to a normal one. We've also provided a function to display the reversed integer.

When you run the program, you'll get the following output:

```
J contains: 3412
K contains: 1234
Q contains: 0034
```

Resolving Type Casting Ambiguities

Before we wrap up our discussion of type casting operators, we need to say something about resolving ambiguities. Because type casting operators can be overloaded, the same problem we had with overloaded functions occurs: that of trying to determine which function to call. It's perhaps more difficult with casting operators than conversion functions, because the calls are often implicit and you may unexpectedly get a compiler error. As we suggested for overloaded functions earlier, don't overdo it when defining your type conversions!

Summary

In this chapter we covered the basics of overloading functions and operators—two useful techniques that enable you to easily expand the flexibility of your C++ programs. We saw how easy it is to define overloaded functions and operators, as long as you don't get carried away and create a lot of ambiguities. We also discovered that there are some restrictions for overloading functions and operators.

The more you work with overloaded functions and operators, the more you'll realize the major benefits that these components provide. The main advantage is that you can process user-defined data types using standard notation.

Exercises

1. What is wrong with the following operator function? (Hint: Remember that + is a binary operator.)

```
class computer {
public:
  int operator+(int a, int b) { return a + b; }
};
```

2. Give an example (besides subscripting) where overloading the function call operator, (), would be useful.

3. Explain why overloading the [] operator would be difficult for subscripting multidimensional arrays, such as

```
a[i, j, k] = 25;
```

4. Implement an association table that maps names (character strings) into numbers. To do this, overload the subscripting operator. Statements such as the following should be supported:

```
assoc t;

t["harry"] = 12;
```

8

Working with Constructor and Destructor Functions

The process of initializing objects created from C++ classes is much more involved than initializing variables in C. Objects are designed to be more general purpose than C variables; therefore, you'll need to develop techniques for encapsulating initialization code. And that's where constructors and destructors come in. We've introduced constructors and destructors in previous chapters. We'll now devote an entire chapter to showing you how to define and use them because of the complexity and special features of these functions.

We'll start by explaining how objects are initialized with constructors. We'll provide a list of important restrictions that you must follow to define and use constructors and destructors. After we cover the basics, we'll move on to some advanced topics, such as using constructors to create an array of objects, creating unnamed objects, working with assignments and initializations, and using constructors as conversion functions.

Here are some of the other highlights of this chapter:

- How to use initializer lists to initialize objects
- How to overload constructors
- How to call constructors with default arguments
- Restrictions on using constructors and destructors
- Techniques for creating arrays of objects
- The differences between assignment and initialization
- How to use dynamic memory with objects

Initializing Objects

Before we start working with constructors and destructors, let's explore how to use initializer lists. Some types of objects can be initialized using the initializer list construct that C supports. Objects created from structures or classes that have only public members (which are essentially the same as structures) can be initialized in this manner. As an example, if we define the structure

```
struct part_rec {
    int partno, double price;
};
```

we can use initializations such as:

```
part_rec widget = { 1015, 1.50 };
part_rec car_parts[2]  = {
  { 333, 4.15 }, { 666, 2.13 }
};
```

Here we've initialized a structure as well as an array containing structures. You can use this technique with structures, arrays, arrays of structures, and nested structures. You can also use partial initializations. In such a case, all of the initial values are not provided.

Note: Global variables or structures not explicitly initialized are always set to zero. However, local variables or variables allocated with the **new** operator are not. You shouldn't rely on such default initializations.

The initializer list technique has some restrictions. For instance, you can't use initializer lists with classes that have constructors or private members. Another restriction is that you can't have more initializers than there are members. (This restriction doesn't apply in C.) For instance, the following initialization generates an error in C++:

```
char msg[10] = "The answer is 42";
```

Remember to leave room for the null character when using strings. For instance, the following statement produces a compiler error in C++ because the string "ABC" requires four bytes:

```
char msg[3] = "ABC";
```

To initialize complex objects created from unions and classes, *constructor* and *destructor* functions are used. Constructor functions specify the initialization code to be executed when an object is created. Destructor functions, on the other hand, specify the code to be executed when an object is no longer used. The constructors and destructors are packaged with the class like other member functions.

Declaring Constructors and Destructors

A constructor function for a class is declared by using the class name as the function name. A destructor also uses the same name, except the name is preceded with the ~ symbol. Let's look at a simple example.

```
class image {
    char *data;
    int wd, int ht;
public:
    image(int w, int h);      // constructor declaration
    ~image(void);             // destructor declaration
};

image::image(int w, int h)    // constructor definition
{
    wd = w; ht = h;           // initializes variables
    data = new char[wd*ht];   // and allocates memory
}

image::~image(void)        // destructor definition
{
    delete[] data;            // frees up memory
}
```

Here we've shown the class definition for **image** and the code for the constructor and destructor functions. The constructor initializes the private variables **wd** and **ht**. It also allocates dynamic memory for the **data** member. Right away you can see that constructors are more powerful than initializer lists. How are constructors invoked? When a variable such as the following is declared

```
image big_picture(1024,1024); // declaration of image
```

the constructor is automatically called. Notice that arguments can be included to initialize the object. Figure 8.1 shows how these arguments match up with those of the constructor. The arguments are used to specify the amount of memory to allocate for the **image** object called **big_picture**.

```
image :: image(int w, int h)
{
  ...
}

image big_picture(1024, 1024);
```

Figure 8.1. Matching the constructor arguments.

The destructor performs the opposite task—it frees up the memory allocated for the **image** object. It is called whenever an **image** object is no longer used. This occurs when the function in which the object is declared returns from execution. If the object is static, that is, not a part of any function, then the destructor is called when the program finishes. Later on we'll explain exactly when the constructor and destructor functions are called.

Note that we placed the constructor in the public section of the class. If we had made it private, we could not have used it to initialize **big_picture**. Similarly, the destructor should also be declared in the public section.

Don't be misled into thinking that constructors can only allocate memory and that destructors can only de-allocate memory. Many objects don't use dynamic memory. The constructors for these objects are used to initialize internal variables. The destructors for these objects are typically not needed. Also, don't forget that C++ structures and unions can have constructors. (This means you can initialize structures with initializer lists or with constructors. Unions can only be initialized with constructors, not initializer lists.)

Note: Don't forget to include the ~ symbol with the destructor function. If you omit this symbol, the compiler will treat the function as a constructor.

Restrictions on Constructors and Destructors

Before we continue our detailed exploration of constructors and destructors, we need to discuss a few restrictions. Constructors and destructors can utilize most of the features available to standard functions. However, you should keep these restrictions in mind when defining constructors and destructors:

- They cannot return a value with the **return** statement.
- Constructors cannot be friend functions, and they cannot be virtual. Destructors, however, can be virtual.
- Constructors can have arguments, but destructors can't.
- Member objects can have constructors, but if they do, the member object's constructor must be called first.
- Unions can have constructors and destructors. However, members of unions cannot.
- Objects that will be stored in arrays must have either a constructor that doesn't use arguments or no constructor at all.

When you work with derived classes, the important rule to keep in mind is that constructors can't be declared as virtual functions. (We'll explain how to handle constructors and destructors in derived classes in Chapter 9.)

How to Call Constructors

Unlike standard functions, constructor functions can be called in several ways. For starters, they can be called explicitly, like any function.

```
image sunset = image(1024, 1024);
```

Here, the object named **sunset** is initialized by an explicit call to the constructor **image()**. Although you can't specify a return value, a constructor in a sense does have one—it returns a reference to the object being created. In our example, **image**() returns a reference to an object created and initialized with the arguments specified. This is shown in Figure 8.2. Objects created by calling a constructor aren't given a name. However, in our example, a name is assigned to the object when the assignment for **sunset** executes.

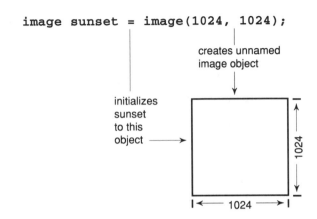

Figure 8.2. Calling a constructor.

You can use a shorthand form for calling a constructor to initialize objects. For example, the following statements are equivalent:

```
image sunset = image(1024, 1024);    // longhand form
image sunset(1024, 1024);            // shorthand form
```

In the second case, **sunset**() is *not* a call to a function named **sunset**(). Instead, it calls the constructor **image**() with the specified arguments.

If a constructor has only a single argument, we don't have to use the function call syntax. We can use the = operator for initialization. For example, suppose we have the following class:

```
class clock {
    long data;
public:
    clock(long seconds) { data = seconds; }
    // public members go here
};
```

There are three ways the constructor **clock()** can then be called:

```
clock timex = clock(43200);   // explicit function call
clock timex(43200);           // shorthand way
clock timex = 43200;          // another way
```

Here we've provided a constructor that initializes a **clock** object with the desired seconds. Now, suppose that you also wanted to be able to initialize a **clock** object by specifying hours, minutes, and seconds. This can be done by declaring another constructor function to overload the original constructor. Let's explore next how this is done.

Overloading Constructors

A constructor can be overloaded like any other C++ function. This feature allows you to provide several versions of a constructor for a single class. Each version can have a different number or type of arguments. This technique is useful for objects that have more than one kind of external representation. For example, you might want to initialize a clock using just seconds or you might want to use hours, minutes, and seconds.

To illustrate how a constructor is overloaded, let's return to the **clock** class. We'll create a program that provides two constructors, one that inputs seconds and one that inputs hours, minutes, and seconds, to initialize **clock** objects. Here is the complete program:

```
#include <stdio.h>
class clock {
    long data;    // time stored in seconds
public:
    clock(long s) { data = s; }   // two constructors
    clock(int h, int m, int s);   // provided
    void hms(int &h, int &m, int &s);
    void display(void);
};

clock::clock(int h, int m, int s)
{
    data = (long)h*3600 + m*60 + s;
}
```

```
void clock::hms(int &h, int &m, int &s)
{
    h  = data/3600;
    s  = data - h*3600;
    m  = s/60;
    s -= m*60;
}

void clock::display(void)
{
    int hr, min, sec;

    hms(hr, min, sec);
    printf("%02d:%02d:%02d\n", hr, min, sec);
}

void main()
{
    // note the two alternate ways to initialize clocks:
    clock timex(13, 55, 46), rolex(12345);

    timex.display();
    rolex.display();
}
```

When run, this program produces

```
13:55:46
03:25:45
```

Notice the following declaration statement in the function **main()**:

```
clock timex(13, 55, 46), rolex(12345);
```

Here, each **clock** object, **timex** and **rolex**, is initialized with a different constructor. The arguments specified with each declaration indicate which constructor is used, as shown in Figure 8.3.

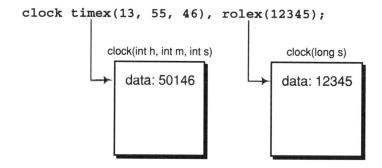

Figure 8.3. Arguments used with the clock() constructor.

To process an overloaded function, the compiler must determine which constructor to call. The rules for determining this were presented in the previous chapter. As we discussed, it's wise not to get too carried away with function overloading, because it can make your code hard to understand. In a complex situation, it may not be so easy to tell which function will be called; this can lead to many surprises. This is particularly true with overloaded constructors that perform dynamic memory allocation operations. We suggest that you try to keep your constructors simple and overload only those constructors that are necessary and useful.

Note: Destructors cannot be overloaded. Because destructors do not accept arguments or return a value, the compiler cannot distinguish between different destructors that have the same name.

Using Default Arguments with Constructors

Constructors can have default arguments. For instance, consider this class:

```
class data_obj {
    int data;
public:
    data_obj(int i = 0) { data = i; }
};
```

The constructor **data_obj()** uses a single argument that is set to zero by default. Because of this declaration, the constructor can be called in one of two ways:

```
data_obj a(25);      // no default
data_obj b;       // default used, b.data set to 0
```

Using this technique, let's return to our **clock** class and specify defaults for the two **clock** constructors:

```
clock::clock(long sec = 0)
{
    data = sec;
}


clock::clock(int hr=0, int min=0, int sec=0)
{
    data = 3600*hr + 60*min + sec;
}
```

In this case, we'll run into trouble because we've allowed ambiguities to creep in. Which constructor should be called for the following declaration: the first one or the second one?

```
clock casio; // compiler error: ambiguous call
```

Because of this ambiguity, the compiler will report an error. The following declaration and statement illustrate an even more subtle problem:

```
clock big_ben(21);
big_ben.display();   // what value is produced?
```

Can you tell which **clock** constructor is called here and what value is returned? You might think that the constructor having a single **long** argument is used. Therefore, the **clock** member **data** would be set to 21, and **display()** would output **00:00:21**. However, the compiler uses the second constructor. Why? The constant 21 is treated as an **integer**, and, although the second constructor has three arguments, it is selected because a type conversion is not required for the first argument. (Recall that it's an **integer**.) The other arguments can use their default values.

To use the first constructor, the **integer** constant must be converted to a **long**. Therefore, the second constructor is the one chosen, even though it has more arguments. The number 21 is then treated as the number of hours. The minutes and seconds default to zero. The resulting output would be **21:00:00**.

As a final note, if all the constructors for a class have at least one argument, and those constructors do not have default arguments, then you must initialize the object with one of them. For instance, you can't write

```
class num {
    int data;
public:
    num(int i) { data = i; }
};


num my_object;     // can't write this, it needs an argument
num my_object(25);  // okay
```

Using Member Objects That Have Constructors

Recall that class members can be user-defined types (objects) as well as basic types (**int, char**, and so on). If such a member also has a constructor, the constructor must be called before the enclosing class's constructor. If the member has a constructor that doesn't use arguments, this call is easily made. (The compiler does the call for you.) What happens if the constructor requires arguments? How are they passed? The following code shows how:

```
class gallery {
public:
    image *picture_of_my_dog;
    image picasso;
    image vangogh;
    gallery(image *i);
};

gallery::gallery(image *i) // constructor for gallery
: picasso(640,480),        // calls image constructor
  vangogh(320,200)         // twice. Note the colon.
{
```

```
        picture_of_my_dog = i;
}
```

The members **picasso** and **vangogh** are initialized by placing calls to their constructors directly after the colon. The calls come immediately after the constructor parameter list and before the opening brace. Figure 8.4 illustrates the placement of each component. Note how we call the member constructors by using the object names. The arguments are supplied just as they are in a standard constructor call. Because we declared the auxiliary member **picture_of_my_dog** as a pointer, we did not have to call a constructor for it.

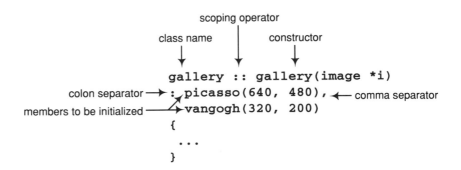

Figure 8.4. Calling member constructors.

Note that the two constructor calls are made before the main body of the class constructor is executed. Contrary to what you might think, the order in which the member constructors are called is determined by the order in which they were declared in the class, and not by the order in which they are listed in the **gallery** constructor definition. Thus, if the **gallery** constructor was defined

```
gallery::gallery(image *i)
: vangogh(320,200),
  picasso(640,480)
{
    picture_of_my_dog = i;
}
```

then the **picasso()** constructor would still be called before the **vangogh()** constructor. This calling order is used because the **picasso** member was declared first in the **gallery** class.

Remember that you don't have to call member functions explicitly if they do not require arguments. They will still be called before the class constructor.

Note: The main object's constructor is called *after* the member constructors. The destructors work in the reverse order.

Using Constructors with Unions

Constructors can be used to initialize unions. This class definition provides an example:

```
union node_elem {
    list *next;
    int data;
    node_elem(list *n) { next = n; }
    node_elem(int d)   { data = d; }
};
```

The trick here is to make sure that the compiler knows which member of the union to initialize. In this case, we used two constructors, one for each type of member. Of course, you must make sure the constructors themselves are not ambiguous.

Unlike structures, has a restriction on the kind of members it can have. Specifically, a union member cannot be an object that has a constructor or a destructor.

When Are Objects Created and Destroyed?

As we've seen, constructors and destructors provide a powerful and convenient method for initializing and destroying objects. However, like any powerful tool, they can be misused. You'll want to know when they are actually called so that you use them properly.

The factor that determines when a constructor and destructor are called is an object's life span. Here are the different life spans an object can have:

- *Automatic objects.* These are objects local to a function, and, as such, are stored on the stack. They exist for the duration of a function.
- *Static objects.* These are objects declared outside of a function. They are created when the program begins and exist for the duration of the program.
- *Dynamic objects.* These are objects residing on the heap. They are created using **new** and destroyed using **delete.**
- *Unnamed objects.* These are objects created temporarily to support an internal expression calculation. Their life-span is implementation-dependent.
- *Member objects.* These are objects that are created and destroyed when the object to which they belong is created and destroyed.
- *Derived class objects.* These are objects created from a derived class. In this case, the base class constructor is called first, before the derived class constructor. Their destructors work in reverse order.

Creating Automatic, Static, and Dynamic Objects

We'll now explore how constructors and destructors are used with automatic, static, and dynamic objects. Let's start by writing a program that shows the differences among these three types of objects. In this program we'll define a class of **beings** that live and die. The constructor performs the birth process by printing a birth announcement; the destructor is used to print an eulogy.

Our program introduces three types of **beings**: mortal, immortal, and artificial. Mortal beings are created by the function **life()**, and they only exist while the function is executing. They are automatic because their life span is limited to the life of the function. The immortal beings are declared statically (outside a function). Although they don't really live forever, they are immortal as far as the function **main()** is concerned. The artificial beings are created on the heap with the **new** operator. Their life span (dynamic) depends on the whims of their creator; that is, they live until **delete** is called. Here is the program:

```
#include <stdio.h>
#include <stdlib.h>
```

```
#include <string.h>
class being {
    char *name;
public:
    being(char *n) {// constructor gives birth
      name = strdup(n);
      printf("%s born, have a cigar!\n", name);
    }
    ~being() { // destructor handles death
      printf("%s died, rest his weary soul!\n", name);
      free(name);
    }
};

void life(char *name)
{
    being mortal(name);
    printf("%s thinks he'll live forever!\n", name);
}

being *science_project(void)
{
    return new being("Frankenstein");
}

being immortal("Zeus");

void main()
{
    being *monster;

    monster = science_project();
    life("Custer");
    delete monster;
}
```

When run, this program produces the output:

```
Zeus born, have a cigar!
Frankenstein born, have a cigar!
```

```
Custer born, have a cigar!
Custer thinks he'll live forever!
Custer died, rest his weary soul!
Frankenstein died, rest his weary soul!
Zeus died, rest his weary soul!
```

Except for dynamic objects and unnamed objects created temporarily in expression calculations, C++ objects are created and destroyed in a specific order:

- Static objects are created in the lexical order in which they appear in the program. They are destroyed in the reverse order. However, if you're using multiple modules that contain static objects, the order in which the objects' constructors are called is undefined.
- Objects declared as static inside a function will be constructed only the first time the function is called. The static object's constructor is not called if the function is never called.
- Automatic objects are created when the function in which they reside is called. They are created in the order in which they appear in the function and destroyed in the reverse order.
- Member objects are created before the class constructor is called. They are destroyed after the class object is destroyed.
- In arrays of objects, the constructors for each element are called in sequence. The destructors work in reverse.

Using Static Objects with Constructors

A C programmer usually thinks of **main**() as the starting point of a program. However, this isn't true, because most implementations set up the command line arguments and other operating system interfaces before the main program executes. In C++, constructors may be called as well. When a static object having a constructor is declared outside a function (as a global variable), its constructor is called before **main**() executes. If an object has a destructor, the destructor is called when the program terminates normally or when the **exit**() function is called. The latter implies that you should never have a destructor that calls **exit**() since this would create infinite recursion.

When you have multiple static objects that are global to a program, you must be careful. If all of the objects are declared in the same source file, then their constructors are called in the order of declaration. However, if the objects are declared in multiple files, the constructor calling sequence is undefined. Therefore, don't rely on the ordering of constructor calls. For example, don't use a static object with a constructor that depends upon another static object that has a constructor.

But don't be afraid of using global static objects with constructors—they can be useful. For instance, you might have a window manager that needs to be initialized before your program starts. You can make your window object global and provide a constructor that initializes the window system by performing tasks such as initializing the window stack, setting up display drivers, and so on. Remember to keep your constructors simple. If a constructor performs too many complex tasks, you might notice a delay when your program starts.

Note: Destructors for global objects are *not* called if you use **abort()** to terminate a program.

Creating Arrays of Objects

If you create an array of objects that have constructors and destructors, you must take special care. You should be aware of the following rules:

- If the object has any constructors, then at least one of the constructors must either take no arguments or take all default arguments.
- A constructor is called for each object in the array in sequence, from first to last.
- The destructor is called for each object in reverse order. If the array is allocated with the **new** operator, then, when **delete** is used, you must use the vector form (**delete[]**).

To illustrate these rules, here's a program that defines an array of objects to process numbers. The constructor initializes the data component of each object to the value of 42. When the program terminates, the destructor is called for each object in the array. We've included **printf()** statements to show you what's going on.

```
#include <stdio.h>
class num42 {
public:
```

```
      int data;
      num42(void) {
        data = 42; printf("\nConstructor called ");
      }
      ~num42(void) {
        printf("\nDestructor called ");
      }
};

void main()
{
    num42 num_array[2];
}
```

This program produces the output

```
Constructor called
Constructor called
Destructor called
Destructor called
```

The compiler keeps track of the number of objects in the array for us because the array was allocated statically. The compiler also knows the number of times to call the destructor. However, dynamic arrays are more difficult to process. For instance, suppose we changed **main**(), as follows

```
void main()
{
    num42 *num_array = new num42[2];
    delete num_array;
}
```

When run, the program now produces:

```
Constructor called
Constructor called
Destructor called
```

In this case, the destructor is called only once. However, it should have been called twice. The compiler doesn't know that it should call the destructor twice, because it doesn't know that **num_array** points to an array of objects instead of a single object. To correct this problem, the **delete** statement should be written as

```
delete[] num_array;
```

The [] signals the compiler that an array is being deleted. The compiler will then look up the appropriate number of elements to delete for you.

Note: Earlier versions of C++ allowed you to define the array size when using **delete**, as in

```
delete [2] num_array;
```

This is no longer allowed in C++ version 2.1.

Creating Unnamed Objects

Temporary objects may be created when an expression is evaluated, but these objects don't have a name. For instance, consider an expression such as **2+3**. The numbers 2 and 3 are like objects. (Although it's important to note that in C++ they're really not implemented as objects, contrary to the way they would be treated in a language such as Smalltalk.) You can think of 2 and 3 as being instances of the class **integer**. Of course, these instances are not assigned a name because they are not associated with a variable. When the expression 2+3 is evaluated, these unnamed objects are created, and, when the result is computed, they are destroyed. This process is illustrated in Figure 8.5. Notice that a number is created by reserving a memory location, such as a register, to store the number. In any respect, you don't have any control over how the number is created and stored. The compiler performs this task on its own.

Now, suppose the operands to the + operator are objects that you defined. Remember that C++ allows you to overload the standard operators to work on user-defined objects. For instance, you can overload + to add two similar objects, as shown in the following program:

```
#include <stdio.h>
struct vector {
```

```
        int dx, dy;
        vector(int a = 0, int b = 0) { dx = a; dy = b; }
    };

    vector operator+(vector &a, vector &b)
    {
        return vector(a.dx + b.dx, a.dy + b.dy);
    }

    void main()
    {
        vector a(3,5), b(4,6), c;

        c = a + b;
        printf("The vector c is: (%d,%d)\n", c.dx, c.dy);
    }
```

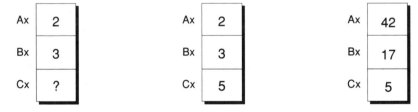

Registers

Ax	2		Ax	2		Ax	42
Bx	3		Bx	3		Bx	17
Cx	?		Cx	5		Cx	5

1. Create operands by loading registers 2. Add 3. Destroy operands by writing over them

Figure 8.5. Adding objects.

In this case, we are adding two vector objects, **a** and **b**, and assigning the result to object **c**. The output created by the program is

```
The vector c is: (7,11);
```

Note the return statement in our **operator+()** function:

```
return vector(a.dx + b.dx, a.dy + b.dy);
```

Here, an unnamed **vector** object is created and then used as the result.

C++ also allows us to add unnamed objects. How? By using constructors and the appropriate **operator+()** functions. Recall how the vector constructors for **a** and **b** were called in the previous program—before the expression is evaluated. Constructors can also be called as part of an expression evaluation. Here's an example:

```
vector c;

c = vector(3, 5) + vector(4, 6);
```

When the expression is evaluated, two unnamed objects of class **vector** are created and initialized to contain the vectors (3,5) and (4,6). When the expression is computed inside the **operator+()** function, another vector is created to hold the result (7, 11). Then, after this result is assigned to **c**, the three unnamed objects are destroyed. Figure 8.6 illustrates the steps involved in processing this expression.

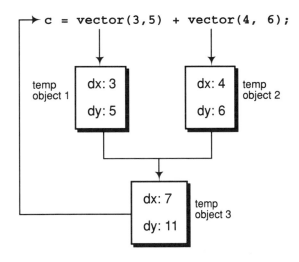

Figure 8.6. Processing the vector expression.

To see how objects are created and destroyed in the context of a program, let's write one that processes numbers. The program uses a simple **num** class that stores an integer and contains a constructor and destructor to print out messages. We've also included another trick. We will use our constructor to support user-defined conversions from **int**s to **num**s.

```
#include <stdio.h>
class num {
    int data;
public:
    num(int i) { // serves as int to num converter
      data = i;
      printf("Constructor called, value %d\n", data);
    }

    ~num() {
      printf("Destructor called, value %d\n", data);
    }

    friend num operator +(num &x, num &y);
};

num operator+(num &x, num &y)
{
    return x.data + y.data;
}

void main()
{
    num a(0);

    a = num(42) + 17;   // hint, trick is here
}
```

This program produces the following output:

```
Constructor called, value 0
Constructor called, value 17
Constructor called, value 42
Constructor called, value 59
Destructor called, value 59
Destructor called, value 17
Destructor called, value 42
Destructor called, value 59
```

The trick comes into play when we add **num(42)** to 17. Remember that function prototypes cause type conversions to be induced, if needed. Here, the number 17 was converted to type **num** before being passed to **operator+()**. Not only did a type cast take place, but an unnamed object of type **num** was also created to hold the value. Two other unnamed objects were created, one to hold **num(42)** and one to hold the result **num(59)**. All these objects were subsequently deleted when they were no longer needed.

Note the order in which the constructors and destructors were called. First, object **a** was created, and then the unnamed objects were created. The unnamed objects were deleted first, and then the object **a** was deleted. The order in which multiple unnamed objects in an expression are created and destroyed is undefined. Don't rely on it!

As shown, the technique of using constructors and destructors in combination with operator overloading can be complex, especially when dynamic objects are used.

Assignment versus Initialization

The difference between assigning values to objects and initializing objects might be unclear at this point. If we were programming in C, the distinction wouldn't be all that important. However, when using C++ we need to be aware of the difference between the two processes, especially if we are using constructors to allocate memory dynamically. Let's take a closer look.

An *assignment* occurs whenever an object that has already been created receives a value through an assignment statement. For example,

```
x = 245;
```

An *initialization*, on the other hand, occurs when an object receives a value at the time it is declared. Here's an example:

```
int x;

x = 25;             // an assignment
clock c(5, 0, 0);   // an initialization
```

Since **x** was declared before it was assigned a value, the statement that follows the declaration (**x = 25**) is an assignment. With the **clock** object **c**, however, its constructor is called at the time the object is declared, and the constructor initializes the object. The distinction is clear enough in this example, but what happens in the following case?

```
int x = 25;      // assignment or initialization?
```

This is actually an initialization. Although the statement looks like an assignment, the variable **x** receives a value at the same time that it is being declared.

Why is this important? To answer this question, consider the following **string** class:

```
#include <string.h>
class string {
public:
    char *data;
    int size;
    void copy(string &s);
    string(int sz) { data = new char[size = sz]; }
    string(string &s) { copy(s); }
    void operator=(string &s) { delete data; copy(s); }
    int len(void) { return size; }
};

void string::copy(string &s)
// make new string look just like old one
{
    data = new char[size = s.size];
    memcpy(data, s.data, size);
}
```

This class contains two types of constructors and an overloaded = operator. The first constructor is used to initialize a string of a specified size; the second is used to initialize a string with a copy of another; and the **operator=()** function is used to handle assignments. We need to pay close attention to the last two functions. The **operator=()** first de-allocates the space currently used by the string before making a copy, whereas the constructor does not. It doesn't have to, because, as a constructor, it is used when the object is first declared. Therefore, memory has not yet been assigned to it. In this case, it is critical that you understand when each function is called. The following example will help you:

```
string s(80); // string(int) constructor called
string t = s; // string(string &) constructor called
s = t;        // operator=() called
```

Take a close look at the last two statements. Although they both look like assignments, the first is in fact an initialization, and, therefore, a constructor is called when the statement executes. Remember how you can call a constructor with one argument by using what appears to be an assignment. In this case, we have two constructors with one argument. One takes an **integer** argument and the other takes a **string&** argument. In the expression **t = s, s** is a **string** and therefore the latter constructor is called.

Now that you've seen the basic differences between assignments and initializations, let's examine these issues in more detail. Initialization takes place under the following conditions:

- When an object is declared
- When an object is passed by value to a function
- When an object is passed by value in a function return statement

An assignment, on the other hand, takes place whenever the = operator is used in a statement that is otherwise not a declaration. Let's review some more examples of initialization.

When an object is passed by value to a function, the formal argument is initialized. How? It gets initialized by copying in the value of the actual argument. Essentially, the formal argument to a function constitutes a declaration, so an initialization takes place. Here's an example:

```
void print(string s)
// string s passed by value, so a copy is made
{
    int i;
    for (i = 0; i<s.len(); i++) putch(s[i]);
}
```

An object returned by a function also constitutes an initialization. In this case, the object specified by the return statement is copied into the object that is the recipient of the function return. It is important to note that no copying takes place if an argument is passed by reference or if the return value is a reference or pointer type. Here's a sample function that illustrates this point:

```
#include <ctype.h>
string uppercase(string &s)
// string argument comes in pass by reference
// no copying takes place during call
{
    int i;
    for (i = 0; i < s.len(); i++) s[i] = toupper(s[i]);
    return s; // now return copy of s after conversion
}
```

Let's look at another example. The next program contains a class with two constructors: One initializes objects with integer values and the other initializes objects with other objects of the class. We've included **printf()** statements in the constructors so you can see what's going on. We've also included a destructor with a **printf()** statement. Here's the program:

```
#include <stdio.h>
class num {
    int id;
public:
    num(int i) {
      id = i;
      printf("First constructor called: \n", id);
    }
    num(num &x) {
      id = x.id;
      printf("Second constructor called: \n",id);
    }
    ~num() { printf("Destructor called: \n", id); }
};

void do_nothing(num x)
{
    printf("Here I am inside function do_nothing\n");
    return;
}
void main()
{
    num a(1);  // first type of constructor called
    num b = a; // second type of constructor called
```

```
     do_nothing(a); // second type of constructor called
}
```

The listing below is produced when the program is run. We've annotated it with comments so you can follow the process.

```
First constructor called:      // via num a(1)
Second constructor called:     // via num b = a
Second constructor called:     // via do_nothing(a)
Here I am inside function do_nothing
Destructor called:  // cleanup for do_nothing() argument
Destructor called:  // cleanup for b
Destructor called:  // cleanup for a
```

Let's slightly modify **do_nothing()** so that we can pass in an object by reference. Note that we've also changed the **return** statement to allow us to pass back a copy of the object **x**.

```
num do_nothing(num &x)
{
  printf("Here I am inside function do_nothing\n");
  return x;
}
```

Using this modified function, the program produces

```
First constructor called:      // via num a(1)
Second constructor called:     // via num b = a
Here I am inside function do_nothing
Second constructor called:     // need copy for return arg
Destructor called:             // no longer need copy
Destructor called:             // cleanup for b
Destructor called:             // cleanup for a
```

Because the argument is now passed to **do_nothing()** by reference, the constructor was not called inside the function until the **return** statement was executed. A copy of the argument was then made in order to pass back the result. Thus, the constructor for this copy was called after the function executed its **printf()** statement.

The Different Types of Constructors

When designing classes, you should have a clear understanding of the different types of constructors available. Table 8.1 presents the four basic types of C++ constructors. This table shows the general form for each constructor. The symbol **X** represents the name of the class to which the constructor belongs, and **T** represents a class name different from **X**. The string **"a1=d1, a2=d2, ..."** represents a number of variable arguments, all of which have defaults.

Table 8.1. Constructor types

Type	General Form
Default constructor	X(void)
	X(a1=d1, a2=d2, ...)
Copy constructor	X(X&, a2=d2, ...)
	X(const X&, a2=d2, ...)
Conversion constructor	X(T, a2=d2, ...)
	X(T&, a2=d2, ...)
	X(const T, a2=d2, ...)
	X(const T&, a2=d2, ...)
General constructor	X(a1, a2, a3, ...)

Default constructors are constructors that can be called without any arguments. This means they take either no arguments or that all their arguments have defaults. Default constructors are used whenever the compiler makes constructor calls automatically, such as for each object in an array or when constructing an object consisting of other member objects (assuming you haven't explicitly called the constructors for the member objects). The compiler will generate a default constructor in the cases where they're needed and you haven't supplied one.

Here are some examples of default constructors:

```
class clock {
    long data;
```

```
public:
   clock(void) { data = 0; } // default constructor
};


// create array of three clocks, all set to zero
clock time_pieces[3]  // default constructor called 3x
class data_obj {
   int data1, data2;
public:
   data_obj(int d1 = 42, int d2=17) { // default
     data1 = d1, data2 = d2;
   }
};


// create a data_obj, defaulting to values of (42,17):
data_obj my_obj;
```

Copy constructors are constructors that are used to copy objects. A copy constructor must be callable by passing a single argument. This argument must be of the same class to which the constructor belongs and it must be passed by reference. If other arguments are present, they must all have defaults. Here are some examples:

```
class clock {
   long data;
public:
   clock(clock &c) { data = c.data; } // copy constructor
};

class string {
   char *data;
   int size, expandable;
public:
   string(void);                      // default constructor
   string(string &s, int e = 0) { // copy constructor
     data = new char[size=strlen(s.data)+1];
     strcpy(data, s.data);
     expandable = e;
   };
};
```

Note: You can use a copy constructor of the form **X(X&)**. However, a constructor of the form **X(X)**, where the argument is passed by value, is not allowed. Such a constructor would cause infinite recursion when called.

You can use copy constructors explicitly, as in the following code:

```
string my_string;
...
string your_string(my_string);
```

However, copy constructors are also called implicitly. For instance, whenever you pass an object by value, a copy constructor is called.

```
void print_str(string s)
{
    // print out the string
}
string s;
...
print_str(s); // copy constructor called to make copy of s
```

Copy constructors are also called when you return an object from a function by value, as in

```
string upper_case(string s)
{
    // convert to upper case
    return s; // copy constructor called
}
string s, t;
...
t = upper_case(s);
```

Conversion constructors are constructors that are callable with a single argument. Unlike copy constructors, this argument must be of a different class than that of the constructor. The argument can be passed by reference or by value. If other arguments are present, they must all have defaults. You've seen conversion constructors in the previous chapter. To refresh your memory, the following class has a conversion constructor that converts a **double** to a **clock** object:

```
class clock {
    long data;
public:
    clock(long d) { data = d; } // conversion constructor
};
```

Another example of a conversion constructor is illustrated by the following **circular_num** class. A **circular_num** object has a value that always stays in a certain upper and lower bound, wrapping around if necessary. Here, we've provided a conversion constructor that takes an ordinary integer and converts it to a **circular_num** object, where the range can be defaulted to (0,9).

```
class circular_num {
    int value, upper, lower;
public:
    circular_num(int v, int l = 0, int u = 9);
    ...
};
```

General constructors are constructors that don't meet the requirements of the other special constructors. We give an example here, once again from the **clock** class:

```
class clock {
    long data;
public:
    clock(int hr, int min, int sec);
};
clock early_alarm(5, 30, 0);
```

A Canonical Form for Classes

When designing classes, there are some general rules you should follow to make your classes as robust as possible. This is particularly true with classes that utilize dynamic memory, as you'll see in this section. You should consider including five types of member functions in your classes: general constructors, default constructors, copy constructors, overloaded assignment operators, and virtual destructors. Table 8.2 lists these functions and summarizes their usage.

Table 8.2. The five important types of class member functions

Function	Reason for Including
General constructor	For general creation and initialization of the object
Default constructor	For implicit initialization of the object, such as when it's included in an array
Copy constructor	To allow objects to be copied during creation
Overloaded assignment	To allow safe assignments between objects
Virtual destructor	To destroy the objects in a safe manner

The **image** class declaration shown here includes an example of each type of member function. (We'll be building this class piece by piece in the following discussion.)

```
class image { // two-dimensional image class
    int wd, ht;
    char *data;
public:
    image(int w, int h);      // general constructor
    image(void);              // default constructor
    image(const image &i);    // copy constructor
    image &operator=(const image &i);  // overloaded
                                        // assignment
    virtual ~image(void);      // virtual destructor
    // other functions go here
};
```

Let's now take a closer look at why you should use these function types in your classes.

Using General Constructors

Almost every non-trivial class will have at least one general constructor that creates objects for the class. Our **image** class has such a constructor, which creates an **image** object and assigns it a size.

```
image::image(int w, int h)
{
    data = new char[(wd = w)*(ht = h)*sizeof(char)];
}
...
image big_picture(1024, 1024);
```

Using Default Constructors

Default constructors are useful for initializing an object to a default state. For instance, you might have "counter" objects that should start out with their sums set to zero.

A default constructor is also useful if you wish to declare arrays of objects. In this case, the default constructor is called for each object when the array is created. As an example, our **image** class has a default constructor that creates images of 128 x 128 pixels.

```
image::image(void)
{
    data = new char[(wd=128)*(ht=128)*sizeof(char)];
}

image gallery[5]; // creates array of five 128x128 images
```

Using Overloaded Assignment Operators

The reasons for using general and default constructors are fairly obvious. However, the reasons for using overloaded assignments, copy constructors, and virtual destructors are not as obvious. These functions are typically used to help manage dynamic memory. Let's take a closer look.

In our **image** class, we store the two-dimensional image data in a one-dimensional array that's allocated on the heap. The general and default constructors perform the memory allocation. We can also define a destructor which de-allocates the **image** data. Here's what the class looks like so far:

```
// image.h: Header file for the class
class image {
    int wd, ht;
    char *data;
public:
    image(int w, int h);
    image(void);
    ~image(void);
    // Other functions go here
};

// image.cpp: Implementation file for the class
image::image(int w, int h)
{
    data = new char[(wd=w)*(ht=h)];
}

image::image(void)
{
    data = new char[(wd=128)*(ht=128)];
}

image::~image(void)
{
    delete[] data;
}
```

Unfortunately, we'll encounter problems if we try to use the class as coded. As we mentioned in the last chapter, we can't use an object in an assignment statement if the object contains pointers. The following program shows what happens if we use an **image** object in an assignment:

```
#include "image.h"
void main()
{
    image nature_scene(128, 128); // allocates 16K
    image art_painting(128, 128); // allocates 16K
```

```
        art_painting = nature_scene;   // pointer copied only!

        // destructors called here, bad news!
}
```

When the images are created, memory is allocated for them on the heap. When we try to assign **art_painting** to **nature_scene**, only the pointer to **art_painting**'s data is copied, as shown in Figure 8.7. The 16K of data originally allocated for **nature_scene** is left dangling, with no reference to it. When the program finishes, the destructors for both **art_painting** and **nature_scene** are called. The data gets de-allocated twice because the objects point to the same data; the result is a mangled heap.

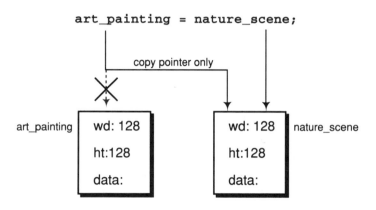

Figure 8.7. Assigning objects with pointers.

We can fix this problem partially by overloading the assignment operator, and ensuring that the entire **image** data gets copied.

```
#include <string.h>
class image {
    int wd, ht;
    char *data;
public:
    image(int w, int h);
    ~image(void);
    image &operator=(const image &i); // overloaded
                                       // assignment
    ... // other functions
```

```
};

image &operator=(const image &i)
// copies one image into another, maintaining the
// heap properly
{
    if (this != &i) { // trap for assignments to self
        if (wd != i.wd && ht != i.ht) {
            // don't reallocate unless you have to
            delete data;
            data = new char[(wd = i.wd)*(ht = i.ht)];
        }
        memcpy(data, i.data, wd*ht*sizeof(char));
    }
    return *this; // return reference to self
}
```

The assignment works by freeing the old **image** data from the heap. It then allocates new storage and copies the incoming **image** data. We don't need to re-allocate memory if the objects are the same size; only the copy operation is performed.

Our assignment operator introduces three special features of which you should be aware. First, note how we test to see if an object is being assigned to itself:

```
if (this != &i) { // trap assignment to self
```

This test is performed by checking to see if the addresses of the source and target objects are the same. The special pointer (**this**) is used to determine the appropriate address for the target object. Although the source object **i** is a reference variable, we must still obtain its address with the expression **&i**.

Note: A reference variable is just a name of an object, and like any object, its address must be obtained in order to assign a pointer to it.

Why should we test that an object isn't being assigned to itself? We don't want to accidently de-allocate its memory and then try to copy its data to newly allocated memory. In general, your assignment operator functions should provide a similar test.

The second feature of our assignment operator function is that it returns a reference to the target object. As mentioned in the last chapter, this allows us to chain assignments together.

```
photograph = art_painting = nature_scene;
```

Finally, the third feature is that we pass in the source **image** by reference and as a constant. This makes the assignment more efficient, and it tells the compiler that we don't plan on modifying the source object.

You should design your assignment operator functions with these three features in mind.

Using Copy Constructors

Our class is almost complete. What's missing? We need a way to handle **images** that are to be created and initialized using another **image** as a model. A copy constructor will do this nicely:

```
image::image(const image &i)
{
    data = new char[(wd = i.wd)*(ht = i.ht)];
    memcpy(data, i.data, wd*ht*sizeof(char));
}
```

Note that our copy constructor is similar to the assignment operator function because it allocates memory for the image and then copies in the source object. The difference here is that we don't have to worry about deleting the old image data because it doesn't exist. As with the assignment operator function, we pass in the source object as a constant reference.

Using our copy constructor, we can write code like the following:

```
image nature_scene(128, 128);  // general constructor called

image art_painting = nature_scene; // copy constructor
```

The last statement we presented is a declaration, as opposed to an assignment such as

```
art_painting = nature_scene;   // Assignment operator
                               // function called
```

Again, you can see why it's critical to understand the difference between initialization and assignment.

Using Virtual Destructors

We can make one more improvement to our **image** class that is related to inheritance and derived classes. (You'll learn more about inheritance in the next chapter, but you should know enough now to follow this discussion.) Notice that we've defined the destructor for the **image** class to be non-virtual.

```
class image {
    ...
    image::~image(void) { delete[] data; }
};
```

However, we should make it virtual, as you'll soon discover.

```
class image {
    ...
    virtual image::~image(void) { delete[] data; }
};
```

To see why, let's derive a new type of **image** class that also has height information for each pixel. To store this information, we'll use a parallel array that we add to the derived class. (We won't show the complete class.) Here's one of the constructors and the destructor:

```
class contour_image : public image { // derived class
    char *z_buffer; // buffer to hold height data
public:
    contour_image(int w, int h); // new constructor
    ~contour_image(void);
    ...
};
```

```
contour_image::contour_image(int w, int h)
: image(w, h) // calls base class constructor
// now, allocate z_buffer
{
    z_buffer = new char[wd * ht * sizeof(char)];
}

contour_image::~contour_image(void)
// delete the additional buffer. Note that the
// base class constructor is called automatically to
// delete the image data itself
{
    delete[] z_buffer;
}
```

Don't worry if you don't understand just how the new constructor and destructor work yet. These details will be explained in the next chapter. Our derived class constructor not only allocates the additional height data (which we've called **z_buffer**), but it automatically calls the base class constructor to allocate the **image** data itself. Also, the derived class destructor not only de-allocates **z_buffer**, but it calls the base class destructor to de-allocate the **image** data as well.

With this new class, we can write code such as

```
contour_image *mountain_map = new contour_image(256, 256);
...
delete mountain_map; // ~contour_image() destructor called
```

There's a problem that can occur, however. Recall how we can point to a derived class object with a base class pointer, as in

```
image *mountain_map = new contour_image(256, 256);
```

Notice how we declared **mountain_map** to be an **image** pointer instead of a **contour_image** pointer, even though we're pointing to a **contour_image** object. This works fine, except when it comes time to delete **mountain_map**:

```
delete mountain_map; // ~image() destructor called here
```

If we don't make the **~image**() destructor virtual, then in the **delete** statement, the **~image**() destructor is called, even though we're pointing to a **contour_image**. As a result, the additional **z_buffer** that was allocated won't get de-allocated. If we make **~image**() virtual, then, when the **mountain_map** is deleted, the **~contour_image**() destructor will be called, as it should. As you can see, you should make your destructors virtual if you are designing a general class.

Other Considerations

In our **image** class example, we copied the **image** data every time an object was initialized or assigned. Remember that the copying also takes place (using the copy constructor) whenever we pass an object by value to or from a function. You can see that a lot of copying can take place, which isn't very efficient.

There are ways around this, but they are beyond the scope of this book. Just for the record, one popular approach is to use reference count schemes. With this scheme, only one copy of each object is kept, whenever possible. If an object is assigned to another object, then instead of a copy taking place, a reference counter is incremented. When the new object is destroyed, the reference counter for the original is decremented. Whenever the reference count goes to zero, the original object can be safely destroyed.

Summary

This completes our in-depth look at constructors and destructors. We started by learning how to declare constructors and destructors for simple objects, and then we learned how to use these devices to initialize objects. You'll need some practice before you learn how to use these new C++ features, because they are different from anything C has to offer.

Exercises

1. Explain why you can't use an initialization list for objects defined from the following class:

```
class employee {
    int age;
    int jobcode;
public:
    char *name;
};
```

To get around this problem, give an example of a constructor that you might write for this class.

2. Given the following class definition:

```
class rect {
    int width, height;
public:
    rect(int w=10, int h=15) { width = w; height = h; }
};
```

show all the possible ways that the constructor can be called.

3. How many times is the constructor for **list_of_nums** called? How many times is the destructor called? Do you get a null pointer assignment? How can you fix the problem?

```
#include <stdio.h>
class list_of_nums {
    int size, *data, cursor;
public:
    list_of_nums(int s) {
      cursor = 0;
      data = new int[size = s];
      printf("Constructor\n");
    }
    ~list_of_nums(void) { delete[] data;
      printf("Destructor\n"); }
    void store(int i)   { data[cursor++] = i; }
    friend int average(list_of_nums l);
};

int average(list_of_nums l)
```

```
    {
        int i, s;
        for (i = 0, s = 0; i < l.cursor; i++) {
          s += l.data[i];
        }
        return s / l.cursor;
    }

    void main()
    {
        list_of_nums scores(10);

        printf("Ready to store\n");
        scores.store(3); scores.store(6);
        printf("Ready for average\n");
        printf("Average score is %d\n", average(scores));
    }
```

4. What are three major problems with the following program?

```
    #include <stdlib.h>
    class image {
        int wd, ht;
        char *data;
    public:
        image(int w, int h) {
          data = new char[wd*ht];
        }
        ~image(void) { delete data; }
    };

    void main()
    {
        image *screen1 = new image(12, 15);
        free(screen1);
    }
```

5. How many times is the **printf** statement called in the following program? Is it the correct number of times?

```
#include <stdio.h>
struct point {
    int x, y;
    point(void) { x = 0; y = 0; }
    point(int a, int b) { x = a; y = b; }
    ~point(void) { printf("Destructor called\n"); }
};

void main()
{
    point *coordinates = new point[5];
    delete coordinates;
}
```

How would you fix this problem?

6. In exercise 5, why did we need a constructor without arguments?

Inheritance and Class Hierarchies

In previous chapters we presented the basic building blocks of C++, including classes, objects, functions, and overloaded operators. However, we haven't covered one important piece of the object-oriented programming puzzle yet—*inheritance*. Inheritance is the feature that sets object-oriented programming apart from traditional programming because it allows us to extend and reuse existing code without having to rewrite the code.

We'll start our discussion by reviewing the basic principles of inheritance that we introduced in earlier chapters. After the review, we'll explore the mechanics of inheritance. Next, we'll present more complex examples of inheritance and we'll discuss some advanced techniques, including abstract classes, dynamic inheritance, and multiple inheritance.

Here are some of the other highlights:

- How to write reusable code
- Techniques for deriving classes
- How to write a general purpose file compression program
- How to define and use polymorphic objects

A Quick Look at Inheritance

Inheritance is at work all around you. For example, consider the way children share their parents' physical traits. Although children resemble their parents, they are also different. The inheritance process shows that some traits are shared and others become changed.

Inheritance is a useful and natural technique for organizing programs. As an example, consider a pop-up menu. Such a menu has much in common with a user-interface window. A pop-up menu has a rectangular border, a cursor or input selector, a position on the screen, and so on. You could say that a pop-up menu is a special type of window, because it inherits its basic attributes from a window.

In C++, inheritance is accomplished by taking a class (known as a *base class*) and *deriving* new classes from it. Each *derived class* inherits the members of the *base class* (including data and functions). The derived class can also modify or add to the base members. This process can continue so that a derived class can also serve as a base class from which other derived classes are defined. Thus, we can build up class hierarchies, where each class can serve as a parent or root for a new set of classes. Figure 9.1 presents an example of a class hierarchy.

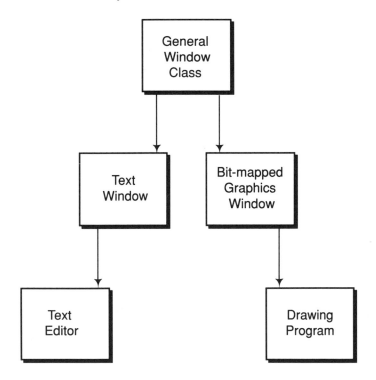

Figure 9.1. A class hierarchy.

> **Note:** Base classes are sometimes called *parent classes* or *super classes*. Also, derived classes are sometimes called *child classes* or *subclasses*.

Inheritance can be used to help write reusable code and to represent the relationships between types and subtypes (classes and subclasses). These two uses of inheritance are often intertwined, as you'll see next.

Writing Reusable Code

We'll now create a simple class called **sigma** and then we'll reuse (extend) it. The **sigma** class is used to create objects that keep a running total of numbers:

```
#include <stdio.h>
class sigma { // sums up numbers
public:
    float sum;
    sigma(void)                { sum = 0.0; }
    virtual void input(float d) { sum += d; }
    virtual void display(void) {
       printf("The sum is: %5.2f\n", sum);
    }
};

void main()
{
    sigma x;

    x.input(17.0); // feed in some numbers to be summed
    x.input(25.0);
    x.display();   // display the sum
}
```

This program produces the following output:

```
The sum is: 42.00
```

Now, suppose a statistician wanted to use the program to calculate the *average* of a set of numbers. Instead of rewriting the program, you could use inheritance to make these changes. The following program shows how this is done:

```
// This portion of the code stays the same
#include <stdio.h>
class sigma { // sums up numbers
public:
    float sum;
    sigma(void)                        { sum = 0.0; }
    virtual void input(float d)     { sum += d; }
    virtual void display(void) {
        printf("The sum is: %5.2f\n", sum);
    }
};

// additional code to extend the sigma class
class mu : public sigma { // finds average as well
public:
    int n;
    mu(void) { n = 0; }
    virtual void input(float d);
    virtual void display(void);
};

void mu::input(float d)
{
    sigma::input(d); // reuse existing code
    n++;             // add to it
}

void mu::display(void)
{
    sigma::display(); // reuse existing code
    // Add to the code
    float avg = n ? sum / n : 0;
    printf("The average is: %5.2f\n", avg);
}

// A slightly modified main program
void main()
```

MSVC·GRP

```
{
    mu x; // use derived object instead

    x.input(17.0); // feed in some numbers to be summed
    x.input(25.0);
    x.display();    // display the sum and average
}
```

When you run the program, you'll see the following results:

```
The sum is: 42.00
The average is: 21.00
```

The program was easy to modify because we only needed to add a new class, **mu**. This class inherits the members of the **sigma** class. We achieved this by deriving **mu** from **sigma**. Figure 9.2 highlights the syntax used for this derivation. (You may want to go back and review Chapter 3 if you forgot how this syntax works.)

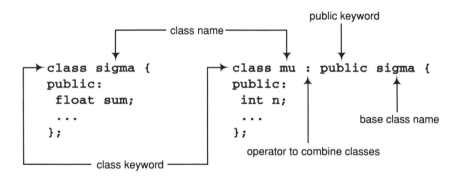

Figure 9.2. The components of the mu and sigma classes.

The class **mu** inherits all of **sigma**'s attributes, including the members **sum**, **sigma::input()**, and **sigma::display()**. Recall that a derived class can add both data and functions to the base class. The **mu** class adds the members **n**, **mu::input()**, and **mu::display()**. Figure 9.3 illustrates this inheritance.

Note: In C++, inheritance can only be used to add features to a base class; you can't use inheritance to remove members.

mu class

```
int n;
mu();
input();
display();
```

sigma class

```
float sum;
sigma();
input();
display();
```

Figure 9.3. The mu class derived from sigma.

Note that **mu** has two functions named **input()**, and two named **display()**. These two sets of functions were declared virtual. Therefore, **mu**'s versions of **input()** and **display()** override **sigma**'s versions. But notice how **mu**'s versions chain back to **sigma**'s as the **mu::input()** function.

```
void mu::input(float d)
{
    sigma::input(d); // reuse existing code
    n++;             // add to it
}
```

This chaining technique allows us to write reusable code. We have also used this technique with the **mu::display()** function.

```
void mu::display(void)
{
    sigma::display(); // reuse existing code
    // Add to the code
    float avg = n ? sum / n : 0;
    printf("The average is %5.2f\n", avg);
}
```

The code we reused in this example was short and simple, and therefore inheritance wasn't absolutely necessary. However, in "industrial strength" applications, a substantial amount of code might be reused.

When you write reusable code using inheritance, you are actually *extending* the code, while leaving the original code intact. This process of extending code sets object-oriented programming apart from traditional programming.

Inheritance and Subtypes

Inheritance is also useful for expressing *type* and *subtype* relationships. For instance, a pop-up menu can be considered a subtype of a more general window type. Another example is the relationship between a rectangle and a square. A square is a special type of rectangle whose sides have equal lengths.

You can use a subtype wherever a more general type is used, as the following program illustrates. It defines a rectangle–square class hierarchy and then provides an **area()** function for both rectangles and squares.

```
#include <stdio.h>
class rectangle {
public:
    float wd, ht;
    void init(float w, float h) { wd = w; ht = h; }
};

class square : public rectangle {
public:
    void init(float sz) { wd = ht = sz; }
};

float area(rectangle &r)
{
    return r.wd * r.ht;
}

void main()
{
    rectangle r;
    square s;

    r.init(3, 5);
    s.init(7);
```

```
        printf("Area of rectangle is %5.2f\n", area(r));
        printf("Area of square is %5.2f\n", area(s));
    }
```

This program outputs the following:

```
Area of rectangle is 15.00
Area of square is 49.00
```

This program shows an excellent example of how types and subtypes are intertwined with the technique of reusing code. The **area()** function is shared with rectangles and squares. Recall how a base class pointer or reference can reference a derived class object. Here, **area()** takes a reference to a base class **rectangle** object and, thus, can also work with a derived class **square** object. The function works with both types because **square** is a subtype of **rectangle**.

Details on Using Inheritance

Now that we've explored the basics of inheritance, we'll cover some of the mechanics involved in using inheritance. In particular, you'll learn what's inside a derived class, how to handle duplicate member names, how to use constructors and destructors in derived classes, and how to incorporate information hiding into your class hierarchies. You'll also learn more about the type–subtype relationship between base and derived classes and how this relationship relates to typecasting.

What's inside a Derived Class?

You may be a little confused about which members are in a derived class. This confusion occurs because only the new members are specified when a derived class is declared. If you get confused, just remember this simple rule: *A derived class has all the members of the base class, plus additional ones.* Even if you override a base class function with a derived class version, the base class function is still there. As we saw with our **mu** and **sigma** classes, you can still access the base class function using the scoping operator.

When you use virtual functions, one more hidden member in each class of the hierarchy is present. This member is a pointer to a table of function pointers that handle virtual functions. Each object declared from a class with one or more virtual functions has a virtual function table pointer, and there is one virtual function table for each class. The virtual function table is stored separately from the objects. Figure 9.4 shows a translation from C++ to C for a sample class derivation.

C	C++
| ```c
typedef struct {
  int x,y,radius;
  int (**vptr)();
} circle;

void circle_draw(void);

/* virtual function table */
int (*circle_vtbl[1])() =
{
  (int(*)())circle_draw;
};
typedef struct {
  int circle_x,circle_y;
  int circle_radius;
  int ht;
  int (**vptr)();
} cylinder;

void cylinder_draw(void);

/* virtual function table */
int (*cylinder_vtbl[1])() =
{
  (int(*)())cylinder_draw;
};
``` | ```cpp
class circle {
public:
  int x,y,radius;
  virtual void draw(void);
};

void circle::draw(void);




class cylinder:public circle {
public:
  int ht;
  void draw(void);
};


void cylinder::draw(void);
``` |

Figure 9.4. Translation box for class derivations.

Duplicate Data Member Names

With the **mu** and **sigma** classes, you saw how a base and derived class can have functions with the same name. You also saw how the scoping operator **::** and the properties of virtual functions are used to differentiate between the functions. But what about data? Can a data member be declared in the derived class with the same name as the one in the base class? Yes, although it's probably not desirable. Let's explore an example. The following code shows that **radius** is declared in both the **circle** and **cylinder** classes:

```
class circle {
public:
    float x, y, radius;
};


class cylinder : public circle {
    float ht;
    float radius; // Oops! duplicate member name
};
```

If we were to translate the **cylinder** class into C, it might look like the following:

```
typedef struct {
    float x, y, radius;
    float ht;
    float cylinder_radius
};
```

Note how both **radius** members are in the **cylinder** class, but that, internally, they must have different names. Here, we've arbitrarily assigned the new **radius** member in the **cylinder** class a prefix of **cylinder_**.

Returning to the **circle** and **cylinder** classes, how can we differentiate between the two **radius** members? We'll use the scoping operator just as we would for member functions with the same name. The following statements illustrate how both **radius** members are accessed:

```
cylinder beer_can;
beer_can.radius = 2.5;        // cylinder's version
beer_can.cylinder::radius = 25; // also cylinder's version
beer_can.circle::radius = 3.5;   // circle's version
```

You shouldn't define data members with the same name as we've done. However, sometimes it is unavoidable. When we cover multiple inheritance later on, you'll see that duplicate member names can be quite common.

Once Virtual, Always Virtual

In our **mu** and **sigma** classes, we made **input()** and **display()** virtual, and we used the **virtual** keyword in both the base and derived classes. The **virtual** keyword was not necessary in the **mu** class. Why? Once a function is declared virtual in a base class, it remains virtual for all subsequent derived classes. We can rewrite the **mu** class as follows:

```
class mu : public sigma {
public:
    int n;
    mu(void) { n = 0; }
    void input(float d); // virtual even without the keyword
    void display(void);  // virtual even without the keyword
}
```

Although the **virtual** keyword is optional in such cases, you may want to include it. You'll then know which functions are virtual without having to examine the base class declaration.

One-Way Typecasting

You've learned that a base class pointer can point to a derived class object, even without explicit typecasting. For example:

```
class circle {
public:
    float radius;
};

class cylinder : public circle {
public:
    float height;
};

float circumference(circle *c)
{
    return 6.28 * c->radius;
}
```

```
cylinder piston;
...
float c = circumference(&piston);
```

Here, a pointer to a **cylinder** object is passed to **circumference()**, although this function expects a pointer to a **circle**. No explicit typecast is needed to convert the **cylinder** pointer to a **circle** pointer, because **circle** is **cylinder**'s base. We can use an explicit typecast if we want to.

```
float c = circumference((circle *)&piston); // legal
```

Can we change the typecasting from **circle** to **cylinder**? That is, can we switch from a base class to a derived class? To find out, consider the following function that computes the volume of a **cylinder**:

```
float volume(cylinder *c)
{
    return 3.14 * c->radius * c->radius * c->height;
}
```

What happens if we try to pass a **circle** object to this function? Note that we need to use a typecast, since we're going the wrong direction—from a base class to a derived class.

```
circle ring;
...
float v = volume((cylinder *)&ring); // advisable typecast?
```

Will the call to **volume()** produce meaningful results? No. The **volume()** function accesses not only the **radius** of its input object, but the **height** as well. Unfortunately, **circle**s don't have a height. Thus, we're accessing a member that isn't there. Figure 9.5 illustrates this point. We see that our typecasting is like a street in downtown San Francisco—it only works one way.

Because derived class objects inherit the members of the base class, and can have possibly more members, they are guaranteed to work wherever a base class object works. This is a fortunate result, because it means that any function utilizing a base class object can just as easily utilize a derived class object. We can reuse the function for different object types. This is another example of the power of inheritance in writing reusable code.

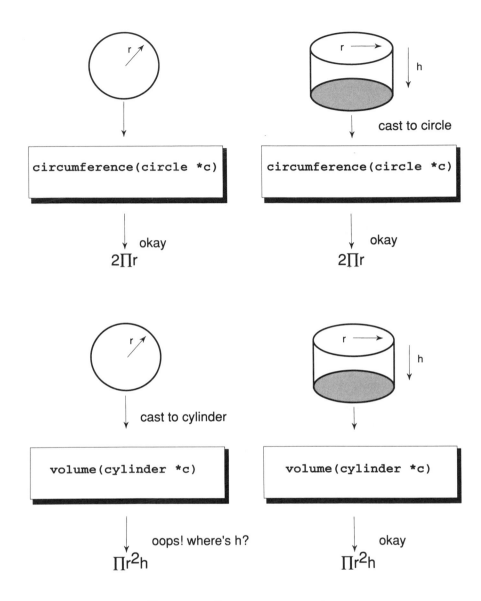

Figure 9.5. One way type casting.

Using Information Hiding

Up to this point, we've been ignoring the issue of hiding class members in derived classes. In this section, we'll show you how to incorporate information hiding into a class hierarchy.

Whenever we derived a class in our previous examples, we used the following syntax:

```
class base { ... };

class derived : public base {
   // ...
};
```

The **public** keyword is used to control how the base class members are treated. In this case, we are saying: *Treat all public members of the base class as being public in the derived class*. The derived class is said to use the base class as a *public base class*. The base class can also be treated as private, by using the **private** keyword.

```
class base { ... };

class derived : private base {
   // ...
};
```

With private base classes, all of the base class members are treated as being private in the derived class, even if some of the members were public in the base class.

When a public base class is used, only the public members of the base class are public in the derived class. The private members stay private. The private members cannot be accessed by the derived class. As an example, consider the following base and derived classes:

```
class cia {
private:
   char *secret_document;
};

class informant : public cia { // public base class
public:
   void leak_to_press(void) {
      printf("%s\n", secret_document); // illegal
   }
};
```

Here, **secret_document** is private to the **cia** class and cannot be used by any other class. Even the derived class **informant**, which uses **cia** as a public base class cannot access **secret_document**. If information hiding didn't work in this manner, you could easily derive a class, such as **informant**, to make private members of the base class public.

You can omit the **public** or **private** keyword when deriving a class. The manner in which the base class is declared determines if it becomes public or private in a derived class. If the base class is declared with the **class** keyword, then it becomes a private base class in a derived class by default. On the other hand, if the base class is declared with the **struct** keyword, it becomes a public base class. That is, we have the following equivalencies:

```
class base_c  { ... };
struct base_s { ... };

class derived_c: base_c <=> class derived_c: private base_c
class derived_c: base_s <=> class derived_c: public base_s

struct derived_s: base_c <=> struct derived_s: private base_c
struct derived_s: base_s <=> struct derived_s: public base_s
```

Fine Tuning Information Hiding

We've used information hiding to make a class public or private. We can also specify which public members of the base class we want to become public in a derived class. To do this, first make the base class private, and then declare the members you would like to make public in the derived class. The members must be declared in the public section of the derived class. Here is the general format:

```
class derived : private base {
    // ...
public:
    base::a_member_of_base;       // now public
    base::another_member_of_base; // also public
    // ...
};
```

The base class member being made public is qualified with the base class name. Note that you leave off all type information for the member—only the name is provided. If the member is a function, you specify only the function name, not its prototype. If you are making an overloaded function public, all functions of that name become public.

Let's apply this syntax to derive a class with selected public members:

```
class square {
public:
    int wd, ht;
    int girth(void) { return wd+ht; }
};

class box3d : private square {
    int depth; // additional member
public:
    square::girth; // base function made public
                   // but wd and ht remain private
};
```

Note: You cannot make a private member of a base class public in a derived class.

Protected Members

You've learned that private members of a base class are not accessible to a derived class. In some situations, you may want a derived class to use the private members of its base class. The distinction between *public* and *private* is too coarse for these situations. Fortunately, C++ provides the **protected** keyword to allow a derived class better access to base class members. A *protected member* can be accessed in a base class and its derived classes. The member is private to all other classes.

Let's return to our **sigma** and **mu** classes to see how protected members can be used. Previously, we made the members public to simplify the code. To follow good design practices, we don't want the **sigma** member **sum** to be public. We would also like the derived **mu** class to access **sum** directly. The solution is to make **sum** a protected member, as shown:

```
class sigma { // sums up numbers
protected:     // note protected keyword
    float sum;
public:
    void sigma(void);
    virtual void input(float d);
    virtual void display(void);
};

class mu : public sigma { // finds average as well
protected:
    int n; // make this protected too
public:
    mu(void) { n = 0; }
    virtual void input(float d);
    virtual void display(void);
}
```

Now, the **mu::display()** function can access **sum** directly in its calculations. The **sum** member remains hidden to all outsiders.

```
void mu::display(void)
{
    sigma::display();
    // Add to the code
    float avg = n ? sum / n : 0; // accessing protected member
    printf("The average is: %5.2f\n", avg);
}
```

Notice that we made the additional data member **n** in our **mu** class protected as well. If we decide to derive a class from **mu**, the derived class will be able to access **n**.

Using Constructors and Destructors in Derived Classes

We explored constructors and destructors in detail in Chapter 8. However, we didn't explain how these special member functions are used with derived classes. There are two important rules related to using constructors and destructors with derived classes:

- When a derived class object constructor is called, it, in turn, must call one of the base class constructors. This call takes place before the body of the derived class constructor executes.

- When a derived class object destructor is called, it, in turn, must call the base class destructor. This call takes place after the derived class destructor body executes.

Note: The rules for calling base class constructors and destructors are analogous to those used in calling the constructors and destructors of nested objects.

Let's take a closer look at the first rule. If a base class doesn't have a constructor, or if it has a default constructor—a constructor that can be called without any explicit arguments—the compiler will make sure the constructor is called. An example of this can be seen with our **sigma–mu** class hierarchy. Note how **sigma** has a default constructor. The **mu** class does not explicitly call this constructor.

```
class sigma {
public:
    float sum;
    void sigma(void) { sum = 0.0; }
    // ...
};

class mu : public sigma {
public:
    int n;
    mu(void) { n = 0; } // implicit call to sigma()
    // ...
}
```

The **mu()** constructor calls the **sigma()** constructor, although you can't tell. This call takes place before the body of **mu()** executes. Therefore, **sum** is set to zero before **n** is. This ordering can be very important; in many cases it makes sense for the base class data to have been initialized before any of the derived class data.

What happens when the base class doesn't have a default constructor? Then, an explicit call must be made to the base class constructor by the derived class constructor. The call is made using the same syntax that we used to call a constructor in a nested object. In this case, the **:** operator plays a significant role.

```
class derived : public base {
    // ...
    derived(<args>) // derived class constructor
    : base(<some other args>) // call base class constructor
    {
        // body of derived constructor
    }
    // ...
};
```

As an example, let's take our **rectangle** and **square** classes from an earlier example and assign them constructors. While we're at it, we'll rewrite the classes to use proper information hiding.

```
class rectangle {
protected:
    float wd, ht;
public:
    rectangle(float w, float h) { wd = w; ht = h; }
};

class square : public rectangle {
public:
    square(float sz)
    : rectangle(sz, sz)
    {
        // nothing else to do
    }
};
```

Take a close look at the **square**() constructor. It calls the **rectangle**() constructor using the **:** syntax before the constructor body. The call to the base class constructor appears before the derived class constructor body because of the order in which the constructors are called. In this case, our derived class constructor has no statements because it only calls the base class constructor.

The **square** class is an example of a special type of derived class called an *interface class*. An interface class provides a special interface to a more general base class. In this case, a **square** is a special type of **rectangle** with equal sides, as enforced by the **square**() constructor. As is often the case with a well-designed interface class, the **square** class does not actually generate any code. Its only member function, the constructor, could easily be an inline function. In many interface classes, the member functions tend to be inline function calls back to the base class. (You'll see more examples of interface classes in Chapter 11 when we discuss parameterized types.)

Since a base class constructor call uses the same syntax as a nested object constructor call, you might wonder what happens if a derived class has a nested object that needs a constructor call. Which constructor gets called first? As it turns out, the base class constructor is called first, then the constructors for any nested objects, followed by the derived class constructor body.

So far, we haven't mentioned anything about destructors. They work as follows: The body of a derived class destructor is always executed first, and then the destructors of any nested objects are called, followed by a call to the base class destructor. That is, the destructors are called in the reverse order in which constructors are called. Since destructors don't have arguments, the nested object and base class constructors are called for you automatically by the compiler.

No Virtual Constructors Allowed

Constructors can't be virtual. The reason is that at the time a derived class constructor is called, the virtual function table pointer stored in the object hasn't been linked up to the table. A constructor should also never call a virtual function.

Calling a virtual function in a base class constructor always results in the base class version of the function being used, regardless if the function was overridden in a derived class. This is true even if it's a derived class constructor that is causing the base class constructor to be called.

An example of this problem is shown in the following program:

```
#include <stdio.h>
class cursor {
```

```
    protected:
        int x, y;
        virtual void init(int xi, int yi) {
           printf("Base init() called\n");
           x = xi; y = yi;
        }
    public:
        cursor(int xi, int yi) { init(xi, yi); }
    };

    class blinking_cursor : public cursor {
    protected:
        void start_blinking(void) {
           // some function to turn blinking on
        }
        virtual void init(int xi, int yi) {
           printf("Derived init() called\n");
           x = xi; y = yi;
           start_blinking();
        }
    public:
        blinking_cursor(int xi, int yi) : cursor(xi, yi) { ; }
    };

    void main()
    {
        blinking_cursor(3, 4);
    }
```

The **cursor** constructor calls the virtual function **init()** to set up the **x** and **y** coordinates. Then, we try to override this function in **blinking_cursor** so that we can also start the **cursor** blinking when the **blinking_cursor** constructor is called. Although this may seem like a clever strategy, it fails miserably. Note what happens when the program runs:

```
Base init() called
```

Since the virtual function table hasn't been set up at the time of the constructor call, the base class constructor only knows about its own functions, and not about any possible overrides in a derived class.

There is a way to get around this type of problem. The strategy is to leave out the **init()** function in **blinking_cursor** and, instead, have the constructor start the blinking directly:

```
class blinking_cursor : public cursor {
protected:
    void start_blinking(void) {
      // some function to turn on blinking
    }
public:
    blinking_cursor(int xi, int yi)
    : cursor(xi, yi) // call base class
    {
        start_blinking(); // turn on blinking
    }
};
```

You'll notice that this new version of **blinking_cursor** is actually smaller and less complicated than the first version, lending credence to the fact that this new version uses the correct technique That notwithstanding, there are cases where having a virtual constructor can be useful. Fortunately, you can simulate virtual constructors to some degree, as you will learn later in this chapter.

Using Virtual Destructors

As you learned in the previous chapter, destructors can be virtual. In any non-trivial class, you should probably make them virtual. This will ensure that the appropriate destructor is called whenever you delete a base class pointer that points to a derived class object.

Creating Class Hierarchies

The class hierarchies we have shown have been quite simple. Our goal was to explain the mechanics of using inheritance without getting bogged down in the details. It's time to see a more realistic example and to learn how to build well-designed class hierarchies.

Suppose you wanted to create some classes to represent gauges found on instrument panels. There are all types of gauges: digital, analog, linear scale, logarithmic scale, and so on. The challenge is to create a class hierarchy for these different types of gauges. The hierarchy should model the relationships among the different gauges in a natural way. This approach will allow us to share as much code as possible.

The first step in creating a hierarchy is to define the different object types to be represented in the hierarchy. We'll also need to identify the common attributes between the object types. Figure 9.6 shows one attempt at organizing the different types of gauges.

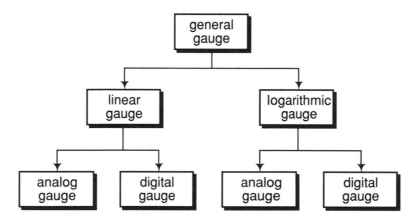

Figure 9.6. A gauge class hierarchy.

Each gauge performs at least two functions: It processes incoming signals, and it displays data. This suggests that each gauge should have the following two functions:

```
process_signal()
display()
```

To determine the data members that should be shared, we need to consider the features that gauges have in common. Here are some suggestions:

Resolution	The number of steps (increments) the gauge has
Scale	The number of steps per unit of input signal
Offset	Where "zero" is on the scale
Needle	The position to indicate current input signal

The last feature, the needle, is the part of the gauge that displays the incoming signal. This needle can be a moving hand on a circular dial, an arrow, or a digital value.

The needle's position or value is a function of the incoming signal, the resolution, the scale, and the offset of the gauge. This function may be linear, logarithmic, or an average or sum of a series of incoming signals over some time period. It could even be something much more complicated.

We've now identified the common attributes of gauges. Let's build a hierarchy. Creating a well-designed class hierarchy requires careful planning. A well-thought-out hierarchy can greatly reduce the coding efforts of a new application. A poorly designed one, on the other hand, can be just as hard to work with as the "spaghetti code" often found in unstructured programs.

In most well-designed hierarchies, the parent or root class should be as general as possible. It shouldn't be general in the sense that it throws in all the features possible for every child class; rather, it should leave as much of the specifics as possible to the child class. The root class should capture only those attributes that are shared between the children, without getting into too many details.

Here's our first attempt at a general **gauge** class:

```
class gauge {
protected:
    float resolution, scale, offset, needle_posn;
public:
    gauge(float r, float s, float o) {
      resolution = r; scale = s; offset = o;
    }
    virtual float process_signal(float signal);
    virtual void display(void);
};
```

We've included the members **resolution**, **scale**, **offset**, and **needle_posn** to represent the state of our gauges. Also, the two virtual functions **process_signal()** and **display()** are provided to control the behavior of the gauges. We've also included a constructor to set up the parameters of the gauge—its resolution, scale, and offset. While we've defined the body of the constructor, we haven't included code for **process_signal()** and **display()**.

We now need to consider an important design issue. The **process_signal()** function is supposed to take the incoming signal and compute a needle position. However, different gauges will compute this function differently; some may use a linear function, others may use a logarithmic one. We can specify a default behavior, such as a linear function of the input signal. However, this method seems contrived The best solution is to use an abstract class and make the function virtual so that the specialized gauge types have to override it. We'll most likely treat the **display()** function in this manner as well, since each gauge type will display its data differently.

Abstract Classes

An *abstract class* is a high-level class that defines the common attributes among a set of derived classes. The abstract class defines the common functions used to interface with all the classes in the hierarchy. By defining these functions, an abstract class establishes the common protocol to be used by all the derived classes. Often, the methods used to support this protocol are just stubs in the abstract class—they don't really do anything. As a result, many abstract classes are not meant to be used directly. Instead, the more specific derived classes should be used.

C++ supports abstract classes by providing *pure virtual functions*. Any class having at least one pure virtual function is considered an abstract class. Pure virtual functions are peculiar because they have no body. The syntax used to declare a pure virtual function may seem unusual—you set the body equal to zero:

```
virtual <return type> <class>::<name>(<args>) = 0;
```

Our general **gauge** class is a good candidate for an abstract class. Here's how we can make the **gauge** class abstract by declaring **process_signal()** and **display()** as pure virtual functions:

```
class gauge {
protected:
    float resolution, scale, offset, needle_posn;
public:
    gauge(float r, float s, float o) {
      resolution = r; scale = s; offset = o;
    }
    virtual float process_signal(float signal) = 0;
    virtual void display(void) = 0;
};
```

A pure virtual function cannot be called since it has no body. Therefore, you can't create an object from an abstract class. How do you use an abstract class and its pure virtual functions? An abstract class is used as a base class. Classes derived from this base are then used to create objects. However, you can (and typically will) use abstract class pointers to point to the derived class objects. The reason for this is to get the maximum amount of polymorphism out of the pointers.

Note: A derived class does not have to override all of the pure virtual functions of the base class. If it doesn't, the derived class becomes an abstract class as well.

Let's step back and consider the abstract **gauge** class we just created. Because virtual functions require some overhead, we don't want to use them unless we have to. On the other hand, if we don't declare the functions virtual now, we can't override them later in derived classes.

It's not uncommon for an abstract class to have data members. Because an abstract class defines a common protocol, it needs only functions to interface to the outside world. You don't want to include members that won't be used by every derived class. This is especially true of data members. On the other hand, if the data members help in the code-sharing process, then you will want to include them. In short, there are tradeoffs involved.

Now that we have defined the general class, we can derive more specific classes. For example, we can derive two classes that override the pure virtual **process_signal**() function to work in a linear and logarithmic fashion.

```
class linear_gauge : public gauge {
public:
    linear_gauge(float r, float s, float o)
    : gauge(r, s, o) { ; }
    virtual float process_signal(float signal);
};

float linear_gauge::process_signal(float signal)
// Compute needle_posn as linear function of input
{
    needle_posn = signal * scale - offset;
    // Handle overflow
    if (needle_posn > resolution) needle_posn = resolution;
```

```
        return needle_posn;
    }

    class logarithmic_gauge : public gauge {
    public:
        logarithmic_gauge(float r, float s, float o)
        : gauge(r, s, o) { ; }
        virtual float process_signal(float signal);
    };

    float logarithmic_gauge::process_signal(float signal)
    // Compute needle_posn as logarithmic function of input
    {
        needle_posn = log10(signal) * scale - offset;
        // Handle overflow
        if (needle_posn > resolution) needle_posn = resolution;
        return needle_posn;
    }
```

Although we overrode **process_signal()** in these two classes, we didn't override the **display()** function. At this stage in the hierarchy, we don't want to commit to the type of display (such as analog versus digital). Because **display()** is a pure virtual function, and we didn't override it our **linear_gauge** and **logarithmic_gauge** classes are also abstract classes.

We're now ready to derive our first **gauge** classes that will be used directly. Let's define a linear digital gauge and a linear analog gauge. (We'll leave the derivation of logarithmic digital and analog gauges as an exercise.) We do this by deriving our new gauge classes from **linear_gauge** and then overriding the **display()** functions as appropriate.

```
    class linear_digital_gauge : public linear_gauge {
    public:
        linear_digital_gauge(float r, float s, float o)
        : linear_gauge(r, s, o) { ; }
        virtual void display(void); // override
    };

    class linear_analog_gauge : public linear_gauge {
    public:
        linear_analog_gauge(float r, float s, float o)
```

```
          : linear_gauge(r, s, o) { ; }
          virtual void display(void); // override
     };
```

We can now define the new **display()** function; but first, a few words should be said about writing constructors for the two derived classes. Note how each constructor has to call the base class constructor for **linear_gauge**. In turn, the **linear_gauge** constructor must call the **gauge** constructor. Each time you derive a new class, you may have to define one or more new constructors. The only time you don't have to do this is when the base class has a default constructor. This is not the case with our **gauge** class, because its constructor requires three parameters.

Note: If a base class has constructors but does not have a default constructor, then any class derived from the base must have at least one constructor, and each of the derived class constructors must call one of the base class constructors.

We can now define the **display()** functions for our gauges and use them in a program. To make our code portable, we'll be using the standard I/O routines to display the gauges. Here is the complete program:

```
#include <stdio.h>
#include <math.h>
// The abstract gauge class
class gauge {
protected:
    float resolution, scale, offset, needle_posn;
public:
    gauge(float r, float s, float o) {
      resolution = r; scale = s; offset = o;
    }
    virtual float process_signal(float signal) = 0;
    virtual void display(void) = 0;
};

// The abstract linear gauge class
class linear_gauge : public gauge {
public:
```

```
    linear_gauge(float r, float s, float o)
    : gauge(r, s, o) { ; }
    virtual float process_signal(float signal);
};


// The abstract logarithmic gauge class
class logarithmic_gauge : public gauge {
public:
    logarithmic_gauge(float r, float s, float o)
    : gauge(r, s, o) { ; }
    virtual float process_signal(float signal);
};


class linear_digital_gauge : public linear_gauge {
public:
    linear_digital_gauge(float r, float s, float o)
    : linear_gauge(r, s, o) { ; }
    virtual void display(void); // override
};


class linear_analog_gauge : public linear_gauge {
public:
    linear_analog_gauge(float r, float s, float o)
    : linear_gauge(r, s, o) { ; }
    virtual void display(void); // override
};


// Class implementations
float linear_gauge::process_signal(float signal)
// Compute needle_posn as linear function of input
{
    needle_posn = signal * scale - offset;
    // Handle overflow
    if (needle_posn > resolution) needle_posn = resolution;
    return needle_posn;
}


float logarithmic_gauge::process_signal(float signal)
// Compute needle_posn as logarithmic function of input
{
```

```
    needle_posn = log10(signal) * scale - offset;
    // Handle overflow
    if (needle_posn > resolution) needle_posn = resolution;
    return needle_posn;
}


void linear_digital_gauge::display(void)
// Use "digital" display. Make it auto-sizing.
{
    int i;
    float maxnum = resolution * scale;
    int wd = log10(maxnum) + 1;
    for (i = 0; i<wd+2; i++) putchar('-');
    printf("\n|%*d|\n", wd, (int)needle_posn);
    for (i = 0; i<wd+2; i++) putchar('-');
    putchar('\n');
}


void linear_analog_gauge::display(void)
// Make an analog display
{
    int i, start, end;

    start = offset;
    end   = resolution;
    for (i = start; i <= end+2; i++) putchar('-');
    putchar('\n'); putchar('|');
    for (i = start; i <= end; i++) {
        if (i % 5) putchar('.');
        else if (i % 10) putchar('*');
        else putchar('0' + i / 10);
    }
    putchar('|'); putchar('\n'); putchar('|');
    for (i = start; i <= end; i++) {
        if (i == (int)needle_posn) putchar('^');
        else putchar(' ');
    }
    putchar('|'); putchar('\n');
    for (i = start; i <= end+2; i++) putchar('-');
    putchar('\n');
}
```

```
void main()
{
    linear_digital_gauge ldg(50.0, 1.0, 0.0);
    linear_analog_gauge  lag(50.0, 1.0, 0.0);

    ldg.process_signal(35.0);
    ldg.display();
    putchar('\n');
    lag.process_signal(35.0);
    lag.display();
}
```

Here's the output from the program:

```
-----
|  35|
-----


-------------------------------------------------------
|0....*....1....*....2....*....3....*....4....*....5|
|                                          ^        |
-------------------------------------------------------
```

Dynamic Inheritance

We left the derivation of logarithmic analog and digital gauges in the previous section as an exercise. If you try to derive these gauges, you'll encounter some problems in trying to share code. In particular, you'll discover that the analog and digital **display**() functions are (or could be) identical for both linear and logarithmic gauges. This code is difficult to share among the derived classes.

The problem lies with the type of inheritance created using class derivations. Since the classes are derived at compile-time, the resulting inheritance is called *static inheritance*. There is another form of inheritance which isn't precisely determined until run-time. This is called dynamic inheritance. It turns out that dynamic inheritance is just the technique needed in our guage classes.

C++ doesn't directly support dynamic inheritance. However, you can simulate it by incorporating a base class object inside another class. The new class takes on the role of a derived class and may contain additional members. Because the new class incorporates the base class object, it inherits all the attributes of the base class.

The trick to setting up dynamic inheritance in C++ involves using pointers. Instead of placing a base class object inside another class, you point to it. If the pointer you are using is a base class pointer, you can point to any object type in that base classes' hierarchy. Since a pointer is used, you can defer your choice until run-time.

How can we use this technique with our gauge classes? To answer this, we must first reorganize the gauge class hierarchy. Recall that gauges are made of two components: a signal processing unit that takes the input signal and maps it onto the needle position, and a display device that takes the needle position and displays it. We have two types of signal processors: linear and logarithmic. We also have two types of display devices: analog and digital. This suggests that we have two class hierarchies: one for the signal processors, and one for the display devices. These hierarchies are shown in Figure 9.7. (For our purposes, we'll treat the display device as the gauge itself.)

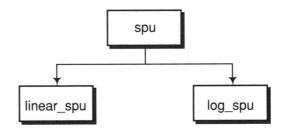

(a) Signal processing class hierarchy

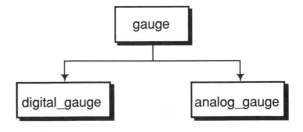

(b) Gauge class hierarchy

Figure 9.7. The two class hierarchies.

To share as much code as possible, we can combine these two hierarchies using dynamic inheritance. Inside each gauge you'll find a pointer to a base class signal processing object. At run-time, we'll determine which specific type of signal processor to use. The following program shows the complete setup:

```
#include <stdio.h>
#include <math.h>
/////////////////////////////////////////////
// Define the signal processing hierarchy
/////////////////////////////////////////////
class spu { // abstract signal processing unit
protected:
    float resolution, scale, offset;
public:
    spu(float r, float s, float o);
    virtual float process(float signal) = 0;
    float num_steps(void) { return resolution; }
    float factor(void)    { return scale; }
    float start(void)     { return offset; }
};

class linear_spu : public spu {
public:
    linear_spu(float r, float s, float o)
    : spu(r, s, o) { ; }
    virtual float process(float signal);
};

class log_spu : public spu {
public:
    log_spu(float r, float s, float o)
    : spu(r, s, o) { ; }
    virtual float process(float signal);
};

/////////////////////////////////////////////
// Define the gauge hierarchy
/////////////////////////////////////////////
class gauge { // abstract gauge class
```

```
    protected:
        spu *spu_obj;          // pointer to signal processing unit
        float needle_posn;   // position of needle on gauge
    public:
        gauge(spu *s) { spu_obj = s; needle_posn = 0.0; }
        virtual float process_signal(float signal); // common to
                                                     // all gauges
        virtual void display(void) = 0; // note: pure virtual!
    };


    class digital_gauge : public gauge {
    public:
        digital_gauge(spu *s) : gauge(s) { ; }
        virtual void display(void);
    };


    class analog_gauge : public gauge {
    public:
        analog_gauge(spu *s) : gauge(s) { ; }
        virtual void display(void);
    };


    ////////////////////////////////////////////
    // Implement the member functions
    ////////////////////////////////////////////
    spu::spu(float r, float s, float o)
    // Constructor for abstract signal processors
    {
        resolution = r;
        scale = s;
        offset = o;
    }


    float linear_spu::process(float signal)
    // Use a linear function to process signal
    {
        float p = signal * scale - offset;
        if (p > resolution) p = resolution; // overflow
        return p;
    }
```

```
float log_spu::process(float signal)
// Use a logarithmic function to process signal
{
    float p = log10(signal) * scale - offset;
    if (p > resolution) p = resolution; // overflow
    return p;
}


float gauge::process_signal(float signal)
// Set needle position to signal processor output
{
    return needle_posn = spu_obj->process(signal);
}


void digital_gauge::display(void)
// Use "digital" display
{
    int i;
    float maxnum = spu_obj->num_steps() * spu_obj->factor();
    int wd = log10(maxnum) + 1;

    for (i = 0; i<wd+2; i++) putchar('-');
    printf("\n|%*d|\n", wd, (int)needle_posn);
    for (i = 0; i<wd+2; i++) putchar('-');
    putchar('\n');
}


void analog_gauge::display(void)
// Use an analog display
{
    int i, start, end;
    start = spu_obj->start();
    end   = spu_obj->num_steps();
    for (i = start; i <= end+2; i++) putchar('-');
    putchar('\n'); putchar('|');
    for (i = start; i <= end; i++) {
        if (i % 5) putchar('.');
        else if (i % 10) putchar('*');
        else putchar('0' + i / 10);
    }
```

```
        putchar('|'); putchar('\n'); putchar('|');
        for (i = start; i <= end; i++) {
            if (i == (int)needle_posn) putchar('^');
            else putchar(' '); }
        putchar('|'); putchar('\n');
        for (i = start; i <= end+2; i++) putchar('-');
        putchar('\n');
    }

void main()
{
    // Create a logarithmic digital gauge
    digital_gauge dlog_gauge(new log_spu(10.0, 1.0, 0.0));
    // Create a linear analog gauge
    analog_gauge alin_gauge(new linear_spu(50.0, 1.0, 0.0));
    dlog_gauge.process_signal(150.0);
    dlog_gauge.display();
    putchar('\n');
    alin_gauge.process_signal(35.0);
    alin_gauge.display();
    // Note: the two spu objects have not been deleted
}
```

When run, this program produces the following output:

```
----
|  2|
----


------------------------------------------------------
|0....*....1....*....2....*....3....*....4....*....5|
|                                      ^            |
------------------------------------------------------
```

Let's examine this program. First, we create a signal processing unit class hierarchy with the classes **spu**, **linear_spu**, and **log_spu**. These classes utilize most of the data members that used to reside in the gauge classes (**resolution**, **scale**, and **offset**) in order to process the signal. The two derived classes override the virtual **process()** function to provide linear and logarithmic operations.

Second, we create the new gauge hierarchy. Each gauge has a **needle_posn** and a pointer to a **spu** object. We must use a base class **spu** pointer so that we can point to either a **linear_spu** or a **log_spu** object. Each gauge has a constructor for initializing the **spu** object pointer. The gauges have **process_signal**() functions which update **needle_posn** using the embedded **spu** objects. In addition, the gauges have virtual **display**() functions, which are overridden in the derived classes to support analog and digital displays.

To create a gauge, we first declare an object from either the **analog_gauge** or **digital_gauge** class. (Note that we can't create an object of type **gauge**, since **gauge** is an abstract class.) In the constructor call for our object, we dynamically create a **linear_spu** or a **log_spu** object, and pass in its address. (Again, we can't create a **spu** object, since **spu** is an abstract class.) The combination of the type of **gauge** object and the type of **spu** object we choose determines the overall type of gauge that is created. In our program, we create a logarithmic digital gauge and a linear analog gauge.

Virtual Constructors Revisited

Although you can't make a constructor virtual, you can produce some of the effects of a virtual constructor. One is the ability to determine the type of object being created at run-time. Our **linear_gauge**() and **analog_gauge**() constructors work this way. By passing in the appropriate type of signal processing object, we are creating new gauge types dynamically.

```
// Create a logarithmic digital gauge
digital_gauge dlog_gauge(new log_spu(10.0, 1.0, 0.0));

// Create a linear analog gauge
analog_gauge alin_gauge(new linear_spu(50.0, 1.0, 0.0));
```

Constructors that use this technique are sometimes referred to as *virtual constructors*. Note that these constructors are not virtual in the strictest technical sense.

Improving Our Gauges

One problem with our gauges and their "virtual constructors" is that we must explicitly create dynamic **spu** objects in the constructor call. However, we never actually delete these objects in our main program. We need a better way to process these embedded objects.

```
class linear_digital_gauge : public digital_gauge {
public:
    linear_digital_gauge(float r, float s, float o)
    : digital_gauge(new linear_spu(r, s, o)) { ; }
    virtual ~linear_digital_gauge(void) { delete spu_obj; }
};

class log_digital_gauge : public digital_gauge {
public:
    log_digital_gauge(float r, float s, float o)
    : digital_gauge(new log_spu(r, s, o)) { ; }
    virtual ~log_digital_gauge(void) { delete spu_obj; }
};

class linear_analog_gauge : public analog_gauge {
public:
    linear_analog_gauge(float r, float s, float o)
    : analog_gauge(new linear_spu(r, s, o)) { ; }
    virtual ~linear_analog_gauge(void) { delete spu_obj; }
};

class log_analog_gauge : public analog_gauge {
public:
    log_analog_gauge(float r, float s, float o)
    : analog_gauge(new log_spu(r, s, o)) { ; }
    virtual ~log_analog_gauge(void) { delete spu_obj; }
};
```

When you examine these classes you might do a double take, since we've now come full circle. We have explicitly derived, using static inheritance, linear digital guages, linear analog guages, and so on. But we did it by also mixing in dynamic inheritance. By doing this, we avoided having to duplicate the code for the **display**() functions, or for the **process**() functions. As a bonus, our new high-level classes contain very little code being mostly a few inline function calls. As a result, the classes have minimal overhead.

Our strategy is to create a specific gauge type by first inheriting a digital or analog gauge. Then, the creation of dynamic **spu** objects is encapsulated in the constructors. Each class also has a destructor that deletes the appropriate **spu** object. We can now write statements such as the following, without worrying about how the embedded **spu** object is created and deleted:

```
linear_digital_gauge ldg(50.0, 10.0, 0.0);
log_analog_gauge lag(10.0, 1.0, 0.0);
```

You can see that we've successfully hidden all the tricky details.

IS-A versus HAS-A Relationships

Static and dynamic inheritance have other differences which can be expressed in terms of two relationships called *IS-A* and *HAS-A*.

An IS-A relationship is determined by a type–subtype relationship. An example of an IS-A relationship is our rectangle–square example. A square IS-A rectangle because it can be used wherever a rectangle can. Note that IS-A works one way. It's not true that a rectangle IS-A square, since there are rectangles that certainly aren't squares.

A HAS-A relationship is determined by nested objects. For example, our gauges contain signal processing objects. Thus, a gauge HAS-A signal processor. It doesn't make sense to say that a gauge IS-A signal processor. (Although you could argue that point.)

Based on these two descriptions of IS-A and HAS-A, we can conclude that an IS-A relationship is created by static inheritance, whereas a HAS-A relationship is created by dynamic inheritance.

Multiple Inheritance

In our inheritance examples, each derived class is derived from a single parent. This technique is called *single inheritance*. A class can also be derived from multiple parents. This technique is called *multiple inheritance*. Figure 9.9 shows some examples of multiple imheritance. Note that multiple inheritance doesn't necessarily mean that you are using multiple derivations—that is, deriving a class from a derived class. Our gauge class hierarchy used multiple derivations. However, at each step, only one parent was directly involved. For multiple inheritance, two or more parents must be used.

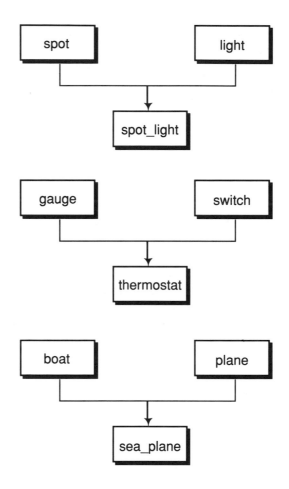

Figure 9.9. Examples of multiple inheritance.

To achieve multiple inheritance in C++, you use the same class derivation syntax as you did for single inheritance, except that you can list several base classes instead of just one. For example, suppose we have a **spot** class and a **light** class. We can derive a **spot_light** class from them as follows:

```
class spot { // a circular spot class
public:
    float radius;
    spot(float r) { radius = r; }
    float area(void);
```

```
};

class light { // a class representing light
public:
    float intensity;
    light(float i) { intensity = i; }
    void shine(void);
};

class spot_light : public spot, public light { // two bases
public:
    spot_light(float r, float i) : spot(r), light(i) { ; }
};
```

Notice how **spot_light** has two base classes: **spot** and **light**. Also note that the constructor for **spot_light** calls both base class constructors.

A class derived from multiple parents takes on the properties of all the parents and is a subtype of them all. Take, for example, the **spot_light** class. A **spot_light** *IS-A* **spot**, and it *IS-A* **light**. A **spot_light** has an area like a **spot** does, and a **spot_light** can shine like a **light** can. Therefore, a **spot_light** can play both roles. Here is an example:

```
spot_light fame_enhancer(17.0, 42.0);
// Access spot members
float r = fame_enhancer.radius;
float a = fame_enhancer.area();

// Access light members
float i = fame_enhancer.intensity;
fame_enhancer.shine();
```

What Multiple Inheritance Is Not

Now that you know what multiple inheritance is, what isn't it? Consider our gauges. They are composed of both signal processing units and display devices. Could we then say that gauges manifest multiple inheritance? The way to answer this is to consider whether or not gauges can take on the roles of both a signal processor and a display device. As you might surmise, they can. However, the role of being a signal processor is subservient to that of being a display device. The two roles aren't on equal terms. It's more correct to say that a gauge HAS-A signal processor, rather than to say it IS-A signal processor. Thus, we can conclude multiple inheritance is not being used.

We *can* use gauges in a multiple inheritance scheme. Consider, for example, the furnace thermostat in your house. Most thermostats are composed of a gauge, from which you can read the current room temperature, and a switch, which controls the current to the furnace. The thermostat plays both roles, and neither one is subservient to the other. This suggests that we can create a thermostat class by deriving it from both a gauge class and a switch class. In fact, we'll do just that later on. But first, you need to learn more about the nuts and bolts of multiple inheritance.

Working with Multiple Inheritance

The more you work with multiple inheritance, the more you'll encounter tricky problems. The main one involves dealing with member names from separate base classes that, once they are merged in the derived class, cause naming conflicts. Also, a problem is often encountered where the same base class is actually inherited more than once in a derived class. The question here is: Should the members of the base class be duplicated in the derived class, or should only one copy of them exist?

To see these problems firsthand, let's look at a simple class hierarchy that illustrates the major points. This hierarchy involves deriving a **cooler** class from two classes: **sparkling_water** and **juice**.

```
class sparkling_water {
public:
    float amt, co2_content;
    sparkling_water(float a, float cc) {
      amt = a; co2_content = cc;
    }
    void bubble(void);
};

class juice {
public:
    enum fruit { apple, orange, cherry };
    fruit flavor;
```

```
      float amt, juice_content;
      juice(float a, float jc, fruit f) {
        amt = a; juice_content = jc; flavor = f;
      }
      void make_fruitier(float new_jc);
};

class cooler : public sparkling_water, public juice {
public:
    float mix_ratio;
    cooler(float a, float m, float cc, float jc, fruit f)
    : sparkling_water(a*(1-m), cc), juice(a*m, jc, f)
    {
      mix_ratio = m;
    }
};
```

The **sparkling_water** class keeps track of the amount of water, **amt**, and the CO2 content or ratio, **juice_content**. A **bubble**() function is provided (which we don't define) to simulate the water fizzing. The **juice** class keeps track of the amount of liquid, **amt**, the ratio of juice to water, **juice_content**, and the flavor of the juice. A **make_fruitier**() function is provided (which we don't define) to increase the juice content. Both of the classes have constructors to initialize their members.

The **cooler** class has both the properties of sparkling water and fruit juice because it is derived from the two classes. It keeps track of the mix ratio, **mix_ratio**, between the amount of sparkling water and fruit juice. Notice that the **cooler** constructor, like any derived class constructor, must call the constructors of its base class(es). In this case, two such base class constructors must be called, and we use the parameters **m** and **a** (mix ratio and amount), along with the other parameters to determine what to pass to the base class constructors.

Being derived from the two parents **sparkling_water** and **juice**, the **cooler** class has all the members of each parent, as well as its own **mix_ratio** member. In particular, it has the following members:

```
sparkling_water::amt;
sparkling_water::co2_content;
sparkling_water::bubble();
juice::flavor;
```

```
juice::amt;
juice::juice_content;
juice::make_fruitier();
cooler::mix_ratio
```

Here are some examples of a **cooler** class accessing some of these members:

```
cooler sundance;

sundance.co2_content = 0.05;
sundance.juice_content = 0.10;
sundance.bubble();
```

Ambiguous Member Names

You might have noticed that a cooler object has two **amt** members, one from each of its parents. You can't reference **amt** directly because the reference is ambiguous. This is a common problem with multiple inheritance. The problem can be eliminated if you don't use ambiguous members in your derived classes. However, if you want to use such members, you can qualify their name with the appropriate base class name.

```
sundance.amt = 20.0;                    // error: ambiguous.
sundance.sparkling_water::amt = 20.0;  // ok
sundance.juice::amt = 20.0;             // ok too
```

Note that these same rules apply to any member functions from the different classes having the same name.

Virtual Base Classes

With multiple inheritance, you can create very complicated class hierarchies. One problem that surfaces is inheriting from the same base class more than once. To do so directly is an error.

```
// Error, duplicate base class
class breakfast_drink : public juice, public juice {
```

```
    // Members go here
};
```

However, you can indirectly inherit from the same base class more than once. Consider the following **wine_cooler** class:

```
class wine : public sparkling_water {
public:
    grape_amt;
    // ...
};


class wine_cooler : public wine, public cooler {
    // ...
};
```

Since both the **wine** and **cooler** classes are derived from the **sparkling_water** class, the **wine_cooler** class inherits from **sparkling_water** twice. This means that a **wine_cooler** object has two copies of each member of **sparkling_water**. A **wine_cooler** object has two **co2_content** members and three **amt** members—the third comes from the **juice** class inherited by the **cooler** class. The problem with these duplicate copies is that there is no way to differentiate between them.

You won't want to have duplicate copies of a base class in most situations. C++ accommodates this by providing *virtual base classes*. A derived class receives one copy of the members from a virtual base class, even if it indirectly inherits from the base class more than once.

To define a virtual base class, you use the **virtual** keyword when listing the base class in a derived class declaration. Then, any classes using the derived class are guaranteed to receive only one copy of the virtual base class. Here's an example of how we can change our **wine_cooler** example to have only one copy of **sparkling_water**:

```
// Note how sparkling_water is declared virtual here
class cooler : virtual public sparkling_water, public juice {
    // ...
};

// Note how sparkling water is declared virtual here
class wine : virtual public sparkling water {
```

```
    // ...
};

class wine_cooler : public wine, public cooler {
    // ...
};
```

Since **sparkling_water** was declared as a virtual base class in both **cooler** and **wine**, when **wine_cooler** is derived from both of these classes, it gets only one copy of **sparkling_water**.

Note: The use of the **virtual** keyword for virtual base classes has nothing to do with the use of the **virtual** keyword for virtual functions. The meaning of the word virtual is overloaded here.

When you combine multiple inheritance and virtual bases with virtual functions, and throw in member access control, overloaded functions and operators, and user-defined conversions, you can end up with a very complex system. The rules for combining all of these features are intricate and subtle. We don't have space to cover all of the rules in this book. In fact, we recommend that you consider multiple inheritance to be an advanced feature of C++ and only attempt using it once you have a good grasp of the fundamentals of C++.

That having been said, let's see if we can apply multiple inheritance in a more realistic setting. To do so, we'll revisit our gauge classes once again.

Making Thermostats

In this section we'll show you how to use multiple inheritance to create a **thermostat** class using a **gauge** and a **switch** class as a base. Here's how our thermostats will work: Whenever a temperature signal is processed, we monitor the resulting position of the thermostat's needle. If the needle falls below a certain threshold, we turn a switch on, presumably allowing current to flow to a furnace. Then, when the needle rises above a certain threshold, we turn the switch off. The program in Listing 9.1 shows the complete code.

To define our **thermostat** class, let's first define the **gauge** and **switch** classes. For the **gauge** class, we won't go through the derivations we did earlier. Instead, we'll define a linear digital gauge directly:

```
class gauge { // a linear digital gauge
protected:
    float resolution, scale, offset, needle_posn;
public:
    gauge(float r, float s, float o);
    float process_signal(float signal);
    void display(void);
};
```

The program listing gives the definitions of the gauge member functions. For the sake of brevity, we've simplified the **display()** function from what you've seen before to simply print out the needle position.

We can define a class for switches as follows:

```
class on_off_switch {
protected:
    int closed;              // on/off state
public:
    on_off_switch(void)     { closed = 0; }
    void turn_on(void)      { closed = 1; }
    void turn_off(void)     { closed = 0; }
    float connect(float v) { return closed ? v : 0.0; }
};
```

The **on_off_switch** class has an internal member storing the on/off state of the switch. The state is initialized to off by the **on_off_switch()** constructor and is controlled by the **turn_on()** and **turn_off()** functions. The switch state is used by the **connect()** function in determining whether to allow the value passed in (presumably a current) to be returned or to return a 0.

Now comes the interesting part. Here the **thermostat** class is defined using multiple inheritance:

```
class thermostat : public gauge, public on_off_switch {
protected:
    float low, high; // operating threshold temperatures
public:
    thermostat(float r, float s, float o, float l, float h);
    void sample_temp(float ts);
};
```

The **thermostat** class adds the two members **low** and **high**, which are used to control the turn-on and turn-off points of the furnace switch. The constructor sets up the gauge parameters. It also initializes the switch to off and sets up the **low** and **high** control points.

```
thermostat::thermostat(float r, float s, float o,
                       float l, float h)
: gauge(r, s, o) // set up inherited gauge
// on_off_switch constructor called implicitly
{
    low = l; high = h; // initialize control points
}
```

Note how the **gauge()** constructor is called explicitly by the **thermostat()** constructor. The **on_off_switch()** constructor is called implicitly because it is a default constructor.

The interesting function to examine in the **thermostat** class is **sample_temp()**.

```
void thermostat::sample_temp(float ts)
// Sample raw temperature signal and process it
{
    // Convert signal into temperature units, and
    // determine needle position
    process_signal(ts);
    // Control switch accordingly
    if (needle_posn <= low) turn_on();
    if (needle_posn >= high) turn_off();
}
```

This function takes a raw temperature signal as input and calls **process_signal()** to convert it into temperature units. The function also determines the position of the needle for the gauge. Then, the needle position is checked to see if it has crossed one of the control points. If it has, either the **turn_on()** or **turn_off()** function is called, as appropriate.

You can see from the **sample_temp()** function that our **thermostat** really does act like both a **gauge** and an **on_off_switch**. The direct call to **process_signal()** is utilizing the gauge portion, and the direct calls to **turn_on()** and **turn_off()** are utilizing the **on_off_switch** portion.

The **main()** function also shows that a **thermostat** object plays the roles of both a **gauge** and an **on_off_switch**.

```
void main()
{
    // Initialize gauge parameters, and switch control points
    thermostat ts(120.0, 1.0, 0.0, 50.0, 75.0);

    for (int i = 0; i<ntemps; i++) {
        ts.sample_temp(temps[i]);
        ts.display();
        // Pass 10 amps of current through the switch and
        // display outcome
        printf("The furnace current is %5.2f amps\n\n",
                ts.connect(10.0));
    }
}
```

The thermostat **ts** acts like a gauge when **gauge**s **display()** is called. The thermostat also acts like a switch when the **on_off_switch**es' **connect()** function is called to pass current through the thermostat.

Listing 9.1

```
///////////////////////////////////////////////////
// Thermostats defined with multiple inheritance
///////////////////////////////////////////////////
#include <stdio.h>
class gauge { // we'll define a linear digital gauge
protected:
    float resolution, scale, offset, needle_posn;
public:
    gauge(float r, float s, float o);
    float process_signal(float signal);
    void display(void);
};
```

```
gauge::gauge(float r, float s, float o)
{
    resolution = r; scale = s; offset = o;
    needle_posn = 0;
}


float gauge::process_signal(float signal)
{
    needle_posn = signal * scale - offset;
    if (needle_posn > resolution) needle_posn = resolution;
    return needle_posn;
}


void gauge::display(void)
{
    printf("The temperature is %5.2f degrees\n", needle_posn);
}


class on_off_switch {
protected:
    int closed;               // on/off state
public:
    on_off_switch(void)     { closed = 0; }
    void turn_on(void)      { closed = 1; }
    void turn_off(void)     { closed = 0; }
    float connect(float v)  { return closed ? v : 0.0; }
};


class thermostat : public gauge, public on_off_switch {
protected:
    float low, high; // operating threshold temperatures
public:
    thermostat(float r, float s, float o, float l, float h);
    void sample_temp(float ts);
};


thermostat::thermostat(float r, float s, float o,
                        float l, float h)
: gauge(r, s, o) // set up inherited gauge
// Inherited switch constructor called implicitly
```

```
{
    low = 1; high = h; // initialize thresholds
}

void thermostat::sample_temp(float ts)
// Sample raw temperature signal and process it
{
    // Convert signal into temperature units, and
    // determine needle position

    process_signal(ts);

    // Control switch accordingly
    if (needle_posn <= low) turn_on();
    if (needle_posn >= high) turn_off();
}

// Thermostat simulation
const int ntemps = 5;
float temps[ntemps] = { 68.0, 49.0, 60.0, 78.0, 68.0 };

void main()
{
    // Initialize gauge parameters, and switch control points
    thermostat ts(120.0, 1.0, 0.0, 50.0, 75.0);

    for (int i = 0; i<ntemps; i++) {
        ts.sample_temp(temps[i]);
        ts.display();
        printf("The furnace current is %5.2f amps\n\n",
                ts.connect(10.0));
    }
}
```

Stop Reinventing the Wheel

To close out the chapter, we're going to take another look at how inheritance allows us to reuse code. In this case, we won't be reusing the code that represents an object, but, rather, some code that uses an object. In the next section, we'll show you how to design reusable functions. To do this, we'll present an example of a function that compresses character data. We'll be able to use the function for different applications, such as compressing data stored both in files and in memory.

Designing a General Compression Algorithm

The first step in defining a compression function is to think about it at a very high level. Conceptually, our compression function takes character data as input, compresses it, and then outputs the compressed data. We can think of this data as coming from a buffer. Thus, the function prototype for our compression function is as follows:

```
void compress(buffer &in, buffer &out);
```

Here, **buffer** is a class used to represent character data. Inside **compress()**, we'll need a way of taking a character out of the input buffer, and a way to place a character into the output buffer.

```
c = in.get();
out.put(c);
```

How do we make our function general enough to work with files and memory? We do this by defining **buffer** to be an abstract class, and then we derive both file buffer and memory buffer classes. We'll also need to make **get()** and **put()** virtual, so that they will perform the appropriate operations for the type of buffer involved. Then, when we want to call the **compress()** function, we declare a buffer of the appropriate derived type and pass a reference to it. (A pointer would work as well.)

Thus, the secret to making **compress()** reusable involves using a pointer or reference to a base class buffer object and using virtual functions such as **get()** and **put()**. The combination of these two techniques brings about the desired reusability.

We can't overemphasize the importance of passing a pointer or reference to the buffer, as opposed to just passing the buffer by value. Besides the obvious inefficiencies of passing parameters by value, it's only by using a pointer or reference that we can fully exploit the polymorphism inherent in the virtual functions. Had we just passed the buffer by value, then the base class versions of **get()** and **put()** would be used, which isn't what we want.

(Actually, this would not be allowed anyway, since **buffer** is an abstract class, and **get**() and **put**() are pure virtual and have no function bodies.)

An Abstract Buffer Class

Let's now fill in the details of the strategy just outlined in the previous section. We'll start by defining an abstract buffer class, and then we'll design our compression algorithm. Here is the abstract buffer:

```
////////////////////////////////////////////////////////
// Abstract buffer class (buff.h)
////////////////////////////////////////////////////////
#ifndef H_BUFF
#define H_BUFF
class buffer {
public:
    virtual void reset(void) = 0;    // resets the buffer
    virtual int eob(void) = 0;       // tests for end of buffer
    virtual int get(void) = 0;       // gets next character
    virtual int put(int c) = 0;   // puts character onto buffer
    virtual long xfrcnt(void) = 0;   // returns # of chars
                                     // transferred
};
#endif
```

Our abstract buffer class consists entirely of pure virtual functions. We've provided functions to reset the buffer (presumably to start the reading or writing to the buffer from the beginning), to test for end-of-buffer, to read or write characters to the buffer, and to keep track of the number of characters read or written. This last function will allow us to compute the amount of compression achieved.

A Data Compression Algorithm

We can now define our compression algorithm so that it supports the abstract class **buffer**. It's helpful to implement the algorithm before defining the more specific file and memory buffer classes. By doing this, we can test our abstract class to make sure that it has the right protocol (function interface) before we derive the other classes. Also, since we're writing the algorithm using abstract buffers, the algorithm won't rely accidentally on unnecessary details about the type of buffer used. Thus, we'll ensure that the compression algorithm will be as general purpose as possible.

The algorithm we're going to use here performs two types of compression. The first type, which we'll call *WordStar compression*, comes from the popular WordStar word processing program. It works by combining the spaces between words with the characters in the words. This is done by setting the upper bit of a byte used to represent a character. (The high bit is not needed to represent characters in the ASCII character set.) Any byte that has the high bit set (that is, is greater than 127) is interpreted as a space, followed by a character whose value is the result of stripping off this high bit. We are actually storing two items in a byte—a space and a character. Figure 9.9 illustrates how the letter *e* is stored with a space in this manner and how the algorithm is applied to compress the letter.

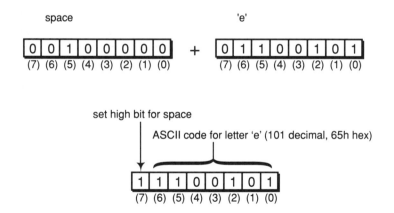

Figure 9.9. Compressing a character and a space.

The second type of compression we'll use is called *run-length compression*. It works by combining sequences of repeated characters into a three-byte sequence. Figure 9.10 shows an example.

Figure 9.10. The run-length compression technique.

Our compression algorithm implements both of these compression techniques. It uses special codes to instruct a companion function (the decompressor) how to expand the data to its original form. (We'll leave the decompressor as an exercise.) The compression codes used are as follows:

FF – NN – CC	Repeat character CC NN times
FE – NN	Repeat space character NN times
FD – CC	Use character CC as is (escape flag)
80 <= XX >= FC	Space followed by character CC = XX + 7F

The last line above shows a range of codes from 0x80 to 0xFC. These codes are used in the WordStar compression. They represent two characters: a space, followed by a character whose value is obtained by stripping off the high bit. Note that we can't use codes 0xFD and above for this, since they are already reserved. Thus, WordStar compression can only be used on characters up to 0x7C. (Note that 0x7C = 0xFC + 0x7F.)

The following C++ function defines our compression algorithm and uses the abstract buffer class given earlier. The algorithm uses a one-character lookahead, so that it can tell when to kick in the compression logic. We need to know when we've ended a run of repeated characters or when we've started the next word. The variables **currchar** and **nextchar** are used for this reason.

```
///////////////////////////////////////////////////////////
// rlcfunc.cpp: The compression algorithm
///////////////////////////////////////////////////////////
#include <stdio.h>
#include <string.h>
#include <stdlib.h>
#include "buff.h"
void compress(buffer &txtin, buffer &txtout)
{
    int i, rc = 0, currchar, nextchar;

    currchar = nextchar = txtin.get();
    while(currchar != EOF) {
        if (currchar != nextchar) { // end of run length ?
            // is run length worth compressing?
            if (rc > 1 && (rc > 3 || currchar >= 0x80)) {
                if (currchar == ' ') {
                    txtout.put(0xfe); // multiple space marker
```

```
                        txtout.put(rc);    // run length count
              }
              else {
                 txtout.put(0xff);      // run-length marker
                 txtout.put(rc);        // run-length count
                 txtout.put(currchar); // character repeated
              }
               currchar = nextchar; nextchar = txtin.get();
           }
          else { // not worth compressing
             if (currchar >= 0x80) {
                 // we have a single graphics character
                 // so, prefix with escape marker
                 txtout.put(0xfd);
                 txtout.put(currchar);
                 currchar = nextchar;
                 nextchar = txtin.get();
             }
             else { // handle sequences of 3 or less
                 // Take care of all but last char
                 if (rc > 1) txtout.put(currchar);
                 if (rc > 2) txtout.put(currchar);
                 // Possible "Wordstar compression"
                 if (currchar == ' ' && nextchar != EOF &&
                    nextchar < 0x7d) {
                     // fold space and char into one byte
                     // and advance twice
                     txtout.put(nextchar + 0x80);
                     currchar = txtin.get();
                     nextchar = txtin.get();
                 }
                 else {
                     // can't do any compression so,
                     // just store and advance
                     txtout.put(currchar);
                     currchar = nextchar;
                     nextchar = txtin.get();
                 }
             }
          }
       }
```

```
            rc = 0; // start run-length count over
        }
        else { // same character, so keep advancing
          nextchar = txtin.get();
        }
        if (++rc == 256) {            // inc, handle overflow
           txtout.put(0xff);      // run-length marker
           txtout.put(255);       // run length
           txtout.put(currchar);  // character to repeat
           rc = 1;                // start count over
        }
     }
  }
}
```

A Memory Buffer Implementation

Now that we have defined our compression algorithm, we need to define the specific buffer types. First, we'll define a memory buffer object that operates on data stored in memory. The code is split into two parts: the class definition (mbuff.h) and the class implementation (mbuff.cpp).

```
////////////////////////////////////////////////////
// Derived memory buffer class definition  (mbuff.h)
////////////////////////////////////////////////////
#include <string.h>
#include <stdlib.h>
#include "buff.h"
#ifndef H_MBUFF
#define H_MBUFF
class mem_buff : public buffer {
protected:
    // additional data members
    int cursor, capacity;
    unsigned char *data;
    // private methods
    int init(int size);
    int copy(char *mem, int size);
public:
    // additional methods
```

```
            void close(void) { delete data; data = 0; }
            mem_buff(void)    { cursor = capacity = 0; data = 0; }
            ~mem_buff(void)   { close(); }
            int open(char *m, int n) { return copy(m, n); }
            int open(char *str) { return copy(str, strlen(str)); }
            int open(int size)  { return init(size); }
            void display(void);
            // overridden methods
            void reset(void) { cursor = 0; }
            int eob(void)     { return cursor >= capacity; }
            int get(void);
            int put(int c);
            long xfrcnt(void) { return cursor; }
        };
        #endif


        ///////////////////////////////////////////////////
        // Methods for memory buffer class   (mbuff.cpp)
        ///////////////////////////////////////////////////
        #include <stdio.h>
        #include "mbuff.h"
        int mem_buff::init(int size)
        // Returns 1 if successful, otherwise 0
        {
            // might already be allocated
            if (data == 0) data = new unsigned char[capacity = size];
            cursor = 0;
            return data != 0;
        }


        int mem_buff::copy(char *mem, int size)
        // Returns 1 if successful, otherwise 0
        {
            int r = init(size);
            if (r) memcpy(data, mem, capacity);
            return r;
        }
        void mem_buff::display(void)
        {
            int i;
```

```
        for (i=0; i<cursor; i++) putchar(data[i]);
    }
    int mem_buff::get(void)
    {
        if (cursor < capacity)
            return data[cursor++]; else return EOF;
    }

    int mem_buff::put(int c)
    {
        if (cursor < capacity) {
            data[cursor++] = c;
            return c;
        }
        else return EOF;
    }
```

Because the abstract class does not have variables, our **mem_buff** class buffer adds them to support a character array buffer. These variables include ***data**—a pointer to a character array—and **cursor**, which serves as an index. We've also used some internal routines, such as **copy()**, to help support the three types of constructors. The internal routines allow us to specify an existing array to copy, to use a null-terminated character string, or to have a buffer allocated for us. The most important functions are **get()**, **put()**, **eob()**, and **xfrcnt()**, which are overridden from the base class. These maintain and test the internal cursor so that the end of the buffer is detected properly and so that we can keep track of the number of characters passing through the buffer.

A File Buffer Implementation

Our file buffer class (**file_buff**) is similar to the **mem_buff** class, except that the **file_buff** constructor just initializes some internal variables. Also, before using a **file_buff** object, we must explicitly open a file for it using **open()**, and we must close the file when we're finished. The **open()** function takes the same arguments that the standard I/O function **fopen()** takes—a file name and the access mode.

As with the **mem_buff** class, we split up the code into a header file (fbuff.h) and a implementation file (fbuff.cpp):

```
/////////////////////////////////////////////////////
// Derived file buffer class   (fbuff.h)
/////////////////////////////////////////////////////
#include "buff.h"
#ifndef H_FBUFF
#define H_FBUFF
#include <stdio.h>
class file_buff : public buffer {
protected:
    // additional data members
    FILE *handle;
    long cnt;
public:
    // additional methods
    int open(char *name, char *mode);
    void close(void) {
       if (handle) fclose(handle); handle = 0;
    }
    file_buff(void)  { cnt = 0; handle = 0; }
    ~file_buff(void) { close(); }
    // overridden methods
    void reset(void) { rewind(handle); }
    int eob(void)    { return feof(handle); }
    int get(void);
    int put(int c);
    long xfrcnt(void) { return cnt; }
};
#endif


/////////////////////////////////////////////////////
// Methods for file buffer class (fbuff.cpp)
/////////////////////////////////////////////////////
#include "fbuff.h"

int file_buff::open(char *name, char *mode)
// Returns 1 on success, 0 on error
{
    cnt = 0;
    if (!handle) {
        if((handle = fopen(name, mode)) == 0) {
```

```
            printf("Error opening file %s\n", name);
            return 0;
        }
    }
    return 1;
}


int file_buff::get(void)
{
    int c;
    if ((c = fgetc(handle)) != EOF) cnt++;
    return c;
}


int file_buff::put(int c)
{
    cnt++;
    return fputc(c, handle);
}
```

Putting It All Together

Now we can write a program that puts all the pieces together. This program takes a character buffer, compresses it, and writes it to a file.

```
//////////////////////////////////////////////////
// rlc.cpp: Memory to file compression program
//////////////////////////////////////////////////
#include "mbuff.h"
#include "fbuff.h"
// From rlcfunc.cpp:
void compress(buffer &txtin, buffer &txtout);

void main()
{

    mem_buff inbuff;
    file_buff outbuff;
```

```
        inbuff.open("this      is   a test of rrrruunnnleeeeength "
                    "compression");

        outbuff.open("test.fil",  "w");

        compress(inbuff,  outbuff);

        long  incnt  =  inbuff.xfrcnt();
        long  outcnt  =  outbuff.xfrcnt();
        printf("%ld vs %ld saving %3.0f%%\n",
               outcnt,  incnt,
                (float)(incnt-outcnt)/(float)incnt*100.0);

        inbuff.close();
        outbuff.close();
}
```

When run, this program outputs the following:

```
44  vs  54  saving   19%
```

The output file **test.fil**, if viewed by a hex dump program, would look as follows:

```
74 68 69 73 FE 05 69 73    this..is
20 E1 F4 65 73 74 EF 66     ..est.f
F2 72 72 72 75 75 6E 6E    .rrruunn
6E 6C FF 05 65 6E 67 74    nl..engt
68 E3 6F 6D 70 72 65 73    h.ompres
73 69 6F 6E                 sion
```

Summary

Inheritance sets object-oriented programming apart from more traditional approaches. In this chapter, you saw how inheritance can make your programs more expressive in modelling the relationships among the objects being used. You saw different types of inheritance, such as static inheritance, dynamic inheritance, single inheritance, and multiple inheritance. Each type has its uses, but they all provide you with the same two advantages:

- Inheritance allows you to elegantly express type–subtype relationships;

- Inheritance allows you to extend existing code and reuse it in new ways, all without modifying the existing code.

Exercises

1. Given the following simple **calculator** class:

```
class calculator {
public:
    virtual int add(int a, int b) { return a + b; }
    virtual int sub(int a, int b) { return a - b; }
};
```

derive a new class that adds memory to the class so that the result of the calculation can be stored. Also, add new functions, such as

```
int add_to_mem(int a)
```

to use the memory.

2. Using the following classes and declared pointers:

```
struct circle {
    int radius;
};

struct cylinder : public circle {
    int height;
};

circle *cirptr, cir;
cylinder *cylptr, cyl;
```

which of the following statements are legal?

```
cirptr = &cyl;
cylptr = &cir;
cirptr = cylptr;
cylptr = cirptr;
```

3. Suppose you were creating a system of classes to support screen windows in both text mode and graphics mode. Explain why multiple inheritance would be useful. Also, explain how you can get around having to use multiple inheritance.

4. What's wrong with the constructors given for the following classes? Are the destructors okay? How could you fix the classes? (Hint: For the destructors, think about what happens when you point to a **string80** object with a **string** pointer, and then call **delete** using that pointer.)

```
struct string {
    int size;
    int *data;
    virtual void allocate(int size) {
        data = new int[size = s];
    }
    virtual void deallocate(void) { delete data; }
    string(int s) { allocate(s); }
    ~string(void) { deallocate(); }
};

struct string80 : public string {
    int static_data[80];
    void allocate(int s) { size = s; data = static_data; }
    void deallocate(void) { ; }
    string80(void) : string(80) { ; }
    ~string80(void) { ; }
};
```

The C++ Stream I/O System

In addition to the standard C I/O routines, such as **printf**() and **scanf**(), C++ supports a more object-oriented I/O system. Up to this point, we haven't used this I/O system for two reasons. First, we didn't want to confuse you by introducing too many new concepts at once. Second, the C++ stream I/O system uses many of the advanced features of C++, such as overloaded operators and virtual functions. By now, you should be ready to learn how to put the C++ stream I/O system to work.

We'll start with a brief tour of the C++ stream I/O system. Then, we'll cover the system in detail, starting with low-level techniques and moving on to high level ones. Our first stop will be the character-level functions, including **get**() and **put**(). Next, we'll discuss stream states and how you can monitor and control these states. We'll also explore the high-level >> and << operators, which have been overloaded for performing input and output operations with objects. You'll first learn the basics of using these operators, such as the built-in formatting functions, and then we'll show you how you can customize the operators for your own objects. Finally, you'll learn how to read and write to files, using both sequential and random access techniques.

The main topics of this chapter include:

- How to use the low-level stream I/O functions
- Techniques for testing stream states
- How to use the high-level stream operators >> and <<
- How to perform formatted input and output
- How to use the >> and << operators for your objects

• How to perform file I/O
• Techniques for in-memory formatting

Note: The C++ stream I/O library is not a built-in language feature; it is supplied as a "standard" library. Because some of the features of this library are implementation-dependent, you may encounter slight differences from the material presented here and the features your compiler provides.

A Brief Journey down the Streams of C++

The most visible feature of the C++ stream I/O system is the *stream operators* >> and <<. These operators are used to perform input and output, respectively. The >> and << operators are the right-shift and left-shift operators found in C. They have been overloaded in C++ to support I/O operations. (Recall that Chapter 7 discusses how operators are overloaded.) Here's our first program that shows how simple stream I/O is performed:

```
#include <iostream.h>
void main()
{
    int x;

    cin >> x;  // input x from standard input stream
    cout << x; // output x to standard output stream
}
```

The translation box in Figure 10.1 illustrates how this program corresponds with a C program. The program inputs an integer from the stream **cin** and sends the number back to the stream **cout**. Here, **cin** and **cout** are considered *stream objects* and play similar roles to the C **stdin** and **stdout** variables. In fact, the following stream objects are often predefined. (The exact ones are implementation-dependent.)

Object	Description	C Equivalent
cin	Standard input	stdin
cout	Standard output	stdout
cerr	Standard error	stderr

```
C                          C++

/* standard C I/O */       // C++ stream I/O

#include <stdio.h>         #include <iostream.h>

void main()                void main()
{                          {
  int x;                     int x;

  scanf("%d", &x);           cin >> x;
  printf("%d",x);            cout << x;
}                          }
```

Figure 10.1. Translation box for stream I/O.

C++ supports many types of stream objects. A complex class hierarchy is utilized, as shown in Figure 10.2. This class system is defined in the header file **iostream.h**, which you *must* include whenever you're using the C++ stream I/O system. This header file is analogous to the standard C **stdio.h** header file.

Note: C++ provides three other related header files, named **iomanip.h**, **fstream.h**, and **strstrea.h**. You may have to include these files when using certain stream I/O features.

As Figure 10.2 indicates, the stream I/O class hierarchy is quite complex. It uses multiple inheritance and utilizes as many as 16 classes. Before you get scared away by this system, you should know that you don't need to use all of these classes.

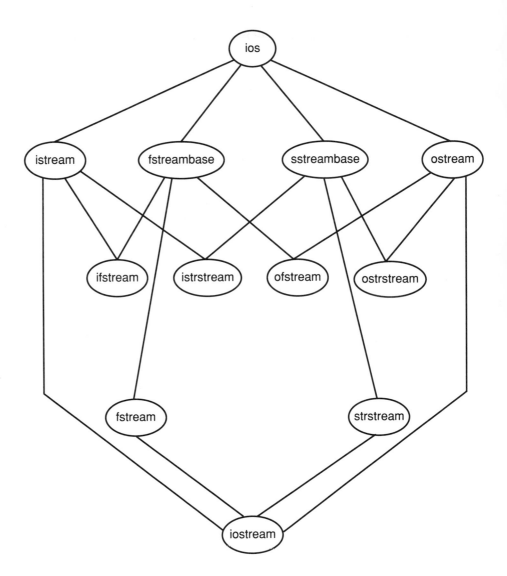

Figure 10.2. The C++ stream I/O class hierarchy.

The classes **istream**, **ostream**, and **iostream** are used to define input, output, and input/output stream objects. The **cin** and **cout** objects are defined from derived classes of **istream** and **ostream** (specifically, **istream_ withassign** and **ostream_withassign**). You'll be working with these object types directly in your programs. When using files, you'll use the derived classes **ifstream**, **ofstream**, and **fstream** in similar ways. You can also perform in-memory formatting by using the **strstream** class.

The C++ stream I/O system provides data buffering. To handle this, the classes **streambuf**, **filebuf**, and **strstreambuf** are used. You won't normally need to be concerned with these classes. The stream classes, such as **istream** and **ostream**, include objects from these buffer classes and use them internally, taking care of the details for you.

To use stream objects such as **cin** and **cout**, you use the stream operators **>>** (for input) and **<<** (for output) and use objects as operands. As supplied, the stream operators work with the basic data types, such as integers, floats, and strings. For each of these types, the stream operators have been overloaded to provide the conversion from these built-in types to sequences of characters.

Let's look at an example. The following program inputs numeric data of different types (**int** and **double**) and outputs strings as well:

```
#include <iostream.h>
void main()
{
    double price;
    int qty;

    cout << "Enter part quantity: ";
    cin >> qty;
    cout << "Enter price of part: $";
    cin >> price;
    cout << "Total order comes to : $" << qty*price << "\n";
}
```

Here's a sample run:

```
Enter part quantity: 32
Enter price of part: $4
Total order comes to: $128
```

If you type in and run this program, you'll notice that any spaces you enter before the number are skipped.

The last statement of the program illustrates that multiple operations can be combined into a single statement. For example,

```
cout << a << b << c;
```

sends the objects **a**, **b**, and **c** to the output stream, one after the other.

Our program uses default formatting for the variables **qty** and **price**. You can specify your own format. This program shows how you can format a number using a format similar to the **printf()** format string of "%4.1f":

```
#include <iostream.h>
#include <iomanip.h>
void main()
{
    double num = 10.5;
    cout << "Stocks have risen ";
    cout << setw(4) << setprecision(1) << num << " percent\n";
}
```

If you bought your stocks at the right time, you'll be happy to see the message printed by this program:

```
Stocks have risen 10.5 percent
```

Functions such as **setw()** and **setprecision()** are called *I/O manipulators*. They are also part of the C++ stream I/O system. To use such manipulators, you must include the header file **iomanip.h**, as we did in our program.

You can also perform I/O at a lower level than that provided by the stream operators. For example, you can use functions such as **get()** and **put()**. These functions work on a character-by-character basis. Using these functions, here's a way to copy data from one stream to another:

```
// Stream to stream copy using get() and put()
#include <iostream.h>
void main()
{
    int c;
    // Copy until end of input is reached
    while((c = cin.get()) != EOF) cout.put(c);
}
```

Notice that we're accessing the stream objects **cin** and **cout** directly, using standard member function call notation. This process is illustrated in Figure

10.3. In this case, the functions **get()** and **put()** take the place of the >> and << operators.

```
while(cin.get(c)) cout.put(c));
```

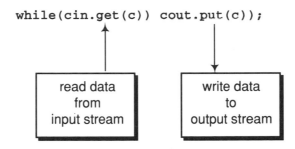

read data
from
input stream

write data
to
output stream

Figure 10.3. Using get() and put() to perform low-level I/O.

Because the stream operators can be overloaded, you can customize them for your own use. Later on, we'll show you how to create clock objects and then output them using the stream operators. Here is a sample of the kinds of things you can do:

```
clock tower_clock(4, 30, 0);
cout << "The time is " << tower_clock << "\n";
```

The second statement generates output such as the following:

```
The time is 04:30:00 AM
```

The **tower_clock** object is processed by the second << operator in such a way that each of the object's components—hours, minutes, and seconds—is displayed.

In addition to using the standard input and output streams, you can also read and write to files. Here is an example:

```
#include <fstream.h>
void main()
{
    fstream dest;

    dest.open("test.fil", ios::out | ios::trunc);
    dest << "Secret code for today is 'send me money'\n";
```

```
        dest.close();
    }
```

In this program, we create an output file object named **dest** using the class **fstream**. Note that **fstream**, like all the file object classes, is defined in **fstream.h**. (You must include this file when performing stream I/O with files.) Fortunately, file objects also use the same stream operators for input and output that we used for the standard input and output objects **cin** and **cout**. The C++ I/O system is designed to work the same way for all stream objects.

This completes our quick tour of the C++ stream I/O system. We'll now cover the I/O system in more detail, starting with the character-level stream functions.

Using the Character-Level Stream Functions

The character-level functions are used to read and write characters and strings. They operate at a lower level than the stream operators because they can't format data. They are useful because they provide more direct control over I/O. Table 10.1 lists the character-level I/O functions provided. Table 10.2 shows how some of these functions correspond with the standard C I/O functions.

Table 10.1 Character-level I/O functions

---

ostream &put(char c);
Inserts a character into the output stream. Returns the output stream.

int get(void);
Extracts the next character from the input stream and returns it. An EOF is returned on end of input.

int peek(void);
Returns the next character from the input stream without extracting it. An EOF is returned on end of input.

istream &putback(char c);
Pushes character **c** back onto the input stream. The input stream object is returned.

istream &get(signed char &c);
istream &get(unsigned char &c);
Extracts the next character from the input stream. The input stream object is returned.

istream &get(signed char *s, int n, char t = '\n');
istream &get(unsigned char *s, int n, chat t = '\n');
Extracts up to **n** characters into **s**, stopping when the termination character is found. The termination character is not extracted or stored in **s**. Returns the input stream object.

istream &getline(signed char *s, int n, char t = '\n');
istream &getline(unsigned char *s, int n, char t = '\n');
Extracts up to **n** characters into **s**, stopping when the termination character is found. The termination character is extracted but is not stored in **s**. Returns the input stream object.

istream &ignore(int n, int t = EOF);
Extracts and discards up to **n** characters, or until the termination character **t** is found. The termination character is left on the input stream. The input stream object is returned.

int gcount(void);
Returns the number of characters extracted in the last extraction.

Table 10.2. Translations for analogous C and C++ character-level I/O calls

C++ Call	C Call
c = cin.get();	c = fgetc(stdin);
cin.putback(c);	ungetc(c, stdin);
cout.put(c);	fputc(c, stdout);

As you study Table 10.1, you'll see that the input functions belong to the **istream** class. The single output function, **put()**, belongs to the **ostream** class. Note how the **get()** function is overloaded and can read single characters or a string of characters. The **getline()** functions are slightly different. They read the termination character (although it isn't stored in the string), whereas the **get()** functions do not read this character.

As Table 10.2 shows, some of the functions are similar to those found in C. For instance, a third form for **get()**, which takes no parameters, but returns an **int** representing the character read is provided. This function is analogous to the C **fgetc()** function. In addition, the **getline()** functions are similar to the C **fgets()** function except for one important difference: The **getline()** functions don't store the termination character on the string, whereas **fgets()** does.

Let's explore how the other two forms of **get()** (which return stream objects) operate. The next program reads text, line by line, from the standard input stream and writes the same text back out, with line numbers, to the standard output stream. The text is also truncated to 40 characters per line.

```
// A line numbering program using C++ stream I/O.
#include <iostream.h>
#include <iomanip.h>

char buff[41];

void main()
{
    int lno = 0;
    char c;

    // loop until eof or error
    while(cin.get(buff, 41)) { // reads up to one line
      do {                         // scan to newline character
        if (!cin.get(c)) break; // might be at eof though
      } while(c != '\n');
      cout << setw(4) << ++lno << ": " << buff << "\n";
    }
}
```

Here is a sample output of the program. In this case, we're using the program text as the input.

```
1: // A line number program using C++ stream I/O.
2: #include <iostream.h>
3: #include <iomanip.h>
4:
```

```
 5: char buff[41];
 6:
 7: void main()
 8: {
 9:    int lno = 0;
10:    char c;
11:
12:    // loop until eof or error
13:    while(cin.get(buff, 41)) { // reads up
14:      do {                      // scan to
15:         if (!cin.get(c)) break; // might b
16:      } while(c != '\n');
17:      cout << setw(4) << ++lno << ": " <<
18:    }
19: }
```

Although this program is short, many of the C++ stream I/O features are used. The outer **while** loop reads up to one line of text using the string form of **get()**. The loop terminates after 40 characters are read or when a new line is encountered. Note that **get()** takes three parameters. The third parameter, which specifies the termination character, is set to the newline character (**\n**) by default. The inner **do** loop reads the rest of the line using the character form of **get()**, in case the outer loop didn't encounter the end of the line.

After the line is read, it is written back out with a line number attached to the front. For this operation, we're using the high-level stream operators. We're also using the I/O manipulator **setw()** to format the line number to four digits. For this function, we need to include the header file **iomanip.h**.

Note: You can mix both the high-level stream operators and the low-level character I/O functions in a program.

The outer **while** loop executes until the end of the stream is detected or an error occurs. The inner loop also checks for the same condition in case it needs to terminate early.

Testing the State of the Stream

The line numbering program uses the following test in the outer **while** loop:

```
while (cin.get(buff, 41)) { // ... }
```

How does this test work? We are using a trick that involves a conversion operator. Let's explore this further.

First, note that most of the stream I/O functions listed in Table 10.1 return a reference to a stream object. In fact, they return the same stream object from which they are called. Therefore, the I/O functions operate as follows:

```
istream& istream::input_func( <Args> )
{
    // ...
    return *this;
}
```

or

```
ostream& ostream::output_func( <Args> )
{
    // ...
    return *this;
};
```

In the call **cin.get()**, a reference to **cin** is returned. At this point, a conversion operator defined for the **istream** class kicks in. This conversion operator converts the stream object reference into a **void** pointer. The **void** pointer is then tested for nonzero status in the **while** loop. The trick is that the conversion operator tests the state of the stream and returns zero if an error is detected. Here's a peek at how the conversion operator is defined:

```
istream::operator void *() {
    return fail() ? 0 : this;
}
```

The conversion operator uses a special member function named **fail()**. This function returns a value of 1 if an end-of-file marker or a stream error is encountered. Based on the result of **fail()**, either a null pointer or a pointer to the **istream** object is returned. Because a valid object pointer is never 0, the only way the result can be 0 is if the stream is in a **fail** state. Thus, the **while** loop executes until the stream input fails. The following sample code summarizes this procedure:

```
istream &temp;
temp = cin.get(buff,41);
while (temp.operator void *()) { // ... }
```

Another operator that can test the state of the stream is defined. Recall the following test in the inner loop of our line numbering program:

```
do {                          // scan to newline char
    if (!cin.get(c)) break;   // might have an error!!
} while (c != '\n');
```

The **if** statement uses the overloaded operator function **istream::operator!()**, which is defined as:

```
int istream::operator!() {
    return fail();
}
```

This operator function is more straightforward than **operator void *()**. It simply returns 1 if **fail()** is true; otherwise, it returns 0. Recall how unary operator functions such as **operator!()** work as member functions. The **if** statement above translates to

```
if ( (cin.get(c)).operator!() ) break;
```

Note that **get()** returns the stream object **cin**, from which the **operator!()** function is called. It is as though we coded

```
istream &temp;
temp = cin.get(c);
if (temp.operator!()) break;
```

The **ostream** class has similar operators defined. Also, note that these operators will work with the **>>** and **<<** I/O operators because they return references to stream objects, as you'll soon learn.

The component that makes our end-of-stream operator functions work is the function **fail()**. This function is only one of a group of functions available to test the state of a stream. We'll examine them in a moment, but first let's look at the stream state itself.

The stream state is stored in a variable included in each stream object. This variable can have one of the following states, as listed in Table 10.3. These states are gathered up into the following enumerated type:

```
enum io_state { goodbit = 0, eofbit = 1, failbit = 2,
                badbit = 4, hardfail = 128 };
```

Table 10.3. States for streams

State	Value	Description
good	0	Normal working order
eof	1	Pointer is at the end of the buffer
fail	2	Operation failed; stream usable if error is cleared
bad	4	Invalid operation attempted; stream may be usable if error is cleared
hardfail	128	Unrecoverable error

The differences between the last three states are subtle. The **fail** state indicates a condition such as detecting the end of a file. The stream can be used again if the error is cleared. The **bad** state usually indicates an invalid operation was attempted, such as reading a letter where a digit was expected. In this case, the stream might be corrupted (with characters lost) but *can* be made usable if the stream state is cleared. In contrast, the **hardfail** state indicates that some type of irreversible error occurred.

To set and test the stream state, a set of functions is provided for both the **istream** and **ostream** class. They are listed in Table 10.4.

For convenience, you'll probably be using the two operator functions most of the time to test the **fail()** status of the stream, as we showed earlier. However, you can use the other functions. For instance, here's a version of our stream copy program which uses **get()**, **put()**, and **good()**:

```
#include <iostream.h>
void main()
{
    char c;
```

```
         // copy from stream to stream
    while (1) {
       cin.get(c);
       if (cin.good()) cout.put(c); else break;
    }
 }
```

Table 10.4. Functions for testing the state of a stream

Function	Description
int rdstate();	Returns current stream state
int good();	Returns 1 if in good state
int eof();	Returns 1 if at end of file
int fail();	Returns 1 if failbit, badbit, or hardfail is set
int bad();	Returns 1 if badbit or hardfail is set
void clear(int s = ios::goodbit)	Clears or sets the state (default clears state to good)
operator void *();	Returns NULL if fail() returns 1
int operator !();	Returns 1 if fail() returns 1

Normally, the error status is set for you by the predefined stream functions. However, you might want to set the status yourself. You can do so by using the **clear()** function. This function is somewhat misnamed. Not only can you clear the stream state to **good**, you can set the state to any value you desire. Note that when a stream error does occur, you must clear the stream state (set it to **good**) in order to continue using the stream.

Now that we've shown the stream state functions, you might be wondering how they can be used in a program. One example is a program that must validate user input. The following program tries to parse a function call of the form **func(arg)**. Take notice of how the program tests the state of the stream at every step and how it even sets the state to **fail** itself if the proper syntax isn't entered. Also notice that the program skips to the end of a line when it encounters invalid input and tries again.

```
    // Sample parsing program using stream state tests
    #include <iostream.h>
```

```
#include <ctype.h>
istream &parse_name(istream &strm, char *name)
// Looks for identifier name up to 8 characters
{
    int i = 0;
    char c;

    while(1) {
      if (i < 8) {
        if (strm.get(c)) {
            if (isalnum(c)) {
                name[i++] = c; // collect up name
            }
            else {
                strm.putback(c); // might be '(' or ')' or \n
                break;
            };
          }
        }
      }
    name[i] = 0; // null terminate string
    return strm;
}

istream &parse_func(istream &strm, char *fname, char *arg)
// Looks for a function with a single arg. The function
// name and argument name are restricted to 8 characters.
{
    char c;

    if (parse_name(strm, fname)) {
        if (strm.get(c)) {
            if (c == '(') {
                if (parse_name(strm, arg)) {
                    if (strm.get(c)) {
                        if (c != ')') {
                            strm.putback(c);
                            strm.clear(ios::failbit);
                        }
                    }
```

```
                    }
               }
               else {
                   strm.putback(c);
                   strm.clear(ios::failbit);
               }
           }
        }
    }
    return strm;
}


void main()
{
    char fname[9], arg[9], c;

    cout << "Enter function call: ";

    while(cin) { // while stream okay
       if (parse_func(cin, fname, arg)) break;
       cout << "Invalid input, need syntax func(arg)\n";
       cin.clear(); // clear stream state
       while(cin.get(c) && c != '\n') { ; } // skip to eol
    }
    cout << "Function read is " << fname << "("
         << arg << ")" << "\n";
}
```

Notice how the function **parse_func()** sets the stream state to **fail**:

```
strm.clear(ios::failbit);
```

To access the enumeration **failbit**, we had to qualify it with the class name **ios**. Why? The enumerated type **io_state** is nested inside the class declaration for **ios**.

Here's a sample run of the program:

```
Enter function call: sin( pi)  // (spaces not permitted)
Invalid input, need syntax func(arg)
sin(pi)
Function read is sin(pi)
```

You'll be seeing this style of validated input again, but now it's time for us to move on to the main topic of this chapter—the stream operators **>>** and **<<**.

Using the Stream Operators

In this section we'll show you how to input and output standard C++ data types (**int**, **char**, and so on) using both default formatting and your own formatting. Then, we'll show you how to customize the stream operators to output user-defined objects.

The secret behind the stream operators is that they have overloaded operator functions. Here are the basic forms for these overloaded functions:

```
istream &istream::operator>>(istream &strm,
                             object_type &object)
{
    // Do the operation ...
    return strm;
}

ostream &ostream::operator<<(ostream &strm,
                             object_type object)
{
    // Do the operation ...
    return strm;
}
```

The operator functions for **>>** are members of the class **istream.** This class defines the stream objects for input operations. Likewise, the operator functions for **<<** are members of the class **ostream**, which defines the stream objects for output. Default operator functions are provided for inputting and outputting the simple C++ data types, as shown in Table 10.5. These operator functions use default formatting for each of the built-in types, which we present in terms of the familiar **scanf()** and **printf()** formats.

While you're looking over Table 10.5, note how the default input formats are the same as the ones used for simple **scanf()** inputs.

Table 10.5 Default formats for the built-in types

Type	Default Format	Type	Default Format
signed char	"%c"	unsigned char	"%c"
char *	"%s"	unsigned char *	"%s"
short	"%hd"	unsigned short	"%hu"
int	"%d"	unsigned int	"%u"
long	"%ld"	unsigned long	"%lu"
float	"%.g"	double	"%.lg"
long double	"%.lg"	void *	"%p"

When data is read into a variable of a given type, all the white space (tabs, spaces, and newlines) up to the first valid character of that type's ASCII representation is skipped. Likewise, the scanning stops when the first nonvalid character for that type is found. The following program shows some examples of this:

```cpp
#include <iostream.h>
#include <string.h>
struct pet_data {
    char name[80];
    int age;
};

pet_data database[3];
void main()
{
    int i, n = 0;

    while (n < 3) {
      cout << "Enter name of pet (or quit): ";
      cin  >> database[n].name;
      if (!strcmp(database[n].name, "quit")) break;
      cout << "Enter pet's age: ";
      cin >> database[n].age;
      n++;
    }
    cout << "\nThe pet database contains: \n\n";
```

```
      for (i = 0; i < n; i++)
        cout << database[i].name << ", age "
               << database[i].age << "\n";
   }
```

Here's a sample run:

```
Enter name of pet (or quit): fido
Enter pet's age: 2
Enter name of pet (or quit): bubba
Enter pet's age: 4
Enter name of pet (or quit): quit
The pet database contains:
fido, age 2
bubba, age 4
```

A few problems might surface when the **>>** operator is used with the built-in types. Things can get fouled up in a hurry if the input format isn't correct. For instance, when reading strings, you can't easily include white space Note what happens to our program with the following input:

```
Enter name of pet (or quit): my friend flicka
Enter pet's age: Enter name of pet (or quit): Enter pet's
age: Enter name of pet (or quit): Enter pet's age: my, age 0,
age 0,
age 0
```

The input scanner stopped reading the pet's name after it read the word "my." It then tried to read in the pet's age starting with the word "friend." Since this failed, it skipped the input, and the program went around the loop again, up to three times. You've probably encountered similar problems when using C's **scanf()**. The solution in C++ is to use the string version of **get()** and to test the stream state, as you learned how to do in previous sections. As an exercise, see if you can apply this technique to fix our sample program.

Chaining the Stream Operators

As we've already shown in numerous examples, you can combine several input or output operations together in a single statement, such as

```
cout << "Your order comes to " << amt << " dollars\n";
```

You might be wondering how this chaining works. Let's take a closer look at the definition of the stream operators to see if we can figure it out.

Remember that the stream operators `<<` and `>>` are binary. The first operand is the stream object, and the second is the object to input or output. For the built-in types, the stream operators are overloaded using member functions, so the first argument is the hidden **this** pointer. Thus, the following example shows equivalent ways to call the `<<` function for integers:

```
cout << 42;              // one way
cout.operator<<(42);     // another way
```

Recall that most of the stream I/O functions return a reference to a stream object. For example, the output operator function for integers looks like the following:

```
ostream& ostream::operator<<(int i)
{
    // somehow output integer
    return *this;
}
```

The pointer **this** references the stream object that serves as the hidden first argument. The **this** pointer is also returned from the output function. Therefore, the stream coming in is the stream returned. This arrangement allows the output operations to be chained together. For example, in the statement

```
cout << "The ultimate answer: " << 42;
```

the `<<` operator, which binds to the left, could be translated into the corresponding function calls

```
(cout.operator<<("The ultimate answer: ")).operator<<(42);
```

The leftmost operator executes and outputs the character string. After this, a reference is returned to the **cout** stream object so that its `<<` function can be called again for the integer **x**. This process is illustrated in Figure 10.4. It's as though the following calls took place:

```
ostream &temp;
temp = cout.operator<<("The ultimate answer: ");
temp.operator<<(42);
```

The resulting output is

```
The ultimate answer: 42
```

The input operator can be chained in a similar fashion.

Note: Keep in mind that the **>>** operator also groups from left to right.

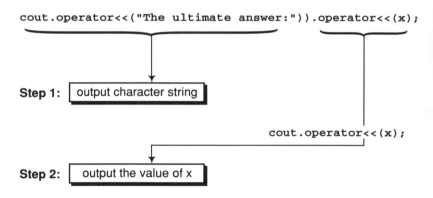

Figure 10.4. Outputting data with the << operator.

Performing Formatted Output

In addition to the default formatting available, you can control the formatting yourself. Each stream has an associated formatting state that determines the formatting to be used. Like the error state, the formatting state is a combination of bit flags. Table 10.6 shows the formatting bits available. These bits can be set using what are called the *I/O manipulators*. These are functions that can be used in conjunction with the stream operators to control the formatting. Table 10.7 shows the common I/O manipulators available.

Note: To use any of the I/O manipulators that take parameters, you must include the header file **iomanip.h**. For the other manipulators, you only need to include **iostream.h**.

Table 10.6. Formatting flags

Flag	Value	Action
skipws	0x0001	Skips white space on input
left	0x0002	Left justifies output
right	0x0004	Right justifies output
internal	0x0008	Uses padding after sign or base indicator
dec	0x0010	Uses decimal base for conversion
oct	0x0020	Uses octal base for conversion
hex	0x0040	Uses hexadecimal base for conversion
showbase	0x0080	Shows base indicator on output
showpoint	0x0100	Always shows decimal point and trailing zeros on floating-point output
uppercase	0x0200	Uses uppercase for outputing hex digits
showpos	0x0400	Adds '+' to positive integers on output
scientific	0x0800	Uses exponential floating notation
fixed	0x1000	Uses fixed-point floating notation
unitbuf	0x2000	Flushes all streams after output
stdio	0x4000	Flushes cout, cerr after output

The most commonly used manipulators are **setfill()**, **setprecision()**, and **setw()**, which control how numbers appear on output. The **setfill()** manipulator controls what character is used for padding. The **setprecision()** manipulator controls how many digits to use after the decimal point, and **setw()** sets the total width of the number. For instance, here's a short program that outputs some numbers using a fill character of '0', a field width of 6, and a precision of 2. This format is equivalent to using the **printf()** format of "%06.2f."

```
#include <iostream.h>
#include <iomanip.h>
void main()
{
    cout << setfill('0') << setprecision(2);
```

```
        cout << setw(6) << 42.17 << '\n';
        cout << setw(6) << 3.14159 << '\n';
    }
```

The output from this program is:

```
042.17
003.14
```

Table 10.7. The common I/O manipulators

Manipulator	I/O Direction	Action
dec	in/out	Sets the base to decimal
oct	in/out	Sets the base to octal
hex	in/out	Sets the base to hexadecimal
ws	in	Skips white pace characters
endl	–	Inserts new line, flush stream
ends	–	Inserts a null byte
flush	–	Flushes the stream
setbase(int b)	in/out	Sets conversion base
setiosflags(long f)	in/out	Sets specified formatting bits
resetiosflags(long f)	in/out	Resets specified formatting bits
setfill(char c)	out	Sets the fill character
setprecision(int n)	out	Uses n digits after decimal point
setw(int w)	in/out	Sets total field width

You might wonder why we called **setw**() for each output. Most of the formatting states stay set once they've been changed. However, the field width gets reset to zero after each input or output. (A field width of zero instructs the function to use whatever width is necessary to output the number.) Each time you wish to output a number at a fixed width, you must use the **setw**() manipulator explicitly.

Performing Formatted Input

You'll notice from Table 10.7 that many of the manipulators work for input as well as output. The **setw**() manipulator is one of them. You can use it whenever you wish to control how many characters are read into a string. As you might surmise, this means you can prevent the input from overflowing a buffer used to hold input data. The following program shows how **setw()** is used:

```
// Program to read in a file name safely
#include <iostream.h>
#include <iomanip.h>
void main()
{
    char fname[13];

    cin >> setw(13); // 13 = 12 characters + 1 null byte
    cin >> fname;
    cout << "The file name is: '" << fname << "'\n";
}
```

When reading strings, only non-whitespace characters are stored in the string. Also, leading whitespace characters are skipped.

Another set of manipulators that can be used for input as well as output are those that control the number base. For instance, here is a program that inputs a hex number and then outputs it in octal:

```
#include <iostream.h>
#include <iomanip.h>
void main()
{
    unsigned x;

    cout << "Enter hex number: ";
    cin >> hex >> x;
    if (!cin) {
        cout << "Not a valid hex number\n";
        cin.clear();
    }
    else
        cout << "The number in octal is: " << oct << x << "\n";
}
```

When a hex number is read, all leading whitespace is skipped, and then digits are read until the first non-hex digit is found. (The non-hex digit is left on the input stream.) If the first non-whitespace character is not a valid hex digit, then the stream is set to the **fail** state. Thus, you can check for valid input, as we did in our program. Here are some sample runs of the program:

```
Enter hex number: 30something
The number in octal is: 60


Enter hex number: x15
Not a valid hex number
```

Similar rules apply for reading in octal and decimal numbers.

You can also use the **setbase()** manipulator for setting the base, where you pass in the number representing the base. For instance, 8 indicates octal, 10 indicates decimal, and 16 indicates hexadecimal. You can also use 0, which specifies that standard C parsing rules for numbers should be applied. That is, a number starting with 0 is treated as octal, a number starting with 0x is treated as hex, and all others are treated as decimal. The following program illustrates this feature:

```cpp
#include <iostream.h>
#include <iomanip.h>
void main()
{
    unsigned x;
    cout << "Enter a number: ";
    cin >> setbase(0) >> x;
    cout << "The number in decimal is: " << x << '\n';
}
```

Here are some sample runs of this program:

```
Enter a number: 42
The number in decimal is: 42


Enter a number: 052
The number in decimal is: 42
```

```
Enter a number: 0x2A
The number in decimal is: 42
```

Setting the Formatting Flags Directly

Some of the formatting flags don't have their own special manipulators to set them. For instance, Table 10.6 indicates that a **skipws** flag is provided; however, Table 10.7 lists no special manipulator for this flag. For these flags, you can use the manipulators **setiosflags()** and **resetiosflags()**. You can pass a bit mask to be used for setting and resetting the flags. For example, the following statement shows how you can turn off the skipping of white space:

```
cin >> resetiosflags(ios::skipws);
```

Note that we can use the flag bit named **skipws**, but that we must qualify it with the class name **ios** because the flag names are nested in the class declaration.

You can also set or reset more than one flag at a time. For instance, here's how you can output a number in a right-justified, capitalized, hex format:

```
unsigned x = 0xab;

cout >> setiosflags(ios::right | ios::hex | ios::uppercase);
cout >> '(' >> setw(4) >> x >> ')';
```

This would result in the following output:

```
(  AB)
```

Overloading the Stream Operators

In previous sections you've seen how to use the built-in formatting routines to enhance the stream operators. However, we haven't begun to tap the real power available. One of the main advantages to the C++ style of stream I/O is that you can overload the stream operators and customize them for your own user-defined objects.

To overload the stream operators, you must define your own operator functions. These functions must be defined in a special way, as shown:

```
// For input
istream &operator>>(istream &strm, object_type &object)
{
    // somehow read in object
    return strm;
}


// For output
ostream &operator<<(ostream &strm, object_type object)
{
    // somehow write out object
    return strm;
}
```

First, your operator functions must pass the appropriate type of stream object type as the first parameter, and the second parameter should be the object to be input or output. Second, the operator function should pass back the stream object. This allows the operators to be chained and also makes it easy to test the state of the stream after the I/O operation.

Note: For the input operator function, you must pass the input argument by reference so it can be modified properly. For the output operator function, you can define the output argument so that it can be passed either by value or by reference.

Let's write our first program to overload the input and output operators. The program defines a structure to represent points and then overloads both the **>>** and **<<** operators to work with points. We've also coded the input routine so that it can accept only a specific syntax, which is *x,y*, for each point entered.

```
// Overloaded input and output example for points
#include <iostream.h>
struct point {
    int x, y;
    void set(int a, int b) { x = a; y = b; }
```

```
        point(void) { set(0,0); }
        point(int a, int b) { set(a,b); }
};

ostream &operator<<(ostream &strm, point p)
{
    return strm << "(" << p.x << "," << p.y << ")";
}


istream &operator>>(istream &strm, point &p)
// Input routine for points. Looks for x,y pattern
{
    int x, y;
    char c;

    if (strm >> x) {  // read first int just fine
        if (strm >> c) { // look for comma
            if (c == ',') { // yes, we found one
                if (strm >> y) { // read 2nd int just fine
                    p.set(x, y);  // so set point
                    return strm;  // return stream in good state
                }
            }
        }
    }
    strm.clear(ios::failbit);  // set stream to fail state
    return strm;
}


void main()
{
    point p;
    char c;

    cout << "Enter new window location: ";
    // validation loop
    while(1) {
        if (cin >> p) break; // point read successfully
        cout << "Point entered wrong, please use x,y\n";
```

```
        cin.clear(); // reset stream state, read to eol
        while(cin.get(c) && c != '\n') { ; }
    }
    cout << "New window location is: " << p << "\n";
}
```

Let's step through this program. First, take a look at the overloaded **operator<<()** function. We've taken special care to use the stream object passed in, rather than using **cout**. This insures that the proper stream linkage is maintained. And contrary to what you might think, recursion does not enter into the picture when we use the **<<** operator inside our **<<** operator function, because the arguments in this case are never **point** objects. The input function, **operator>>()**, also uses the same technique of stream linkage; it uses its sister **operator>>()** functions as well.

You should also study the **operator>>()** function carefully because it illustrates a useful method for handling input errors. It is written so that the values for the **point** coordinates can be entered only in a predefined format—two integers separated by a comma. It relies on the fact that the predefined input operator function for integers generates an error if an integer is not read after whitespace characters are skipped. It then reads in a character and checks to make sure the character read is a comma. Only then does it try to read in another integer. If the input is in the correct format, the point is updated and the stream is returned in the **good** state. Otherwise, the stream is set to the **fail** state (in case it isn't already) before it is returned. The main program sets up a **while** loop that exits only if our operator function says it's okay to exit. Otherwise, an error message is printed and the program tries to read more data.

Since we've just shown you how to perform a simple pattern recognition operation with input data, let's compare it to what can be done with C's **scanf()** function. Suppose you wished to enter dates with a format of mo–day–yr. You can get **scanf()** to accept this pattern with the following statement:

```
scanf("%d-%d-%d", &mo, &day, &yr);
```

Notice that this format forces the input of a date to have dashes between the numbers. You might be tempted to do a similar thing with the **>>** operator:

```
cin >> mo >> '-' >> day >> '-' yr;
```

This won't work because we're trying to read a value into the constant '-' in the second application of the >> operator. The way to handle this type of input is use a method similar to the one we used to read the **point** objects. That is, we must read individual fields and test the stream state each time.

Note: One reason for using >> and << is that they provide a greater degree of type checking than **printf()** and **scanf()**. The arguments to >> and << are checked at compile-time. The arguments used with the **printf()** and **scanf()** functions, on the other hand, are not type-checked.

Using Virtual I/O Functions

The real advantage of overloading the stream operators is that you can also apply virtual functions to support polymorphic input and output. Of course, we couldn't do this with the **scanf()** and **printf()** families of functions provided with C. Because the operator functions << and >> aren't virtual (they are only overloaded in the classes **ostream** and **istream**), you might be wondering how we can create virtual I/O functions.

To see this, let's try to build a virtual output function. We'll overload the << operator. The trick is that we'll pass a pointer to the object to be output rather than the object itself. Inside the function we'll call a member function, which happens to be virtual, to perform the output. Here's an example, which outputs the current time of a clock:

```
ostream &operator<<(ostream &strm, clock *clk)
{
    return clk->display(strm); // display() can be virtual
}
```

This function formats **clock** objects. Note that the **clock** pointer **clk** can point to an object of any derived class of **clock**. Thus, if **display()** is virtual, a different version of it might be used for any given **clock** object. This same trick will also work if you pass the object using a reference argument.

```
// Note how we're passing a reference to a clock!!
ostream &operator<<(ostream &strm, clock &clk)
{
    return clk.display(strm); // display() can be virtual
```

```
                                               // here too
    }
```

To see this in action, let's borrow our familiar clock example from previous chapters and derive a new type of clock that prints the letters AM or PM after the time and uses a twelve-hour clock instead of a twenty-four-hour clock.

```
///////////////////////////////////////////////
// Polymorphic clock output example
///////////////////////////////////////////////
#include <iostream.h>
#include <iomanip.h>
///////////////////////////////////////////////
// Basic 24-hour clock class
///////////////////////////////////////////////
class clock {
protected:
    int hr, min, sec;
public:
    clock(int h, int m, int s) { hr = h; min = m; sec = s; }
    virtual ostream &display(ostream &s);
};

ostream &clock::display(ostream &strm)
// Virtual function to display the time with a 24-hour
// format. The hour field has blank padding; the other
// fields use a '0' fill character.
{
    return strm << setfill(' ') << setw(2) << hr << ":"
                << setfill('0') << setw(2) << min << ":"
                << setw(2) << sec;
}

ostream &operator<<(ostream &strm, clock *c)
// This operator function calls a virtual function.
// Note: This function is not a member function.
{
    return c->display(strm);
}
```

```
//////////////////////////////////////////////
// 12-hour clock
//////////////////////////////////////////////
class ampm_clock : public clock {
public:
    ampm_clock(int h, int m, int s) : clock(h, m, s) { ; }
    virtual ostream &display(ostream &strm);
};

ostream &ampm_clock::display(ostream &strm)
// Function to override the clock display() function
// to include an AMPM indicator.
{
    int amflag, hrold = hr; // save hour setting

    if (hr < 12) amflag = 1; else { amflag = 0; hr -= 12; }
    clock::display(strm); // call base class version
    if (amflag) strm << " AM"; else strm << " PM";

    hr = hrold; // restore hour setting
    return strm;
}

void main()
{
    clock military_time(17, 30, 45), *the_time;
    ampm_clock civilian_time(17, 30, 45);

    the_time = &military_time;
    cout << the_time << "\n";
    the_time = &civilian_time;
    cout << the_time << "\n";
}
```

This program produces

```
17:30:45
 5:30:45 PM
```

Note: The method of using virtual output functions will also work with virtual input functions.

Stream File I/O

We have used the standard input and output streams for our programs in this chapter. We can also make our examples work with files by replacing **cin** and **cout** with appropriate stream objects attached to files.

The three stream file classes available for file I/O are **ifstream**, **ofstream**, and **fstream**. They are used for file input, file output, and file input/output. These classes are defined in the header file **fstream.h**, which you must include to use file I/O. In this book, we'll be using **fstream** exclusively because it supports both input and output.

Note: The **fstream.h** header file incorporates the **iostream.h** header file. You don't need to include **iostream.h** explicitly when using **fstream.h**.

Here is an example of how you can create a file, open it for output, and write text to it. We'll soon be explaining the features illustrated in the program.

```
#include <fstream.h>
void main()
{
    fstream myfile;

    myfile.open("test.fil", ios::out | ios::trunc);
    if (!myfile) { cout << "Error opening test.fil\n");
    }
    else { myfile << "Here is some test data\n";
        myfile.close();
    }
}
```

Table 10.8 provides the five basic functions you can use in conjunction with **fstream** objects.

When opening an **fstream** file, you must specify an open mode parameter. This parameter is made up of a number of flags which you can OR together, as given in Table 10.9. The flag names used are nested inside the **ios** class; thus, you must qualify them with the **ios** name when referencing them. For instance, in our sample program, we opened up the file for output, and truncated the file if it already existed, with the following flags:

```
ios::out | ios::trunc
```

There is also a permission mode parameter which grants read/write access. Normally, the default of allowing reading and writing is sufficient, so you don't have to include this parameter.

Table 10.8. The five basic fstream functions

fstream(void);
Constructor to initialize an fstream object. Does not open the file.

fstream(char *fn, int omode, int pmode = S_IREAD|S_IWRITE);
Creates an **fstream** object, and opens the file **fn**, using the specified open and permission modes.

~fstream(void);
Destructor that flushes the file buffer and closes the file (if not already closed).

void fstream::open(char *fn, int omode, int pmode = S_IREAD|S_IWRITE);
Opens the file **fn**, using the specified open and permission modes.

void fstream::close(void);
Closes the file if not already closed.

Table 10.9. Open mode definitions

Mode	Value	Description
in	0x01	Open for reading
out	0x02	Open for writing
ate	0x04	Seek to end of file upon opening
app	0x08	Open in append mode
trunc	0x10	Truncate file on open if it already exists

nocreate	0x20	File must exist at open, or open fails
noreplace	0x40	File must be new at open, or open fails
binary	0x80	Don't translate carriage return/line feed pairs (the opposite of text mode, the default)

You'll notice from Table 10.8 that you can open a file using one of two techniques: Open the file at the time the constructor is called or use the **open**() function. In our sample program, we used the latter technique. We could have opened the file with the constructor. Also, the destructor will automatically close the file for us. Thus, we could write the program in a simpler fashion.

```
#include <fstream.h>
void main()
{
    fstream myfile("test.fil", ios::out | ios::trunc);
    if (!myfile) {
        cout << "Error opening test.fil\n");
    }
    else {
        myfile << "Here is some test data\n";
    }
    // File closed automatically by destructor
}
```

It's best to separate the opening and closing of the file from the constructor and destructor. That way, you have finer control over the file status. For instance, it's possible to close the file and then use the same **fstream** object to open another one. For example:

```
fstream yourfile;
yourfile.open("aaa.fil", ios::out | ios::trunc);
yourfile.close();
yourfile.open("bbb.fil", ios::out | ios::trunc);
```

Random Access I/O

Although stream objects are normally used to perform stream-oriented I/O (that is, sequential access), you can perform random access I/O as well. Table

10.10 shows some of the functions available for this purpose, and Table 10.11 shows some definitions available for determining the type of seek mode to use.

Table 10.10. Random access routines

Input routines

istream &istream::seekg(long ofs, seek_dir mode);
long istream::tellg(void);
istream &istream::read(signed char *s, int nbytes);
istream &istream::read(unsigned char *s, int nbytes);

Output routines

ostream &ostream::seekp(long ofs, seek_dir mode);
long ostream::tellp(void);
ostream &ostream::write(const signed char *s, int nbytes);
ostream &ostream::write(const unsigned char *s, int nbytes);

Table 10.11. Seek modes

enum seek_dir {
  beg = 0, // Seek relative to beginning of file
  cur = 1, // Seek relative to current file position
  end = 2   // Seek relative to end of file
};

These modes are defined inside the class ios.

These random access routines are similar to the ones provided in the **stdio** C libary. However, note that there are two seek routines, **seekg()** and **seekp()**—one for the input position, and one for the output position. Likewise, there are two functions to return the stream positions, **tellg()** and **tellp()**, for input and output positions, respectively.

When seeking to a file location, you must specify the seek mode, using the enumerated type **seek_dir**. The values given in Table 10.11 are similar to the SEEK_BEG, SEEK_CUR, and SEEK_END constants in the **stdio** C library.

Let's see these routines in action. The following program defines a **part** structure and then writes out some parts to different locations in the file. It then closes the file and tries to read these parts back in. As a check, the parts are then displayed on the standard output, using a customized **<<** operator function (just to give you more practice at designing your own formatting routines). The program outputs the following:

```
Widget   Super Deluxe    .    159.99
Gadget   Ultra Magnum         249.95
Gizmo    Turbo Professional    69.99
```

```cpp
// Sample program storing a parts database
// using random access I/O
#include <fstream.h>
#include <iomanip.h>
struct part {
    char name[9];
    char model[21];
    double price;
};


ostream &operator<<(ostream &strm, part &p)
// Operator to output a part in a tabular
// format
{
    // Output the part name left-justified
    strm << setiosflags(ios::left);
    strm << setw(8) << p.name;
    // Output the part model left-justified
    strm << setiosflags(ios::left);
    strm << setw(20) << p.model;
    // Output the price right-justified
    strm << setiosflags(ios::right);
    strm << setw(6) << setprecision(2) << p.price;
    return strm;
}


part parts_list[3] = {
    { "Widget", "Super Deluxe", 159.99 },
    { "Gadget", "Ultra Magnum", 249.95 },
```

```
        { "Gizmo",   "Turbo Professional", 69.99 }
};

void main()
{
    fstream f;
    int i;

    // Open the file in binary mode
    f.open("parts.fil", ios::out | ios::binary);

    // Write the parts to the 17th, 18th and 19th records
    for (i = 0; i<3; i++) {
        f.seekp((17+i)*sizeof(part), ios::beg);
        f.write((const char *)&parts_list[i], sizeof(part));
    }
    f.close();

    // Now, try reading them back in
    f.open("parts.fil", ios::in | ios::binary);
    for (i = 0; i<3; i++) {
        f.seekg((17+i)*sizeof(part), ios::beg);
        f.read((char *)&parts_list[i], sizeof(part));
    }

    // Display the parts to the standard output
    for (i = 0; i<3; i++) cout << parts_list[i] << '\n';
}
```

In-Memory Formatting

The C++ stream I/O library provides a way to format directly to and from memory buffers, similar to the way that **sprintf()** and **sscanf()** are used in C. The **strstream** class is used for this purpose. It is defined in the header file **strstrea.h**, which you must include if you wish to perform in-memory formatting.

> **Note:** The **strstrea.h** header also includes the **iostream.h** header; thus, you don't need to include both **strstrea.h** and **iostream.h**.

You can create a **strstream** object in two ways using the following constructors:

```
// Create a stream object attached to a dynamic buffer
strstream(void);

// Create a stream object attached to an existing buffer
// of size n, and use the I/O mode specified
strstream(char *b, int n, int mode);
```

With both ways, you can perform both input and output to the stream. Here's a simple example:

```
// Sample program showing in memory formatting
#include <strstream.h>
void main()
{
    char buff[80];
    strstream s(buff, 80, ios::out);
    int the_answer = 42;

    s << "The answer is: " << the_answer;
    cout << buff; // just to see if it worked
}
```

This program outputs the following:

```
The answer is: 42
```

Summary

In this chapter you learned how to use the flexible C++ stream I/O system. We started by presenting a tour of the new I/O features that the C++ stream system provides. Then, we explored the standard input and output stream objects, as well as techniques for performing file and in-memory I/O. We presented numerous examples to show you how to use the stream input and output operators >> and <<. We also showed you how to customize these operators for your own objects.

By now, you should know how to use stream objects and operators to enhance the I/O capabilities of your programs. In the next chapter, we'll take a different approach to I/O—record-oriented I/O.

Exercises

1. Write an arithmetic expression parser using a combination of the stream operators and functions. Make sure that you test the stream state for failures when performing input and output operations.

2. Study the **iostream.h**, **fstream.h**, and **strstream.h** header files included with your compiler. If you have the source code to the stream methods, study those also. Notice how multiple inheritance is used extensively by the stream I/O class system.

3. Implement an I/O system similar to that given in this chapter, except make it work for your favorite interactive windowing environment. (Hint: The stream metaphor might not be the most appropriate method, but could it work? Also, how would you incorporate both mouse and keyboard inputs?)

4. It's possible to write your own I/O manipulators. Study the documentation that came with your compiler on how to do this, and write some manipulators of your own to set up printer codes (such as page eject, font sizes, etc.) for your printer.

Record-Oriented File I/O

In the previous chapter you learned how to use the flexible C++ stream I/O system to create general-purpose stream I/O objects. In keeping with the philosophy of C, the C++ I/O classes are built on top of C++ and are accessed through a set of standard header files and libraries. This means that you can also define your own I/O system with user-defined classes. And that's exactly what we're going to do next.

Our goal is to show you how to implement a record-oriented file I/O system. With this type of system, we'll be able to read and write random access records. To pull this off, we'll be exploiting many of the object-oriented features of C++. We'll also be introducing some more advanced features, such as *templates* and *parameterized types*, which you haven't seen yet.

We'll start this chapter by introducing the concept of a record-oriented I/O system. Then, we'll develop a program that uses simple record-oriented I/O techniques. Our next stop is templates and parameterized types. Here we'll cover a new technique for creating reusable code, which we'll apply to our file system application. We'll spend the remainder of the chapter showing you how to develop a general-purpose inventory program.

Here are some of the highlights of this chapter:

- How to use objects to support record-oriented files
- How to use templates to implement parameterized types
- How parameterized types relate to inheritance
- Techniques for creating an inventory program

The Limits of Stream I/O

Stream-oriented I/O is appropriate for many applications; however, some applications require more flexible I/O capabilities. For instance, suppose we need to maintain an inventory of the parts that a computer company has in stock. One way to do this is to store the parts in a random access, fixed-length record file. Figure 11.1 illustrates a sample format of the file type we have in mind.

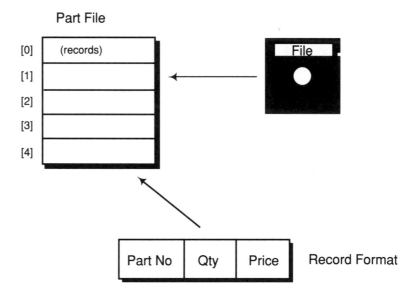

Figure 11.1. A sample record-oriented file.

The system we're using here is considered a *record-oriented file I/O system* because the file is arranged into a series of multibyte sections called *records*. The main advantage of using this system is that we can randomly access any record location for a read or write operation.

What we really want is a way to support files of different record types. For instance, we might want a file of customer data or a file of personnel data. Unfortunately, C++ does not directly support this type of record I/O. However, it's easy to get around this restriction by using classes and developing our own system.

Let's look at a few lines of code to illustrate what we want our record-oriented I/O system to do.

```
struct part {
    int partno, qty;
    double price;
};

file_of<part> inventory;
part p;

inventory.open("yr1989.inv", update);
inventory.read(&p, 1);
p.qty--;
inventory.write(&p, 1);
inventory.close();
```

The first statement after the structure declaration declares an inventory file object whose records are of type **part**. We then use this file object to open up a file, read the first part from the file, update the part quantity, write it back to the file, and close the file. This represents the typical update process we might use to keep our inventory database up-to-date.

One of the statements,

```
file_of<part> inventory;
```

probably doesn't make much sense to you yet because it doesn't look like any C++ statement we've used before. What does **file_of<part>** mean? It *represents* the type of our **inventory** object. Recall how objects are declared in general:

```
type_of_object object;
```

For instance, we might have

```
int i;
part p;
window w;
```

The only thing different about **file_of<part>** is that, instead of being just a simple type identifier, it includes a parameter—**part**. Actually, our declaration is an example of what is known as a *parameterized type*.

What do parameterized types have to do with our record I/O system? They let us conveniently support files with different record types. To see how this works, we'll first need to examine the basic features of record-oriented I/O systems. Then, we'll see how to incorporate parameterized types into our I/O system.

Getting Started with Record-Oriented Files

As with many general-purpose systems, such as our record I/O file system, you should first design a general class and then use this class to derive more specific classes. This approach helps you to consider what the essential features of your system are and encourages you to apply an object-oriented, building-block approach to solving your problems. That's what we'll do here.

Before we write any code we'll need to determine the operations that our objects must perform. That is, we need to come up with a list of methods for our class definition. For our record-oriented files, we'll need to perform the following operations:

- Declare a file object using a specified record size
- Open and attach a file to the file object
- Seek to any record in the file
- Read and write any record in the file
- Handle errors
- Close the file

In addition to these methods, we'll need to determine the data and state variables that our record objects will require. For instance, we'll need to be able to keep track of the record size, the current record, the name of the file, and the file handle. Now that we know our requirements, we can put together a general class.

```
/////////////////////////////////////////////////////
// recfile.h: General record I/O file class header
/////////////////////////////////////////////////////
#ifndef H_RECFILE
#define H_RECFILE
#include <stdio.h>
enum access_mode { f_create, f_update };
```

```
class recfile {
protected:
    // state variables
    FILE *fp;         // standard I/O file pointer
    char *name;       // name of thc file
    int recsize;      // record size in bytes
    long curr_rec;    // current record (count by zero)
    int opened;       // file open status
public:
    // methods
    recfile(int recsize = 1);
    ~recfile(void) { close(); }
    virtual int open(char *fname, enum access_mode mode);
    virtual int close(void);
    int isopen(void) { return opened; }
    long seek(long recno, int seek_mode=SEEK_SET);
    long rw(
       int dir, void *data, unsigned nrecs, long recno
    );
    virtual void err_handler(int errtype, ...);
};
#endif
```

Let's start with the data members of **recfile**, and then we'll look at its functions. First, note that the file pointer **fp** is declared as type **FILE *** We did this because we're going to use the standard C I/O system for our basic file access operations. Our **recfile** class simply serves as a wrapper that is placed around the standard I/O system so that we can perform more high-level I/O operations. Specifically, we want to make it easy to perform record-oriented reads and writes.

Let's now walk through each of the methods of our **recfile** class. We'll start with the constructor and destructor.

```
///////////////////////////////////////////////
// recfile.cpp: Implementation of recfile class
///////////////////////////////////////////////
#include <string.h>
#include <stdarg.h>
#include <errno.h>
#include "recfile.h"
```

```
recfile::recfile(int recsize)
// Creates a record file object. Defaults to
// one-byte records-(character I/O).
{
    name = NULL; fp = NULL;
    recfile::recsize = recsize;
    opened = 0;
}
```

Our constructor initializes all of the state variables, sets up the record size of the file, and sets the file status to "not open." The destructor is declared inline in the class declaration. It's quite simple. All it does is call **close()** to insure that the associated file is closed when we no longer need the object. We certainly don't want to keep any open files hanging around!

After a **recfile** object is initialized, we need a way to open and attach the file to the initialized object. We'll also need a way to close the file after we are finished with it. The methods **open()** and **close()** are designed to handle these tasks.

```
int recfile::open(char *fname, enum access_mode mode)
// open the file using standard C I/O
// returns the open status
{
    close(); // in case already opened
    if (mode == f_create) {
        // create, truncate if already exists
        fp = fopen(fname, "w+b");
    }
    else {
        // test for existence first
        fp = fopen(fname, "r");
        if (fp != NULL) {
            fclose(fp);
            fp = fopen(fname, "r+b");
        }
    }
    if (fp == NULL) {
        err_handler(2, fname);
        opened = 0;
    }
```

```
    else {
       name = new char[strlen(fname)+1];
       strcpy(name, fname);
       opened = 1;
    }
    return opened;
}

int recfile::close(void)
// returns 1 if successful, else 0
{
    if (opened) {
       if (fclose(fp) == 0) {
           opened = 0;
          delete[] name;
        }
       else err_handler(3);
    }
    return !opened;
}
```

The **open()** function takes two arguments: a filename and an access mode. The filename is a character string, and the access mode is an enumerated type with the following values:

Value	Description
f_create	Creates the file and opens it for reading and writing. If the file already exists, the file is cleared.
f_update	Opens an existing file for reading and writing. If the file doesn't exist, an error occurs.

In **open()**, notice that the file is opened with the standard C **fopen()** function. Also, the open status flag is set and the filename and file pointer are stored. Before the new file is opened, the function checks to see if a file is already open. If this is the case, the currently opened file is closed before the new file is opened. This makes our **recfile** object more robust. You can think of it as an insurance policy against accidentally losing data.

The **close()** function uses the standard **fclose()** function to close a file. It also frees up the allocated space for the filename. Both functions return 1 if successful; otherwise, the **err_handler()** function is called and 0 is returned.

Once a file is opened, it can be accessed by **seek()** and **rw()**. Let's explore these functions next.

```
long recfile::seek(long recno, int seek_mode)
// Moves the file pointer to the record offset recno,
// using seek_mode (which should be either SEEK_SET,
// SEEK_CUR, or SEEK_END). Returns -1 and reports if
// there's an error; otherwise it returns the new record
// position.
{
    long newpos = recno * recsize;
    if (opened) {
        if ((newpos = fseek(fp,newpos,seek_mode)) == -1) {
            err_handler(4, recno);
            return -1;
        }
        return curr_rec = newpos / recsize;
    }
    err_handler(1);
    return -1;
}


long recfile::rw(int dir, void *d, unsigned nr, long recno)
// Reads/writes nr records in/out of buffer d at record
// recno. If iodir = 1, it does a write; otherwise it does
// a read. If recno = -1, it means to read/write from
// the current position. Returns 0 if error; otherwise the
// number of bytes moved is returned. The recno offset is
// always from the beginning of the file (unless it is -1,
// which means current position).
{
    long recsmoved;

    // Always do a seek so that fread() and fwrite() work
    // properly.
    // Seek either to current record or to specified one.
    if (opened) {
```

```
        if (recno == -1) {
          if (seek(0L, SEEK_CUR)) return 0;
        }
        else {
          if (seek(recno, SEEK_SET)) return 0;
        }
        if (dir == 1)
            recsmoved = fwrite(d, recsize, nr, fp);
            else recsmoved = fread(d, recsize, nr, fp);
        if (recsmoved != nr) err_handler(5,dir,recno);
        return recsmoved;
    }
    else {
      err_handler(1);
      recsmoved = 0;
    }
    return recsmoved;
  }
```

The **seek()** function calls **fseek()** and takes the same type of settings for the **seek_mode** argument: SEEK_SET, SEEK_CUR, and SEEK_END. However, the offset is interpreted as the number of records rather than the number of bytes. Therefore, the **recsize** is used as a multiplier. The current record position is returned, or -1 is returned in case of an error. (We couldn't use 0 for an error indicator, because 0 is a valid record position.) If there is an error, the **err_handler()** is called.

The **rw()** function is used to both read and write records. The I/O mode (read or write) is supplied with the first argument, **dir**. If **dir** is set to 0, a read operation occurs; setting it to 1 causes a write to occur. Arguments are also provided to specify the record position (**recno**) and the number of records to read or write (**nr**). Note that we check the **recno** argument for a special code (-1) to determine if we should use the current record, which we also keep track of in the variable **curr_rec**.

The data is transferred to and from the memory pointed to by the void pointer **d**. However, the function assumes that enough space has been allocated for the data. The derived classes that we'll develop later will do this for us.

Note that when mixing random access reads and writes, you must always do an intervening seek so that the file buffer is flushed properly, as we do in **rw()**. The function does the I/O operation by calling either **fread()**

or **fwrite()**. It checks for an incomplete transfer (that is, not enough records read or written) and calls **err_handler()** in case of an error. If the operation is successful, **rw()** returns the number of records transferred.

As you might have noticed, all our functions call **err_handler()** in case of an error. This function takes the error type as the first parameter, along with a varying number of other parameters.

```
char *dirnames[2] = { "read", "write" };
void recfile::err_handler(int errtyp,...)
{
    va_list arg_ptr;
    int dir;
    long rec;
    char *s;

    va_start(arg_ptr, errtyp);
    switch (errtyp) {
      case 0: fprintf(stderr,"No error\n"); break;
      case 1: // never opened file
        fprintf(stderr,"Trying to access unopened file\n");
        break;
      case 2: // error opening
        s = va_arg(arg_ptr, char *);
        fprintf(stderr, "%s: %s\n", strerror(errno), s);
        break;
      case 3: // error closing file
        fprintf(stderr,"%s: %s\n", strerror(errno), name);
        break;
      case 4: // error seeking
        fprintf(stderr,"%s: %ld\n", strerror(errno),
                va_arg(arg_ptr, long));
        break;
      case 5: // error reading or writing
        dir = va_arg(arg_ptr, int);
        rec = va_arg(arg_ptr, long);
        fprintf(stderr,"Incomplete %s at %ld for file %s\n",
                dirnames[dir], rec, name);
        break;
    }
```

```
        va_end(arg_ptr);
    }
```

A **switch** statement is used to control how the error is processed. In all cases, an error message is formatted and written to **stderr**. Note that we've made **err_handler()** virtual so that we can change the way it works by deriving another class. But this isn't the only way to make a flexible error handler. Another technique is to use a global function pointer and then initialize it to point to a default function. If you wished to change the error handling action, you could just point to a different function.

Now that we've defined our general class, let's put it to use. Here is a program that opens up a file of parts, writes out a part to the fifth record, and then reads the part back and displays the data that has been read.

```
/////////////////////////////////////////
// Simple record-oriented file example
// Be sure to link with recfile.cpp
/////////////////////////////////////////
#include "recfile.h"
class part {
protected:
    int partno, qty;
    double price;
public:
    part(int n, int q, double p) {
      partno = n; qty = q; price = p;
    }
    void display(FILE *f) {
      fprintf(f, "partno: %4d  qty: %5d  price: $%f\n",
              partno, qty, price);
    }
};

void main()
{
    recfile f(sizeof(part));
    part p(1, 100, 249.99);

    f.open("test.fil", f_create);
    f.rw(1, &p, 1, 5); // write one part to record #5
```

```
        f.rw(0, &p, 1, 5); // read it back in
        p.display(stdout);
        f.close(); // optional; destructor would do it for us
   }
```

To compile and run this program, make sure that you include the **recfile.h** file, which has the class declarations, and that you link the program with **recfile.cpp**, which contains the class methods.

If you look at the main program, you might discover that it's not as high level as we promised. Sure, you don't have to perform the file position calculations yourself (the class does it), but you must compute the record size (which we've done with **sizeof()**). Also, when using **rw()** you must pass a pointer to the part structure and hope that you get it right, since the **rw()** prototype specifies a void pointer for this slot. How can we improve this situation? One way is to derive a new class specifically for parts files.

```
/////////////////////////////////////////
// Example of derived parts file class
// Be sure to link with recfile.cpp
/////////////////////////////////////////
#include "recfile.h"
class part {
protected:
    int partno, qty;
    double price;
public:
    part(int n, int q, double p) {
      partno = n; qty = q; price = p;
    }
    void display(FILE *f) {
      fprintf(f, "partno: %5d  qty: %5d  price: $%6.2f\n",
               partno, qty, price);
    }
};

// Derived class for parts files
class parts_file : public recfile {
public:
    parts_file(void) : recfile(sizeof(part)) { ; }
    long read(part &p, long recno = -1) {
```

```
        return rw(0, &p, 1, recno);
     }
     long write(part &p, long recno = -1) {
        return rw(1, &p, 1, recno);
     }
};

void main()
{
    parts_file f;
    part p(1, 100, 249.99);

    f.open("test.fil", f_create);
    f.write(p, 5);
    f.read(p, 5);
    p.display(stdout);
    f.close();
}
```

Note how we were able to reuse all of the functions of the base class **recfile**. We added three new functions: **parts_file()**, **read()**, and **write()**. The first function is a new constructor that calls the base constructor with the proper record size. (Remember that since our base constructor has an argument, we *must* call it.) Then we added the functions **read()** and **write()**, which provide a higher-level interface to the **rw()** function. These functions let us pass the parts by reference. In this case, we can only read or write one part at a time.

Why did we really need to derive this new class? We wanted to provide the proper type casting from our specific **part** type to the unspecified type used in the **recfile** class. Note how **read()** and **write()** pass along a **part** pointer to the **rw()** function, which uses a **void** pointer. Also, notice how the constructor handles the record size initialization for us by using the size of the part structure.

Note: A typical use of a derived class is to provide a type casting interface to a more general base class. The derived class is often referred to as an *interface class*.

Although this approach works well, it's not as general purpose as it could be. For example, suppose we wanted to create a file of **client** records, where **client** is a user-defined structure. We'd have to derive yet another class to handle this new structure. In fact, for every new type of file we introduce we must derive a special class. Although we could create these new classes by copying the derived class definition and then modifying it, there is a better way. It's now time to reveal our secret weapon—parameterized types.

We're going to construct a second program, which uses parameterized types, that is much more general purpose than the program we first introduced. But before we do, let's take a detour and find out what parameterized types are all about.

Parameterized Types and Templates

A parameterized type is a general type that is composed of other subtypes. You can think of the subtypes as being parameters to the main type. Although you might not realize it, you have used parameterized types before.

One example of a parameterized type is an array. An array is a data structure that consists of a continuous sequence of objects of some subtype. For example, you can have an array of **int**s, an array of **float**s, an array of **part**s, and so on. Another example of a parameterized type is a simple stack. The stack element type would serve as a parameter to the main stack type. You could then have a stack of **int**s, a stack of **float**s, a stack of **part**s, and so on.

Arrays are the only built-in parameterized type that C++ provides. However, you can create your own parameterized types using the **template** construct. You can think of a template as a sort of macro-ized structure, where the subtypes are passed in as parameters.

Note: We'll be using the terms *template* and *parameterized type* interchangeably throughout this discussion because the two terms mean the same thing. (C++ uses templates to implement parameterized types.)

You can define a template by placing the **template<>** descriptor before a class or function definition. The **template<>** descriptor specifies the parameters to be used in the template. The parameters can be either types or constant expressions. For example, the following program shows how you can define and use a simple stack template:

```
#include <stdio.h>
// Define stacks of type T, size S
template<class T, int S>
class stack {
private:
    T data[S];
    int cursor;
public:
    stack(void)    { cursor = -1; }
    void push(T d) { data[++cursor] = d; }
    T pop(void)    { return data[cursor--]; }
};

void main()
{
    stack<int, 10> s; // declare stack of 10 ints

    s.push(25);
    s.push(17);
    printf("First pop:  %d\n", s.pop());
    printf("Second pop: %d\n", s.pop());
}
```

Take a look at the **template** prefix used with the **stack** class declaration:

```
template<class T, int S>
```

Notice that parameters are passed to a template by placing them between the angle brackets **<>**. Two types of parameters are supported: types and constants. A type name is specified by prefixing it with the keyword **class**. (Recall that classes are types.) For constants, you specify the type of constant you wish to be allowed.

In our example, we passed the class (or type) **T** and the integer **S** The **T** parameter represents the type of elements we want to store in our stack. The **S** parameter specifies the size of the stack. Notice how these parameters are used in the **stack** template to define the array used to hold stack data:

```
T data[S];
```

Here, we're using a statically allocated array. Also, notice how we use the type **T** in the **push()** function.

```
void push(T d) { data[++cursor] = d; }
```

How are templates used? To see how, we'll need to explore how templates relate to what we already know—classes and objects. A template is to a class what a class is to an object. Recall that an object is an instantiation of a class. A class is an instantiation of a template. You can think of a template as being a sort of meta-class from which you can create a family of classes.

A class is instantiated from a template when the compiler encounters the class being defined from the template. For example, we can define a **stack** class to hold 10 **int**s with the following notation:

```
stack<int, 10> // define a specific type of stack
```

This notation (a template name followed by parameters placed between angle brackets) can be used wherever a type name is used. For instance, we can declare an object of type **stack<int, 10>** as we did in our sample program.

```
stack<int, 10> s; // declare stack of 10 ints;
```

This type of declaration causes a specific class to be generated, and then it creates an object of that class. In a sense, the compiler builds the following code:

```
class int_stack {
private:
    int data[10];
    int cursor;
public:
    stack(void)       { cursor = -1; }
    void push(int d) { data[++cursor] = d; }
    int pop(void)     { return data[cursor--]; }
};

int_stack s;
```

Notice how **T** was replaced everywhere with **int** and **S** was replaced with 10. Also, a unique name was given for the stack.

You can also make templates out of functions. In a sense, you end up with *meta-functions*. Once instantiated, a unique function is generated using the template arguments. For example, if we hadn't declared the stack functions inside the class declaration, we would have needed to declare them outside as template functions. Here's how we could have declared them:

```
template<class T, int S>
stack<T, S>::stack(void)
{
    cursor = -1;
}

template<class T, int S>
void stack<T, S>::push(T d)
{
    data[++cursor] = d;
}

template<class T, int S>
T stack<T, S>::pop(void)
{
    return data[cursor--];
}
```

There are three issues to notice here. First, we had to specify the class name for each of the member functions using the parameterized form, **stack<T, S>**. Why? We did this so that the member functions are associated with the correct class. Second, we specified the constructor as

```
stack<T, S>::stack(void) // this way
```

and not as

```
stack<T, S>::stack<T, S>(void) // not this way!
```

That is, the function name doesn't require the template syntax.

Third, none of our functions relied on the template parameter **S**, but we had to specify it anyway in order to uniquely identify the class.

For our **stack<int, 10>** class, the following functions would be generated (we've used an arbitrary class name of **int_stack**):

```
int_stack::int_stack(void) { cursor = -1; }

void int_stack::push(int d) {  data[++cursor] = d; }

int int_stack::pop(void) { return data[cursor--]; }
```

Templates and Derived Classes

As you might surmise from the previous section, using templates can cause a lot of code to be generated, albeit direct and efficient code. For example, for each **stack** class instantiated from the **stack** template, a complete set of functions is generated. There are two ways to reduce the amount of code being generated: Use inline functions, which we did for our stack class, and create templates from derived classes.

The second technique works as follows: First, define a base class that implements most of the code to be shared between the derived classes. Classes derived from this base class are meant to be **interface** classes, as mentioned earlier. These interface classes do nothing more than the necessary type casting needed for a specific class type. Typically, the required functions can be made inline. Second, instead of explicitly defining a series of derived classes, define a single derived class as a template. Then, when derived classes are instantiated from this template, very little extra code (if any) is actually generated.

We can use this technique with our **recfile** class. Recall how we derived a special class to handle files of parts:

```
class parts_file : public recfile {
public:
    parts_file(void) : recfile(sizeof(part)) { ; }
    long read(part &p, long recno = -1) {
      return rw(0, &p, 1, recno);
    }
    long write(part &p, long recno = -1) {
      return rw(1, &p, 1, recno);
    }
};
```

We can actually generalize this derived class to work for files of any type by making it a template. We'll give this template the name **file_of** to indicate its generality.

```
template<class T>
class file_of : public recfile {
public:
    file_of(void) : recfile(sizeof(T)) { ; }
    long read(T &p, long recno = -1) {
      return rw(0, &p, 1, recno);
    }
    long write(T &p, long recno = -1) {
      return rw(1, &p, 1, recno);
    }
};
```

With this template in hand, we can generate numerous specialized file classes (and objects) quite easily. For instance,

```
file_of<part> inventory;        // file of parts
file_of<int>  numbers;          // file of integers
file_of<customer> customers;    // file of customer records
```

Because the template uses all inline functions, no overhead is incurred by all of these new classes, either in run-time speed or in code space. (The compiler will slow down slightly because it must generate all of the class definitions.)

Using our newly discovered templates, we can now create a simple parts file program, as follows:

```
///////////////////////////////////////
// Example of file template class
// Be sure to link with recfile.cpp
///////////////////////////////////////

#include "recfile.h"
class part {
protected:
    int partno, qty;
    double price;
```

```
public:
    part(int n, int q, double p) {
       partno = n; qty = q; price = p;
    }
    void display(FILE *f) {
       fprintf(f, "partno: %5d  qty: %5d  price: $%6.2f\n",
                partno, qty, price);
    }
};

template<class T>
class file_of : public recfile {
public:
    file_of(void) : recfile(sizeof(T)) { ; }
    long read(T &p, long recno = -1) {
       return rw(0, &p, 1, recno);
    }
    long write(T &p, long recno = -1) {
       return rw(1, &p, 1, recno);
    }
};

void main()
{
    file_of<part> f;
    part p(1, 100, 249.99);

    f.open("test.fil", f_create);
    f.write(p, 5);
    f.read(p, 5);
    p.display(stdout);
    f.close();
}
```

This example shows you how powerful parameterized types can be when they are combined with inheritance and derived classes. In fact, let's take a closer look at how inheritance and parameterized types are related, before we present our inventory program.

Relationship between Templates and Inheritance

As we've shown in the previous section, templates or parameterized types are often used in conjunction with inheritance and derived classes. The result is so powerful because both techniques, parameterized types and inheritance, are really ways to share or reuse code. These techniques are fundamentally different, but complementary, as you'll discover next.

Inheritance allows us to reuse or share code at the object code level. That is, the source code needs to be compiled and turned into object code only once for a given class. The object code is then shared between the derived classes. In contrast, with templates, the code is shared at the source level. That is, the source for the template is copied and then slightly altered for each instantiated class. Thus, we can get many different object code modules from the same template source.

From this analysis, you can see that inheritance is more efficient when it comes to saving code space. However, inheritance usually causes more run-time overhead, particularly when virtual functions are used. On the other hand, templates are much more code-intensive. However, they usually generate faster code, since the resulting classes and their members can be used directly, without any extra overhead. By using inheritance and templates together, though, you can get the best of both worlds—compact *and* fast code, as you saw in the last section.

Another difference between inheritance and templates is how they affect the shape of a class hierarchy tree. Inheritance is a way of vertically organizing classes, and templates provide a horizontal organization. To see this, recall our record I/O classes. Figure 11.2 shows the hierarchy that was created.

At the top of the hierarchy is our general class, **recfile**. Below it is our derived template, **file_of<>**. Below this are the specific instances of our template. The thing to notice is that class derivation (inheritance) causes the hierarchy tree to grow downward, or vertically. Templates cause the tree to grow sideways, or horizontally. Note that none of the leaf classes is more specific than the others. They all exist at the same level. Their single parent, being more general, exists at a higher level.

A Complete Inventory Program

After you've digested the previous discussion of templates and parameterized types, type in the inventory program presented in Listings 11.1 and 11.2.

We'll be providing a quick explanation of the program's components, and then we'll give you the complete program listings.

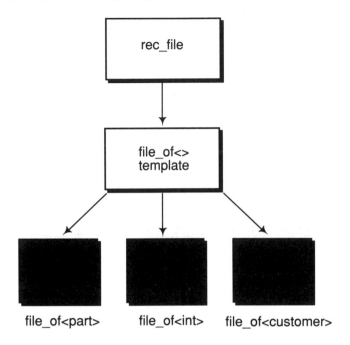

Figure 11.2. Relationship between inheritance and parameterized types.

Our program, called **db++**, implements a complete inventory system that allows you to maintain a database of parts. What's unique about this program is that it puts together all the topics that we have been exploring in this chapter, including record-oriented I/O and parameterized types.

Using the **file_of<>** template we introduced earlier as a base, we'll derive the class **db**. This class is used to maintain our parts database, and our program maintains this database through an interactive menu session. The menu is shown in Figure 11.3.

For our **db++** program, we've borrowed the **part** class from earlier examples. However, we have greatly extended it to make our program more useful. We've added constructors, operator functions, and input and output methods for the parts. Here's the new class declaration:

```
/////////////////////////////////////////
// parts.h: Parts class header
/////////////////////////////////////////
```

```
db++ at your service:

c   Create database
o   Open existing database
f   Find part
u   Update part
a   Add part
d   Delete part
l   List parts
q   Quit
h   Help


>
```

Figure 11.3. The menu for the db++ inventory program.

```
#ifndef H_PART
#define H_PART
#include <iostream.h>
#include <iomanip.h>
class part {
protected:
    // The data
    int partno, qty;
    float price;
public:
    // The methods
    friend ostream &operator<<(ostream &strm, part &p);
    friend int same_key(part &a, part &b);
    void set(int p, int q, float c) {
      partno = p; qty = q; price = c;
    }
    void copy(part &p) { set(p.partno, p.qty, p.price); }
    part(void) { set(-1,0,0); } // defaults to "null part"
    part(part &p) { copy(p); }
    part(int p, int q, float c) { set(p,q,c); }
    void operator=(part &p) { copy(p); }
    int isnull() { return partno == -1; }
```

```
        int get_key(void) { return get_partno(); }
        int get_partno(void);
        int get_qty(void);
        int get_price(void);
        void input(void);
};
#endif
```

We've added new ways to initialize parts, including an overloaded assignment operator, and some interactive routines to input the part data from the terminal. We've also included a test for a null part, which is used to help us delete parts from the database. If a part is deleted, the corresponding record data is set to a null code so that the record can be located and reused when we add inventory parts.

The **db** class picks up where **file_of<>** left off. The **file_of<>** methods perform low-level operations, such as reading and writing records. To create a higher-level database application, we need methods to perform operations, such as adding a part, deleting a part, locating a part, and so on. Here is the class declaration for our **db** class:

```
class db : public file_of<part> {
protected:
    unsigned nrecs;  // number of slots available in file
    unsigned nitems; // number of valid items
public:
    db(void) { nitems = 0; nrecs = 0; }
    void update_header(void);
    void read_header(void);
    int open(char *fname, enum access_mode mode);
    int close(void);
    unsigned search(part &p);
    unsigned add(part &p);
    unsigned del(part &p, unsigned recno = 0);
    unsigned update(part &p, unsigned recno = 0);
    void list(ostream &strm);
};
```

In this class we must keep track of both the number of records available in the file and the number of parts stored. We also have two auxiliary functions, **update_header()** and **read_header()**, which we use to access the first record of the file. In this record, we store the number of records and number of parts, so that we can close the file, open it again, and pick up where we left off. We have overridden the virtual functions **open()** and **close()** so that we can do this header maintenance.

There are five basic operations that can be handled by our **db** class (besides opening and closing files):

search	Search by part number for a given part
add	Add a new part (duplicates are not checked)
del	Delete a part
update	Update a part
list	List all parts in the file

The methods for this class and the **part** class are given in Listings 11.1 and 11.2. But before you study them, take a closer look at the **db** class declaration.

```
class db: public file_of<part>  {
    // ...
};
```

Note that this class is derived from the **file_of<>** template. We also instantiated the record type to **part**.

What we end up with is a database class that specializes in parts. You might be wondering if we could have made the **db** class a template as well. We could have. In fact, here's an example:

```
template<class T>
class db : public file_of<T> {
protected:
    unsigned nrecs;  // number of slots available in file
    unsigned nitems; // number of valid items
    public:
    db(void) { nitems = 0; nrecs = 0; }
    void update_header(void);
    void read_header(void);
    int open(char *fname, enum access_mode mode);
    int close(void);
    unsigned search(T &p);
    unsigned add(T &p);
```

```
        unsigned del(T &p, unsigned recno = 0);
        unsigned update(T &p, unsigned recno = 0);
        void list(ostream &strm);
};
```

Then, we could declare a complete family of database classes.

```
db<part> parts_db;

db<client> clients_db

db<bank_accounts> accounts_db;
```

Note that whatever type we use in our parameterized database must have member functions such as **same_key()**, **makenull()**, and **isnull()**.

As you study the methods implemented for the **db** class, you'll notice we use about every trick available in C++. As such, our **db++** system serves as a comprehensive example of C++ programming. Notice that while we've developed a record-oriented file system here, we also use the C++ stream package. We use the stream I/O for the interactive part of the program where we query for part information. Thus, we're mixing two types of I/O in the same program.

Listing 11.1

```
///////////////////////////////////////////////////
// parts.cpp: Parts class implementation
///////////////////////////////////////////////////
#include "parts.h"
//
// Non-member functions
//
void skip_to_eol(istream &s)
{
    char c;
    s.clear(); // set to good state
    while(s.get(c) && c != '\n') { ; }
}
```

```
ostream &operator<<(ostream &strm, part &p)
{
    if (p.isnull()) return strm << "Null part";

    strm << "Partno: " << setw(5) << p.partno << "   ";
    strm << "Qty: " << setw(5) << p.qty << "   ";
    strm << "Price: " << setw(6)
         << setprecision(6) << p.price;
    return strm;
}

int same_key(part &a, part &b)
{
    return a.partno == b.partno;
}

//
// Member functions
//

int part::get_partno(void)
// Returns 1 if valid input, 0 otherwise
{
    cout << "Partno: ";
    if (cin >> partno) return 1;
    return 0;
}

int part::get_qty(void)
// Returns 1 if valid input, 0 otherwise
{
    cout << "Qty: ";
    if (cin >> qty) return 1;
    return 0;
}
int part::get_price(void)
// Returns 1 if valid input, 0 otherwise
{
    cout << "Price: ";
    if (cin >> price) return 1;
```

```
          return 0;
      }

void part::input(void)
{
    while (1) {
       if (get_partno()) {
           if (isnull()) break;
           if (get_qty()) {
               if (get_price()) break;
           }
       }
       // must have had error
       cout << "Invalid input, press return -- try again:\n";
       skip_to_eol(cin);
    }
}
```

Listing 11.2

```
///////////////////////////////////////////////////
// Sample parts inventory program (dbpp.cpp)
// Be sure to link with recfile.cpp and parts.cpp
///////////////////////////////////////////////////
#include <iostream.h>
#include <iomanip.h>
#include <stdio.h>
#include <string.h>
#include <stdlib.h>
#include <stdarg.h>
#include <errno.h>
#include "recfile.h"
#include "parts.h"


//////////////////////////////////////////
// Define template for record I/O files
//////////////////////////////////////////
template<class T>
class file_of : public recfile {
```

```
public:
    file_of(void) : recfile(sizeof(T)) { ; }
    long read(T &data, long recno = -1) {
      return rw(0, &data, 1, recno);
    }
    long write(T &data, long recno = -1) {
      return rw(1, &data, 1, recno);
    }
};


//////////////////////////////////////
// Derive db of parts class
//////////////////////////////////////
class db : public file_of<part> {
protected:
    unsigned nrecs;   // number of slots available in file
    unsigned nitems; // number of valid items
public:
    db(void) { nitems = 0; nrecs = 0; }
    void update_header(void);
    void read_header(void);
    int open(char *fname, enum access_mode mode);
    int close(void);
    unsigned search(part &p);
    unsigned add(part &p);
    unsigned del(part &p, unsigned recno = 0);
    unsigned update(part &p, unsigned recno = 0);
    void list(ostream &strm);
};


void db::read_header(void)
// Read header info from record 0
{
    part p;      // make fake part
    read(p, 0); // read into it
    // Pull out nrecs and number of items
    memcpy(&nrecs, &p, 2);
    memcpy(&nitems, ((char *)&p)+2, 2);
}


void db::update_header(void)
```

```
                  // Update record 0, which contains number
                  // of records and number of valid parts
                  {
                      part p; // make fake part
                      memcpy(&p, &nrecs, 2); // copy header data
                      memcpy(((char *)&p)+2, &nitems, 2);
                      write(p, 0); // store at record 0
                  }

              int db::open(char *fname, enum access_mode mode)
              // Let the base class do the open, and then
              // read in the header info
              {
                  recfile::open(fname, mode);   // notice chaining
                  if (opened && mode == f_update)
                     read_header();   // get header data
                  return opened;
              }

              int db::close(void)
              // Update the header and then
              // let base class close the file
              {
                  if (opened) update_header(); // synchronize header
                  return recfile::close();      // let base class do close
              }

              unsigned db::search(part &p)
              // Searches sequentially through the file for
              // part. Looks for matching part numbers.
              // Returns record number of part, or zero.
              {
                  unsigned r;
                  part q;

                  for (r = 1; r <= nrecs; r++) {
                      if (read(q,r) && same_key(p, q)) {
                          p = q;
                          return r;
                      }
                  }
```

```
        return 0;
}


unsigned db::add(part &p)
// Searches for empty slot (null part)
// Doesn't check for duplicates!!
// Returns new record number, or 0 if error
{
    unsigned r;
    part q;         // make a null part
    r = search(q);  // search for one in database
    if (r) {
        if (write(p, r)) { // add part p to db
            nitems++;
            update_header(); // store nitems
            return r;
        }
    }
    else { // must expand the file before adding part p
        if (write(p, nrecs+1)) {
            nrecs++; nitems++;
            update_header(); // store nitems
            return nrecs;
        }
    }
    return 0;
}


unsigned db::del(part &p, unsigned recno)
// Delete part from the file (part set to null).
// If recno = 0, then search for part first;
// otherwise, ignore part parameter and write to the recno.
// Returns recno of part deleted, or 0 if error.
{
    unsigned r;
    if (recno) r = recno; else r = search(p);
    if (r) {
        part q; // make null part
        write(q, r); // write to file
        nitems--;
        update_header(); // store nitems
```

```
        }
        return r;
}


unsigned db::update(part &p, unsigned recno)
// Update part at recno with new data.
// If recno = 0, then search for part.
// Returns recno of part updated, or 0 if error.
{
        unsigned r;
        if (recno) r = recno; else r = search(p);
        if (r) {
                write(p, r); // write to file
        }
        return r;
}


void db::list(ostream &strm)
{
        int cur_rec, parts_seen;
        part p;

        for (cur_rec = 1, parts_seen = 0;
              cur_rec <= nrecs && parts_seen < nitems;
              cur_rec++) {
                read(p, cur_rec);
                if (!p.isnull()) {
                        strm << p << "\n"; parts_seen++;
                }
        }
}


////////////////////////////////////////////////////////
// Okay, now come the interactive session routines
////////////////////////////////////////////////////////
void menu(void)
{
        cout << "\ndb++ at your service:\n\n";
        cout << "c  Create database\n";
        cout << "o  Open existing database\n";
        cout << "f  Find part\n";
```

```
    cout << "u  Update part\n";
    cout << "a  Add part\n";
    cout << "d  Delete part\n";
    cout << "l  List parts\n";
    cout << "q  Quit\n";
    cout << "h  Help\n\n";
}

int get_action(void)
{
    char action;
    cout << "> ";
    cin.clear();
    cin >> action;
    return action;
}

//
// Here is the main control:
//
int do_action(db &f, int act)
{
    part p;
    char c, fname[80];
    unsigned rec;

    // Don't try operations if file isn't opened
    if (act != 'q' && act != 'c' &&
        act != 'o' && act != 'h' && !f.isopen()) {
      cout << "Database not opened\n";
      return act;
    }
    switch(act) {
      case 'q': // quit
        cout << "Closing down database ...\n";
        f.close();
      break;
      case 'c': // create
        cout << "Enter file name: ";
        cin.get(c); // read past newline first
        cin.get(fname,80);
```

```
            f.open(fname, f_create);
        break;
        case 'o': // open existing
          cout << "Enter file name: ";
          cin.get(c); // read past newline first
          cin.get(fname,80);
          f.open(fname, f_update);
        break;
        case 'f': // find
        cout << "Find ";
          if (p.get_key()) {
            if ((rec = f.search(p)) != 0) {
              cout << "Part found at rec " << rec << "\n";
              cout << p << "\n";
            }
            else {
              cout << "Part not found\n";
            }
          }
        break;
        case 'u': // update
          cout << "Update ";
          if (p.get_key()) {
            if ((rec = f.search(p)) != 0) {
              cout << p << "\n";
              cout << "Enter new part info: \n";
              p.input();
              if (!p.isnull()) {
                // Note: by using rec here, we can
                // also rename part number
                if (f.update(p, rec))
                    cout << "Part successfully updated\n";
                    else cout << "Error updating part\n";
              }
              else cout << "Part not changed\n";
            }
            else cout << "Part not found\n";
          }
        break;
        case 'a': // add
          cout << "Enter part to add below: \n";
```

```
                    p.input();
                    if (!p.isnull()) {
                        if ((rec = f.add(p)) != 0) {
                            cout << "Part stored at rec " << rec << "\n";
                            cout << p << "\n";
                        }
                    }
                break;
            case 'd': // delete
                cout << "Delete ";
                if (p.get_key()) {
                    if ((rec = f.search(p)) != 0) {
                        cout << p << "\n";
                        cout << "Do you still wish to delete? ";
                        cin >> c;
                        if (c == 'y' || c == 'Y') {
                            if (f.del(p, rec))
                                cout << "Part deleted\n";
                            else cout << "Error deleting part\n";
                        }
                        else cout << "Part not deleted\n";
                    }
                    else cout << "Part not found\n";
                }
                break;
            case 'l': // list parts
                f.list(cout);
                break;
            case 'h':
                menu();
                break;
        }
        return act;
}

// Finally, our (small!) main program
void main()
{
    db f;
    int i;
```

```
      menu();
      while(1) {
        i = get_action();
        if (i == 'q') break;
        do_action(f, i);
      }
    }
```

Summary

In this chapter you learned how to extend the standard C++ I/O system by implementing a record-oriented file I/O program. We discovered that records provide a useful structure for representing data, because they can be randomly read and written.

We started out by exploring the basics of record-oriented files and then we built a simple program that processes record-oriented files. To increase the flexibility of our record-oriented file system, we introduced parameterized types and templates. As we learned, parameterized types provide a useful feature to help us create shareable code. Finally, in the last part of the chapter we created an inventory program that uses record-oriented I/O and parameterized types.

Exercises

1. We used a virtual function for the error handler in the **rec_file** class. Show how you can change this error handling system by creating a default error handling function, which you call with a function pointer. This method allows you to customize the error handling by pointing to your own function.

2. In this chapter we discuss making the **db** class a parameterized type as well. Implement it this way.

3. In the **db** class, we search for parts by sequentially scanning the records in the file. Improve on this by incorporating a better search strategy, such as storing the records in a binary tree form.

4. Implement a variable-length record I/O system. Could you derive one from the **rec_file** class?

12

A Simulation Project Using C++

Imagine that you've been climbing a mountain for the last few days and then you finally get to the top. You look out over the plush green valley that stretches for miles, and the only things that are on your mind are the view and the feeling that you've worked really hard to accomplish an important goal. Hopefully, that's the way you're feeling now, because you've arrived at the last chapter and have reached the top of the C++ mountain.

What you see when you look out from the top of this mountain are all the topics you've mastered—classes, constructors, inline functions, overloaded functions, inheritance, and so on. The list is extensive. Now we're in a position to do something fun and interesting with what we know.

In this chapter we'll develop an animated simulation of a car control system. This system will contain a speedometer with a moving needle, a digital odometer, command centers to speed up and slow down the car, and marquee-style arrows that show us the information flow between these objects.

To create this program, we'll start by building a set of screen device classes to support our simulation. Then, we'll introduce some gauges to show you how to use the screen device classes. Next, we'll create a unique turtle object to help us draw lines on the screen. We'll be using this turtle to produce animation effects. Our last stop is the car simulation program, which uses all the other classes we'll introduce in this chapter.

Here are the main features of this chapter:

- How to write more complex C++ programs
- How to create screen device classes to support display devices

- How to use turtle objects to draw on the screen
- Techniques for performing animation

Overview of the Simulation Program

Figure 12.1 shows what the screen for our simulation program looks like. To get this simulation up and running, we'll need to build a set of general and specialized classes. Here's a quick look at the classes we'll be using:

- A system of screen display classes, which includes a memory-mapped IBM PC display class, and an IBM screen class that uses ANSI.SYS codes
- A system of gauge classes, including analog and digital gauges
- A system of turtle classes, including one that provides a marquee-style lights animation
- A pulse generator class
- An accelerator class
- A car simulation class

Figure 12.2 shows how these classes will be combined to make up our car simulation.

Note: The simulation program is designed to run on an IBM PC with a text mode display. But because of the way the program is designed, it can easily be changed to run on other computer systems.

Building Screen Devices

We're going to need a way to display information on the screen for our simulation program. What's significant about our program is that it uses animation techniques to demonstrate the simulation. If you have ever tried to write an animation program, you already know how difficult it is to perform sophisticated screen I/O operations. Fortunately, we now have objects on our side, and objects turn out to be great building blocks for creating animation effects.

We'll start by showing you how to use object-oriented techniques to build screen device objects. These objects serve as device drivers that allow us to communicate with different screen devices.

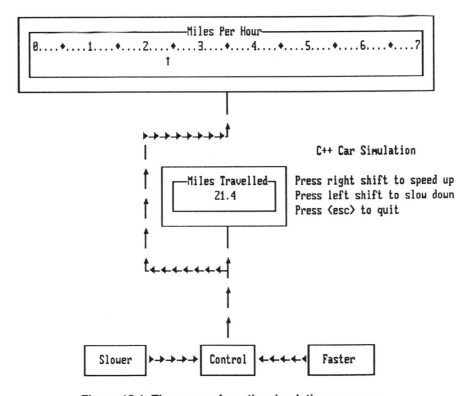

Figure 12.1. The screen from the simulation program.

Although our program is designed to work with the IBM PC screen, it can easily be adapted to other computer systems. All you need is a computer system that allows you to perform operations such as controlling the position of the cursor and printing a character where indicated by the cursor.

We'll start by constructing a set of screen device classes, as shown in Table 12.1, that progress from the general to the specific. The first screen class is device-independent. The other two classes, on the other hand, implement simple device drivers for IBM PC-specific screen devices. The **ibm_screen** class implements a memory-mapped device driver that makes it possible for us to communicate directly with the PC screen. The last class, **ansi_screen**, implements a device driver that works with the DOS ANSI.SYS driver. What's important about the more specific classes is that they are derived from the general class **screen_device**. If you want to support other screen devices, you can easily implement a new driver by deriving a class from **screen_device**. We've included Figure 12.3 to show you how the three classes are related.

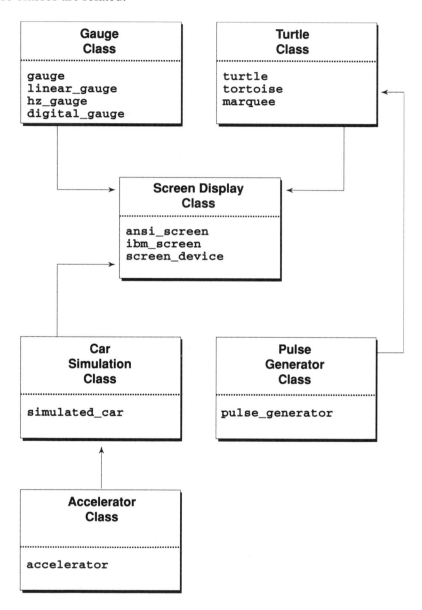

Figure 12.2. The relationship between the simulation classes.

Table 12.1. Screen I/O classes

Class Name	Description
scrcen_dcvice	Generic screen device driver
ibm_screen	Memory-mapped device driver
ansi_screen	ANSI.SYS-style device driver

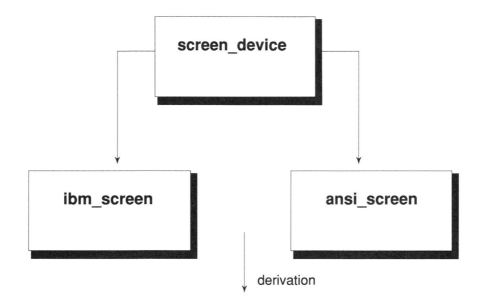

Figure 12.3. Relationship between the screen device classes.

The Screen Device Class Header File

Now that we've introduced you to the screen device classes that we'll be using, let's roll up our sleeves and write the code for them. Our first job is to construct a header file, called **screen.h**, that will serve as the home for our screen device classes. Because of the size and complexity of this file, we'll put it together in four parts. But remember when you later run the simulation program or other programs that need this file, that it will be up to you to join the four parts. We'll remind you about this later.

Note: The method we'll use to present classes in this chapter follows the step-by-step building block approach we just introduced. Keep in mind that whenever a reference is made to a file (either by an **#include** directive or in the comments), be sure to use all of the parts presented for that file.

Let's start by first looking at our generic **screen_device** class. Here is the rundown of its features:

- Supports a text display mode, but it could easily be adapted to support a graphics mode
- Supports random access cursor control
- Allows you to write characters to any screen location
- Provides horizontal and vertical line fills
- Provides box-drawing capabilities
- Supports text attributes, including highlighting, underlining, and reverse video

Note that we've designed our screen device so that, along with the more basic functions, it has built-in methods for drawing lines and boxes. This brings up one of the issues in designing classes like our screen devices. What should be built-in and what should be left to the user? The choice has a lot to do with what kind of hardware might be underneath the device driver. Some display hardware is capable of drawing boxes and lines by itself. Here, we decided to include the line- and box-drawing functions in our generic class. The application program need not be concerned about whether it's done in software or in hardware.

The design that we've introduced is typical of many object-oriented windowing systems where the primitive graphics functions are provided by the display devices. The more complex shapes and figures are not directly supported, because they can be built up from the more primitive ones by the user.

The **screen_device** is not actually the first component that we'll put in the **screen.h** header file. We'll need to build the foundation first by defining a set of constants to support the screen device driver. With this in mind, here's the first part of our **screen.h** file:

```
///////////////////////////////////////////////////////
// Display device header file  (screen.h: 1 of 4)
///////////////////////////////////////////////////////
// We use the following preprocessor directives to keep
```

```
// the header files from being recompiled needlessly.
// Remember to have the #endif directive at the end of
// part 4!

#ifndef SCREENH
#define SCREENH
#include <stdio.h>
enum graphics_symbol {
    ulc   = 0xda,   // upper left-hand corner
    llc   = 0xc0,   // lower left-hand corner
    urc   = 0xbf,   // upper right-hand corner
    lrc   = 0xd9,   // lower right-hand corner
    ltee  = 0xb4,   // left-handed tee
    rtee  = 0xc3,   // right-handed tee
    uptee = 0xc1,   // tee pointing up
    dntee = 0xc2,   // tee pointing down
    hzbar = 0xc4,   // horizontal bar
    vtbar = 0xb3    // vertical bar
};

enum ansi_attr {
    ansi_normal    = 0,    ansi_high      = 1,
    ansi_under     = 4,    ansi_blink     = 5,
    ansi_reverse   = 7,    ansi_invisible = 8
};

enum screen_mode { ibm_mono = 0, ibm_color = 1 };
```

The first component, **graphics_symbol**, defines the extended ASCII codes we'll need to draw lines and corners on IBM PC-compatible displays. We've grouped these codes into an enumerated type so that they could easily be changed to support other hardware display systems. The second enumerated type, **ansi_attr**, includes the attribute codes that are needed for the ANSI.SYS driver. We'll use these codes in all our screen devices to provide a common method to set the screen attributes. Finally, the last enumerated type, **screen_mode**, is used to indicate whether a monochrome or a color graphics card is in use. (This is used only by the **ibm_screen** class.)

We're now ready to move on to part two of the **screen.h** file, which includes the definition for the general or abstract class **screen_device**. This class establishes the methods (functions) and protocols that are common to all of our screen devices. The most important methods are **gotoxy()** and **put()**, which allow us to move an invisible cursor to any screen location and display a character. We'll actually use these two methods to implement the other methods, including **write()**, **box()**, **fillhz()**, and so on. Along with **update_cursor()**, **gotoxy()** and **put()** are the only functions that are hardware-dependent. Because of this, it won't be hard for you to port this code to other environments besides MS-DOS. You'll notice that many of the functions in **screen_device** were declared to be pure virtual. This makes **screen_device** an abstract class. Here is the code for part two of the **screen.h** file:

```
/////////////////////////////////////////////////////
// Abstract display class         (screen.h: 2 of 4)
// Notice the pure virtual functions
/////////////////////////////////////////////////////
class screen_device {
protected:
    int xo, yo; // offset coordinates
public:
    virtual void gotoxy(int x, int y) = 0;
    virtual void put(int c) = 0;
    virtual void putxy(int x, int y, int c) {
      gotoxy(x, y); put(c);
    }
    virtual void clear(enum ansi_attr a = ansi_normal) = 0;
    virtual void set_attr(enum ansi_attr a) = 0;
    virtual void fillhz(int x, int y, int c, int n);
    virtual void fillvt(int x, int y, int c, int n);
    virtual void write(char *s);
    virtual void box(int xul, int yul, int xlr, int ylr);
    virtual void update_cursor(void) = 0;
};
```

The output functions used in this class don't actually move the cursor, which keeps flickering down to a minimum during animation. Instead, an internal cursor is maintained. But our abstract class doesn't even store the cursor coordinates—that's up to the derived classes. The function **update_cursor()** is provided to move the hardware cursor to the stored coordinates when desired.

Note: With the **ansi_screen** class, the hardware cursor is always moved, so **update_cursor**() isn't really needed. Unfortunately, you will always see some flicker.

Several other methods are provided, such as **clear**(), which clears the screen to a desired attribute—bright, dim, reverse video, and so on. Another routine, **set_attr**(), is used to set the attributes dynamically. Finally, a set of offsets, **xo** and **yo**, is provided so that all screen devices will work alike. We assume that the top left-hand corner of the screen is at (0,0), as shown in Figure 12.4. The devices that use other starting values (such as (1,1)) can map to the same coordinates of our model screen by changing the offset coordinates appropriately.

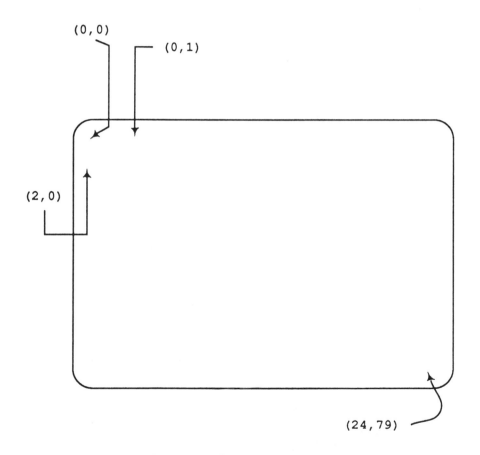

Figure 12.4. Screen coordinates.

Now that we've laid the foundation, we're ready to move on and build the walls, so to speak. Our next task is to use the **screen_device** class to derive the **ibm_screen** class. Recall that this derived class is used to access directly the video memory of the IBM PC's display. As Figure 12.5 shows, each character position on the screen (which we call a *texel*) consists of a character byte followed by an attribute byte. To represent *texel* screen locations, we'll use a structure and then store a texel pointer and video segment variable in our class. Let's next examine the third part of the **screen.h** file to see how this is implemented.

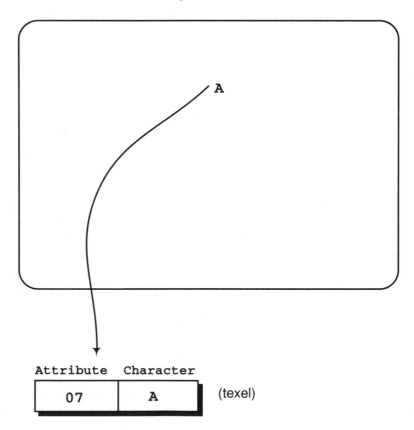

Attribute Character

| 07 | A | (texel) |

Figure 12.5. Representing characters and attributes as texels.

```
//////////////////////////////////////////////////////////
//      Display class for IBM memory-mapped screens
//                   (screen.h: 3 of 4)
//////////////////////////////////////////////////////////
```

```
// Character-attribute mapping for text mode screens
struct texel {
    unsigned char ch, attr;
    texel(int c, int a) { ch = c, attr = a; }
};

class ibm_screen : public screen_device {
    texel *scrptr;
    int wd, ht, cx, cy, video_seg;
    unsigned char attr;
public:
    ibm_screen(screen_mode mode);
    void gotoxy(int x, int y) { cx = x; cy = y; }
    texel &cell(int x, int y) { return scrptr[y*wd + x]; }
    void put(int c);
    void clear(enum ansi_attr a = ansi_normal);
    void set_attr(enum ansi_attr a);
    void update_cursor(void);
};
```

The constructor **ibm_screen()** is used to initialize our texel pointer **scrptr** and the video segment variable **video_seg** to point to the appropriate memory location where the graphics display resides. The constructor's argument, **mode**, indicates the type of display card that is being used—monochrome or color. The starting address for each display type is different. Working our way down the set of methods, **cell()** computes the appropriate texel location from an (x,y) coordinate pair.

In addition to including a constructor and the **cell()** function, we've overridden the virtual functions **gotoxy()**, **put()**, **clear()**, **set_attr()**, and **update_cursor()** so that they will work with our memory-mapped display device. These functions were written to emulate what the ANSI.SYS driver does, so that you can use either an **ibm_screen** object or an **ansi_screen** object. Note that we did not have to override any of the line- or box-drawing functions, since the **screen_device** class can handle these on its own. Thus, we're able to share much of the code.

There are two important variables in our class that we haven't discussed yet—**cx** and **cy**. What are they used for? They store the current coordinates for the internal cursor. The **update_cursor()** function uses these coordinates to move the hardware cursor.

We're now ready to put the last part of our **screen.h** file together. All we have left to do is implement the **ansi_screen** class. This class works with the ANSI.SYS driver. Here is part four of **screen.h**:

```
///////////////////////////////////////////////////////
//          Display class for ansi.sys-style screens
//                  (screen.h: 4 of 4)
///////////////////////////////////////////////////////
class ansi_screen : public screen_device {
public:
    ansi_screen(void);
    void gotoxy(int x, int y);
    void put(int c) { putchar(c); }
    void clear(enum ansi_attr a = ansi_normal);
    void set_attr(enum ansi_attr a);
    void update_cursor(void) { ; } // nothing to do
};
#endif // End of SCREEN.H. Don't forget this!!!!
```

You'll probably notice that this class is fairly simple. We didn't need to add many changes here. In fact, there aren't even any data members, since the ANSI.SYS driver handles all of the screen states for us. Thus, **ansi_screen** serves as an excellent example of a *class wrapper*, which is used to interface to an external driver.

Note: To use **ansi_screen** objects, you must have the ANSI.SYS driver loaded. Consult your DOS manual to see how this is done.

The Screen Device Class Methods

Now that we've seen the class definitions for each of the three screen device classes, we're ready to write the code for the class methods. This time we'll present the code, which is stored in the file **screen.cpp**, in three parts. Again, remember that you must put each part together to make the **screen.cpp** file.

Let's start with the methods for the abstract **screen_device** class.

```
///////////////////////////////////////////////////////
// Methods for screen displays  (screen.cpp: 1 of 3)
///////////////////////////////////////////////////////
```

```
#include <dos.h>
#include "screen.h"

/////////////////////////////////////////////////////
// Methods for generic screen device
/////////////////////////////////////////////////////
void screen_device::fillhz(int x, int y, int c, int n)
{
    int i;
    gotoxy(x, y);
    for (i = 0; i<n; i++) put(c);
}

void screen_device::fillvt(int x, int y, int c, int n)
{
    int i;
    for (i = 0; i<n; i++) putxy(x, y+i, c);
}

void screen_device::write(char *s)
{
    while(*s) put(*s++);
}

void screen_device::box(int xul,int yul,int xlr,int ylr)
{
    fillhz(xul, yul, hzbar, xlr-xul+1);
    fillhz(xul, ylr, hzbar, xlr-xul+1);
    fillvt(xul, yul, vtbar, ylr-yul+1);
    fillvt(xlr, yul, vtbar, ylr-yul+1);
    putxy(xul,  yul, ulc);
    putxy(xul,  ylr, llc);
    putxy(xlr,  yul, urc);
    putxy(xlr,  ylr, lrc);
}
```

The **fillhz()** and **fillvt()** functions, which are used to draw horizontal and vertical lines, are simple. The **box()** function uses them, along with **putxy()**, to draw a box. These functions take full advantage of **gotoxy()**, **put()**, and the enumerated **graphics_symbol** type. But note that **gotoxy()** and **put()** are declared in the **screen_device** class declaration (in **screen.h**) as pure virtual functions. The derived classes are responsible for overriding these functions and providing the actual implementation. Because **screen_device** is abstract, it isn't meant to be used on its own.

Next, we'll write the methods for the memory-mapped **ibm_screen** device class. First, we need to declare some variables, **video_addr** and **video_page**, which reference the appropriate memory locations for the two types of video displays: monochrome and color. The constructor uses these variables to initialize the **scrptr** and **video_seg** variables. We also set up the dimensions of the screen and initialize the internal cursor. Here are the required methods:

```
/////////////////////////////////////////////////////////
//          Methods for memory-mapped IBM PC screen
//                    (screen.cpp: 2 of 3)
/////////////////////////////////////////////////////////
texel *video_addr[2] = {
    (texel *)0xb0000000L, // monochrome
    (texel *)0xb8000000L  // color
};

unsigned video_page[2] = { 0xb000, 0xb800 };
ibm_screen::ibm_screen(screen_mode mode)
{
    scrptr = video_addr[mode];
    video_seg = video_page[mode];
    wd = 80; ht = 25;
    cx = 0; cy = 0; xo = 0; yo = 0;
    attr = 7; // normal white on black
    update_cursor();
}

void ibm_screen::update_cursor(void)
{
    union REGS regs;

    regs.h.ah = 2;            // code for cursor function
    regs.h.bh = video_seg;   // set video page
    regs.h.dl = xo + cx;     // set x coordinates
    regs.h.dh = yo + cy;     // set y coordinates
```

```
        int86(0x10,&regs,&regs); // call bios
}
void ibm_screen::put(int ch)
{
    cell(xo+cx++, yo+cy) = texel(ch, attr);
}


void ibm_screen::clear(enum ansi_attr a)
// Clears the screen using specified ansi_attr
{
    int i, j;

    set_attr(a); // convert and set IBM attributes
    for (i = 0; i<wd; i++) {
        for (j = 0; j<ht; j++)
            cell(i,j) = texel(' ', attr);
    }
}


void ibm_screen::set_attr(enum ansi_attr a)
// Sets internal attribute by mapping ansi.sys-type
// attributes to IBM screen attributes
{
    switch(a) {
      case ansi_normal:
        // force attr to normal
        attr =  0x07;
      break;
      case ansi_high:
        // set foreground high intensity bit
        attr |=  0x08;
      break;
      case ansi_under:
        // set underline on, leave background alone
        // Note: works in monochrome mode only
        attr = (attr & 0xf8) | 0x01;
      break;
      case ansi_blink:
        // set blink bit
        attr += 0x80;
```

```
          break;
        case ansi_reverse:
          // set white on black, leave blink and
          // intensity bits alone
          attr = (attr & 0x88) | 0x70;
        break;
        case ansi_invisible:
          // set foreground c to background c
          attr =  (attr & 0xf0) | (attr >> 4);
        break;
        default: ; // leave attr alone
      }
  }
```

Most of the routines are fairly simple. However, we need to provide some explanation for **update_cursor()** and **set_attr()**. The first function uses a function named **int86()** to make a direct call to the IBM PC's ROM BIOS. If you're familiar with IBM PC programming techniques, you'll probably know what we are doing here. The ROM BIOS contains the critical code that controls the PC. In this case we are calling the ROM BIOS with interrupt 0x10 so that we can move the hardware cursor.

Note: Our program was developed with the Borland C++ compiler, which provides functions such as **int86()** to allow us to access the special features of the PC. If you are using the Borland compiler, you must compile the program using the large memory model.

The **set_attr()** function is the most complicated and emulates some of the features of the ANSI.SYS driver. Note that, except for the **ansi_normal** attribute, the effects of calling **set_attr()** are cumulative. Therefore, this function must mask and shift bits to preserve screen attributes that are already set.

Compared to the **ibm_screen** class, **ansi_screen** is simple, because it shares a lot of code from its base class, **screen_device**. It also relies on the external ANSI.SYS driver to do most of the work. The only thing **ansi_screen** must do is communicate with the ANSI.SYS driver by calling **printf()** to send appropriately formatted strings. Note that since the hardware cursor position is always maintained by ANSI.SYS, the **update_cursor()** function doesn't need to do anything. However, we must define this function because it was declared as pure virtual in **screen_device**. If we leave it as pure virtual, it would make **ansi_screen** an abstract class, which is not what we want. Here is the last part of the **screen.cpp** file:

```
//////////////////////////////////////////////////////////////
// Methods for ansi.sys-style screens (screen.cpp: 3 of 3)
//////////////////////////////////////////////////////////////
ansi_screen::ansi_screen(void)
{
    int i;
    xo = 1; yo = 1; gotoxy(0, 0); // note offset!!
}

void ansi_screen::gotoxy(int x, int y)
{
    printf("\x1b[%d;%df", y+yo, x+xo);
}

void ansi_screen::set_attr(enum ansi_attr a)
{
    printf("\x1b[%dm", a);
}

void ansi_screen::clear(enum ansi_attr a)
{
    set_attr(a);
    printf("\x1b[2J");
}
```

Using the Screen Devices

Let's now put our screen devices to work. We'll use the functions **box()**, **gotoxy()**, **write()**, **put()**, **clear()**, and **update_cursor()** to draw a simple analog gauge, as shown in Figure 12.6. We've presented similar gauges in Chapter 9, and you'll be seeing them again when we build the gauge classes for our simulation program.

To draw our gauge, we must define a **draw_gauge()** function and some sizing parameters. We'll also need a **screen_device** pointer. By using such a base class pointer, we'll be assured that we can use either an **ibm_screen** or an **ansi_screen** device and our **draw_gauge()** function won't know the difference. We suggest that you try the program with both types. And, of course, due to the power of inheritance and polymorphism, you could also define another screen device later, and the **draw_gauge()** function would work just fine with it.

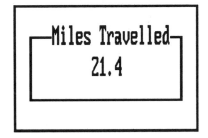

Figure 12.6. Sample digital gauge.

Here is the code for the main program:

```
//////////////////////////////////////////////////////////////
// Example of using a screen object to draw a gauge
// Be sure to link with screen.obj
//////////////////////////////////////////////////////////////
#include <conio.h>
#include <string.h>
#include "screen.h"
void draw_gauge(screen_device *dev,  int x, int y,
                int res, int ofs, char *label = 0)
{
    int i, wd, ht, lx;

    dev->box(x, y, x+res+2, y+3);
    lx = x + (res - strlen(label)+3) / 2;
    dev->gotoxy(lx, y);
    dev->write(label);
    dev->gotoxy(x+1,y+1);
    for (i = ofs; i <= res; i++) {
      if (i % 10 == 0) dev->put(48 + i/10);    // print num
        else if (i % 5 == 0) dev->put(0x04); // or diamond
            else dev->put('.');                // or '.'
    }
}
```

```
void main()
{
    // Uncomment the type of screen device you want
    ibm_screen scr(ibm_color);
    // ansi_screen scr;

    scr.clear();
    draw_gauge(&scr, 10, 5, 55, 0, "Speedometer");
    scr.gotoxy(30, 14);
    scr.write("Press a key...");
    scr.update_cursor();
    getch();
}
```

To run this program, make sure that you first type in the code for the
screen.h and **screen.cpp** files. Remember that we presented these files in
different parts and that you must enter the code for each part in order to
create each of the files. After you create these files, make sure that you save
them in a safe place, because we'll be using them again in this chapter.

Designer Gauges

Next, let's use our screen devices to create a system of gauges. The gauges
we'll implement here are the ones we'll use to develop our simulation
program. Because we've used these types of gauges in Chapter 9 when we
explored inheritance, we won't need to explain again how they work. In fact,
the code that we are using is similar to the code in Chapter 9. The only major
difference is that we've replaced the **printf()** and **putch()** functions with the
appropriate screen device functions, such as **putxy()** and **write()**. We also
exploit the box-drawing and cursor-positioning capabilities of our screen
devices to draw more realistic gauges. Finally, we've added a pointer so that
we can access the screen device on which we wish to draw the gauge.

The class definitions for our gauges are given in the header file **gauge.h**,
and the methods are presented in **gauge.cpp**.

```
//////////////////////////////////////////////////////
//  Gauge class definitions  (gauge.h)
//////////////////////////////////////////////////////
#ifndef GAUGEH
```

```
#define GAUGEH
#include "screen.h"
// Abstract gauge class--note the pure virtual functions.
class gauge {
protected:
    float resolution; // how many ticks the gauge has
    float scale;      // how many ticks per unit
    float offset;     // unit number of first tick
    char overflow;    // set when needle is "pegged"
    char active;      // on/off flag
    virtual float process_signal(float signal) = 0;
    screen_device *dev;
    int xul, yul, np;   // origin of gauge, and needle posn
public:
    gauge(screen_device *dev,float s,float r,float o);
    virtual void draw(int x, int y, char *label = 0) = 0;
    virtual void on(void)  { active = 1; }
    virtual void off(void) { active = 0; }
    virtual float input(float signal) = 0;
};


// Derived class for linear gauges
class linear_gauge : public gauge {
protected:
    virtual float process_signal(float signal);
public:
    linear_gauge(screen_device *dev,float s,float r,float o)
    : gauge(dev, s, r, o) { ; }
};


// Derived class for analog linear gauge
class analog_gauge : public linear_gauge {
public:
    analog_gauge(screen_device *dev,float s,float r,float o)
    : linear_gauge(dev, s, r, o) { ; }
    virtual void draw(int x, int y, char *label = 0);
    virtual float input(float signal);
};


// Derived class for digital linear gauge
```

```cpp
class digital_gauge : public linear_gauge {
protected:
    int box_wd, field_wd, nd;
public:
    digital_gauge(screen_device *dev, float s,
                  float r, float o, int wd, int n)
      : linear_gauge(dev, s, r, o)
    { nd = n; box_wd = wd; field_wd = 0; }
    virtual void draw(int x, int y, char *label = 0);
    virtual float input(float signal);
};
#endif


///////////////////////////////////////////////////////
//  Gauge methods  (gauge.cpp)
///////////////////////////////////////////////////////
#include <conio.h>
#include <string.h>
#include <stdio.h>
#include <math.h>
#include "gauge.h"

// Methods for abstract gauges
gauge::gauge(screen_device *dev,float s, float r, float o)
{
    gauge::dev = dev; scale = s;
    resolution = r; offset = o;
    overflow = 0; np = 0; active = 1;
}


// Methods for linear gauges
float linear_gauge::process_signal(float signal)
// Use linear function to process signal
{
    float posn;
    posn = signal * scale - offset;
    if (posn > resolution) {
       posn = resolution;
       overflow = 1;
    }
    else overflow = 0;
```

```
        return posn;
    }

    // Methods for analog gauges that look something like:
    // |----------------------------------------|
    // |0....5....1....5....2....5....3....5....4...|
    // |                                            |
    // |----------------------------------------|

void analog_gauge::draw(int x, int y, char *label)
{
    int i, wd, ht, lx;
    xul = x; yul = y;
    dev->box(x, y, x+resolution+2, y+3);
    lx = x + (resolution - strlen(label)+3) / 2;
    dev->gotoxy(lx, y); dev->write(label);
    dev->gotoxy(x+1,y+1);
    for (i = offset; i <= resolution; i++) {
      if (i % 10 == 0) dev->put(48 + i/10);
        else if (i % 5 == 0) dev->put(0x04); // diamond
            else dev->put('.');
    }
    input(0.0); // draws needle too
}

float analog_gauge::input(float signal)
// Input and process signal; draw needle too
{
    float x;
    if (active && signal != -1) {
       x = process_signal(signal);
       // erase old needle
       dev->putxy(xul+np+1, yul+2, ' ');
       // then draw new one
       dev->putxy(xul+x+1, yul+2, 0x18);
       np = x;
       return x;
    }
    return -1;
}
```

```
// Methods for digital gauges
void digital_gauge::draw(int x, int y, char *label)
{
    int i, lx;
    float maxnum = resolution*scale;
    field_wd = log10(maxnum) + nd + 2;
    xul = x; yul = y;
    dev->box(x, y, x + box_wd - 1, y+2);
    lx = x + (box_wd - strlen(label)+1) / 2;
    dev->gotoxy(lx, y); dev->write(label);
    input(0.0); // draws needle too
}


float digital_gauge::input(float signal)
// Input and process signal; draw needle
{
    float x;
    int lx;
    char buff[75];
    if (active && signal != -1) {
        x = process_signal(signal);
        sprintf(buff, "%*.*f", field_wd, nd, x);
        lx = xul + (box_wd-field_wd) / 2;
        dev->gotoxy(lx, yul+1); dev->write(buff);
        return x;
    }
    return -1;
}
```

Using Gauges

Our next goal is to take the **gauge** class we just created and build a speedometer. The main program we'll present inputs an integer speed using the stream I/O functions and then sends the speed to our speedometer gauge. Figure 12.7 shows how the screen will look. Note that we must position the hardware cursor after the input prompt by using **update_cursor()**. This must be done before we call the **operator>>()** function. Otherwise, the input routine will get confused and try to read its input from some other screen location. Here's the main program. Type it in and take it for a test drive!

```
//////////////////////////////////////////////////////
// Gauge example (speedo.cpp)
// Be sure to link with gauge.obj, screen.obj
//////////////////////////////////////////////////////
#include <stdlib.h>
#include <iostream.h>
#include "gauge.h"
void main()
{
    char buff[10];
    float speed;
    ibm_screen scr(ibm_color);
    // ansi_screen scr;
    analog_gauge speedometer(&scr, 1.0, 65, 0.0);

    scr.clear();
    speedometer.draw(5, 5, "Ground Speed");
    while(1) {
      scr.gotoxy(25, 15);
      scr.write("Enter speed <q> to quit:         ");
      scr.gotoxy(50, 15); scr.update_cursor();
      cin >> buff;
      speed = atoi(buff);
      if (*buff == 'q') break;
      speedometer.input(speed);
    }
}
```

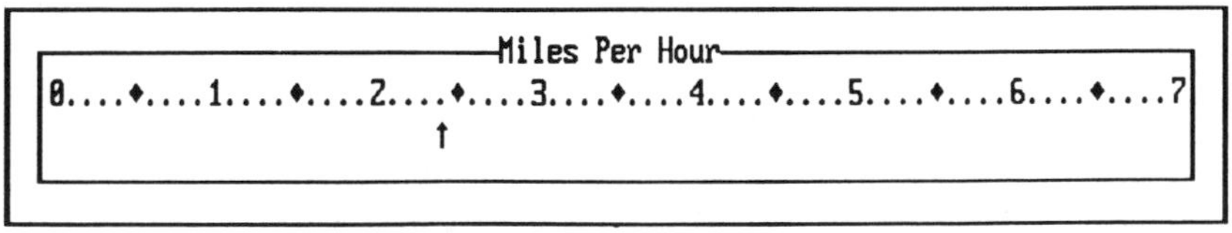

```
┌────────────────────────────────────────────────────────┐
│ ┌──────────────────Miles Per Hour──────────────────────┐ │
│ │0....♦....1....♦....2....♦....3....♦....4....♦....5....♦....6....♦....7│ │
│ │                          ↑                             │ │
│ └──────────────────────────────────────────────────────┘ │
└────────────────────────────────────────────────────────┘
```

Figure 12.7. Processing the speedometer gauge.

Creating Turtles

As you've been working through this chapter, you've probably been wondering when we're going to present the simulation program that we promised at the beginning. Actually, we've been creating the components of the simulation program all along, object by object. It just so happens that we'll need one more object, which we'll call a *turtle* object.

Now you might be wondering what turtles have to do with an automobile simulation program? These objects are actually like drawing pens, and we'll command them to move around the screen and draw lines. We'll use these turtles to draw the wires that connect our gauges and control boxes. Let's first look at the turtle class definition:

```
///////////////////////////////////////////////////
// Turtle class definition          (turtle.h)
///////////////////////////////////////////////////
#ifndef TURTLEH
#define TURTLEH
#include "screen.h"

typedef enum {
    right, down, left, up,
    move, pen_up, pen_down, quit
} turtle_cmd;

class turtle {
protected:
    static enum graphics_symbol corner_matrix[4][4];
    screen_device *scr;
    int xs, ys, x, y, pen_status;
    turtle_cmd orgtc, tc, oldtc, dir, olddir;
    virtual int drawing_char(void);
public:
    virtual void reset(void);
    virtual void draw(void);
    turtle(screen_device *scr, int x=0, int y=0,
           turtle_cmd tc = right);
    virtual int cmd(turtle_cmd tc);
    virtual int cmd(char *s);  // maps chars into codes
};
```

```
#endif  // of TURTLEH

//////////////////////////////////////////////////////
//  Turtle class methods                    (turtle.cpp)
//////////////////////////////////////////////////////
#include <stdio.h>
#include <conio.h>
#include <ctype.h>
#include "turtle.h"

enum graphics_symbol turtle::corner_matrix[4][4] = {
//    r      d      l      u
      hzbar, urc,   hzbar, lrc,    // r
      llc,   vtbar, lrc,   vtbar,  // d
      hzbar, ulc,   hzbar, llc,    // l
      ulc,   vtbar, urc,   vtbar   // u
};

void turtle::reset(void)
{
   x = xs; y = ys; pen_status = 1;
   tc = oldtc = dir = olddir = orgtc;
}

turtle::turtle(screen_device *scr,int x, int y,turtle_cmd c)
{
   turtle::scr = scr;
   turtle::xs = x; turtle::ys = y;
   orgtc = c;
   reset();
}

int turtle::drawing_char(void)
{
   return corner_matrix[olddir][dir];
}

void turtle::draw(void)
{
   if (pen_status == 1) scr->putxy(x, y, drawing_char());
```

```
}
int turtle::cmd(turtle_cmd code)
// Process turtle command. Returns 0 on quit, else 1.
{
    oldtc = tc;
    // compute drawing direction, pen status
    switch(code) {
        case pen_up    : pen_status = 0; break;
        case pen_down : pen_status = 1; break;
        case move:
          if (oldtc == move) {
            switch(dir) {
               case right : x++; break;
               case down  : y++; break;
               case left  : x--; break;
               case up    : y--; break;
            }
          }
          draw();
          tc = move;
          olddir = dir; // commit direction now
        break;
        case quit: return 0;
        default:
          dir = code; // tentatively turn
          tc = code;  // record command
          draw();     // draw in tentative direction
    }
    return 1;
}

int turtle::cmd(char *cmds)
// Converts command string into turtle cmd sequence.
// Returns 0 on encountering quit command, else 1.
{
    char c,i,n, rv = 1;

    while(*cmds && rv) {
        c = *cmds++;
        if (isdigit(c)) { // up to two-digit number allowed
            n = c - '0';
```

```
            c = *cmds++;
            if (isdigit(c)) {
                n = n*10 + c - '0';
                c = *cmds++;
            }
        } else n = 1;
        for (i = 0; i<n && rv; i++) {
            switch(c) {
                case 'r': rv = cmd(right); break;
                case 'd': rv = cmd(down); break;
                case 'l': rv = cmd(left); break;
                case 'u': rv = cmd(up); break;
                case 'm': rv = cmd(move); break;
                case 'o': rv = cmd(pen_up); break;
                case 'n': rv = cmd(pen_down); break;
                case 'q': rv = cmd(quit); break;
                default : rv = 1;
            }
        }
    }
    return rv;
}
```

First, you should find the enumerated type **turtle_cmd**. This variable is used to represent the set of commands that is sent to a turtle to get it to do something. Here's a sample sequence of such commands: *ulmd*. This causes the turtle to perform the following actions:

```
"pen up, turn left, move, pen down"
```

Note that all turn commands are absolute, not relative. For example, left always means left on the screen, right always means right.

Our **turtle** class also uses a constructor to initialize an internal screen device pointer so that it knows which device to use. We also initialize the starting position and orientation of the turtle.

There are two overloaded **cmd()** functions. They control the movement and pen status of the turtle. The first **cmd()** function takes a single **turtle_cmd** argument and, given the history of the turtle movements, determines how to move or turn the turtle. It also determines if a line should be drawn or not. If you look closely at the function, you'll notice that it uses several state variables, such as **tc, oldtc, dir**, and **olddir**, to keep track of the command and direction history of the turtle.

The second **cmd()** function is used as a convenient way of sending a whole sequence of commands to the turtle. Basically, each **turtle_cmd** is mapped to a single character, so a character string can then make up a sequence of commands. Also, keep in mind that you can prefix these commands with a repeat factor, using up to a two-digit number, thus allowing very compact command strings.

The first **cmd()** function calls the function **draw()**, which determines whether or not to draw a line character. The **draw()** function then calls **drawing_char()** to compute the character to be drawn, and then draws it.

The **drawing_char()** function compares the current and previous directions of the turtle and consults a table to determine the type of line or corner character to draw. We have made it virtual so that it can be overridden. (You'll see why a little later.) In fact, we've made most of the functions virtual so your turtles can be adaptable.

Doing Figure Eights

Now that we have a turtle object, let's make it do something. In the next program, we'll create a turtle object and have it draw a series of figure eights on the screen, as shown in Figure 12.8.

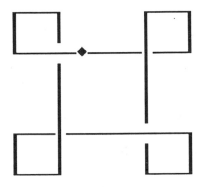

Figure 12.8. Drawing figure eights.

```
/////////////////////////////////////////////////////
// Figure eights turtle example (tommy.cpp)
// Be sure to link with turtle.obj, screen.obj
/////////////////////////////////////////////////////
#include <conio.h>
#include <string.h>
#include "turtle.h"
void main()
{
    int i, j;
    ibm_screen scr(ibm_color);
    // ansi_screen scr;
    turtle tommy(&scr, 35, 10);
    scr.clear();
    tommy.cmd("r12mu3ml5md9mr5mu3ml17md3mr5mu9ml5md3mr7m");
    scr.gotoxy(33, 19);
    scr.write("Press a key...");
    scr.update_cursor();
    getch();
}
```

To run this program, make sure that you include the **turtle.h** file that we presented in the previous section. You'll also need the **screen.h** and **screen.cpp** files to make the turtle do its thing.

Making Turtles Come Alive

Our last turtle, while capable of making interesting designs, isn't too exciting, because it draws so fast that we can't see what it's doing. So, let's take our original turtle class and extend it by deriving a class that animates the drawing action. This is done by overriding the **cmd**() function so that it uses a diamond cursor to draw the line characters. Also, after it draws each character, it waits for a key to be hit before continuing.

The derived class, **tortoise**, provides a good example of inheritance. It reuses as much code from the base class as possible. For example, take a close look at the **cmd**() function we've overridden. Like we've done many times throughout this book with virtual functions, it chains back (or calls) the base class version of the same function and has it do most of the work. All we add to the operation is to draw a cursor and wait for a key to be pressed.

```
///////////////////////////////////////////////////
// Animated turtle example (terry.cpp)
// Be sure to link with turtle.obj, screen.obj
///////////////////////////////////////////////////
#include <conio.h>
#include <string.h>
#include "turtle.h"
///////////////////////////////////////////////////
// Derived turtle class: This one puts out a cursor
///////////////////////////////////////////////////
class tortoise : public turtle {
    turtle_cmd really_old;
public:
    tortoise(screen_device *scr, int x=0, int y=0,
            turtle_cmd tc = right)
    : turtle(scr, x, y, tc) { really_old = olddir; }
    virtual int cmd(turtle_cmd tc);
    virtual int cmd(char *s) { return turtle::cmd(s); }
};

int tortoise::cmd(turtle_cmd code)
// Modifies the drawing sequence by adding a cursor
// and then waits for a key to continue.
// Returns 0 on quit or <esc>, else 1.
{
    int k;
    turtle_cmd temp = olddir;
    olddir = really_old; // must go back two steps
    draw();              // draw old pipe symbol
    really_old = olddir = temp;
    k = turtle::cmd(code);   // draw new one via base method
    // put out diamond cursor
    if (pen_status == 1) scr->putxy(x, y, 0x04);
    if (k == 0) return 0;
    k = getch();
    if (k == 27) return 0; else return 1;
}

void main()
{
```

```
        ibm_screen scr(ibm_color);
        // ansi_screen scr;
        tortoise terry(&scr, 35, 10);

        scr.clear();
        scr.gotoxy(23,19);
        scr.write("Press key to draw, <esc> to quit ...");
        int r;
        do {
          r =

terry.cmd("r12mu3ml5md9mr5mu3ml17md3mr5mu9ml5md3mr6m");
        } while(r);
    }
```

Moving Arrow Marquees

Now that you have seen how easy it is to modify the turtle class, let's do it again. This time, we'll build a marquee class. We've given the class this name because it uses the turtle to draw a series of connected lines, complete with corners, and sprinkles in some arrows along the way. The arrows move around like the moving lights used in a theater marquee. This turtle object might make you think that you're in Vegas! We'll be using these marquee turtles in our simulation to represent the flow of information between gauges.

The **marquee** class example shows the power of inheritance and virtual functions. We can get a dramatically different type of turtle with just a little bit of code. Basically, we add some state variables, override the **drawing_char**() virtual function, and add a **sequence**() function. Here is the **marquee** class with its methods:

```
////////////////////////////////////////////////////////
// Animated marquee class definitions  (marquee.h)
//////////////////////////////////////////////////////// .
#ifndef MARQUEEH
#define MARQUEEH
#include "turtle.h"

// First, a pulse generator class
struct pulse_generator {
```

```
        int cnt, wd;
        void set(int w) { wd = w; cnt = wd - 1; }
        pulse_generator(int w = 1) { set(w); }
        int step(void);
};
// Derive turtle class to have moving arrows
class marquee : public turtle {
public:
        char *path_codes;
        char fast_flip, slow_flip;
        pulse_generator pulse;
        marquee(screen_device *scr, int x, int y, char *pc,
                int delay, turtle_cmd c = right);
        int drawing_char(void);
        void sequence(void);
};
#endif // MARQUEEH


////////////////////////////////////////////////////
// Animated marquee lights class methods (marquee.cpp)
////////////////////////////////////////////////////
#include "marquee.h"
// Methods for pulse generator
int pulse_generator::step(void)
{
    if (++cnt == wd) {
        cnt = 0;
        return 1;
    }
    return 0;
}


// Methods for marquee-style moving arrow turtle
int arrow_chars[4] = { 0x10, 0x1f, 0x11, 0x1e };

marquee::marquee(screen_device *scr, int x, int y,
                 char *pc, int delay, turtle_cmd c)
: turtle(scr, x, y, c), pulse(delay)
{
    fast_flip = 0; slow_flip = 0;
```

```
        path_codes = pc;
    }


int marquee::drawing_char(void)
// Draw a path char, alternating with arrows
{
    int ch;

    if ((fast_flip ^= 1) != 0)
        return turtle::drawing_char();
        else return arrow_chars[dir];
    }


void marquee::sequence(void)
// Draw the whole path once, alternating line
// characters with arrows. The arrows also have
// a slow alternation between sequences.
{
    if (pulse.step()) {   // only draw once in a while
        reset();     // reset turtle posn and dirn
        slow_flip ^= 1;    // toggle the slow flip-flop
        fast_flip = slow_flip; // and init. the fast one
        cmd(path_codes);   // draw complete path
    }
}
```

How does our marquee turtle work? The key are the functions **sequence()** and **drawing_char()**. The **sequence()** function takes a turtle command string (which was initialized by the **marquee** constructor) and calls the base class **cmd()** function to draw the complete path. However, it turns out that **cmd()** calls **drawing_char()**, which we've modified to alternate between drawing line characters and arrows.

This alternation is accomplished by maintaining two flip-flops, which are variables that alternate between the values 0 and 1. The **fast_flip** variable affects the alternation between line and arrow characters and is toggled every time a character is drawn. The **slow_flip** variable is toggled at the start of each sequence. It determines the initial state of **fast_flip**, which in turn determines whether an arrow or line character is drawn first, thus changing the whole pattern of arrows throughout the line path.

Between each sequence, the turtle's position and direction are reset to their starting values. The **slow_flip** variable is toggled, and **fast_flip** is set. However, one other thing happens. Note the **if** statement:

```
if (pulse.step()) { // only draw once in a while
```

This statement calls the **step()** function of another type of object, a *pulse generator*. Every time it is stepped, the pulse generator returns a value. Most of the time, it returns a zero. However, it maintains a counter and, when that counter reaches some limit, it generates a *pulse* by returning a one. Then it goes back to generating zeroes. The pulse generator provides a delay between each complete drawing sequence, thus slowing the animation so you can see it.

True to our object-oriented style, we've made our pulse generator a class and created a pulse generator object to store with our **marquee** object. But what about our flip-flops? Why didn't we make them objects? Because they were so simple, we decided not to.

Animated Spirals

Our next program shows how we can use the marquee turtles. We'll create a marquee object and pass it as a command string so that we can draw a spiral. We'll then move arrows around this spiral to animate it, as shown in Figure 12.9. Here's the program:

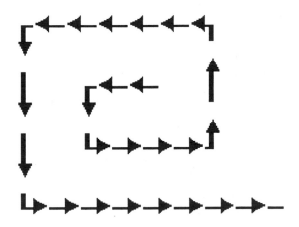

Figure 12.9. An animated spiral.

```
////////////////////////////////////////////////////
// Animated marquee turtle example (marky.c)
// Link with marquee.obj, turtle.obj, screen.obj
////////////////////////////////////////////////////
#include <bios.h>
#include <stdlib.h>
#include <string.h>
#include "marquee.h"
void main()
{
   ibm_screen scr(ibm_color);
   // ansi_screen scr;

   marquee marky(&scr, 35, 10,
                "15md3mr9mu5ml13md7mr17m", 4000, left);

   scr.clear();
   scr.gotoxy(23,19);
   scr.write("Press key to quit ...");
   while(!bioskey(1)) { // quit as soon as key is hit
      marky.sequence();
   }
   bioskey(0);          // get character
}
```

An Object-Oriented Simulation

Finally, we're ready to write the complete car simulation program. Although we're not actually going to move the car, we'll show the flow of commands from the gas and brake pedals to a car control box (which represents the engine and transmission) and then on to an odometer and speedometer.

To implement the program, we'll use all of the classes we've developed in this chapter and, in fact, we're going to use almost every feature that C++ has to offer. We'll also create another class: an odometer, which is derived from the digital gauge type class. The only thing this new class does is intercept the base class **input()** function and sum up the input values. We do this so that the accumulated total can be displayed instead of the current input value. Like most properly derived functions, the process is not complicated.

We've also made an **accelerator** class, which is used to simulate the brakes and the gas pedal. The action of the brakes and gas pedal are combined in the control box, which is represented by the class **simulated_car**. This class takes the acceleration and deceleration signals and combines them to produce a delta value. This value represents the number of miles traveled in one step and is sent to our odometer and speedometer.

Finally, we use our marquee turtles to represent the flow of commands and data through the system. We also use our analog and digital gauges to display the results. Here is the main simulation program:

```cpp
/////////////////////////////////////////////////////
// An object-oriented car simulation (simula.cpp)
// Link with gauge.obj,marquee.obj,turtle.obj,screen.obj
/////////////////////////////////////////////////////
#include <iostream.h>
#include <string.h>
#include <conio.h>
#include <bios.h>
#include <math.h>
#include "marquee.h"
#include "gauge.h"

// A derived digital gauge class the sums up its inputs
class odometer_gauge : public digital_gauge {
    float sum;
public:
    odometer_gauge(screen_device *dev, float s,
                   float r, float o, int w, int n)
    : digital_gauge(dev, s, r, o, w, n)  { sum = 0; }
    virtual float input(float signal);
};

float odometer_gauge::input(float signal)
// An odometer sums up its input
{
    if (signal != -1) sum += signal;
    return digital_gauge::input(sum);
}

// An accelerator class that ramps up to some limit
```

```
struct accelerator {
    int amt, limit;
    accelerator(int l = 1000) { amt = 0; limit = 1; }
    void ramp(int a=1) {
      amt += a;
      if (amt > limit) amt = limit;
    }
    void reset(void) { amt = 0; }
};


// A simulated car class that takes acceleration and
// deceleration commands and adds them together to
// produce the number of miles traveled this step
struct simulated_car {
    float delta;
    simulated_car(void) { delta = 0; }
    float travel(int brakes, int gas);
};


float simulated_car::travel(int brakes, int gas)
{
    if (brakes) delta -= brakes*0.00003;
    if (gas) delta += gas*0.00001;
    if (delta < 0)  delta = 0;
    if (delta > 7)  delta = 7;
    return delta;
}


const int mhz = 25;
void main()
{
    int i, mhz;
    float d;
    ibm_screen scr(ibm_color);
    // ansi_screen scr;

    // Get mhz to estimate delay factors
    scr.clear();
    scr.gotoxy(30, 9);
    scr.write("Car Simulation Program");
```

```
scr.gotoxy(30, 12); scr.update_cursor();
cout << "Enter mhz of your computer: ";
cin >> mhz;
scr.clear();
scr.gotoxy(51,9);
scr.write("   C++ Car Simulation");
scr.gotoxy(51,11);
scr.write("Press right shift to speed up");
scr.gotoxy(51,12);
scr.write("Press left shift to slow down");
scr.gotoxy(51,13); scr.write("Press <esc> to quit");
scr.box(0, 0, 76, 5);
scr.box(26, 10, 49, 14);
scr.box(12, 22, 23, 24);
scr.gotoxy(15, 23); scr.write("Slower");
scr.box(33, 22, 43, 24);
scr.gotoxy(35, 23); scr.write("Control");
scr.box(53, 22, 65, 24);
scr.gotoxy(56, 23); scr.write("Faster");
analog_gauge speedometer(&scr, 10.0, 70.0, 0.0);
speedometer.draw(2, 1, "Miles Per Hour");
odometer_gauge
   odometer(&scr, 0.0006667, 999999.9, 0.0, 20, 1);
odometer.draw(28, 11, "Miles Traveled");
marquee brake_pipe(&scr, 24, 23, "r9m", mhz, right);
marquee gas_pipe(&scr, 52, 23, "l9m", mhz, left);
marquee spd_pipe(&scr, 37, 17,
                    "l15mu10mr16mu3m", mhz*10, left);
marquee odm_pipe(&scr, 38, 21, "u7m", mhz*10, up);
gas_pipe.sequence();
brake_pipe.sequence();
simulated_car car;
accelerator gas(20000/mhz), brakes(25000/mhz);
int key = 0, status = 0;
while(key != 0x011b) {
   key = bioskey(1);
   if (!key) {
      status = bioskey(2);
      if (status & 0x01) {
         gas.ramp();
         gas_pipe.sequence();
```

```
                    } else gas.reset();
                    if (status & 0x02) {
                       brakes.ramp();
                       brake_pipe.sequence();
                    } else brakes.reset();
                    car.travel(brakes.amt, gas.amt);
                    odometer.input(car.delta);
                    speedometer.input(car.delta);
                    spd_pipe.sequence();
                    odm_pipe.sequence();
                    scr.putxy(38, 17, ltee);
                    scr.putxy(38, 14, dntee);
                    scr.putxy(38, 5, dntee);
                 }
               else bioskey(0);
            }
         }
```

Summary

In this chapter we explored the topic of simulation. In particular, we applied most of the C++ programming features that we've presented in this book to create a program that uses animation to simulate a running car. We started the chapter by introducing the basic features of the simulation program, and then we spent some time developing a set of screen device classes. We showed how these classes were used to control screen output on an IBM PC system. Next, we put some gauges together to show you how the screen device classes work. Our next stop was the critical turtle object, which turned out to be the component that brought our animated simulation program to life. Finally, we combined all of the objects and created the simulation program.

We hope the last two chapters have really sparked your interest in C++ programming. The more you work with C++, the more you'll realize the advantages that this language provides over other traditional languages because of its object-oriented nature.

Exercises

1. Using the screen device classes as a base, derive a class that supports bit-mapped graphics.

2. Take the bit-mapped graphics class you developed in exercise 1 and try to build a pop-up window system.

3. Using gauges classes that we presented in this chapter, derive a thermometer type gauge. Set up two different types: one that handles Fahrenheit, the other Celsius.

4. Change the **marquee** turtle class so that it shows the actual data moving down the wires, that is, so it shows numbers representing the values of the signals traveling to the gauges. (Hint: Try implementing a FIFO queue to hold the numbers and add the queue to the **marquee** class.)

Key Differences Between C and C++

The code and explanations in this book are based on Version 2.1 of C++, which is essentially the standard defined in the book *The C++ Programming Language*, second edition by Bjarne Stroustrup (Addison-Wesley). For the most part, C++ is upwardly-compatible with the latest ANSI C standard. However, there are some differences. In this appendix we will be highlighting the key ones to help you make the transition from C to C++.

Specifying Function Prototypes

There is one critical difference between C and C++, and that is how functions with no arguments are specified. In C++, the following function prototype indicates that **f()** has no arguments:

```
int f();
```

In C, this prototype means that **f()** could have any number of arguments. In fact, it's equivalent to writing

```
int f(...);
```

Thus, the following code is an error in C++, but not in C:

```
extern int f();
void main()
```

```
{
    int k;

    k = f(10);
}
```

If you are writing code that you wish to work in both C and C++, the safe way to specify a function with no arguments is to use the **void** keyword:

```
f(void)
```

Likewise, the safe way to specify a function with an unknown number of arguments is

```
f(...)
```

Table A.1 summarizes the differences between C and C++ in this respect.

Table A.1 Specifying parameterless functions in C and C++

Declaration	C Interpretation	C++ Interpretation
f()	f(...)	f(void)
f(...)	f(...)	f(...)
f(void)	f(void)	f(void)

Another crucial difference is that in C++, a function must be defined before it is called. The following program, consisting of the two files **myfunc.c** and **wontwork.c**, would not compile in C++ because we forgot to declare **some_func()** as external:

```
/* File myfunc.c */
double some_func(double a, double b)
{
    return a / 2 * (b + 42.0)
}

/* File wontwork.c.
```

```
    Note no extern declaration for some_func() */
void main()
{
    double a = 5.5, b = 6.7, c = 0.0;

    c = some_func(a,b); /* error, some_func not declared */
}
```

In C, the call to **some_func**() would be handled by defaulting the argument types and the return type to **int**. The result would be a garbled program because the parameter passing would be all wrong.

Even if you did declare **some_func**() as external in **wontwork.c**, you could still make mistakes:

```
/* file wontwork.c */
/* note the erroneous declaration */
extern double some_func(int a, double b);
void main()
{
    double a = 5.5, b = 6.7, c = 0.0;

    c = some_func(a,b);
}
```

Here we incorrectly specified the function prototype for **some_func**(), inadvertently using an **int** where a **double** should go. A C compiler would not catch this error, and neither would the linker. It would happily link up the function call **some_func**() in **wontwork.c** with the function definition in **myfunc.c**. However, this error would be caught in C++ 2.1. See Chapter 5 for coverage of type-safe linkage for an explanation on how this is done.

The Type of Character Constants

In C, the type of a character constant, such as "a", is considered to be **int**. In C++ 2.1, (but not in versions of C++ earlier than 2.0), a character constant is of type **char**. This change was made mainly to allow overloaded functions to work better, in particular the stream operator <<. For instance,

```
cout << 'A';      // prints the letter 'A' in 2.0, but
                  // the number 65 in earlier versions
```

Surprisingly, this change has very little effect when porting code from C to C++. In most cases, you use character constants in statements such as

```
int c;
c = 'A'; // converts to integer 65
```

The conversion to integer works correctly in both C and C++ 2.1. The main difference you will see is when you take the size of a character constant:

```
int k = sizeof('A');    // k = 2 in C, 1 in C++
```

The size of a character constant in C++ is one byte because that's how much room a character takes up. In C, the constant is converted to an integer and, thus, **sizeof**() returns two bytes.

The Types of Enumerations

Suppose you have the following enumerated type:

```
enum fruit { apple, orange, strawberry };
```

In C++, the enumerations **apple**, **orange**, and **strawberry** are given integer values (0, 1, 2), and they are treated as having the type **int**, even though the enumerations as a whole are of type **enum fruit**. Thus, the following is legal in C:

```
enum fruit f;
int i;
f = apple;    /* okay */
i = f;        /* okay, i gets the value 0 */
f = 1;        /* okay, f gets the value 'orange' */
f = 55;       /* what does this mean? */
```

The last statement is erroneous because we are assigning a meaningless value to **f**. There is no **fruit** that has that value. In C++, this would be an error. You can assign an enumeration to an integer in C++, but not the other way around. For instance:

```
enum fruit f;
int i;

f = strawberry;  // okay
i = f;           // okay, i gets the value 2
f = 55;          // compiler error
```

Another difference in the way enumerated types are handled is how they can be nested inside structures. For instance, in C, the following code

```
struct building_block {
    enum tools { brick, mortar, hammer } mytools;
};
```

is the same as

```
enum tools { brick, mortar, hammer };
struct building_block {
    enum tools mytools;
};
```

That is, the enumerated type has the same scope as the **struct building_block**. Thus, the following statement would be illegal:

```
int brick;   /* Error, brick already defined */
```

In C++, this would not be an error. The enumerated type would be hidden in the structure. The reason for this change is that you can now incorporate enumerated types as part of a class, hiding them so that they are only accessible by qualifying their names. For instance, you can say the following in C++:

```
// C++ code:
class building block {
public:
    enum tools { brick, mortar, hammer } mytools;
};
```

```
building_block b;
int brick;    // okay in C++
b.mytools = building_block::brick; // okay if qualified
b.mytools = brick; // error, can't use integer version here
```

Multiple Name Spaces

The last difference has to do with the different name spaces used by the compiler. In C, structure tags have a different name space from other names. However, early versions of C++, structure tags, and all type names for that matter, had the same name space as other names. Thus, code such as the following is legal in C, but it wasn't in early versions of C++:

```
struct bridge {
    double span, height;
};

void bridge(int the_gap);
```

Here, **bridge** is both a structure tag and a function name.

In C++ 2.1, the name space rules have been altered slightly. Code like our previous example will work. However, there are many caveats. For example, a name used as a class name for a class with a constructor cannot be used for anything else. Why not? Remember that constructors of classes have the same name as the class itself. Using that name as the name of another function would result in a conflict, because constructors are functions too. Because there are many exceptions like this one (we can't go into them here), we recommend that you avoid these problems altogether and use names for only one purpose at a time in your programs.

Answers to Selected Exercises

This appendix provides answers to some of the exercises presented throughout the book.

Chapter 2

1. A class is a definition that describes what a certain type of object is. An object is an instance of that class; i.e., a set of memory locations that take on the properties of that class. You may (and typically will) have more than one object instantiated from a class.

2. The five advantages that OOP has over conventional programming are:

   (i)   It supports information hiding (encapsulation).
   (ii) It allows structures (i.e., classes) to inherit properties from other structures.
   (iii) It allows abstract data types to be represented in a more direct fashion.
   (iv) It allows programs to be designed with relatively independent building blocks.
   (v)   By using methods (member functions) to pass "messages" to an object, you can concentrate on what you want the program to do, instead of how it operates.

3. To store the size of the window, the window would have two state variables, **width** and **height**, which can be calculated when the window is created given the size of the text to be displayed in the window.

4. Using information hiding, you need only to be concerned about what you want the class objects to do, and not how the objects are implemented. Only the designer of the class needs to be concerned about how they are implemented. If set up correctly, the designer can change the internals of the class without affecting the user, making the code more portable. The user may have to recompile code after such changes, but the user probably wouldn't have to make any changes to the source itself.

5. A derived class is a sub-class of a base class and it inherits all the properties of the base class.

Chapter 3

1. Here's one way to implement the class:

```
class evaluator {
    float leftnum, rightnum;
public:
    void set_left(float l)  { leftnum = l; }
    void set_right(float r) { rightnum = r; }
    float add(void)         { return leftnum + rightnum; }
    float subtract(void)    { return leftnum - rightnum; }
    float multiply(void)    { return leftnum * rightnum; }
    float divide(void)      { return leftnum / rightnum; }
};
```

4. Here are two typical examples of what you might do:

(i) Package list structures and routines into classes.
(ii) Package window structures and routines into classes.

Chapter 4

1. We'll implement a linked list to store integers as follows:

```c
#include <stdio.h>
class ilist;  // need forward declaration

class inode { // list node
public:
  friend ilist; // ilist can access next pointer
  int i;          // we'll leave the data public
  inode(int v); // a constructor to set data
private:
  // the pointer to next node in the list
  // we'll make it private, so only ilist can
  // access it (it's the class that needs to)
  inode *next;
};

inode::inode(int v)
// constructor to set data in node, zero out next pointer
{
  i = v;
  next = 0;
}

class ilist {
  inode *head; // the head of the list
public:
  ilist(void) { head = 0; }
  ~ilist(void);
  void add(int v);
  void rmv(inode *n);
  inode *search(int v);
};

ilist::~ilist(void)
// destructor which deletes all nodes on the list
{
  inode *p = head, *q;
  while(p != 0) {
    q = p->next; // must save pointer to next node
    delete p;    // delete this node
    p = q;       // point to next node
```

```
        }

}

void ilist::add(int v)
// add to the front of the list by creating a new node, and
// making it the head
{
   inode *p = new inode(v);

   p->next = head; // point to old head
   head = p;            // P is now the new head
}

void ilist::rmv(inode *n)
// Remove node n from the list. The memory for the
// node is not freed, however.
{
   inode *p, *q;
   if (head == 0) return; // no nodes to delete!
   if (n == head) {
      // node is the head, so we need a new head
      p = head->next;
      // alternatively, we could delete the node
      // here, if we wanted to, as follows:
      //
      // delete head;
      head = p;
   }
   else {
      // Walk down the list, looking for the node
      // that needs to be deleted. Need auxiliary
      // pointer that stays one step ahead.
      p = head;
      q = head->next;
      if (q != 0 && q != n) {
         p = q;
         q = q->next;
      }
      if (q != 0) { // we did find the node
         p->next = n->next; // skip around the node
         // alternatively, we could delete the node
```

```
            // here, if we wanted to, as follows:
            //
            // delete n;
        }
    }
}

inode *ilist::search(int v)
// Search and return the first node that has value v in it.
// Returns 0 if node not found.
{
    inode *p = head;
    while(p != 0 && p->i != v) p = p->next;
    return p;
}

main()
{
    ilist list_o_nums;

    list_o_nums.add(42);
    list_o_nums.add(17);
    list_o_nums.add(55);
    inode *matching_node = list_o_nums.search(17);
    if (matching_node == 0)
      printf("Oops: node should be found, but wasn't\n");
     else printf("Matching node contains: %d\n",
                   matching_node->i);
    list_o_nums.rmv(matching_node);
    delete matching_node; // could be done inside rmv()
    matching_node = list_o_nums.search(17);
    if (matching_node != 0)
        printf("Oops: node wasn't removed properly\n");
    // destructor called here implicitly to delete all
    // remaining nodes on the list
    return 0;
}
```

2. Use the constructor to set the head of the list to null, and use the destructor to delete all the nodes in the list, as shown in (1).

3. The function **add1()** will produce an error in trying to access the private member **z** of the **numb2** class. The **numb2** class has no problem accessing the private member **a** of the **numb1** class, since **numb2** was declared as being a friend of **numb1**. Note, however, that **numb1** is not a friend of **numb2**. The friendship only works one way.

4. You could derive **cylinder** as follows:

```
class cylinder : public circle {
public:
  int ht; // add height
  float volume(void) {
    return 3.1416 * radius * radius * ht;
  }
};
```

5. Here's how you can convert the list class into a stack class:

```
class istk {
private: // note which functions are private now
  inode *head;
  void add(int v);
  void rmv(inode *n);
  //// inode *search(int v); // don't need this
public:
  istk(void) { head = 0; }
  ~istk(void);
  void push(int v) { add(v); }
  inode *pop(void) {
    inode *top = head;
    rmv(head);
    return top;
  }
};
```

6. The **delete** statement needs subscripts to signal that an array is being deleted:

```
delete[] yellow_pages;
```

Note that the size is not given; the memory management routines keep track of the size. If you leave out the subscripts when deleting an array, you're telling the compiler you want to delete just one element as pointed to by the pointer. Be careful not to do this unless that's what you want (it probably isn't).

Chapter 5

1. The new **vector_len()** function will look like:

```
int vector_len(vector *v)
{
    return sqrt(v->x * v->x + v->y * v->y);
}
```

The call will look like:

```
printf("vector length: %d\n", vector_list(&dist));
```

2. It prints **0**, since both **i** and **q** are names for the same memory location.

3. The statement

```
&p = 34;
```

is syntactically incorrect. It should read

```
p = 34;
```

Note that this only changes the value of what **p** references; it does not change to what **p** is a reference. (That is, **p** references **i**, and cannot reference any other variable.)

4. The function won't compile because you can't have default arguments that aren't trailing arguments. The only way to write the function and let **i** have a default is to let **j** have a default as well, as in

```
int ultimate_answer(int i = 42, int j = 55, double d = 13)
{
```

```
        return i - d;
    }
```

Chapter 6

1. Try using the **SQ()** macro in the following scenario:

```
#define SQ(x) x*x

int x = 5;
printf("%d\n", SQ(x++));
printf("%d\n", x);
```

Since **x = 5**, you should get 25 for the first number, and then **x** should be incremented to 6. However, when the macro is expanded, the result is:

```
printf("%d\n", (x++)*(x++));
```

Here, we see that **x** gets incremented twice, so **x = 7** when finished. Worse, the expression **(x++)*(x++)** will yield an answer of 5*6 = 30. You could change the macro to an inline function as follows (we've written it for integers):

```
inline int sq(int x) { return x * x; }
```

Now, the two **printf()** statements will yield the correct results of 25 and 6. That's because the value of **x** (5) is copied before being passed to the function. This value is squared and returned (to yield 25), and then **x** is incremented to 6. The inline function is using proper argument passing semantics rather than simple text substitution.

2. We could write our "search" iterator as follows:

```
int_node *int_list_iterator::next(int sv)
// Scan the list until we find a node with the value of sv.
// Start with the node at the cursor, and set the cursor
// to one past the matching node when found.
{
    int_node *p = cursor;
```

```
    while(p) {
      cursor = p->next;
      if (p->data == sv) break;
      p = cursor;
    }
    return p;
}
```

3. In class **clock**, the return type for **sound()** was left off. In such cases, the return type defaults to **int**. However, in class **radio**, **sound()**'s return type was declared to be **void**. Since the return types are different, we've overloaded **sound()** rather than overridden it, which can cause subtle errors because the virtual mechanism is not operating. Fortunately, many C++ compilers will catch this type of mistake and give you either a warning or an error.

   You can fix the problem by putting a return type of **void** on the **sound()** function of **clock**. This type of mistake is easy to make, so be careful when you define virtual functions.

4. The program prints out

```
   First name:
```

   instead of

```
   Well, what is your name?
```

   because in function **doit()**, the **form** parameter was passed by value, rather than by reference, thus, defeating the virtual function mechanism. To fix it, declare **doit()** as follows:

```
   void doit(form &f) // Note &
   {
     f.display();
   }
```

   You could also have written **doit()** as follows, assuming you change the call to **doit()** as appropriate:

```
void doit(form *f) // Note *
{
  f->display();
}
```

Chapter 7

1. Although it looks like we've defined **operator+()** to be a binary operator taking two operands, we've actually defined it to take three. Remember that every class member function has an extra hidden argument. So, for binary operator functions that are class members, the first operand is always the object making the call, and the second operand is the first and only explicit argument in the operator function.

2. You could use () in conjunction with iterators. For instance, in your iterator class, overload the () function to perform the "next" operation:

```
class int_list_iterator {
  // ...
  int operator()() { // Return next int }
};
```

3. You can't use an overloaded [] operator to subscript multdimensional arrays since [] is a binary operator. Since overloaded operator []functions must be class members, the first operand is always the object making the call, leaving only one argument for a subscript. To subscript multi-dimensions, you can overload the () operator, which can accept any number of arguments. (It needs at least one argument, the object making the call.) For example:

```
class two_d_int_array {
  // ...
  int &operator()(int i, int j);
};

class three_d_int_array {
  // ...
  int &operator()(int i, int j, int k);
};
```

Chapter 8

1. Because the class has private members, you can't use an initialization list on it. Here is a constructor to use instead:

```
employee::employee(char *n, int a, int jc)
{
  name = strdup(n);
  age = a;
  jobcode = jc;
}
```

2. Here are the possible ways to call the constructor:

```
rect r;                  // both arguments defaulted
rect r = rect(42);       // last argument defaulted
rect r(42);              // last argument defaulted
rect r = 42;             // last argument defaulted
rect r(42, 17);          // neither argument defaulted
rect r = rect(42,17);    // neither argument defaulted
```

3. The constructor is called once, when **list_of_nums** is first created. However, you'll notice that the destructor is called twice, once after the function **average()** returns, and once when the program finishes. You'll also most likely get a null pointer assignment. What gives? Well, when **average()** is called, **list_of_nums** is passed by value. That means a copy of it is made. Since no copy constructor was included in the class, a default copy constructor is generated, which does a memberwise copy. Unfortunately, the dynamic data isn't copied, only the pointer to it. Now, when the **average()** function returns, the destructor is called for the copy. The destructor then deletes the dynamic data. Then, when the program is about to finish, the destructor is called again, to destroy **list_of_nums** itself. Unfortunately, the dynamic data is deleted again, mangling the heap.

   To fix the problem, you should put in a copy constructor, such as the following:

```
list_of_nums::list_of_nums(list_of_nums &s)
{
  data = new int[size = s.size];
```

```
      memcpy(data, s.data, cursor = s.cursor);
      printf("Copy constructor\n");
}
```

Try adding this constructor and run the program again. Does it work better?

4. First, the constructor never initializes **wd** and **ht**, causing the data to be sized arbitrarily. The constructor should look like the following:

```
image::image(int w, int h)
{
  wd = w; ht = h;
  data = new char[wd*ht];
}
```

Second, the destructor calls **delete** incorrectly, forgetting the brackets. The destructor should be written as follows:

```
image::~image(void)
{
  delete[] data;
}
```

Third, we create a dynamic image by calling **new()**, but destroy it by calling **free()**. Besides the obvious problems of mixing allocation strategies (**new/delete** vs **malloc/free**), the destructor for the image is never called, since **free()** doesn't call destructors. Thus, the data allocated by the image itself is never freed. The **main()** routine should be written as follows:

```
void main()
{
  image *screen1 = new image(12, 15);
  ...
  delete screen1;
}
```

5. The **printf()** statement is called only once, meaning that the destructor is called only once, although it should have been called five times. The problem is that we forgot the brackets on the **delete** statement:

```
delete[] coordinates;
```

Try making this change and running the program again. Now, how many times is the **printf()** statement called?

6. We needed a constructor with no arguments, (i.e., a default constructor) because we wanted to create an array of points. Note that if we took all of the constructors out, that would be okay too, for with any destructors defined, the compiler will generate a default destructor for you. However, the data would not be initialized to any known value.

Chapter 9

1. Here's a calculator with memory:

```
class smart_calculator : public calculator {
  int m;
public:
  // New methods
  smart_calculator(void)  { clear();   }
  int clear(void)         { m = 0;     }
  int store(int v)        { m = v;     }
  int recall(void)        { return m;  }
  int add_to_mem(int a)   { m += a;    }
  int sub_from_mem(int a) { m -= a;    }
};
```

2. The following are legal: (a) & (c). A circle pointer can point to a circle or cylinder object, and can be set to a cylinder pointer, but a cylinder pointer can't point to a circle object, and can't be set to a circle pointer (without typecasting, of course).

3. You might have a general window class that has operations such as **draw()**, **clear()**, **move()**, **write()**, etc. Also, you might have two driver classes, one that interfaces to a text mode screen, one to a graphics mode

screen. Using multiple inheritance, you could merge the general window class with the text mode driver to obtain a text mode window, and then merge the general window class with the graphics mode driver to obtain a graphics mode window. The text and graphics mode windows would override internal virtual functions that do I/O to the drivers by calling the drivers for support. You could get around using multiple inheritance by simply deriving a new window class that incorporates a text mode driver as a member object, and derive a similar class incorporating a graphics mode driver object.

Chapter 10

4. You can make your own stream I/O manipulators as follows. Defining manipulators that take no parameters is easy. For instance, here's how to make a "page eject" output manipulator to work with a PostScript printer:

```
#include <iostream.h>
// define a parameterless output manipulator
ostream &Eject(ostream &os)
{
  return os << " showpage ";
}

main()
{
  cout << Eject; // calling a parameterless manipulator
  return 0;
}
```

You can use a similar form for input manipulator, replacing **ostream** with **istream**.

Defining manipulators that take parameters calls for a little more work. There's no direct way to do it, but there is a trick you can use. Recall that you can overload << and >> to work for your own objects. Using this technique, you can define your manipulator to be a class and then overload << and/or >> to work for objects of that class. The trick is to provide a constructor that has the parameters you are trying to pass to the manipulator. These parameters are stored in the object, to be used later by the overloaded stream operator function. For example, here's how to define and use a manipulator that sets the font for a PostScript printer:

```
#include <iostream.h>
// define a postscript "set font" manipulator
class SetFont {
  int font_size;
  char *font_name;
public:
  SetFont(char *fn, int fs) :  font_size(fs), font_name(fn)
{ }
  friend ostream &operator<<(ostream &s, SetFont &obj);
};

ostream &operator<<(ostream &os, SetFont &obj)
{
  os << obj.font_size << " /" << obj.font_name;
  os << " findfont exch scalefont setfont\n";
  return os;
}

main()
{
  cout << SetFont("Helvetica", 12);
  return 0;
}
```

The iomanip.h header file has some parameterized types defined to try to make the process of declaring manipulator classes a little easier. However, the direct approach just shown is as easy to do, and is a lot less confusing.

Chapter 11

1. To use the function pointer technique, rather than using a virtual function for handling errors, you could do something like the following:

```
// Declare err_handler as a pointer to a function taking
// an int argument followed by unspecified arguments
// and returning void. Put this in recfile.h.
```

```
extern void (*err_handler)(int errtyp, ...);

// In recfile.cpp, forward declare a default error handler.
void default_err_handler(int errtyp, ...);

// In the recfile.cpp file, add the following declaration
// so that err_handler points to the default error handler.
void (*err_handler)(int errtyp, ...) = default_err_handler;

// In recfile.cpp, rename recfile::err_handler to
// default_err_handler, (it's no longer a member).
void default_err_handler(int errtyp,...)
{
  // Code same as in old recfile::err_handler
}
```

Now, if you wanted to redirect the error handling to another function, you could define the following (make sure the arguments match):

```
void your_err_handler(int errtyp, ...)
{
  // your own way of handling errors
}
```

Then, somewhere, (perhaps **main()**), set **err_handler** to point to your error handler:

```
main()
{
  err_handler = your_err_handler;
  ...
}
```

Index

A

B

C

G

H

I

K

L

M

Disk Order Form

If you'd like to use the code presented in this book but don't want to waste your time typing it in, we have a very special offer for you. We are making available a set of diskettes that contain all of the source code for the program listings in this book.

To order your disks, fill out the form below and mail it along with $20 in check or money order, or Visa/MasterCard (orders outside the U.S. add $5 shipping and handling) to:

Azarona Software
C++ Primer Disks
P.O. Box 768
Conifer, CO 80433
(303) 697-1088

Please send me _____ copies of the companion disks for *The Complete C++ Primer* at $20 each. (Orders outside the U.S. add $5 shipping and handling. U.S. funds only.) Please make checks payable to Azarona Software.

Circle format: 5 1/4   3 1/2

Name

Address

City   State   Zip Code

Telephone

Credit Card #   Exp. Date

Name on card   Signature